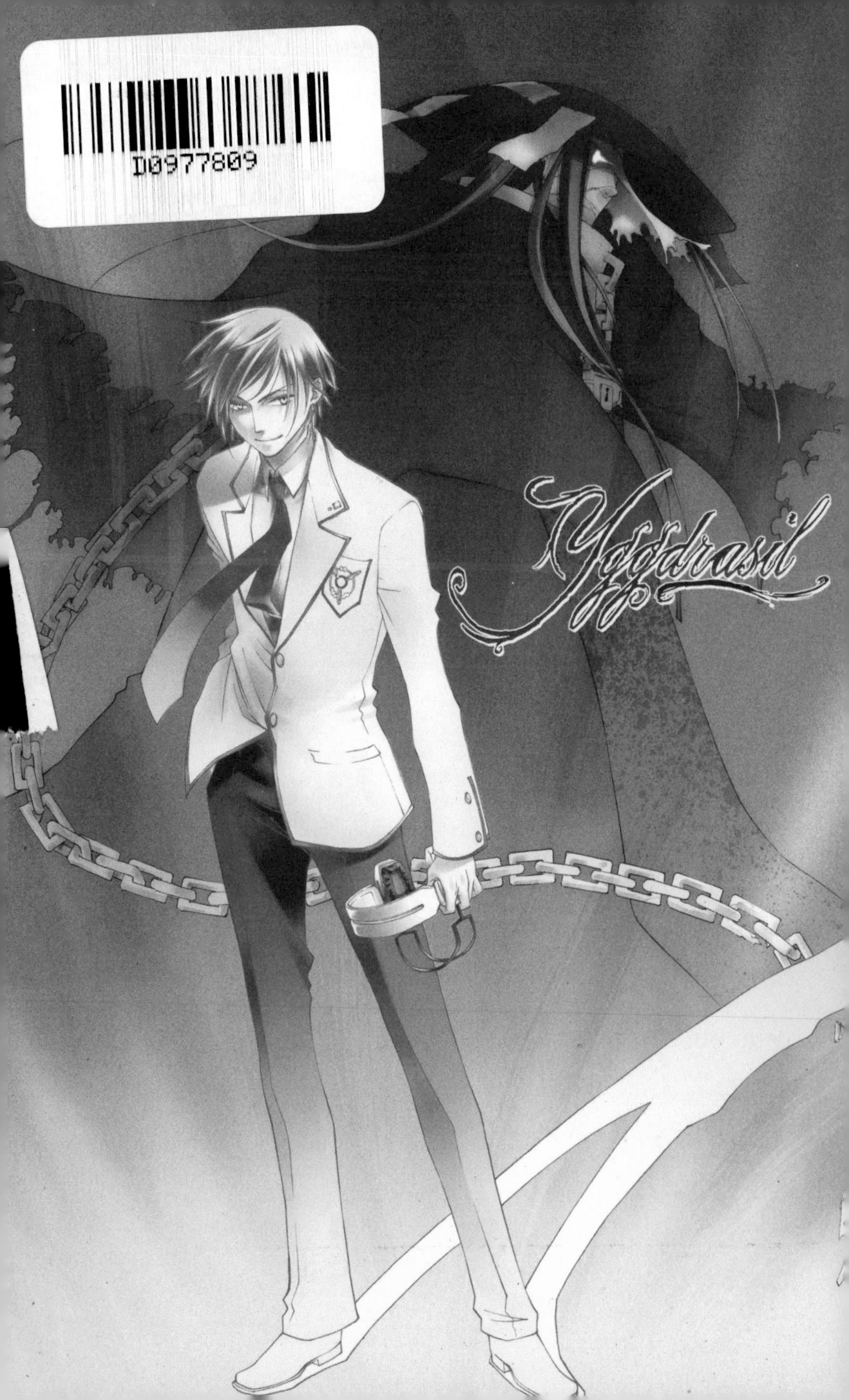
Yggdrasil

Translation – Christine Schilling
Adaptation – Mallory Reaves
Lettering & Retouch – Eva Han
Production Assistant – Suzy Wells
Production Manager – James Dashiell
Editor – Brynne Chandler

A Go! Comi manga

Published by Go! Media Entertainment, LLC

Visit us online at www.gocomi.com
e-mail: info@gocomi.com

ISBN 978-1-933617-91-6

First printed in July 2008

1   2   3   4   5   6   7   8   9

Manufactured in the United States of America.

Yggdrasil

AUTHOR

Lay Mutsuki

Volume 1

go!comi

Concerning Honorifics

At Go! Comi, we do our best to ensure that our translations read seamlessly in English while respecting the original Japanese language and culture. To this end, the original honorifics (the suffixes found at the end of characters' names) remain intact. In Japan, where politeness and formality are more integrated into every aspect of the language, honorifics give a better understanding of character relationships. They can be used to indicate both respect and affection. Whether a person addresses someone by first name or last name also indicates how close their relationship is.

Here are some of the honorifics you might encounter in reading this book:

-san: This is the most common and neutral of honorifics. The polite way to address someone you're not on close terms with is to use "-san." It's kind of like Mr. or Ms., except you can use "-san" with first names as easily as family names.

-chan: Used for friendly familiarity, mostly applied towards young girls. "-chan" also carries a connotation of cuteness with it, so it is frequently used with nicknames towards both boys and girls (such as "Na-chan" for "Natsu").

-kun: Like "-chan," it's an informal suffix for friends and classmates, only "-kun" is usually associated with boys. It can also be used in a professional environment by someone addressing a subordinate.

-sama: Indicates a great deal of respect or admiration.

Sempai: In school, "sempai" is used to refer to an upperclassman or club leader. It can also be used in the workplace by a new employee to address a mentor or staff member with seniority.

Sensei: Teachers, doctors, writers or any master of a trade are referred to as "sensei." When addressing a manga creator, the polite thing to do is attach "-sensei" to the manga-ka's name (as in Mutsuki-sensei).

Onii: This is the more casual term for an older brother. Usually you'll see it with an honorific attached, such as "onii-chan."

Onee: The casual term for older sister, it's used like "onii" with honorifics.

[blank]: Not using an honorific when addressing someone indicates that the speaker has permission to speak intimately with the other person. This relationship is usually reserved for close friends and family.

Table of contents
Yggdrasil ◆ 1

Yggdrasil

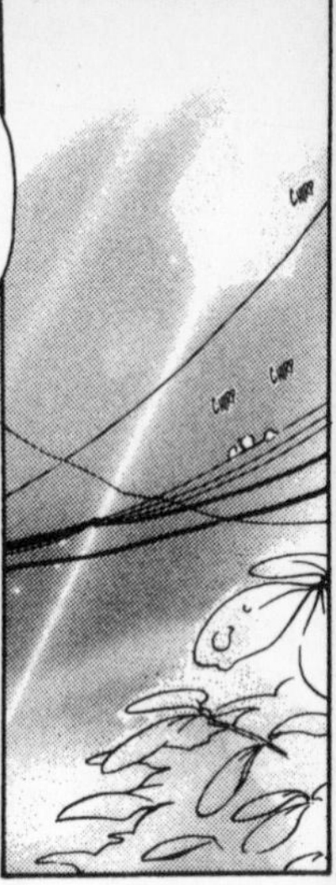

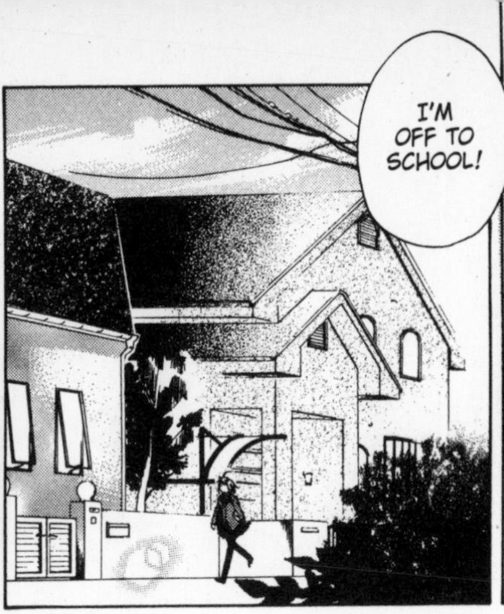
I'M OFF TO SCHOOL!

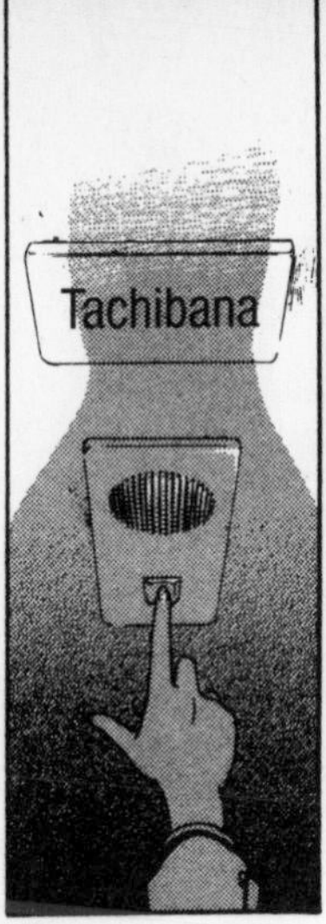
Tachibana

Yggdrasil

Chapter 1

Lay Mutsuki

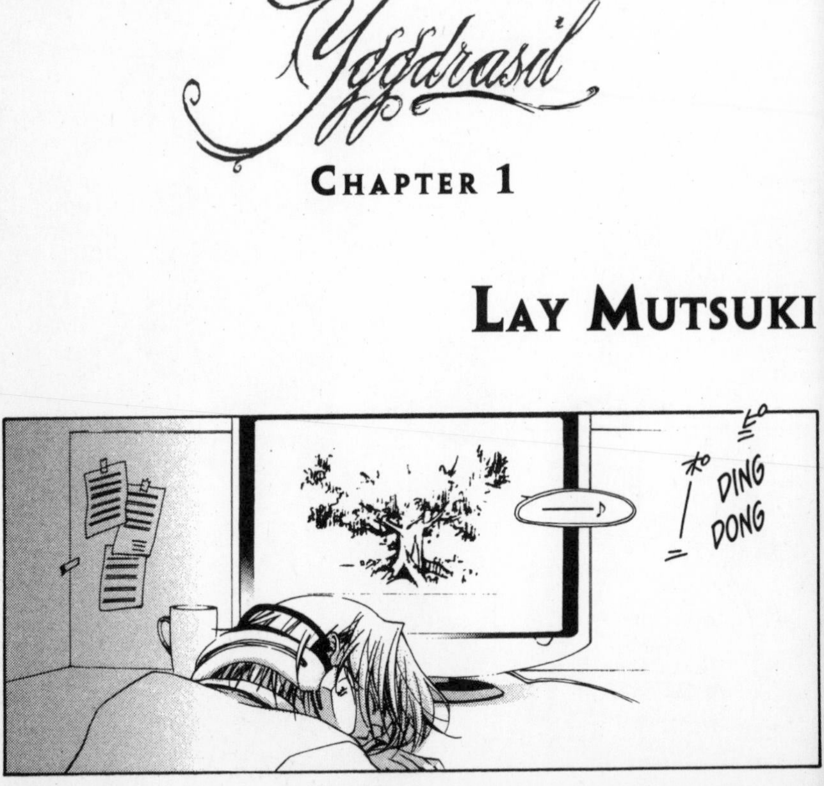
DING DONG

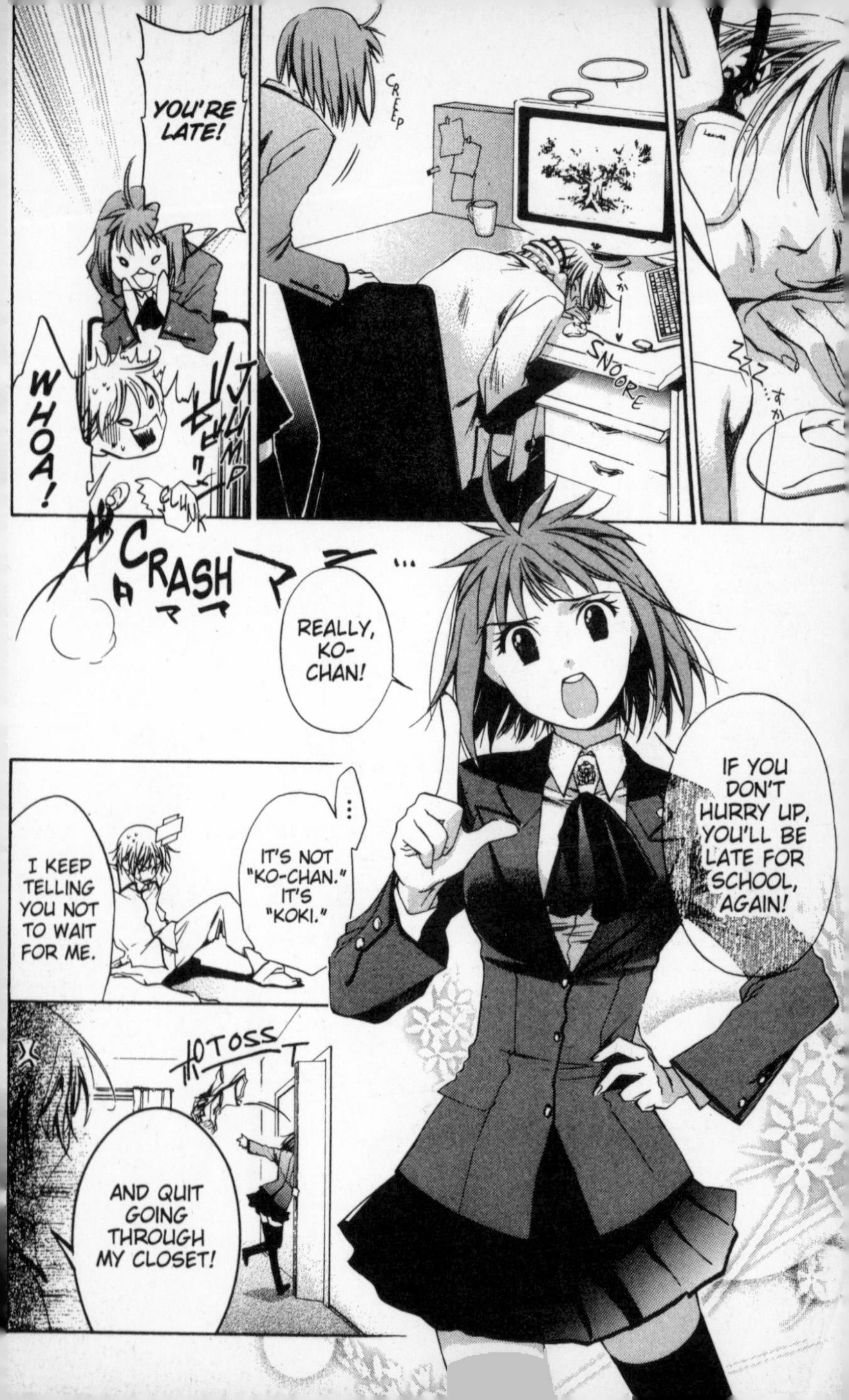
ZZZ
CREEP
SNOORE
YOU'RE LATE!
JUMP
CLUNK
WHOA!
CRASH
...
REALLY, KO-CHAN!
IF YOU DON'T HURRY UP, YOU'LL BE LATE FOR SCHOOL, AGAIN!
...
IT'S NOT "KO-CHAN." IT'S "KOKI."
I KEEP TELLING YOU NOT TO WAIT FOR ME.
TOSS
AND QUIT GOING THROUGH MY CLOSET!

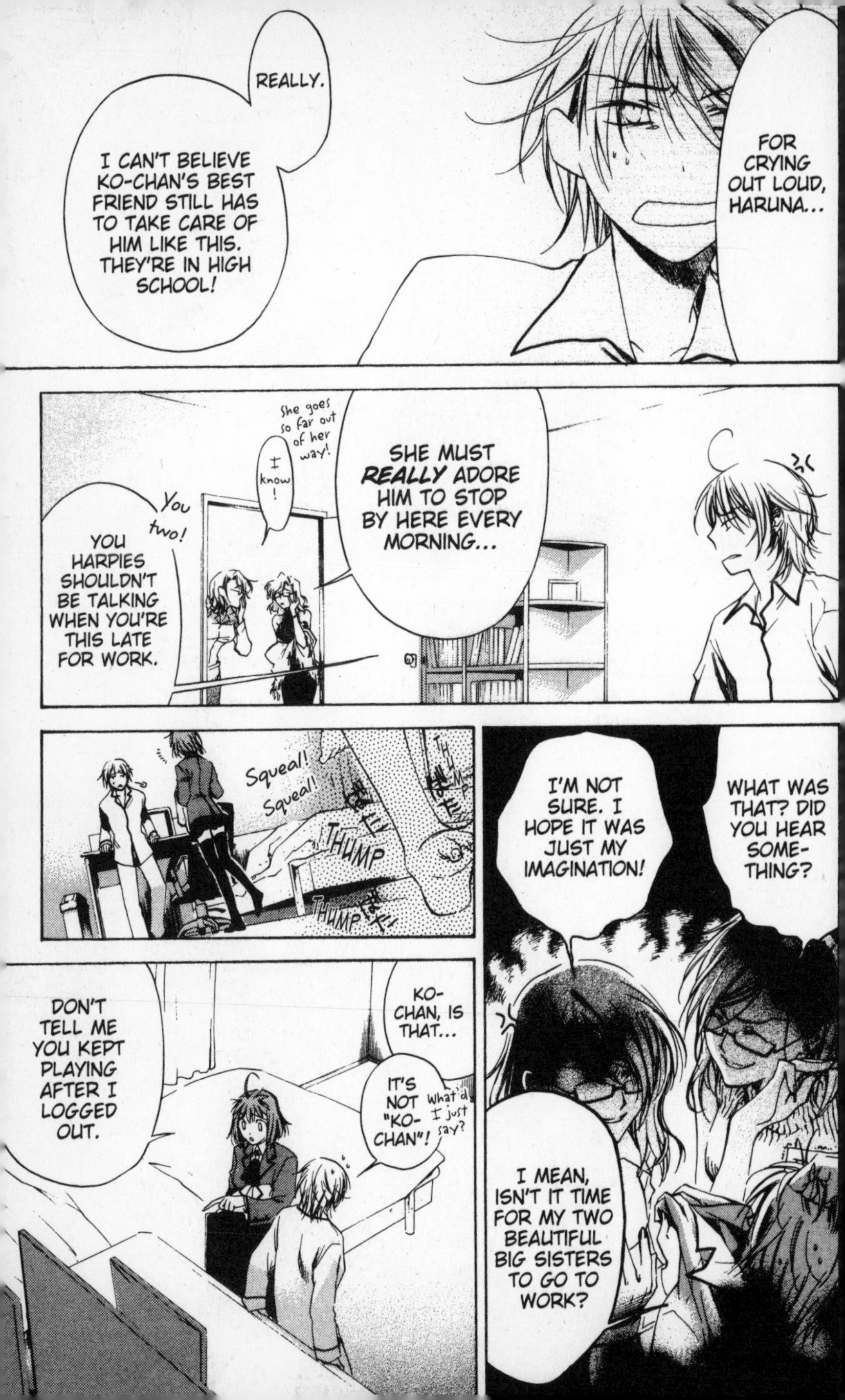
FOR CRYING OUT LOUD, HARUNA...
REALLY.
I CAN'T BELIEVE KO-CHAN'S BEST FRIEND STILL HAS TO TAKE CARE OF HIM LIKE THIS. THEY'RE IN HIGH SCHOOL!
SHE MUST *REALLY* ADORE HIM TO STOP BY HERE EVERY MORNING...
She goes so far out of her way!
I know!
You two!
YOU HARPIES SHOULDN'T BE TALKING WHEN YOU'RE THIS LATE FOR WORK.
WHAT WAS THAT? DID YOU HEAR SOME-THING?
I'M NOT SURE. I HOPE IT WAS JUST MY IMAGINATION!
I MEAN, ISN'T IT TIME FOR MY TWO BEAUTIFUL BIG SISTERS TO GO TO WORK?
THUMP
Squeal! Squeal!
THUMP
THUMP
KO-CHAN, IS THAT...
IT'S NOT "KO-CHAN"!
What'd I just say?
DON'T TELL ME YOU KEPT PLAYING AFTER I LOGGED OUT.

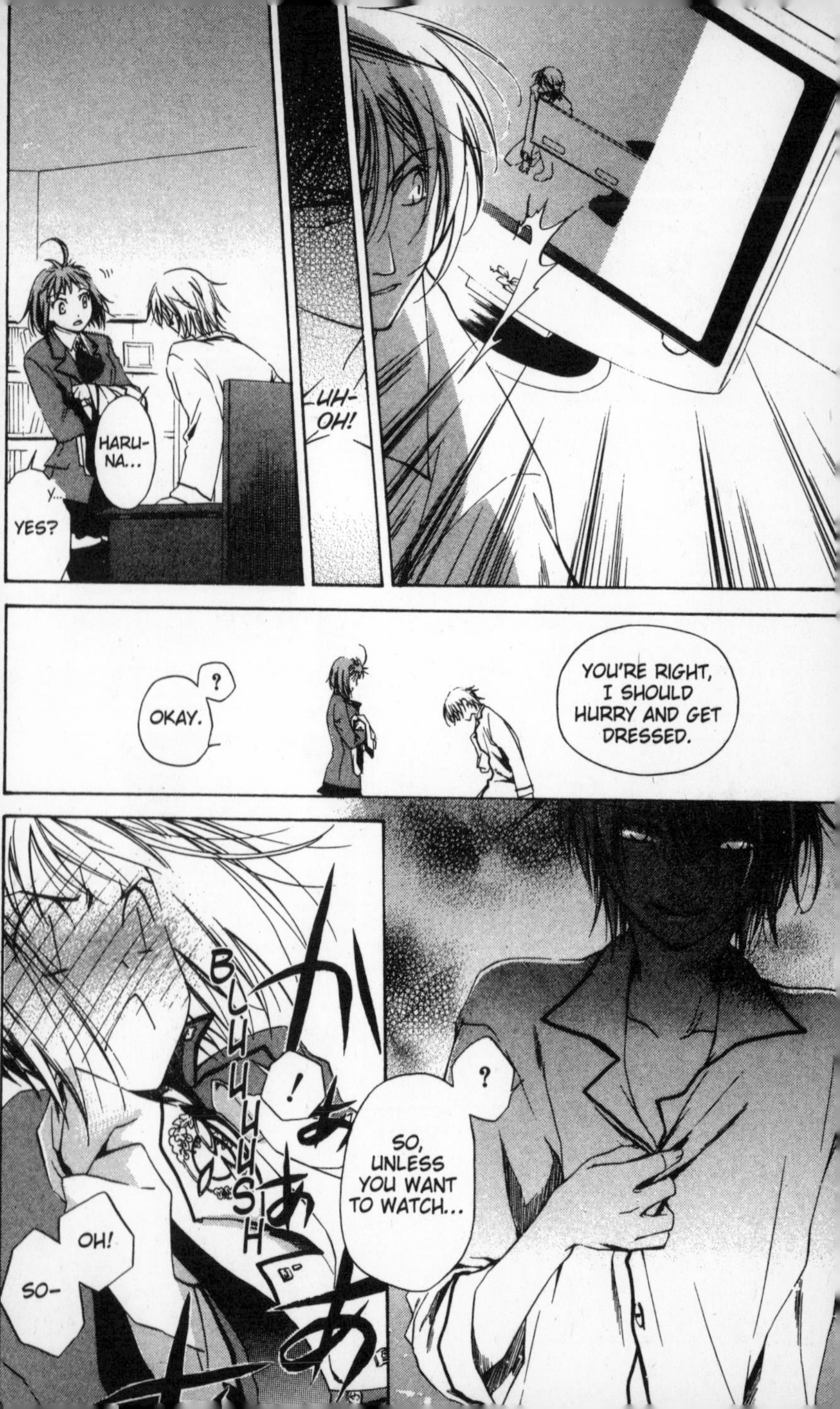
UH-OH!
HARU-NA...
Y... YES?
YOU'RE RIGHT, I SHOULD HURRY AND GET DRESSED.
?
OKAY.
?
SO, UNLESS YOU WANT TO WATCH...
!
BLUUUUSH
OH!
SO-

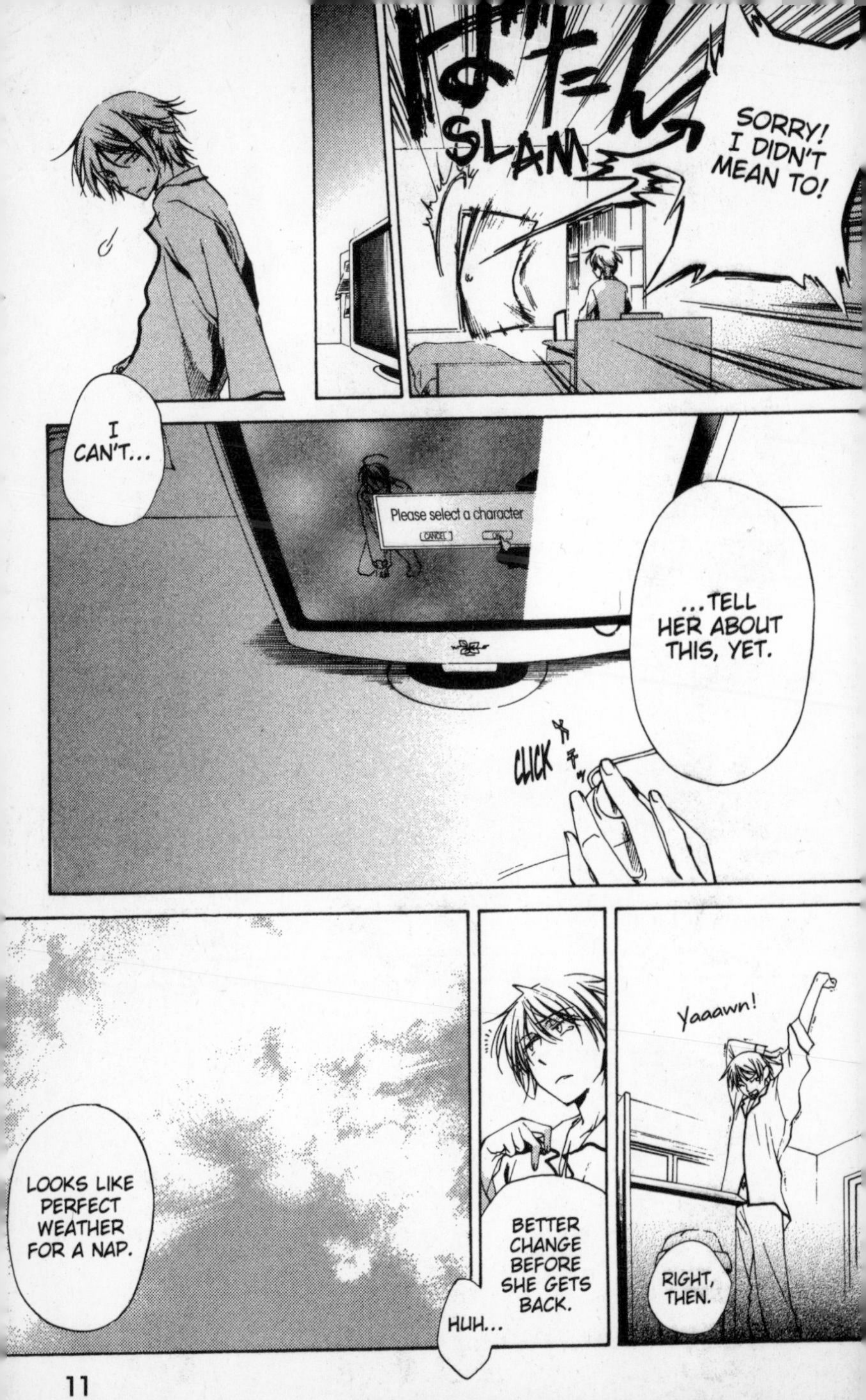
ばたん
SLAM
SORRY! I DIDN'T MEAN TO!
I CAN'T...
Please select a character
CANCEL
...TELL HER ABOUT THIS, YET.
CLICK
Yaaawn!
RIGHT, THEN.
BETTER CHANGE BEFORE SHE GETS BACK.
HUH...
LOOKS LIKE PERFECT WEATHER FOR A NAP.

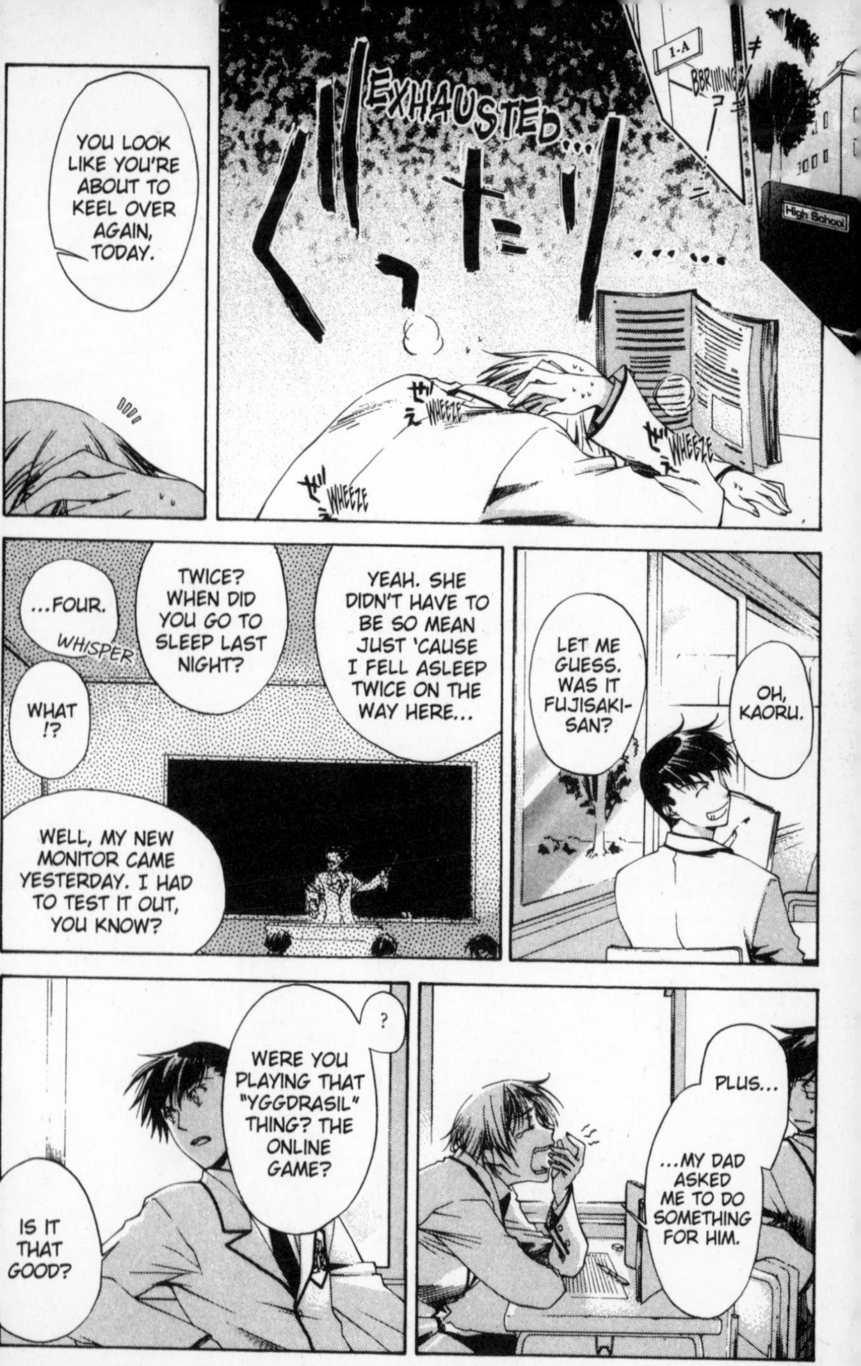

1-A
BBRIIIING
High School
EXHAUSTED...
WHEEZE
WHEEZE
WHEEZE
YOU LOOK LIKE YOU'RE ABOUT TO KEEL OVER AGAIN, TODAY.
OH, KAORU.
LET ME GUESS. WAS IT FUJISAKI-SAN?
YEAH. SHE DIDN'T HAVE TO BE SO MEAN JUST 'CAUSE I FELL ASLEEP TWICE ON THE WAY HERE...
TWICE? WHEN DID YOU GO TO SLEEP LAST NIGHT?
...FOUR.
WHISPER
WHAT !?
WELL, MY NEW MONITOR CAME YESTERDAY. I HAD TO TEST IT OUT, YOU KNOW?
PLUS...
...MY DAD ASKED ME TO DO SOMETHING FOR HIM.
?
WERE YOU PLAYING THAT "YGGDRASIL" THING? THE ONLINE GAME?
IS IT THAT GOOD?

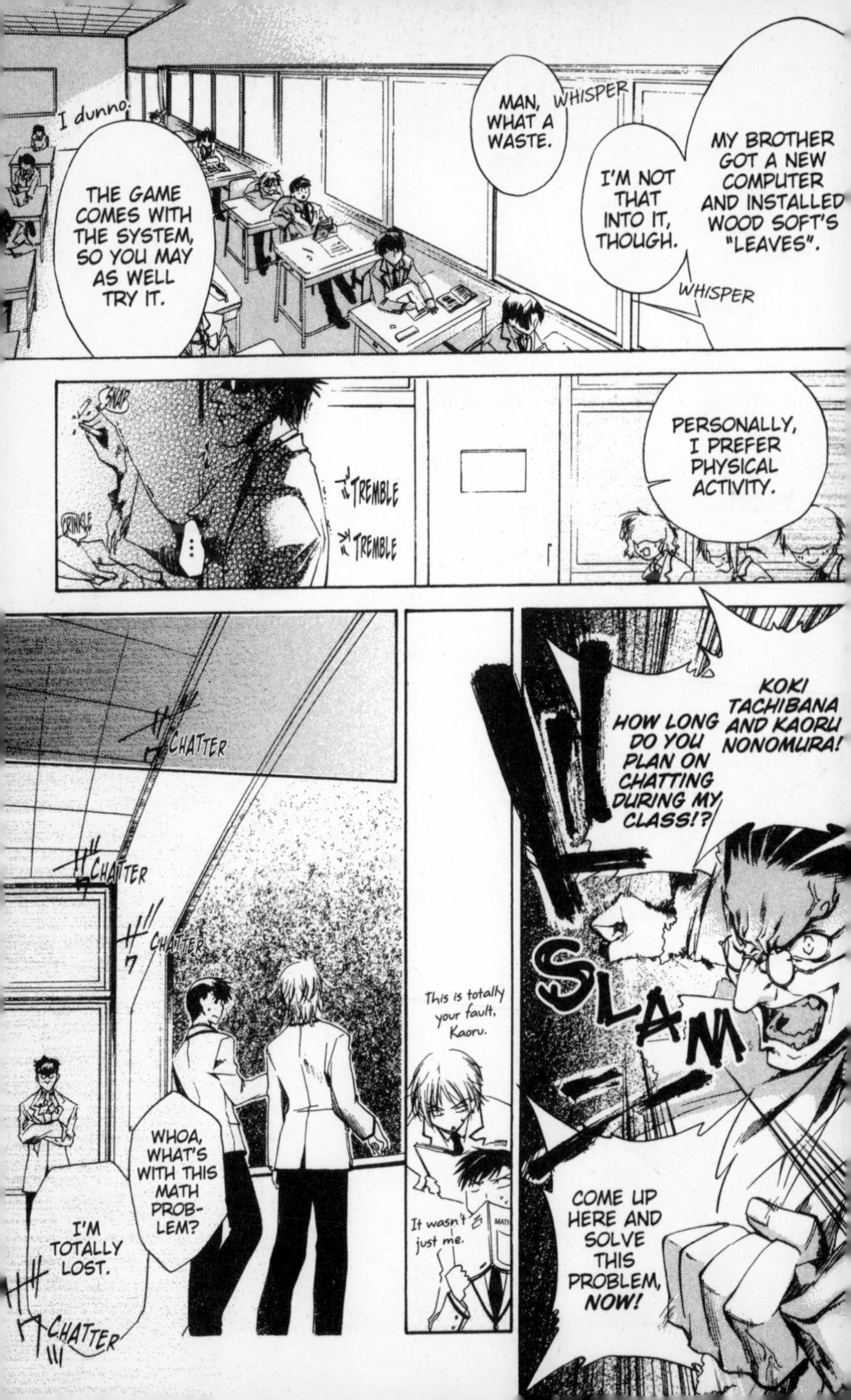
MY BROTHER GOT A NEW COMPUTER AND INSTALLED WOOD SOFT'S "LEAVES".
WHISPER
I'M NOT THAT INTO IT, THOUGH.
MAN, WHAT A WASTE.
WHISPER
THE GAME COMES WITH THE SYSTEM, SO YOU MAY AS WELL TRY IT.
I dunno.
PERSONALLY, I PREFER PHYSICAL ACTIVITY.
TREMBLE
TREMBLE
SNAP
CRINKLE
...
KOKI TACHIBANA AND KAORU NONOMURA!
HOW LONG DO YOU PLAN ON CHATTING DURING MY CLASS!?
SLAM
COME UP HERE AND SOLVE THIS PROBLEM, NOW!
This is totally your fault, Kaoru.
It wasn't just me.
MATH
CHATTER
CHATTER
CHATTER
WHOA, WHAT'S WITH THIS MATH PROBLEM?
I'M TOTALLY LOST.
CHATTER

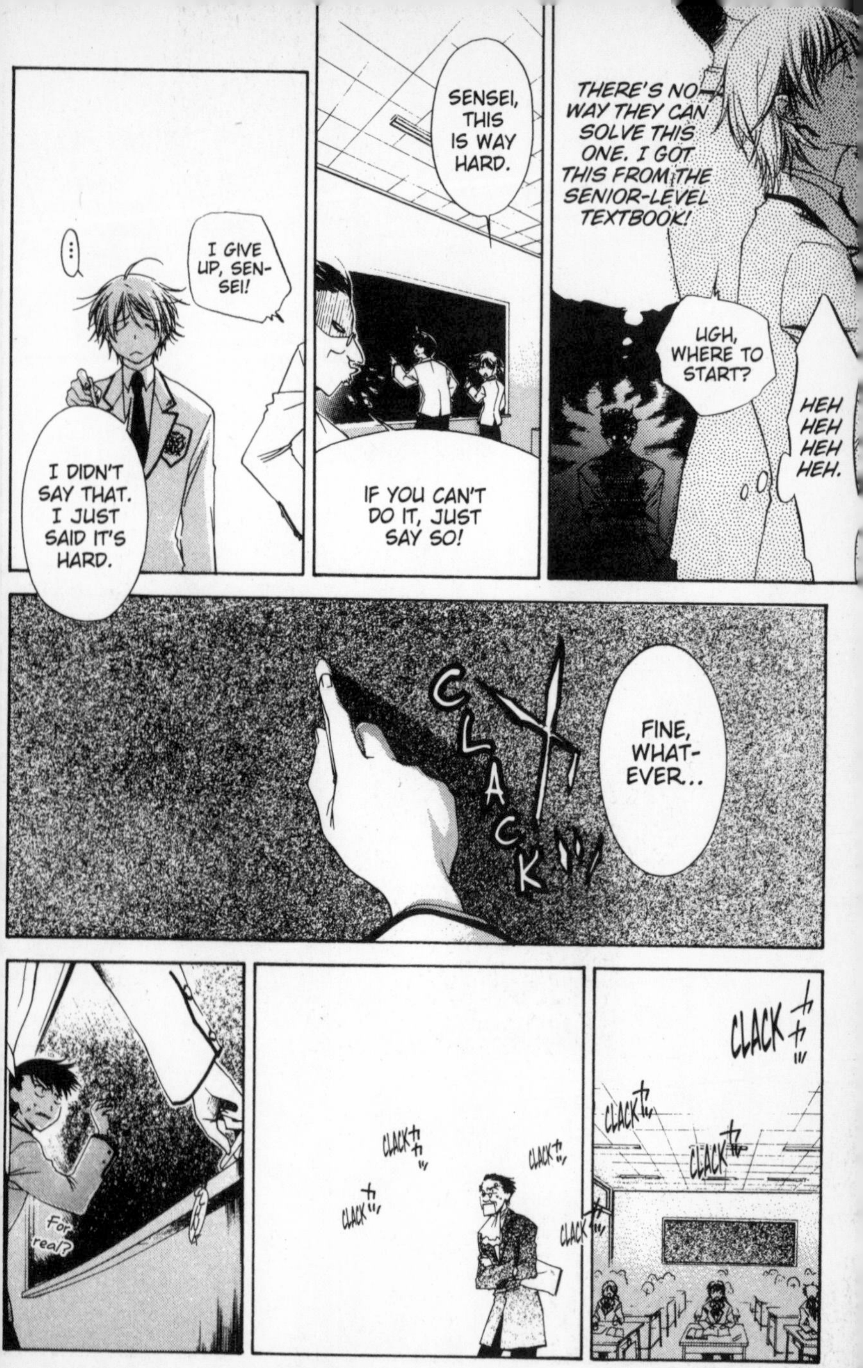
THERE'S NO WAY THEY CAN SOLVE THIS ONE. I GOT THIS FROM THE SENIOR-LEVEL TEXTBOOK!
UGH, WHERE TO START?
HEH HEH HEH HEH.
SENSEI, THIS IS WAY HARD.
IF YOU CAN'T DO IT, JUST SAY SO!
I GIVE UP, SEN-SEI!
...
I DIDN'T SAY THAT. I JUST SAID IT'S HARD.
FINE, WHATEVER..
CLACK CLACK
CLACK
CLACK
CLACK
CLACK
CLACK
CLACK
CLACK
For real?

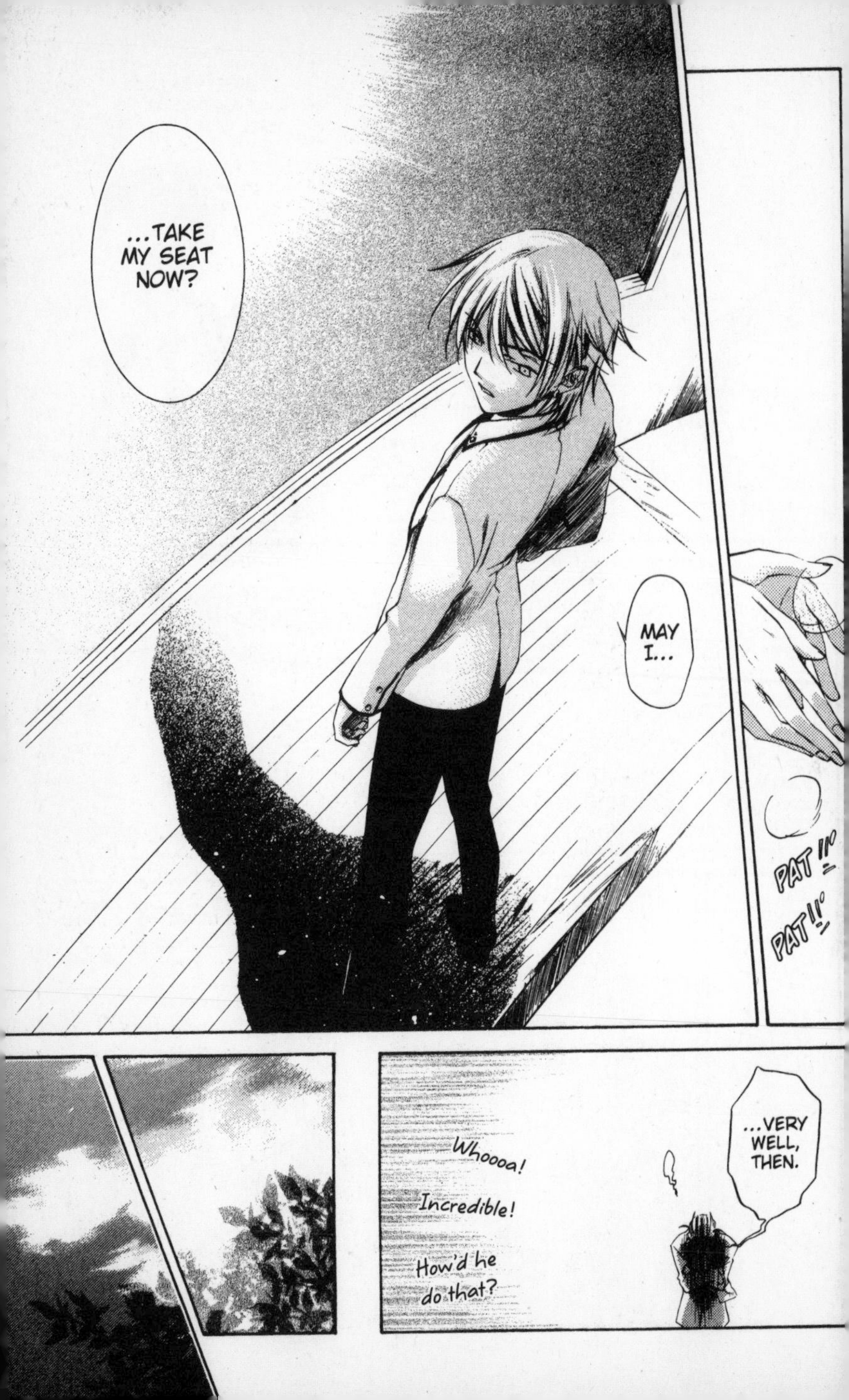
PAT!!
PAT!!
MAY I...
...TAKE MY SEAT NOW?
...VERY WELL, THEN.
Whoooa!
Incredible!
How'd he do that?

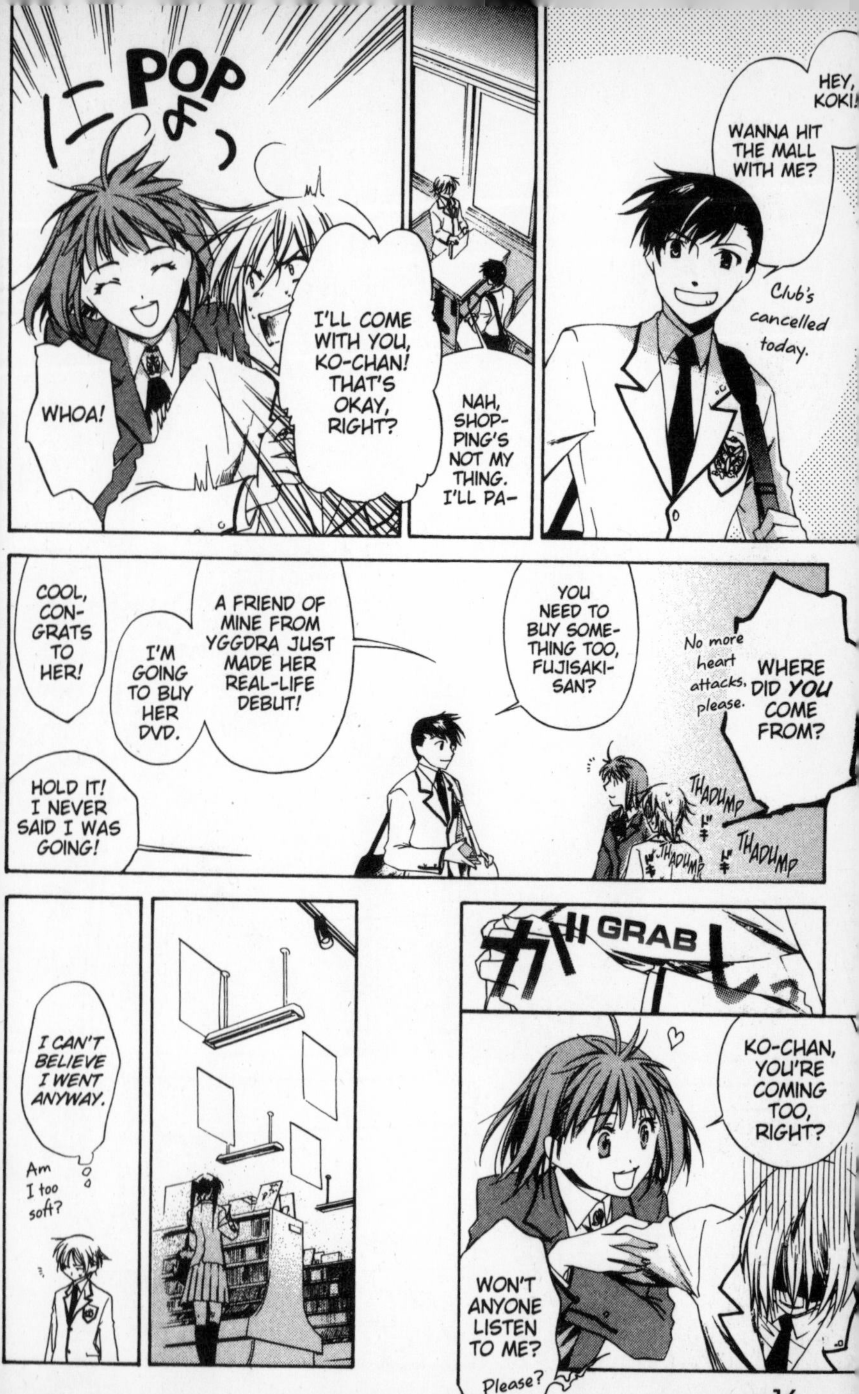
HEY, KOKI! WANNA HIT THE MALL WITH ME?
Club's cancelled today.
NAH, SHOPPING'S NOT MY THING. I'LL PA-
POP
I'LL COME WITH YOU, KO-CHAN! THAT'S OKAY, RIGHT?
WHOA!
WHERE DID *YOU* COME FROM?
No more heart attacks, please.
THADUMP
THADUMP
THADUMP
YOU NEED TO BUY SOMETHING TOO, FUJISAKI-SAN?
A FRIEND OF MINE FROM YGGDRA JUST MADE HER REAL-LIFE DEBUT!
I'M GOING TO BUY HER DVD.
COOL, CONGRATS TO HER!
HOLD IT! I NEVER SAID I WAS GOING!
GRAB
KO-CHAN, YOU'RE COMING TOO, RIGHT?
WON'T ANYONE LISTEN TO ME?
Please?
I CAN'T BELIEVE I WENT ANYWAY.
Am I too soft?

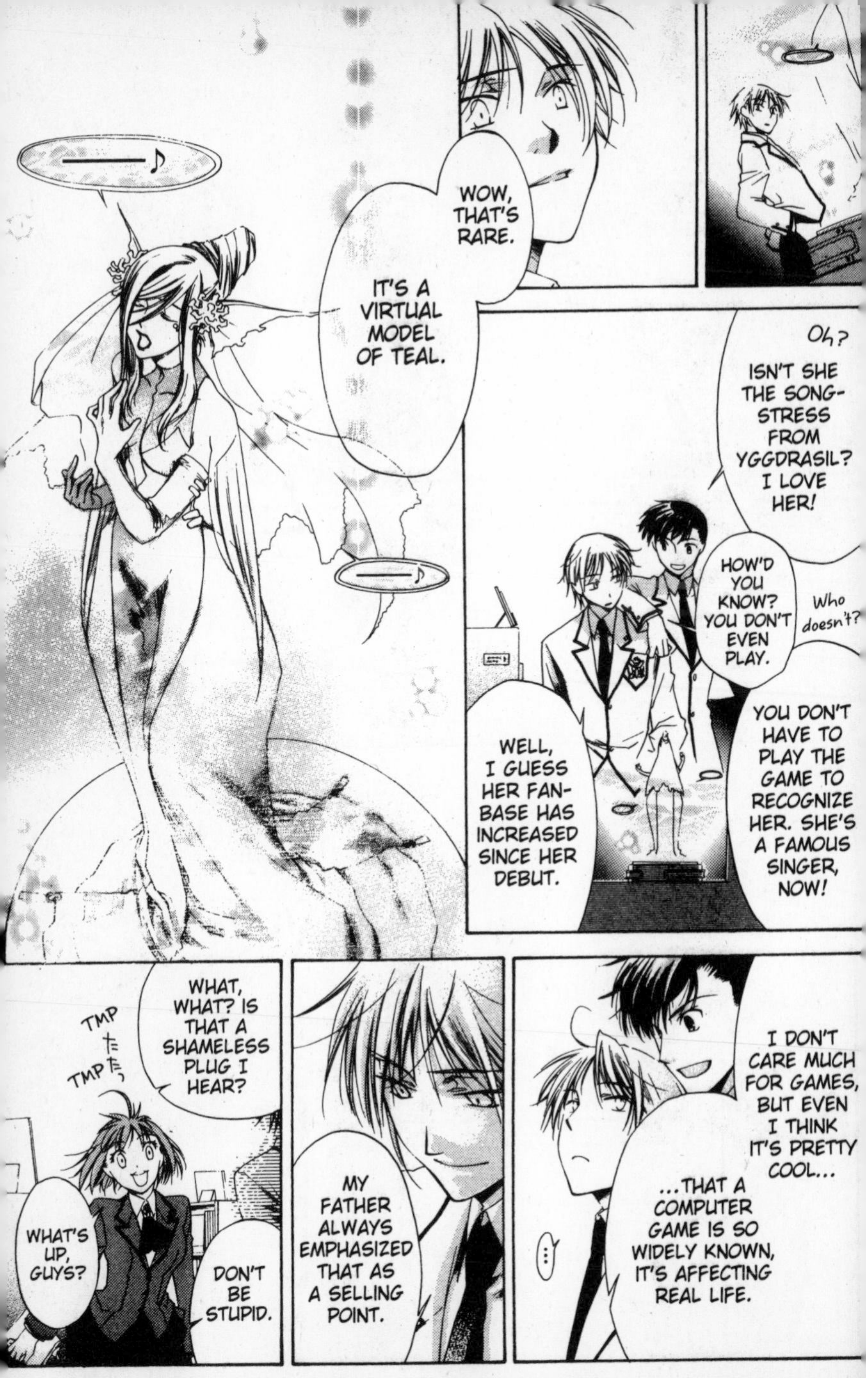

WOW, THAT'S RARE.
IT'S A VIRTUAL MODEL OF TEAL.
Oh?
ISN'T SHE THE SONG-STRESS FROM YGGDRASIL? I LOVE HER!
HOW'D YOU KNOW? YOU DON'T EVEN PLAY.
Who doesn't?
YOU DON'T HAVE TO PLAY THE GAME TO RECOGNIZE HER. SHE'S A FAMOUS SINGER, NOW!
WELL, I GUESS HER FAN-BASE HAS INCREASED SINCE HER DEBUT.
———♪
———♪
I DON'T CARE MUCH FOR GAMES, BUT EVEN I THINK IT'S PRETTY COOL...
...THAT A COMPUTER GAME IS SO WIDELY KNOWN, IT'S AFFECTING REAL LIFE.
...
MY FATHER ALWAYS EMPHASIZED THAT AS A SELLING POINT.
WHAT, WHAT? IS THAT A SHAMELESS PLUG I HEAR?
TMP
TMP
WHAT'S UP, GUYS?
DON'T BE STUPID.

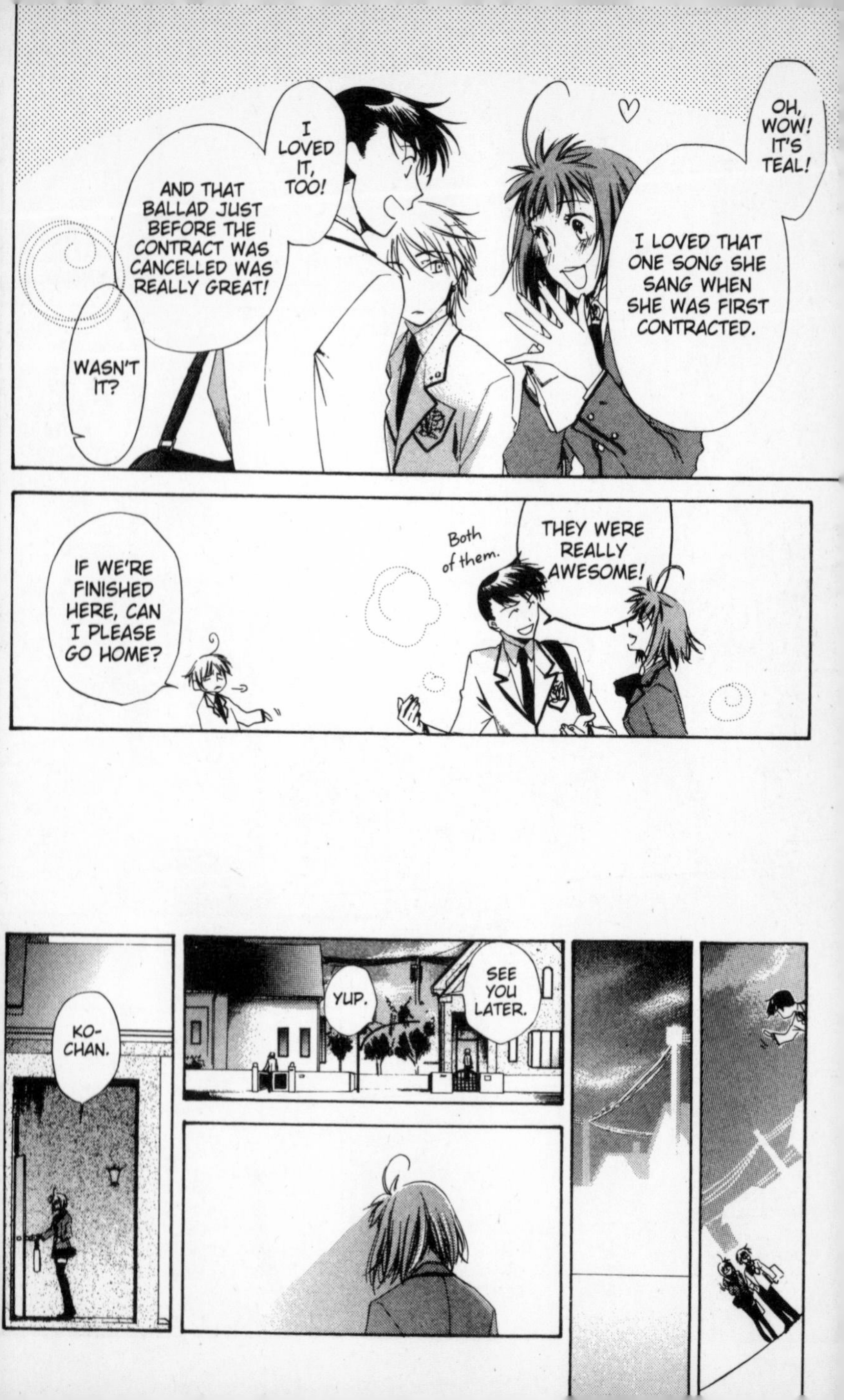
OH, WOW! IT'S TEAL!
I LOVED THAT ONE SONG SHE SANG WHEN SHE WAS FIRST CONTRACTED.
I LOVED IT, TOO!
AND THAT BALLAD JUST BEFORE THE CONTRACT WAS CANCELLED WAS REALLY GREAT!
WASN'T IT?
THEY WERE REALLY AWESOME!
Both of them.
IF WE'RE FINISHED HERE, CAN I PLEASE GO HOME?
SEE YOU LATER.
YUP.
KO-CHAN.

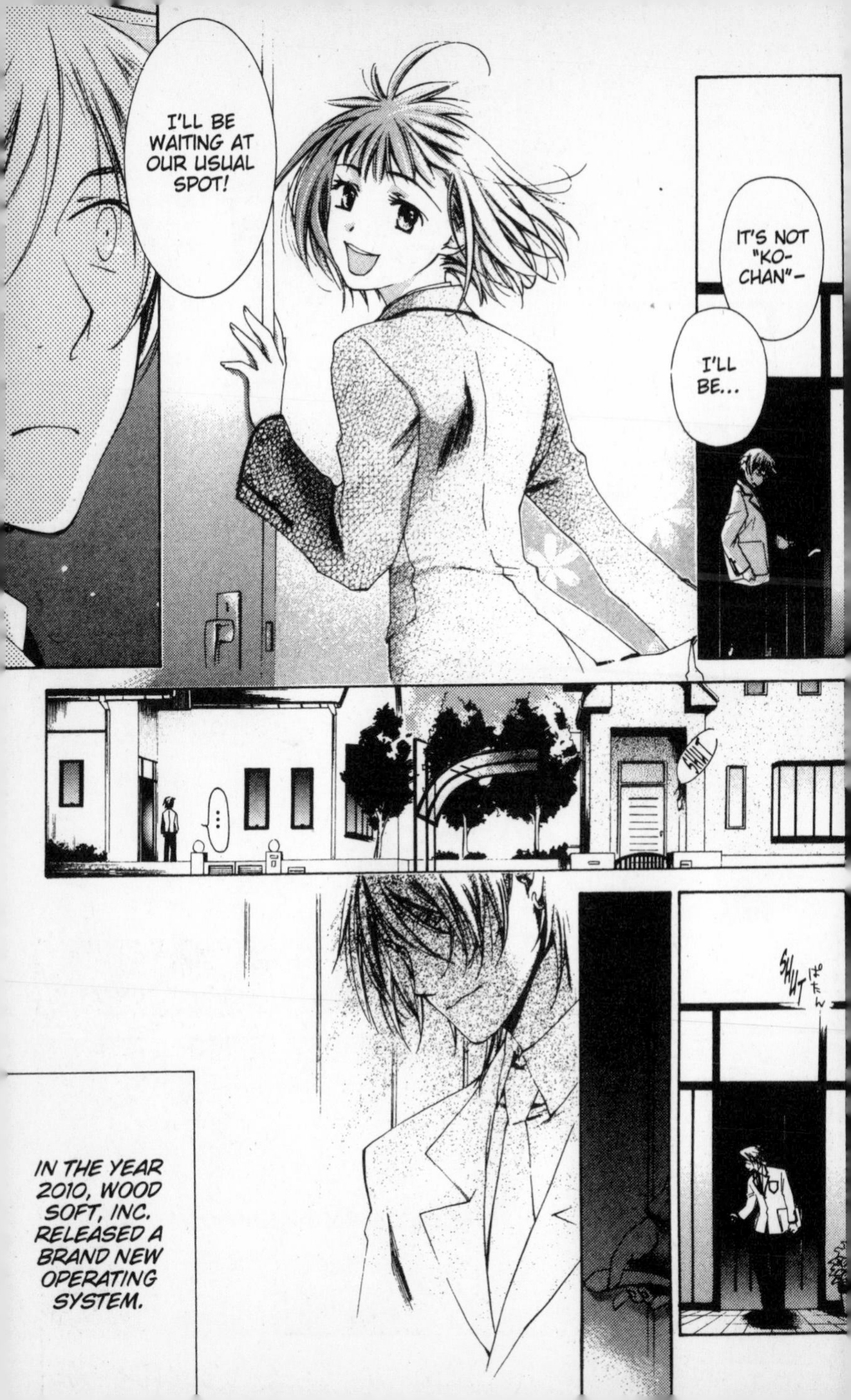
IT'S NOT "KO-CHAN"-
I'LL BE...
I'LL BE WAITING AT OUR USUAL SPOT!
SHUT
...
SHUT ぱたん
IN THE YEAR 2010, WOOD SOFT, INC. RELEASED A BRAND NEW OPERATING SYSTEM.

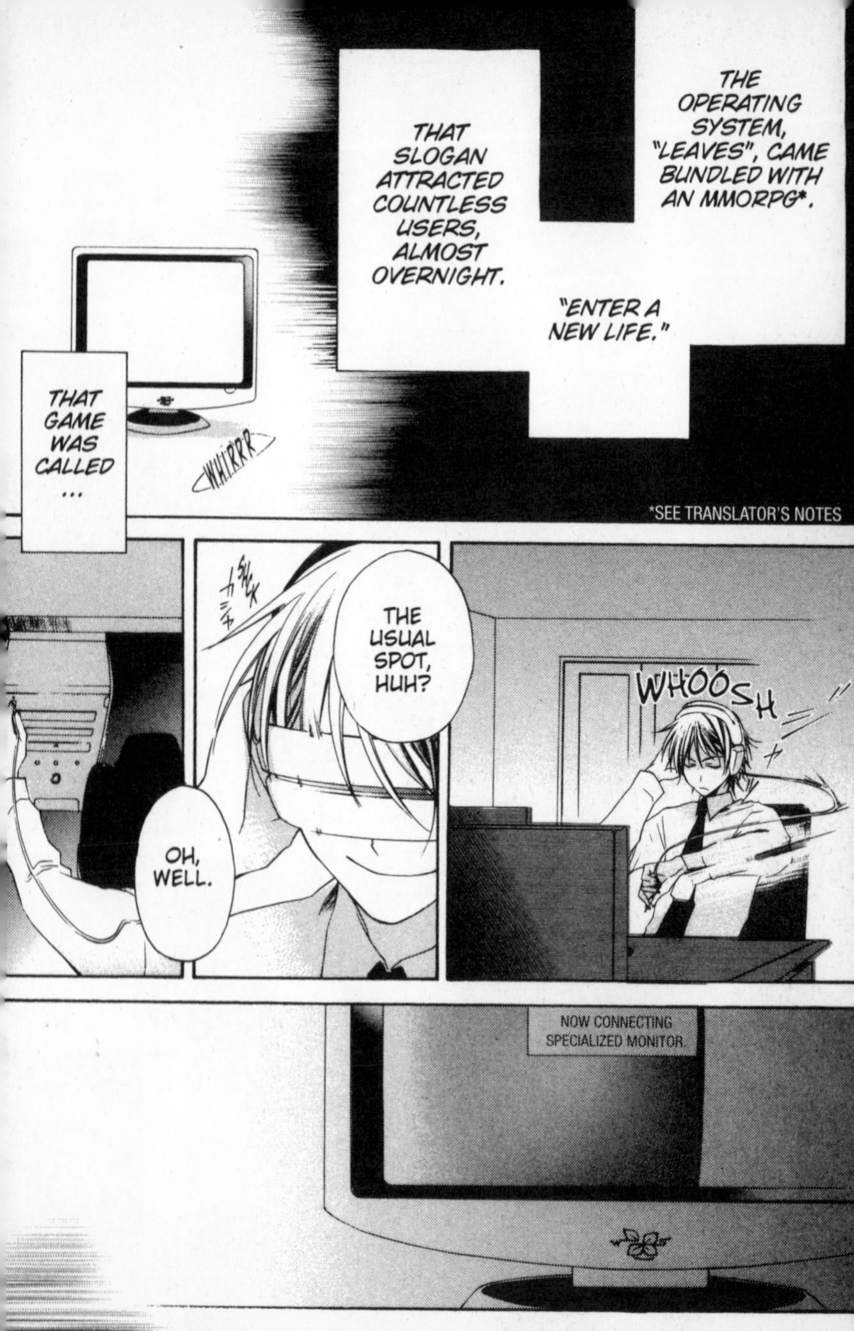
THE OPERATING SYSTEM, "LEAVES", CAME BUNDLED WITH AN MMORPG*.
"ENTER A NEW LIFE."
THAT SLOGAN ATTRACTED COUNTLESS USERS, ALMOST OVERNIGHT.
THAT GAME WAS CALLED ...
WHIRRR
*SEE TRANSLATOR'S NOTES
WHOOSH
SHCK
THE USUAL SPOT, HUH?
OH, WELL.
NOW CONNECTING SPECIALIZED MONITOR.

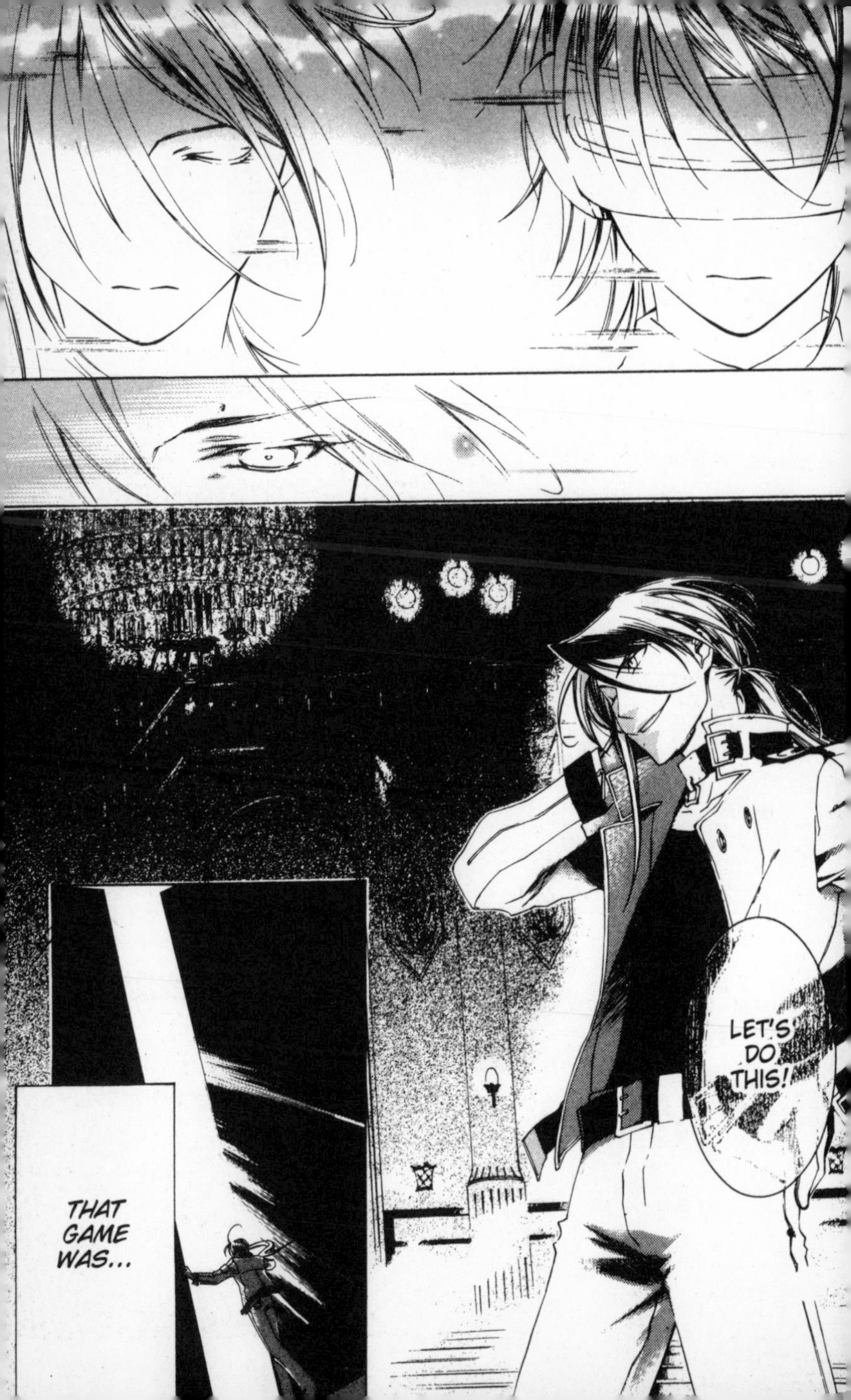
LET'S DO THIS!
THAT GAME WAS...

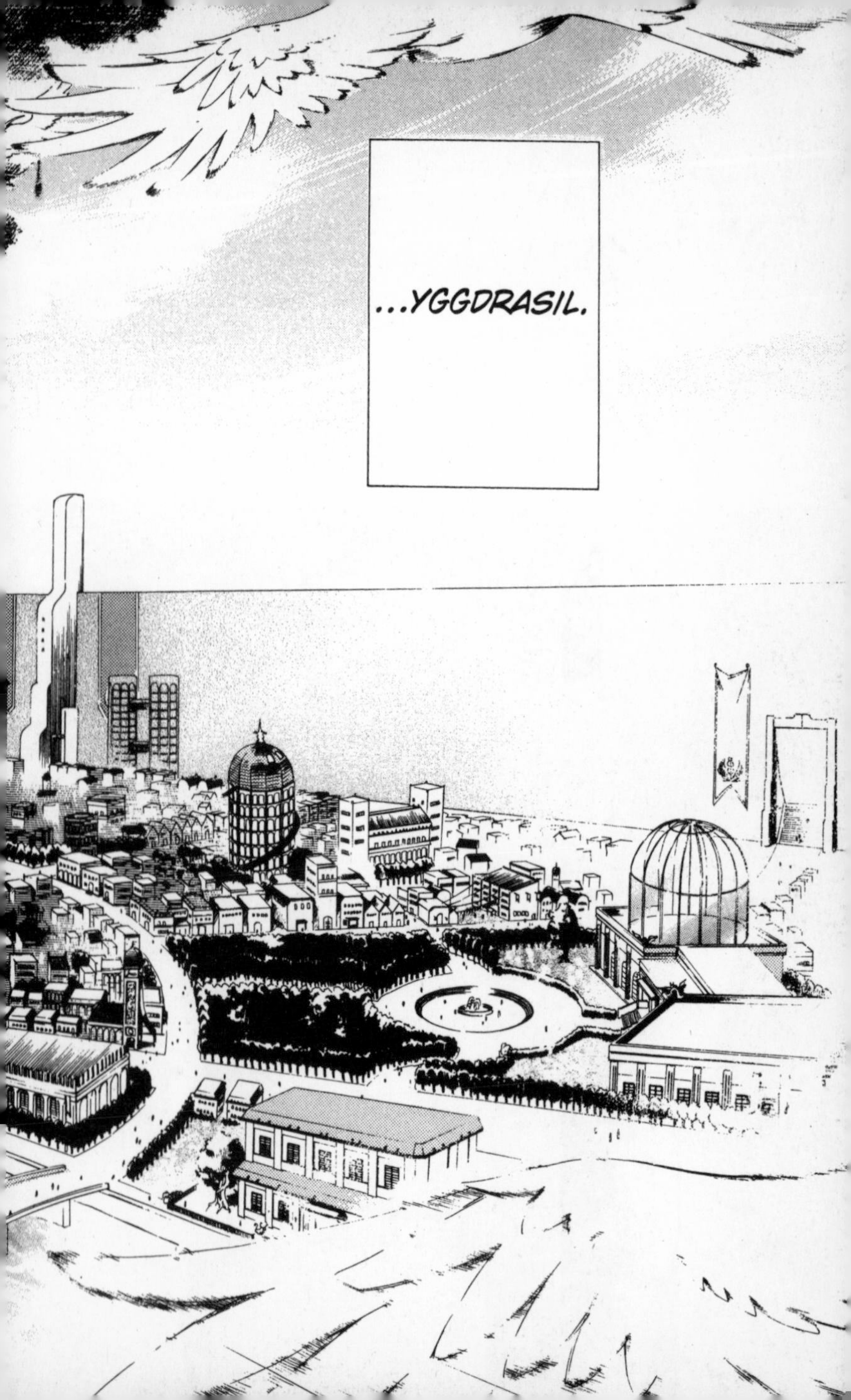
...YGGDRASIL.

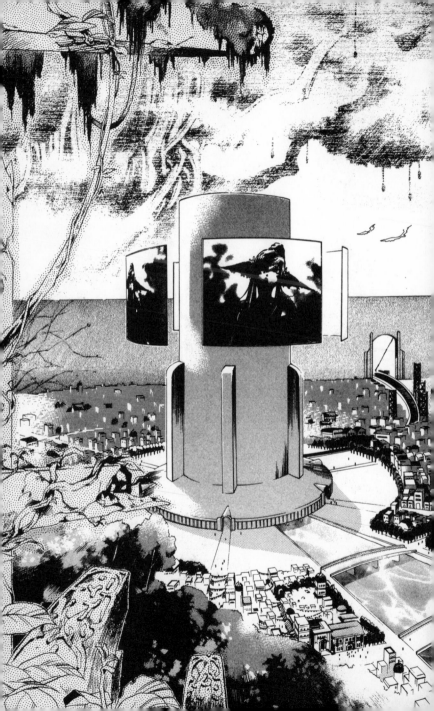

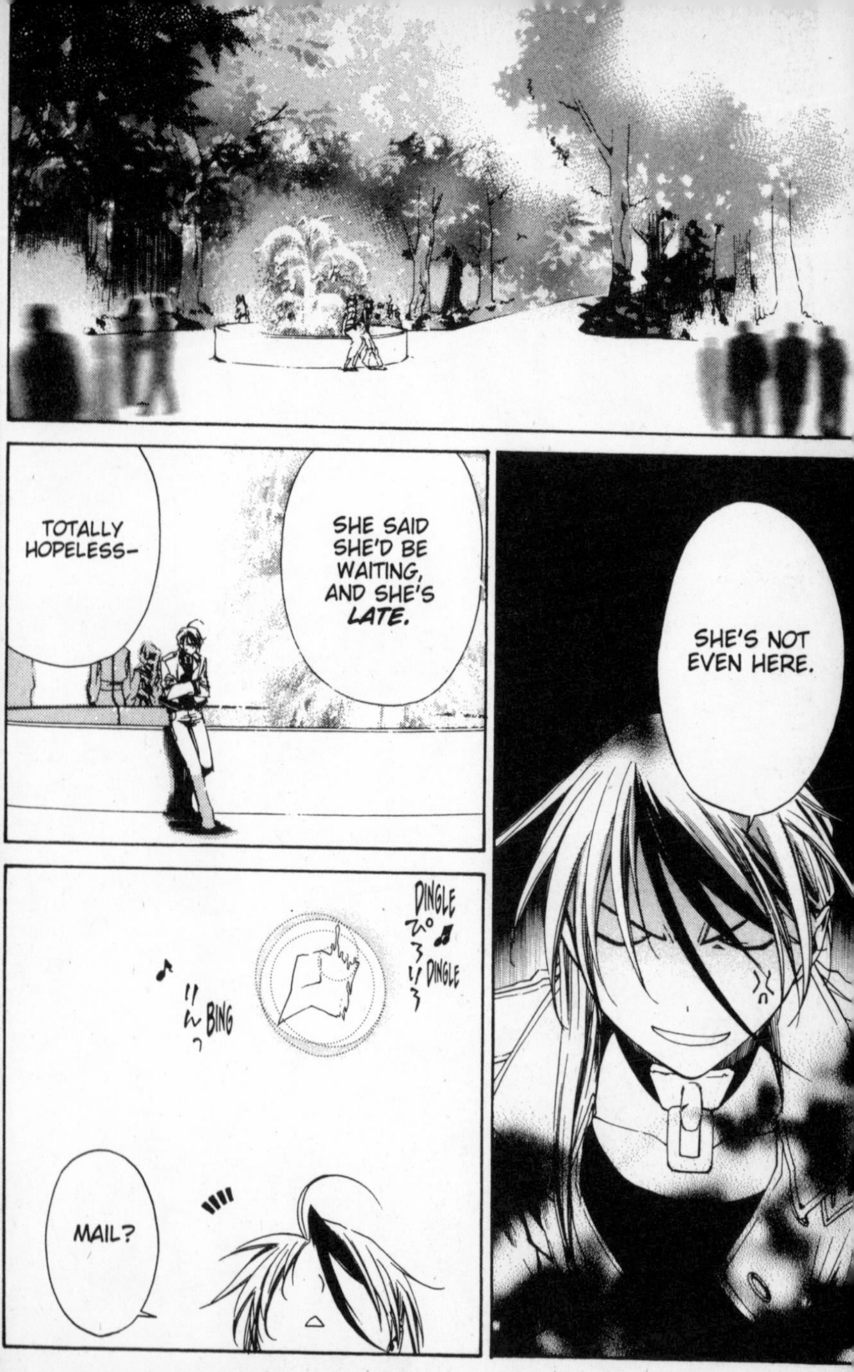
SHE'S NOT EVEN HERE.
SHE SAID SHE'D BE WAITING, AND SHE'S LATE.
TOTALLY HOPELESS-
DINGLE
DINGLE
BING
MAIL?

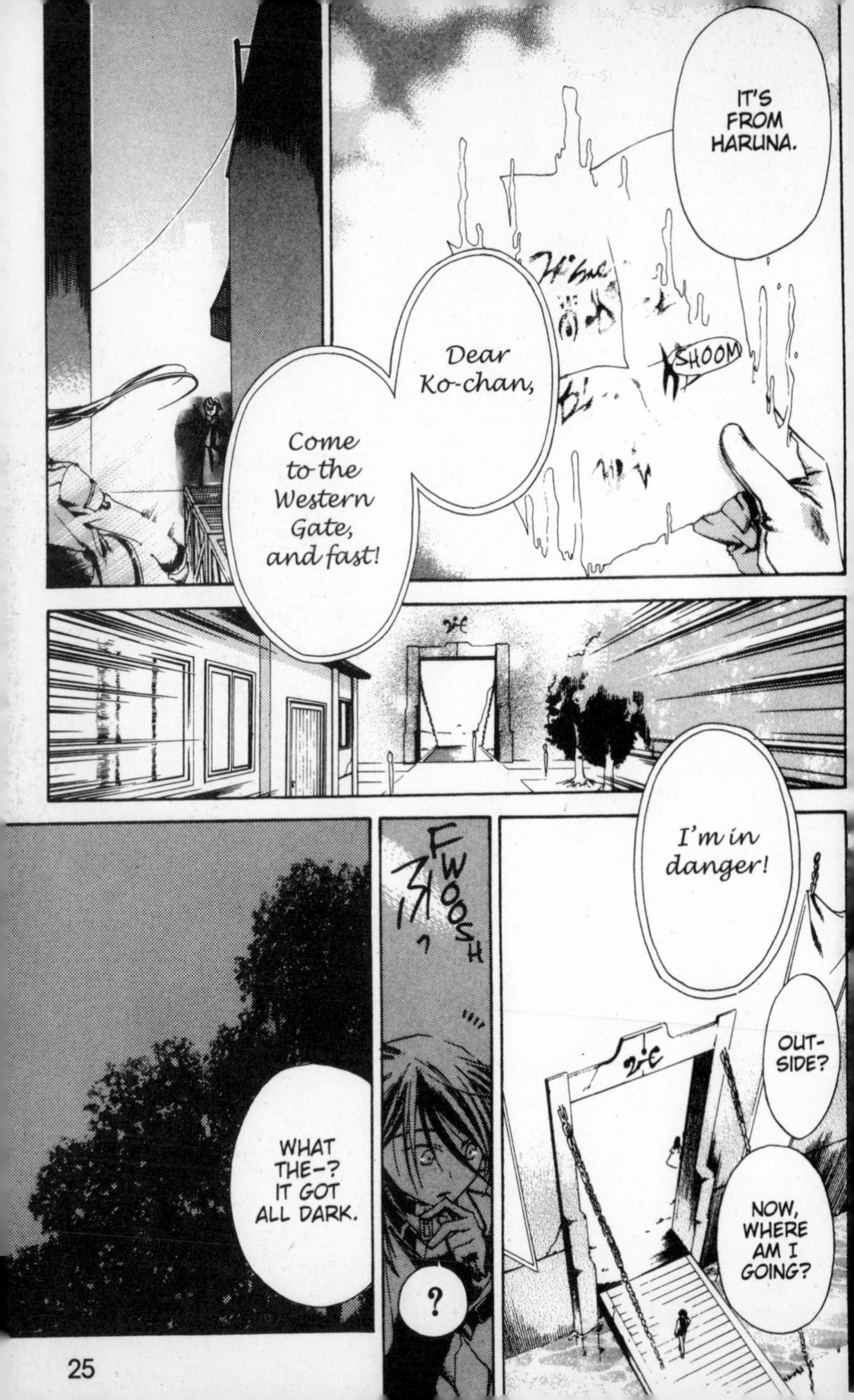
IT'S FROM HARUNA.
SHOOM
Dear Ko-chan,
Come to the Western Gate, and fast!
I'm in danger!
OUT-SIDE?
NOW, WHERE AM I GOING?
FWOOSH
?
WHAT THE-? IT GOT ALL DARK.

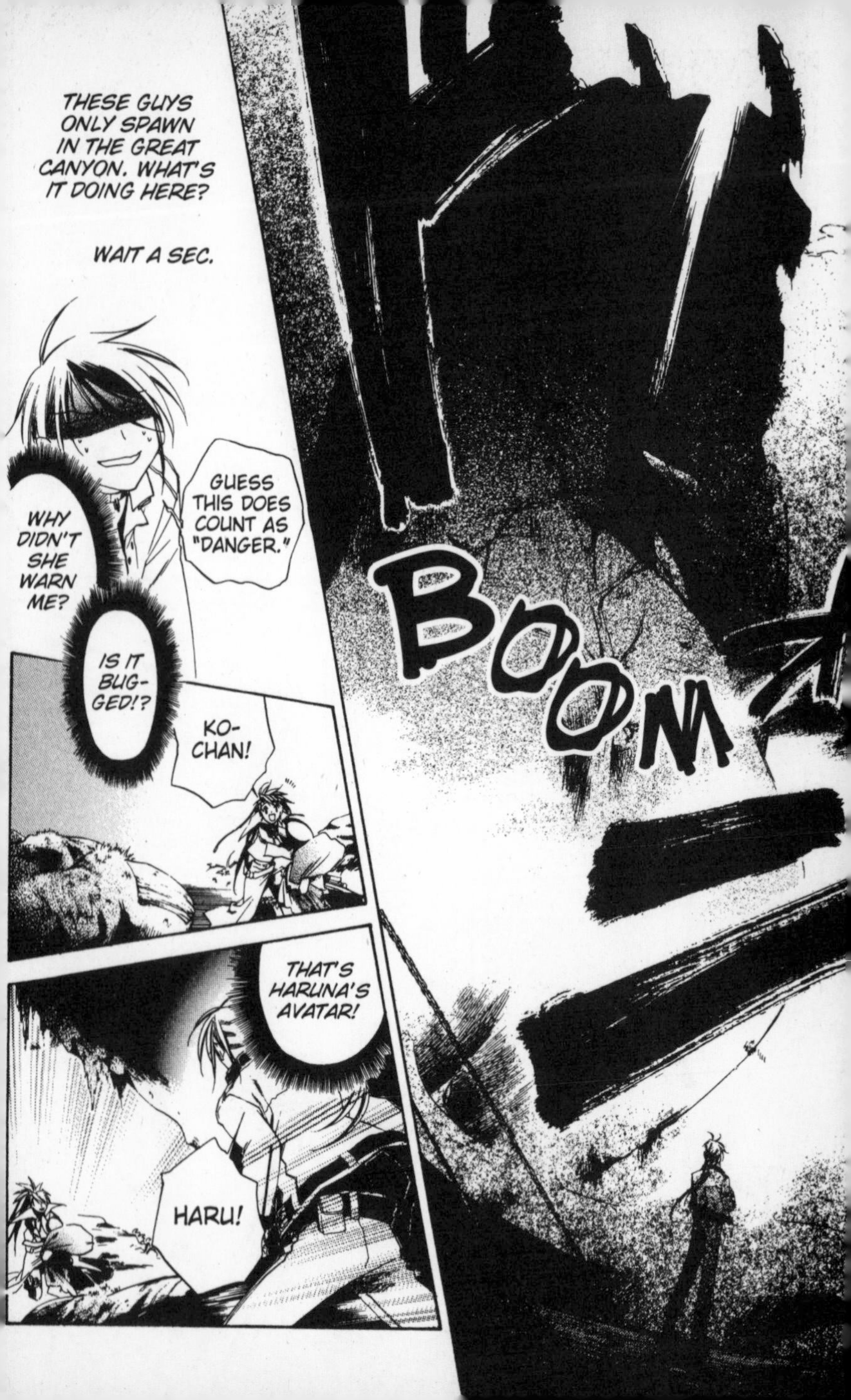
BOOM
THESE GUYS ONLY SPAWN IN THE GREAT CANYON. WHAT'S IT DOING HERE?
WAIT A SEC.
GUESS THIS DOES COUNT AS "DANGER."
WHY DIDN'T SHE WARN ME?
IS IT BUG-GED!?
KO-CHAN!
THAT'S HARUNA'S AVATAR!
HARU!

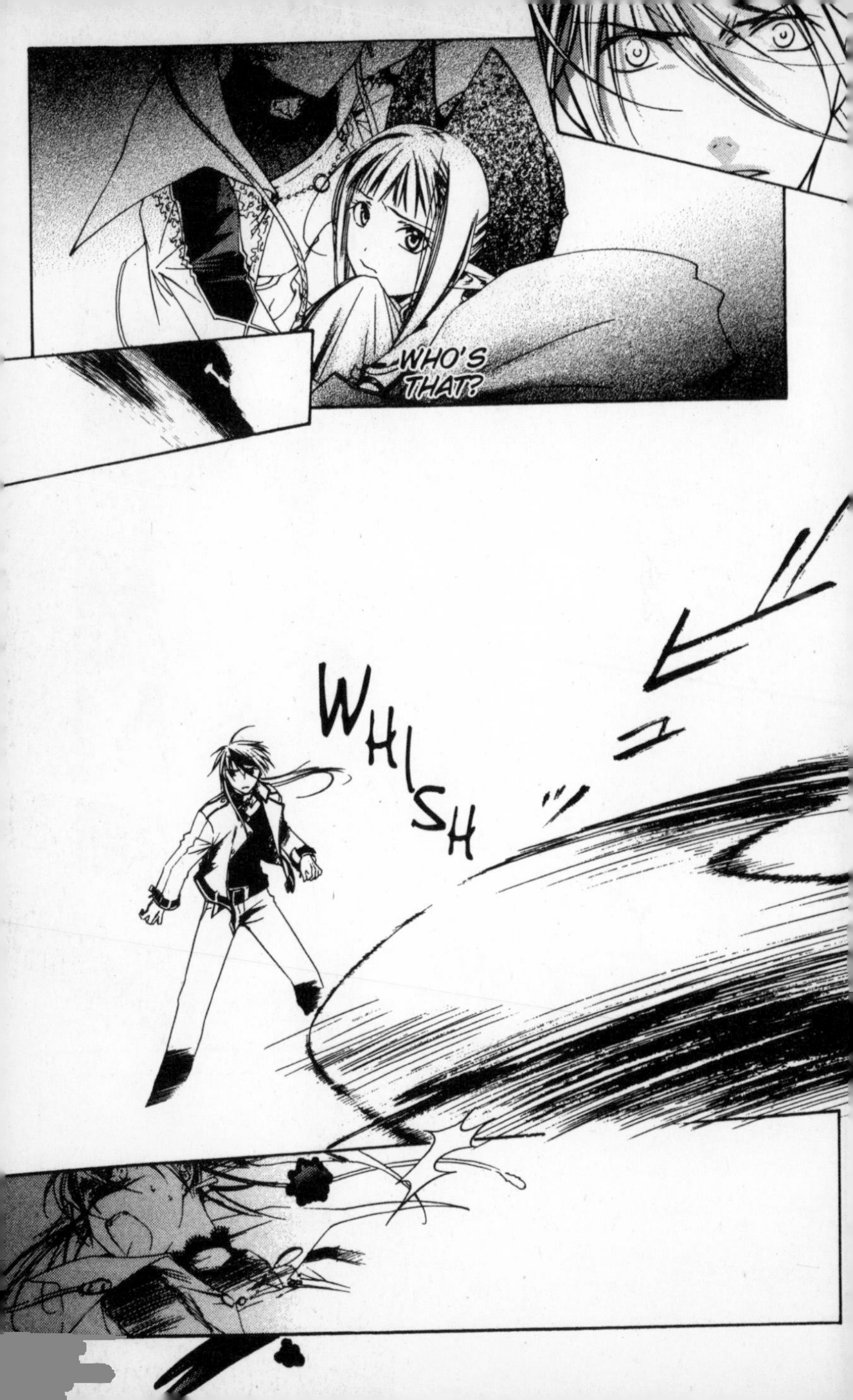
WHO'S THAT?
WHISH

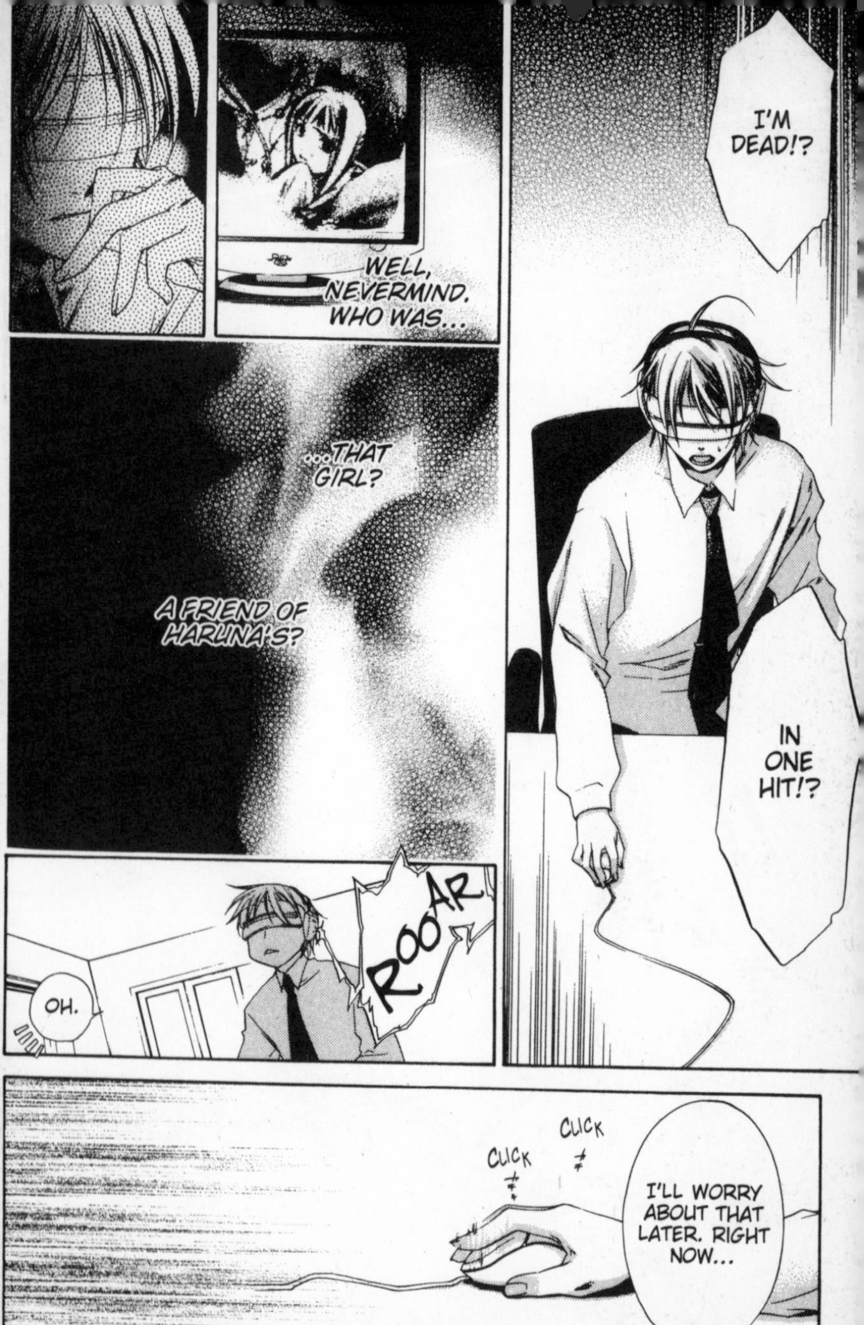
I'M DEAD!?
IN ONE HIT!?
WELL, NEVERMIND. WHO WAS...
...THAT GIRL?
A FRIEND OF HARUNA'S?
ROOAR
OH.
CLICK
CLICK
I'LL WORRY ABOUT THAT LATER. RIGHT NOW...

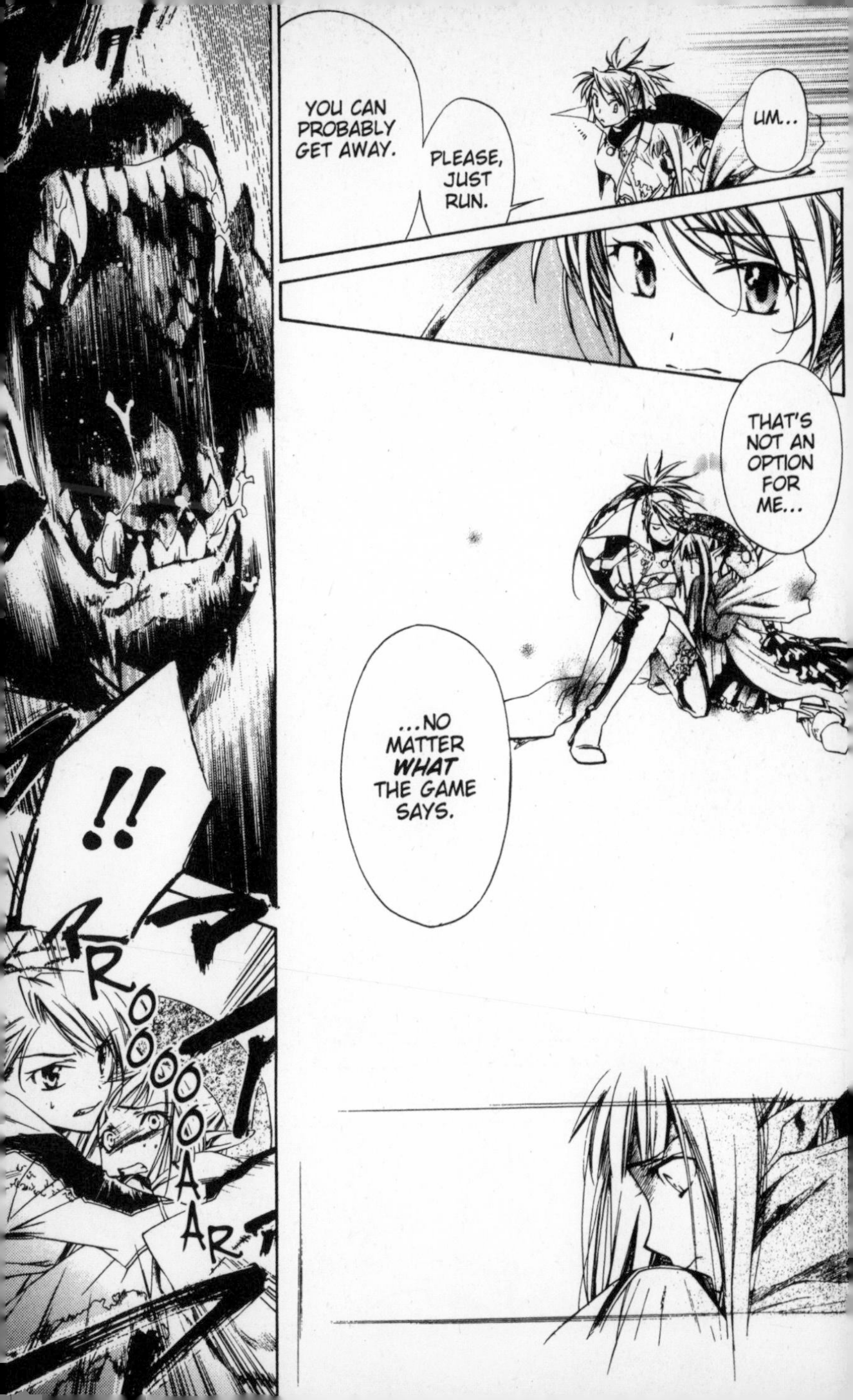
UM...
YOU CAN PROBABLY GET AWAY.
PLEASE, JUST RUN.
THAT'S NOT AN OPTION FOR ME...
...NO MATTER ***WHAT*** THE GAME SAYS.
!!
ROOOOOAAR

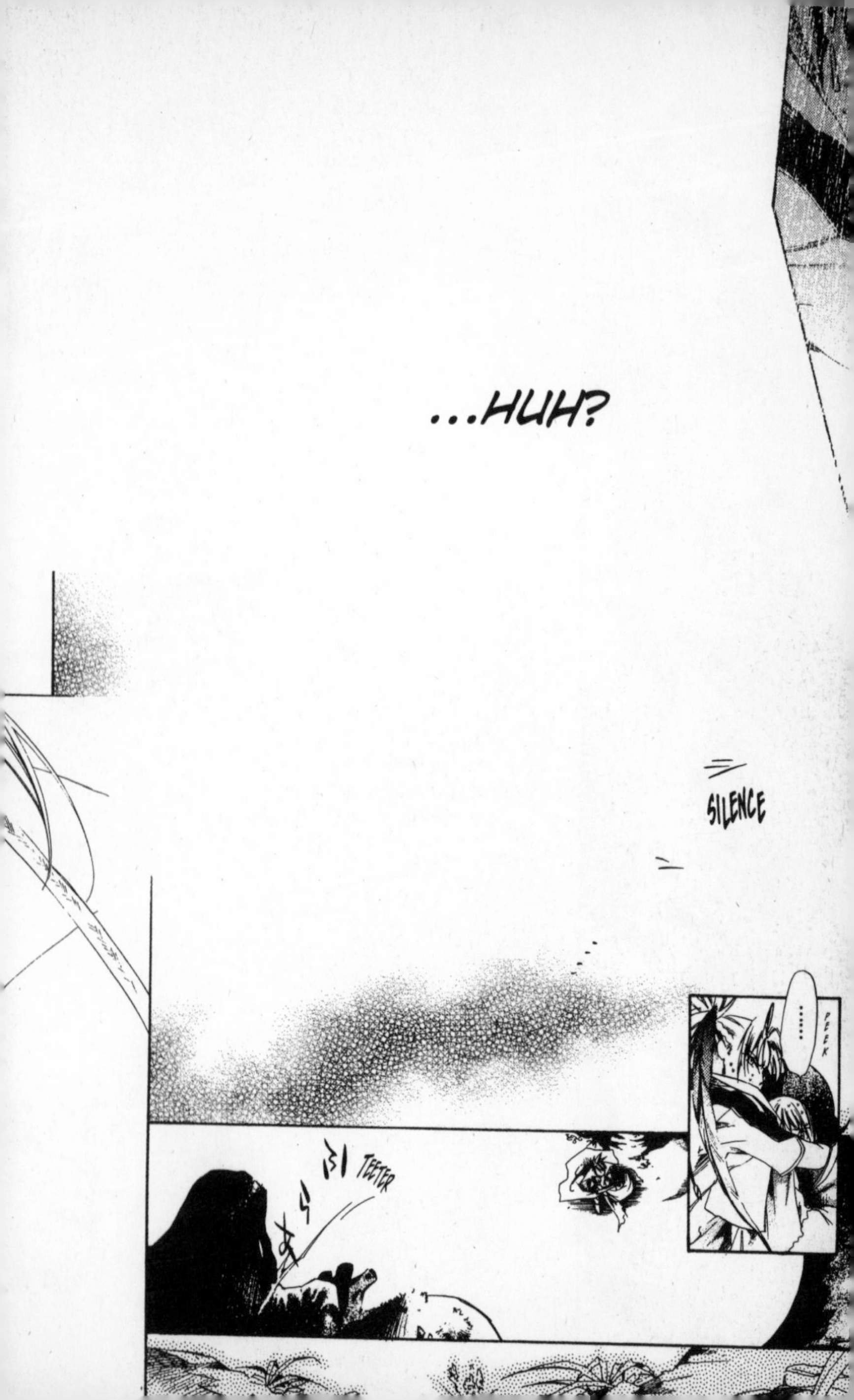
...HUH?
SILENCE
......
PEEK
TEETER

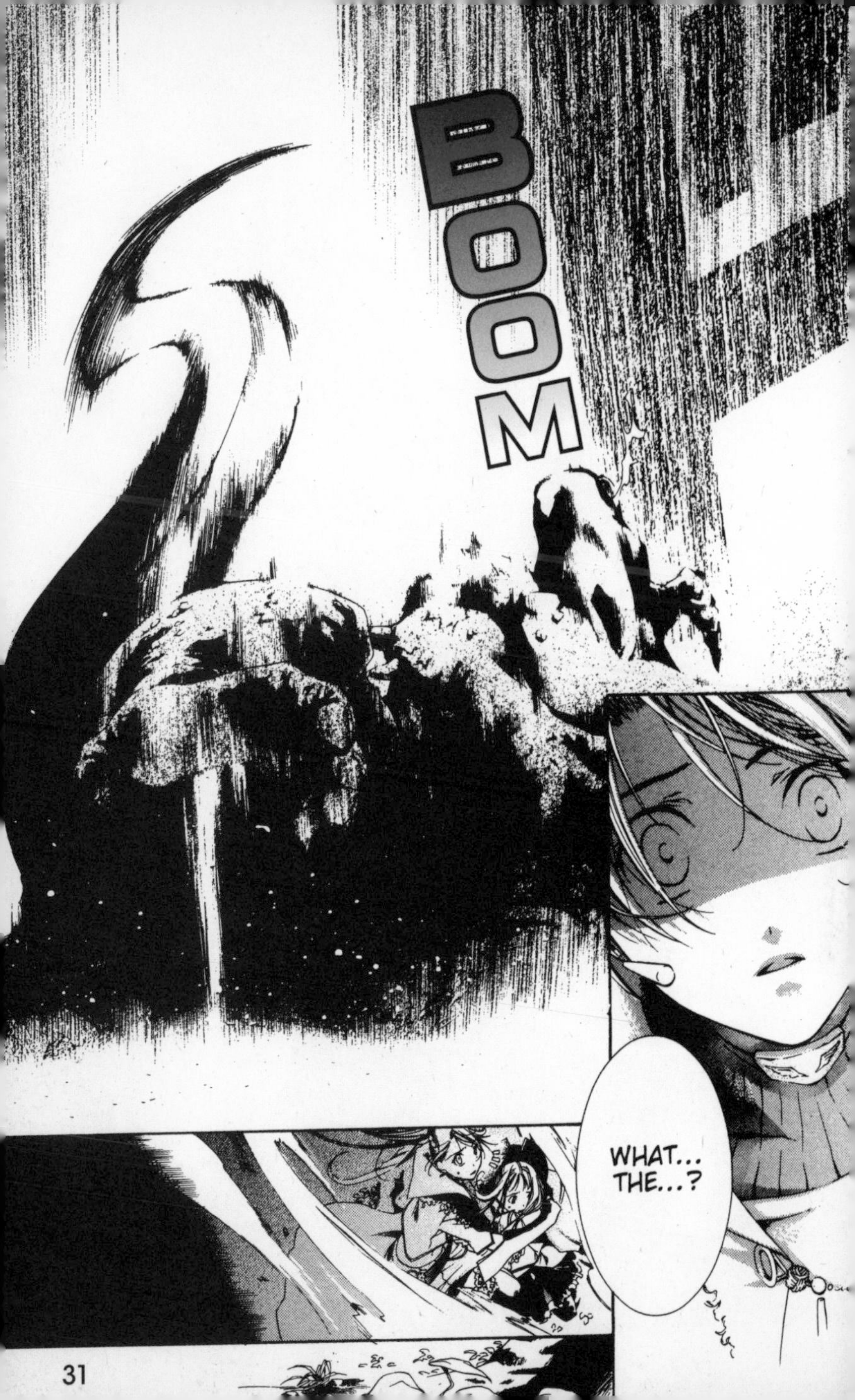
BOOM
WHAT... THE...?

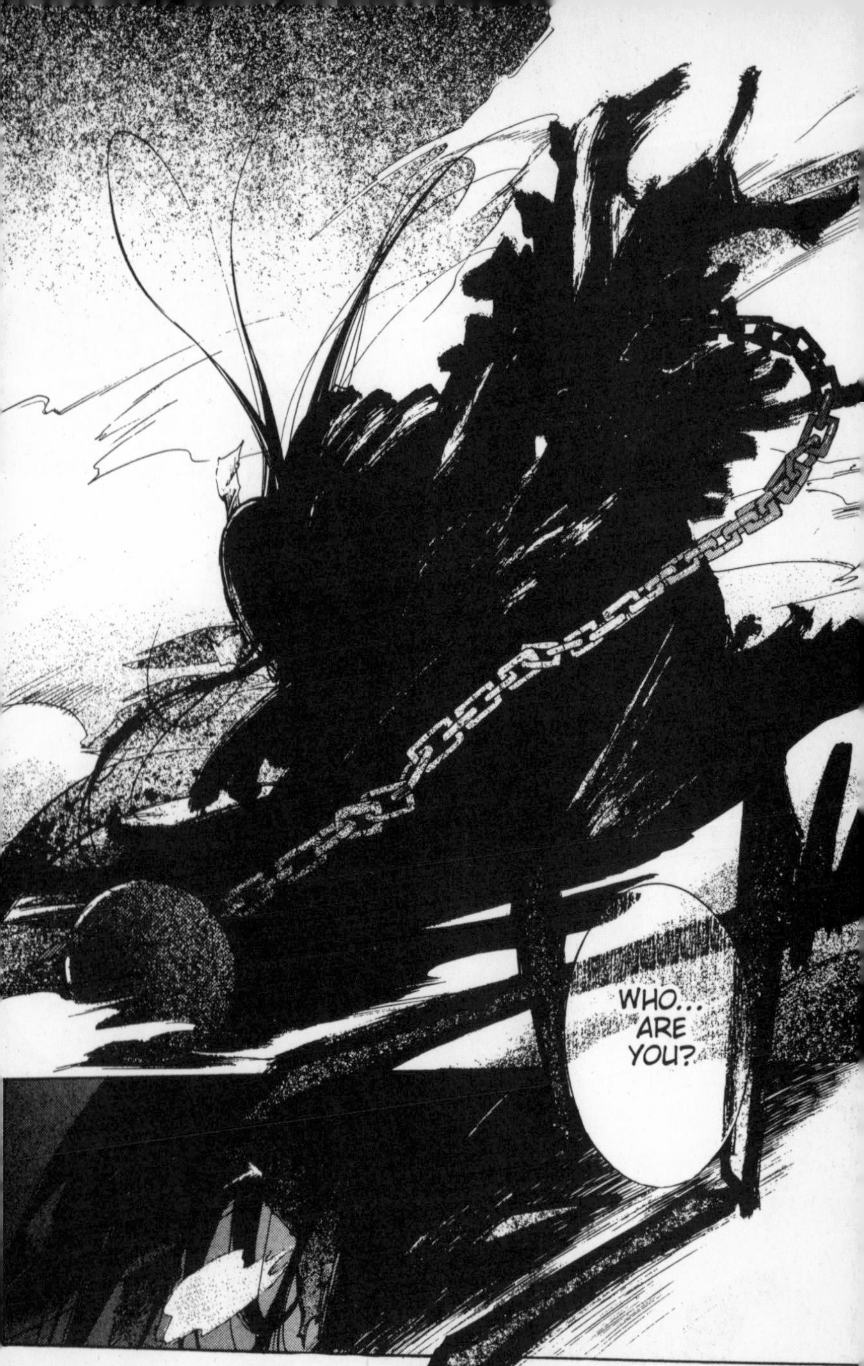
WHO... ARE YOU?

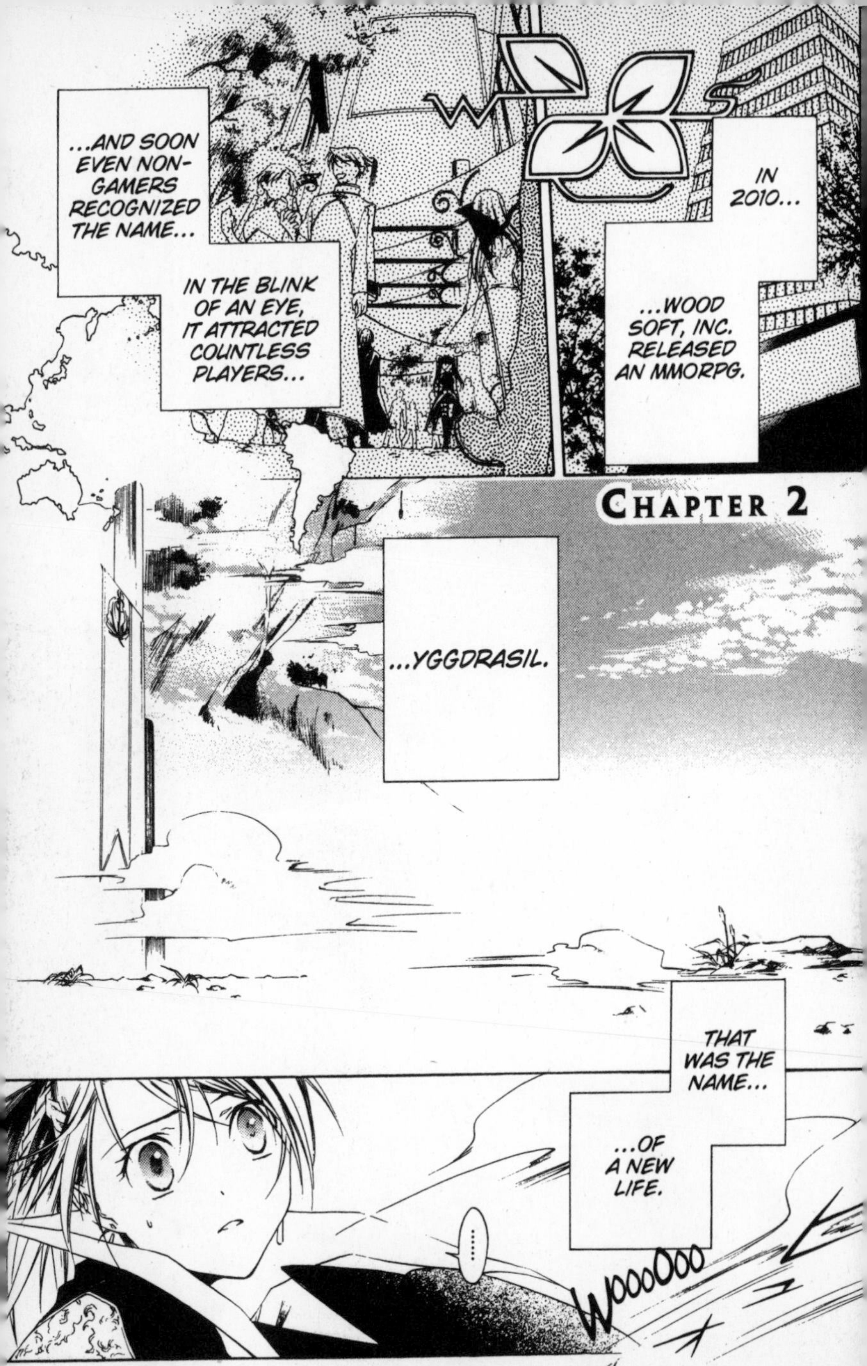
IN 2010...
...WOOD SOFT, INC. RELEASED AN MMORPG.
IN THE BLINK OF AN EYE, IT ATTRACTED COUNTLESS PLAYERS...
...AND SOON EVEN NON-GAMERS RECOGNIZED THE NAME...
CHAPTER 2
...YGGDRASIL.
THAT WAS THE NAME...
...OF A NEW LIFE.
......
WOOOOOO

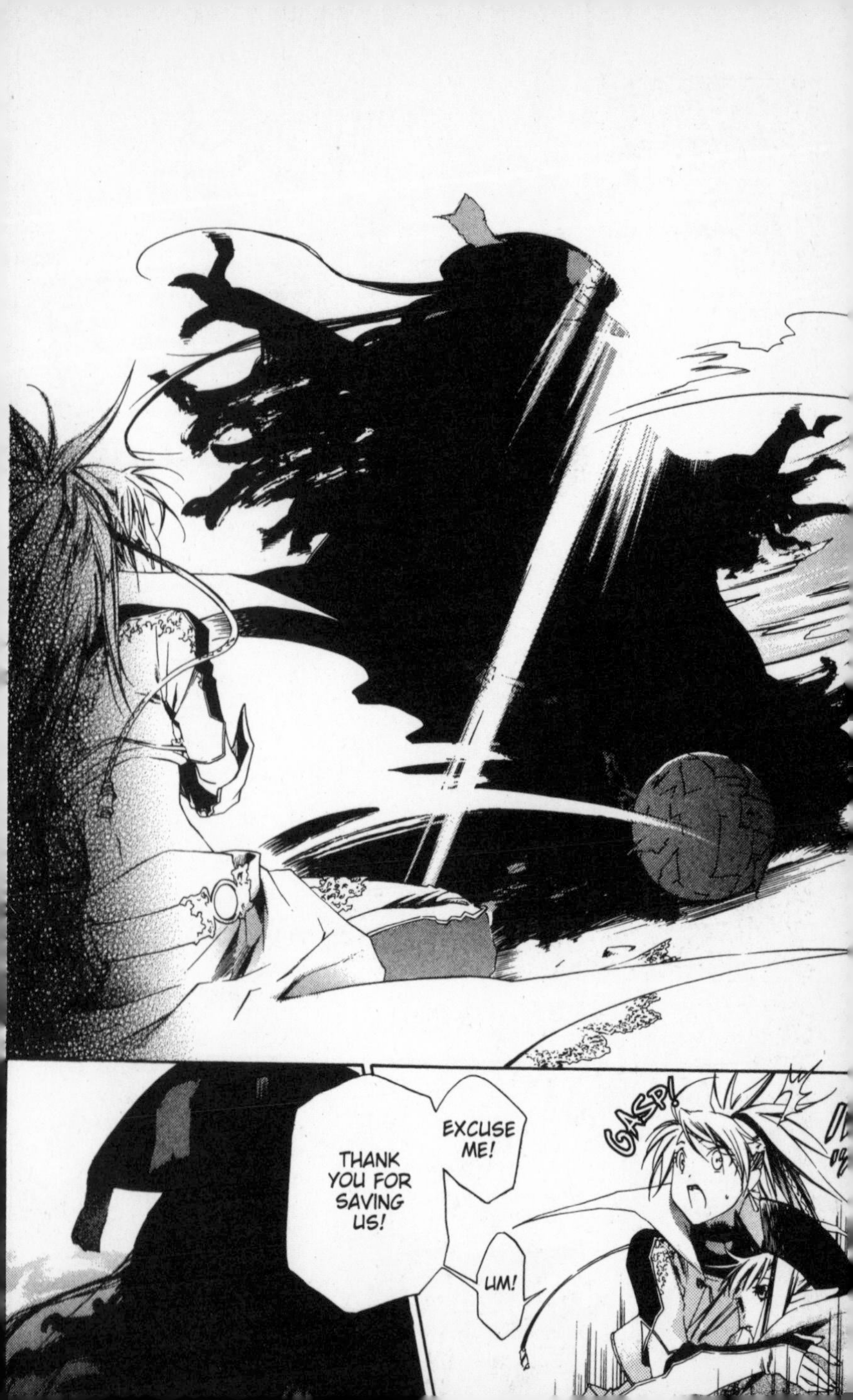
GASP!
EXCUSE ME!
THANK YOU FOR SAVING US!
UM!

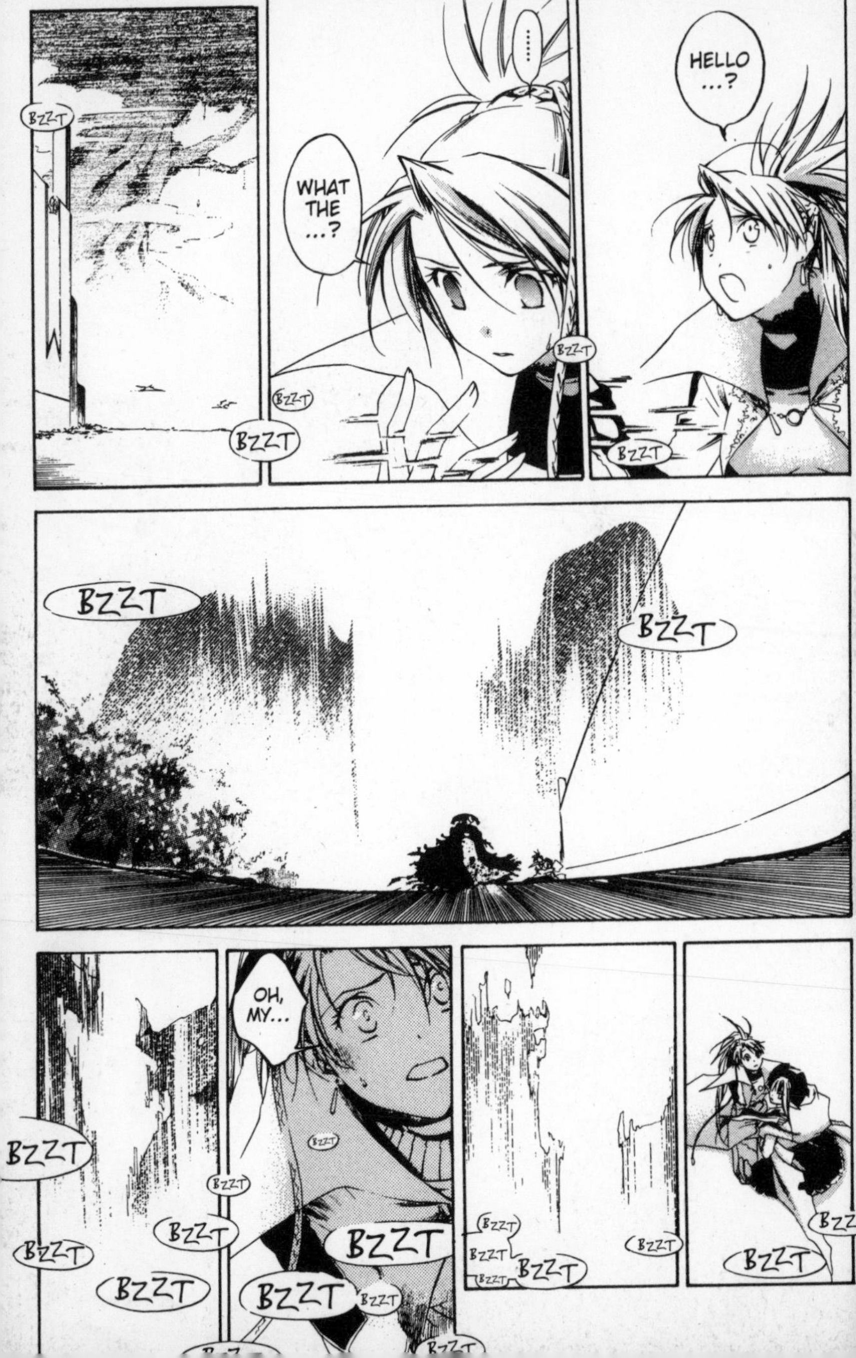

HELLO ...?
BZZT
...
WHAT THE ...?
BZZT
BZZT
BZZT
BZZT
BZZT
BZZT
BZZ
BZZT
BZZT
BZZT
BZZT
BZZT
BZZT
OH, MY...
BZZT
BZZT
BZZT
BZZT
BZZT
BZZT
BZZT
BZZT
BZZT
BZZT

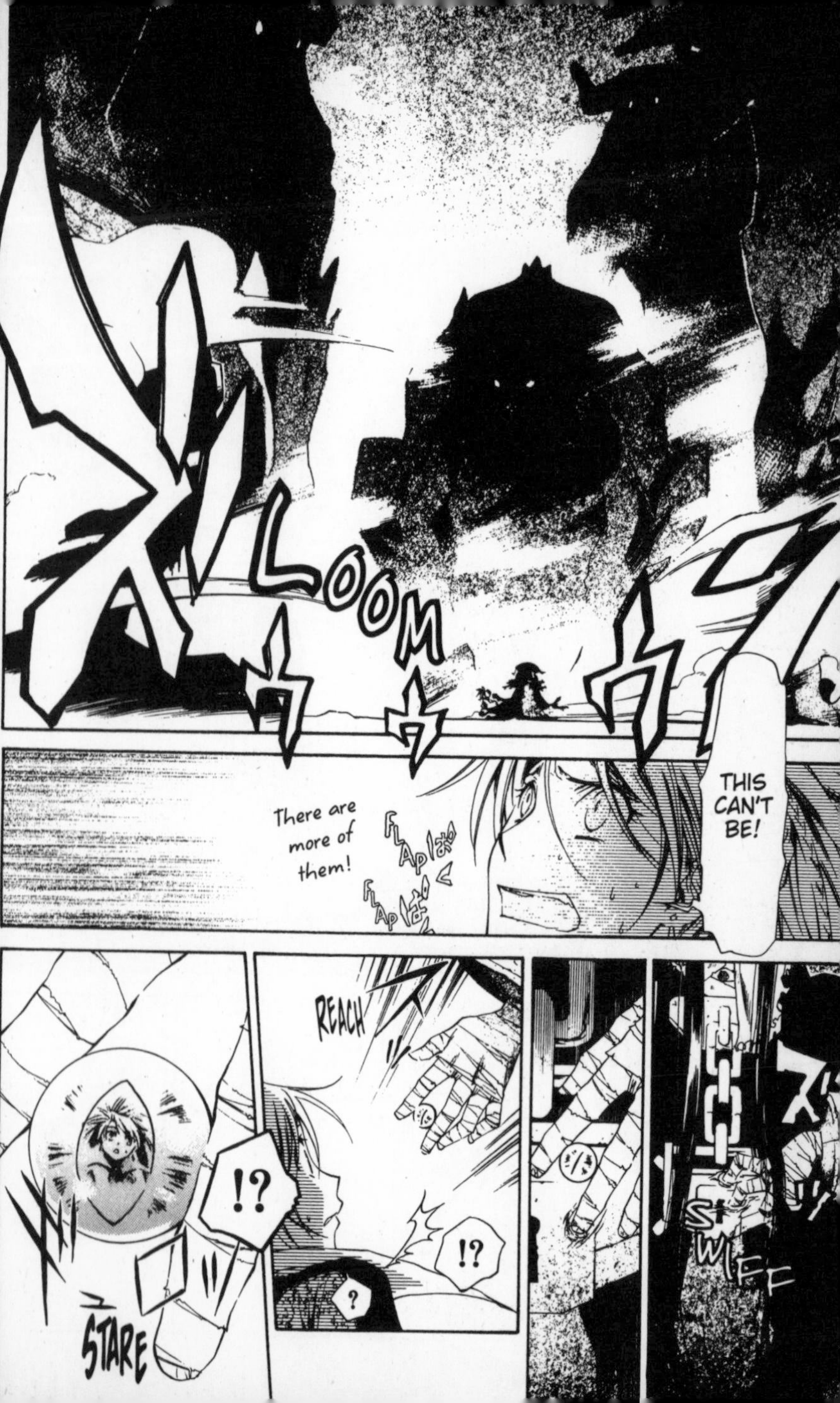
LOOM
THIS CAN'T BE!
FLAP
FLAP
There are more of them!
SWIFF
REACH
!?
?
!?
STARE

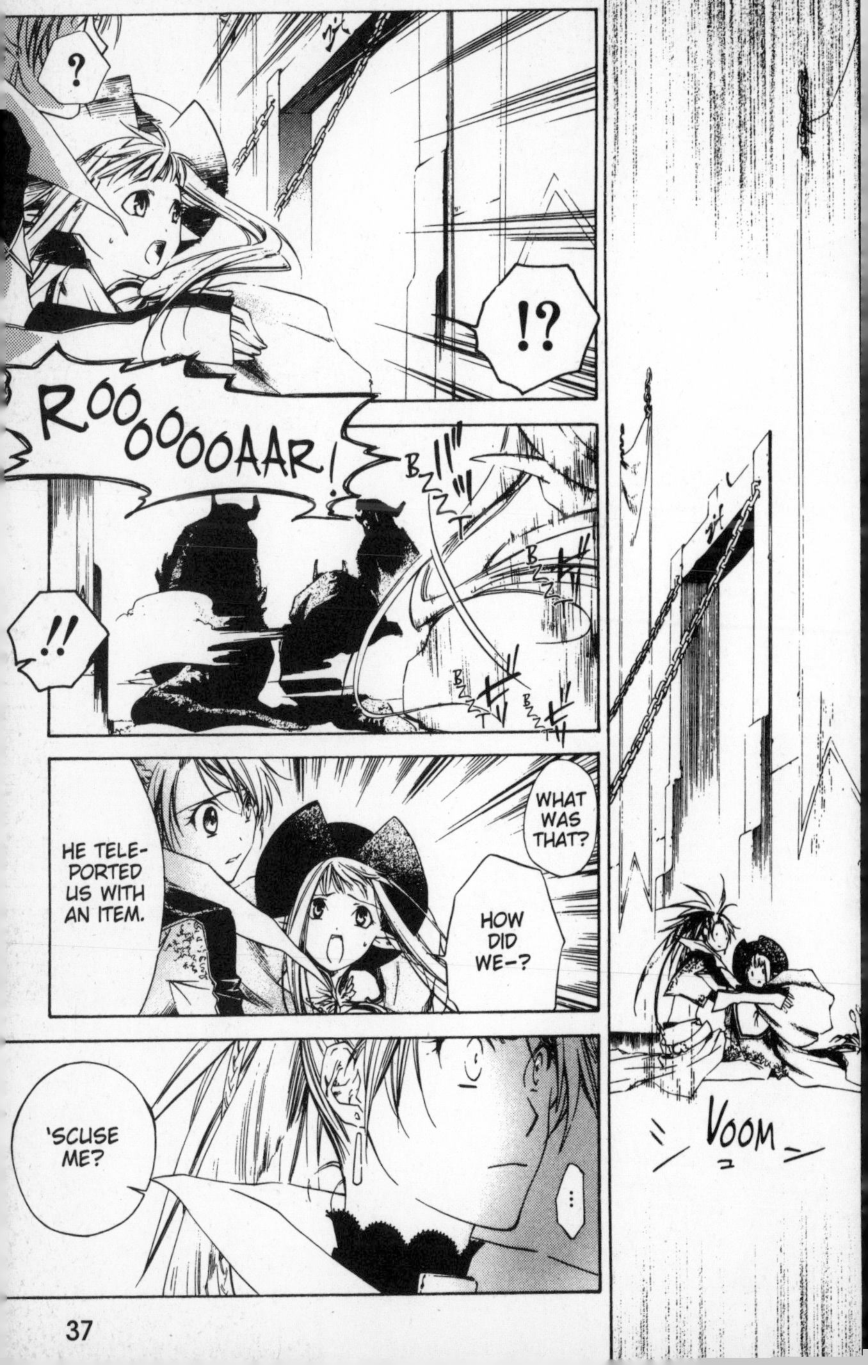
VOOM
?
!?
ROOOOOOAAR!
!!
WHAT WAS THAT?
HOW DID WE-?
HE TELE-PORTED US WITH AN ITEM.
...
'SCUSE ME?

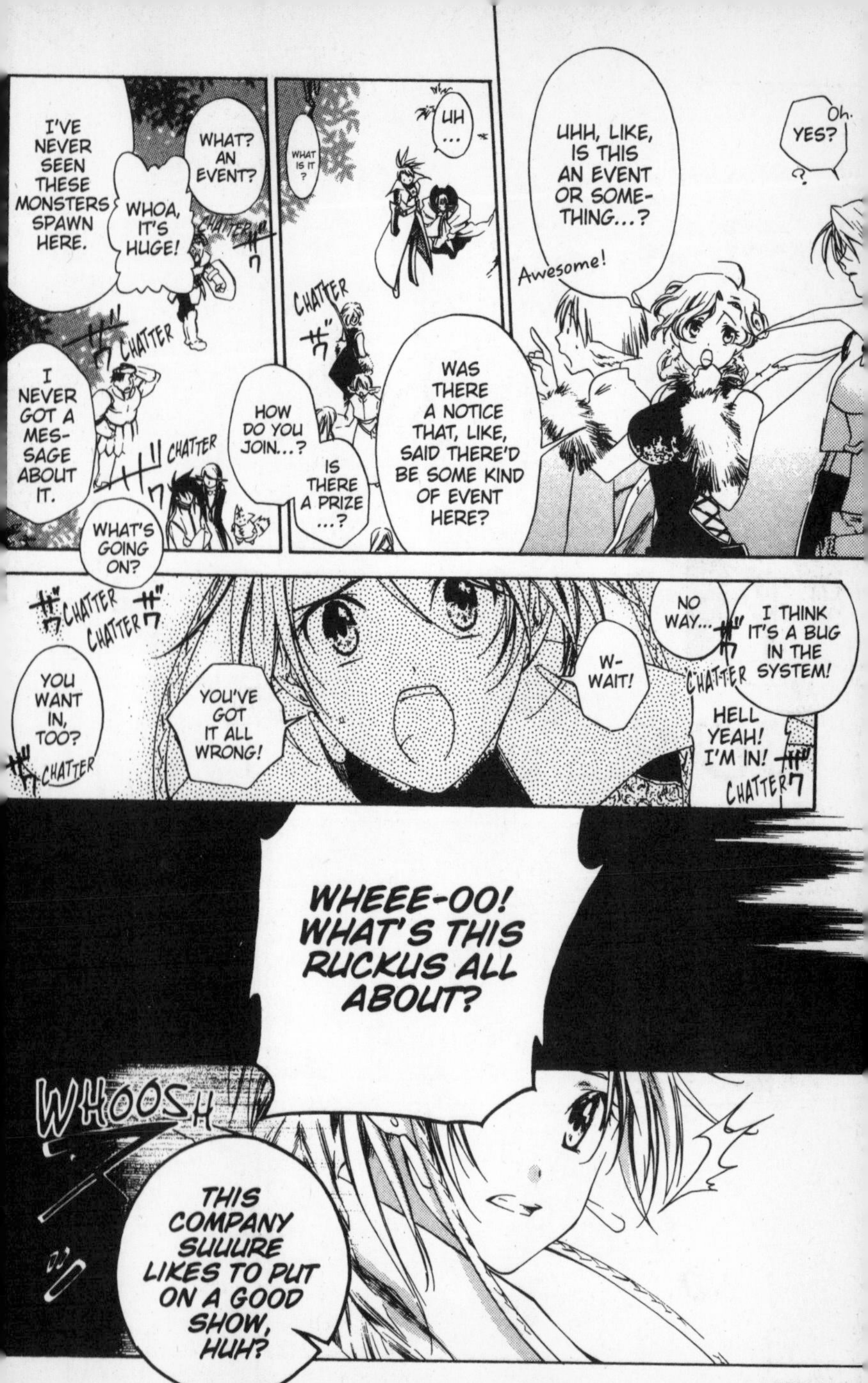

Oh. YES?
?
UHH, LIKE, IS THIS AN EVENT OR SOMETHING...?
Awesome!
WAS THERE A NOTICE THAT, LIKE, SAID THERE'D BE SOME KIND OF EVENT HERE?
UH ...
WHAT IS IT ?
CHATTER
HOW DO YOU JOIN...?
IS THERE A PRIZE ...?
WHAT? AN EVENT?
I'VE NEVER SEEN THESE MONSTERS SPAWN HERE.
WHOA, IT'S HUGE!
CHATTER
CHATTER
I NEVER GOT A MES-SAGE ABOUT IT.
CHATTER
WHAT'S GOING ON?
I THINK IT'S A BUG IN THE SYSTEM!
NO WAY...
CHATTER
HELL YEAH! I'M IN!
CHATTER
W-WAIT!
YOU'VE GOT IT ALL WRONG!
CHATTER
CHATTER
YOU WANT IN, TOO?
CHATTER
WHEEE-OO! WHAT'S THIS RUCKUS ALL ABOUT?
WHOOSH
THIS COMPANY SUUURE LIKES TO PUT ON A GOOD SHOW, HUH?

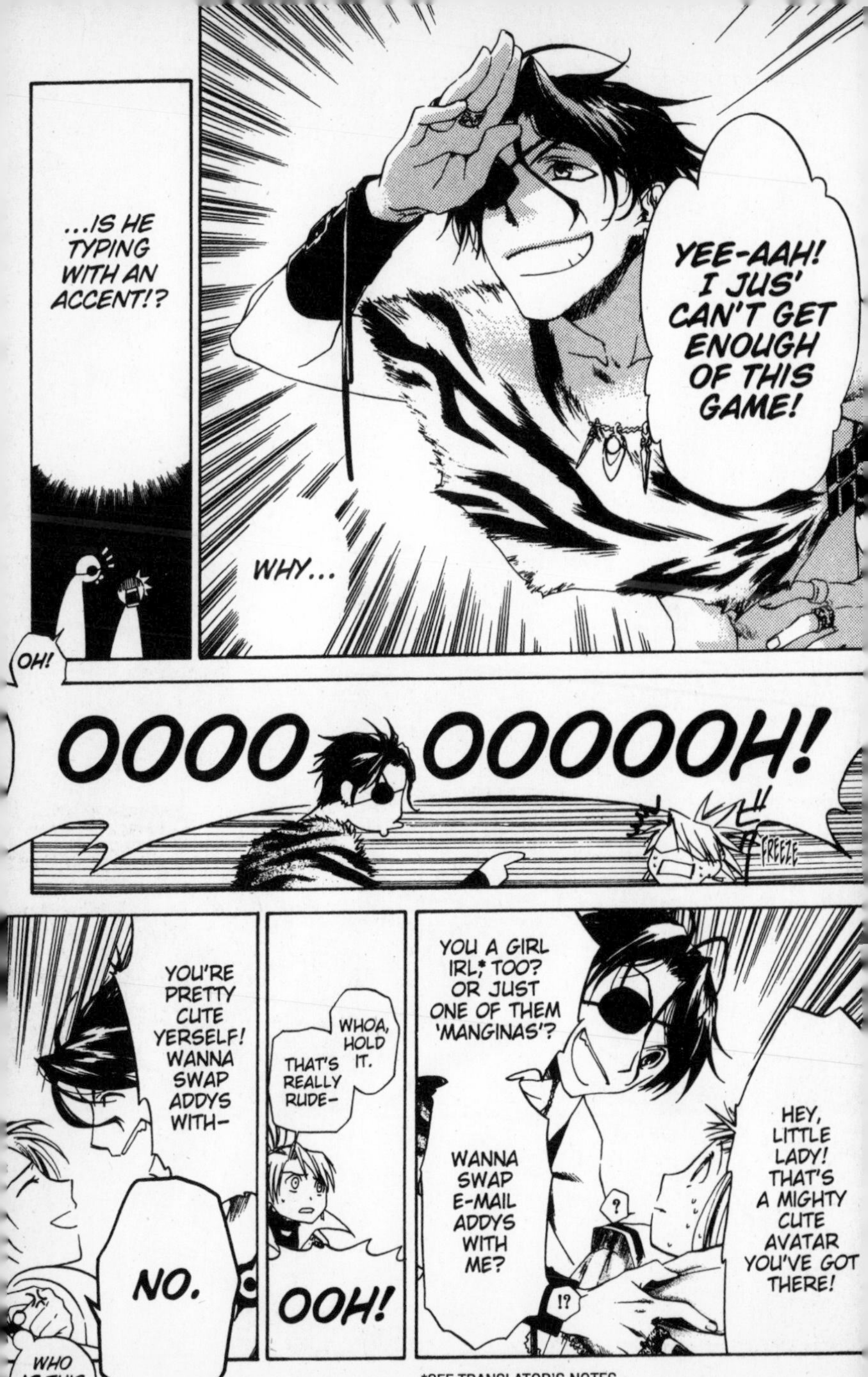
YEE-AAH! I JUS' CAN'T GET ENOUGH OF THIS GAME!
WHY...
...IS HE TYPING WITH AN ACCENT!?
OH!
OOOO OOOOOOH!
FREEZE
HEY, LITTLE LADY! THAT'S A MIGHTY CUTE AVATAR YOU'VE GOT THERE!
?
WANNA SWAP E-MAIL ADDYS WITH ME?
!?
YOU A GIRL IRL,* TOO? OR JUST ONE OF THEM 'MANGINAS'?
WHOA, HOLD IT.
THAT'S REALLY RUDE-
OOH!
YOU'RE PRETTY CUTE YERSELF! WANNA SWAP ADDYS WITH-
NO.
WHO IS THIS GUY?

*SEE TRANSLATOR'S NOTES

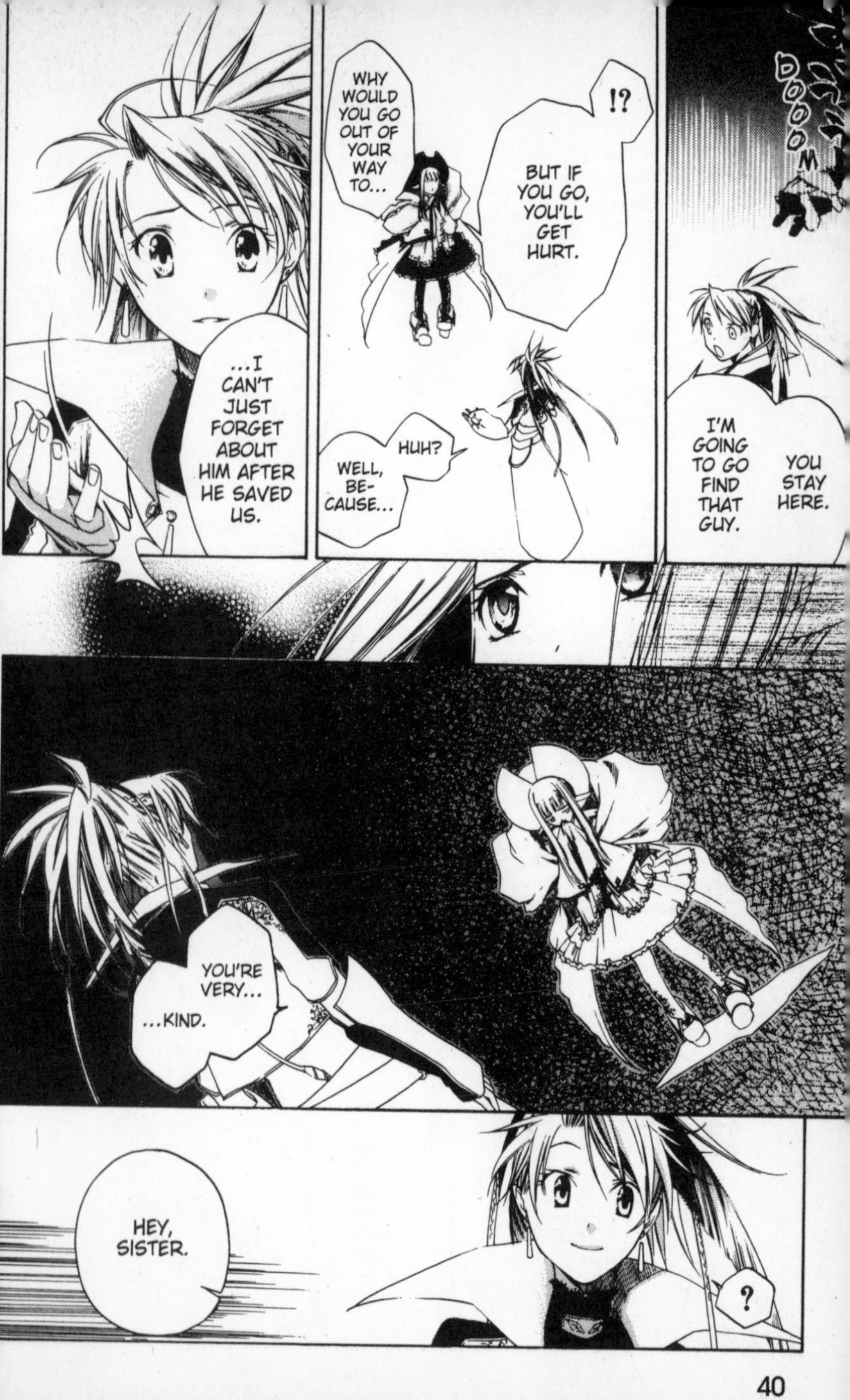
DOOOOM
I'M GOING TO GO FIND THAT GUY. YOU STAY HERE.
!?
BUT IF YOU GO, YOU'LL GET HURT.
WHY WOULD YOU GO OUT OF YOUR WAY TO...
HUH?
WELL, BE-CAUSE...
...I CAN'T JUST FORGET ABOUT HIM AFTER HE SAVED US.
YOU'RE VERY... ...KIND.
HEY, SISTER.
?

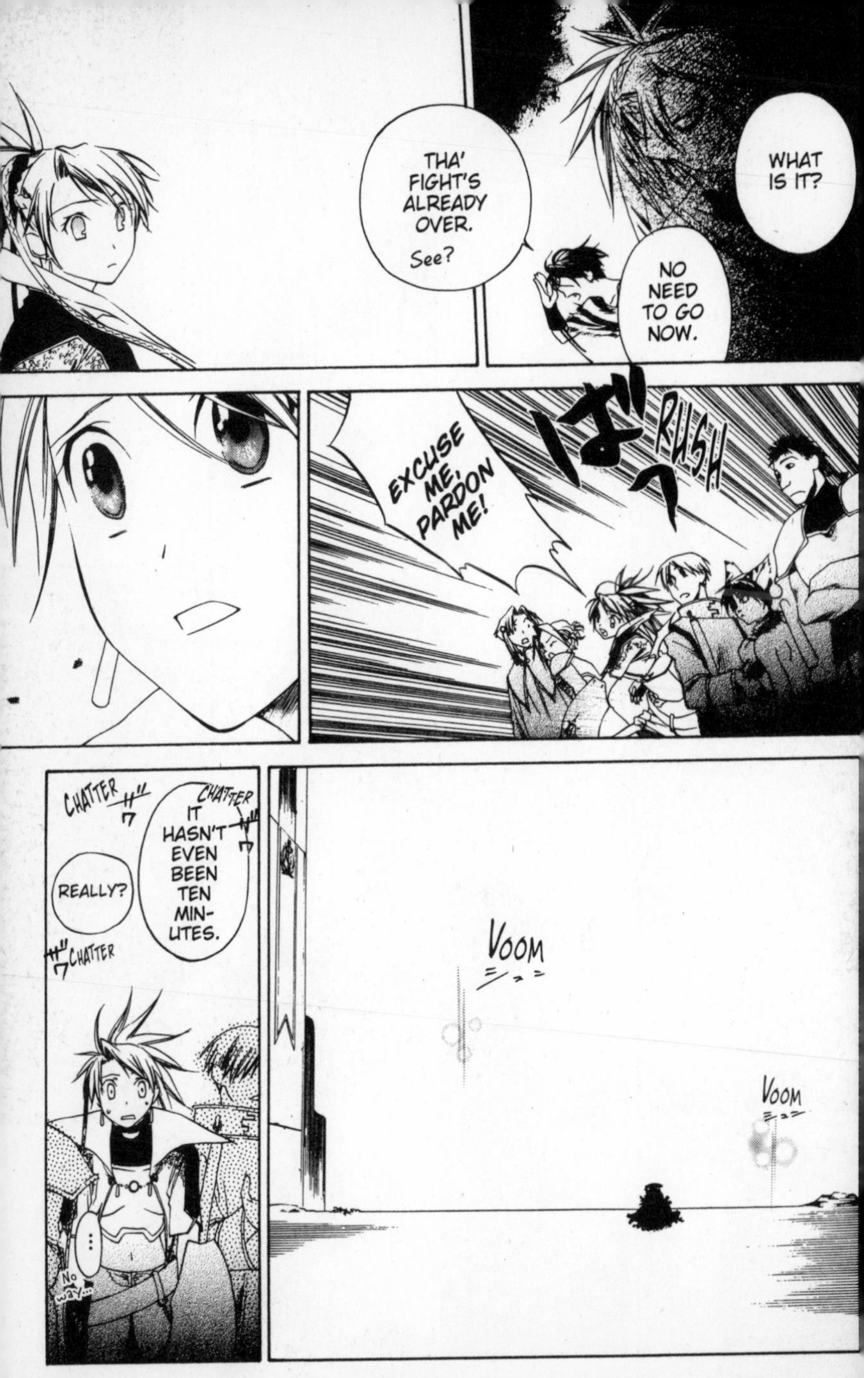
WHAT IS IT?
NO NEED TO GO NOW.
THA' FIGHT'S ALREADY OVER.
See?
ぱっ
RUSH
EXCUSE ME, PARDON ME!
VOOM
VOOM
CHATTER
CHATTER
IT HASN'T EVEN BEEN TEN MIN-UTES.
REALLY?
CHATTER
...
No way...

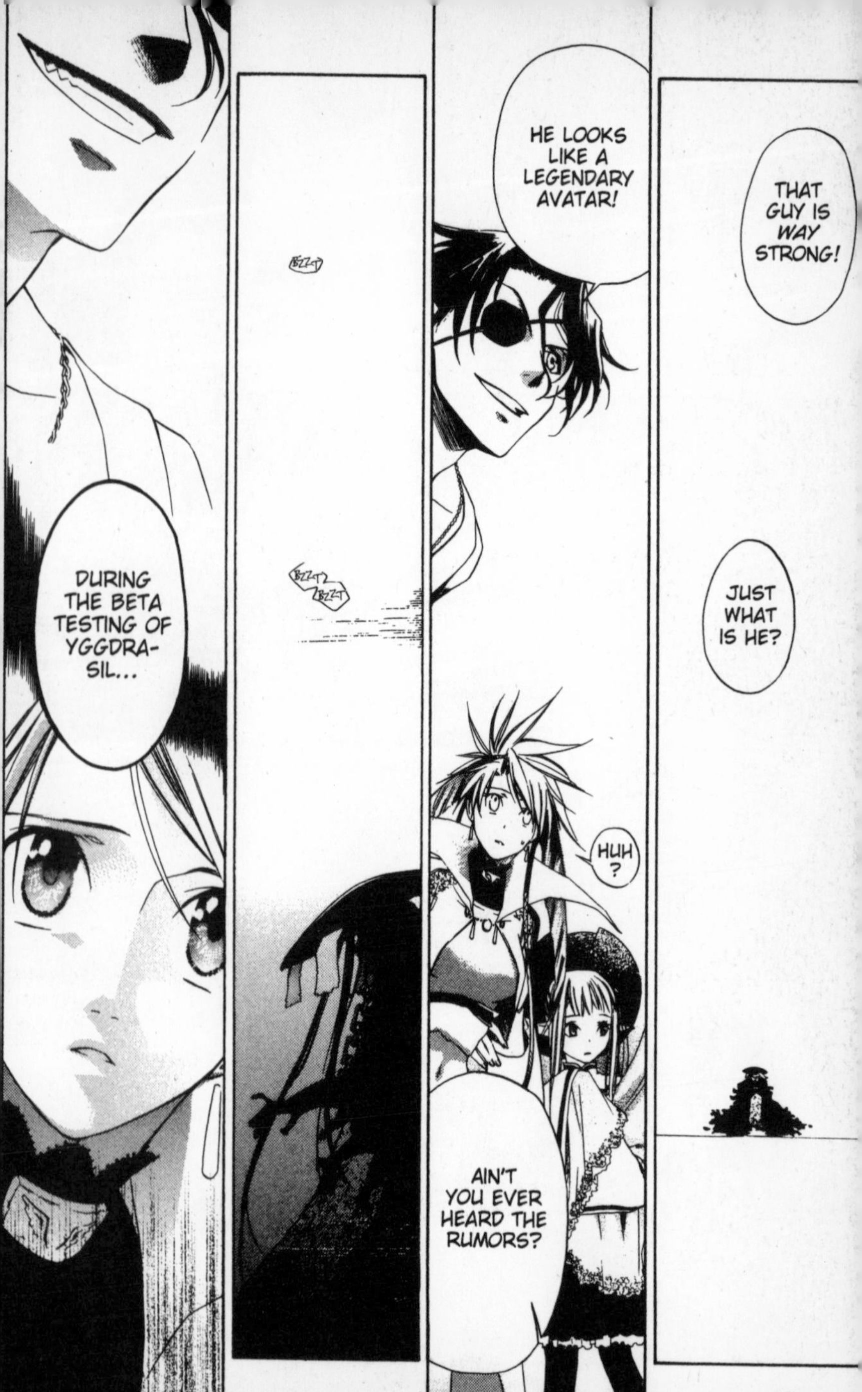
THAT GUY IS WAY STRONG!
JUST WHAT IS HE?
HE LOOKS LIKE A LEGENDARY AVATAR!
HUH?
AIN'T YOU EVER HEARD THE RUMORS?
BZZT
DURING THE BETA TESTING OF YGGDRA-SIL...

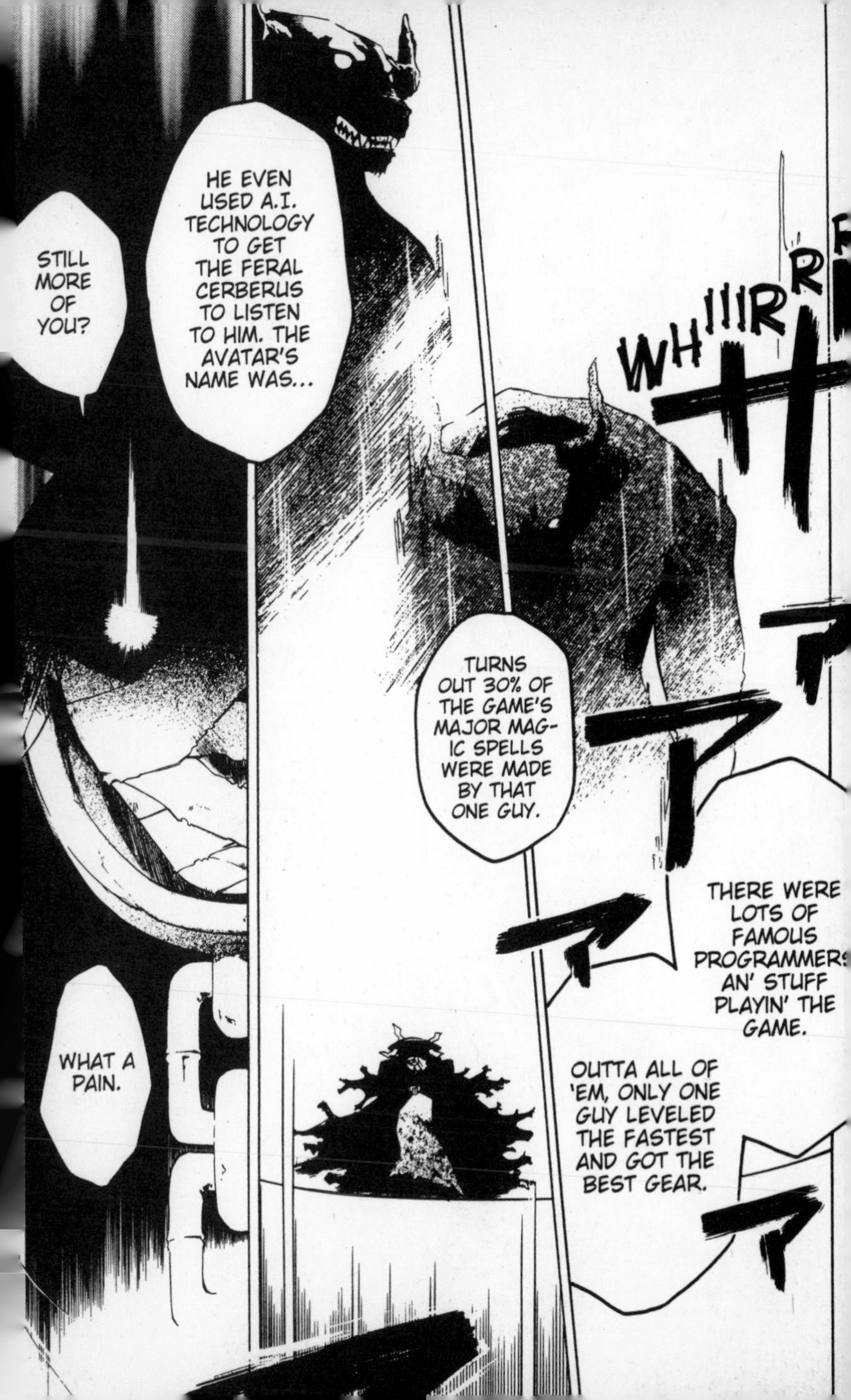
WHIIIRRRR
THERE WERE LOTS OF FAMOUS PROGRAMMERS AN' STUFF PLAYIN' THE GAME.
OUTTA ALL OF 'EM, ONLY ONE GUY LEVELED THE FASTEST AND GOT THE BEST GEAR.
TURNS OUT 30% OF THE GAME'S MAJOR MAG-IC SPELLS WERE MADE BY THAT ONE GUY.
HE EVEN USED A.I. TECHNOLOGY TO GET THE FERAL CERBERUS TO LISTEN TO HIM. THE AVATAR'S NAME WAS...
STILL MORE OF YOU?
WHAT A PAIN.

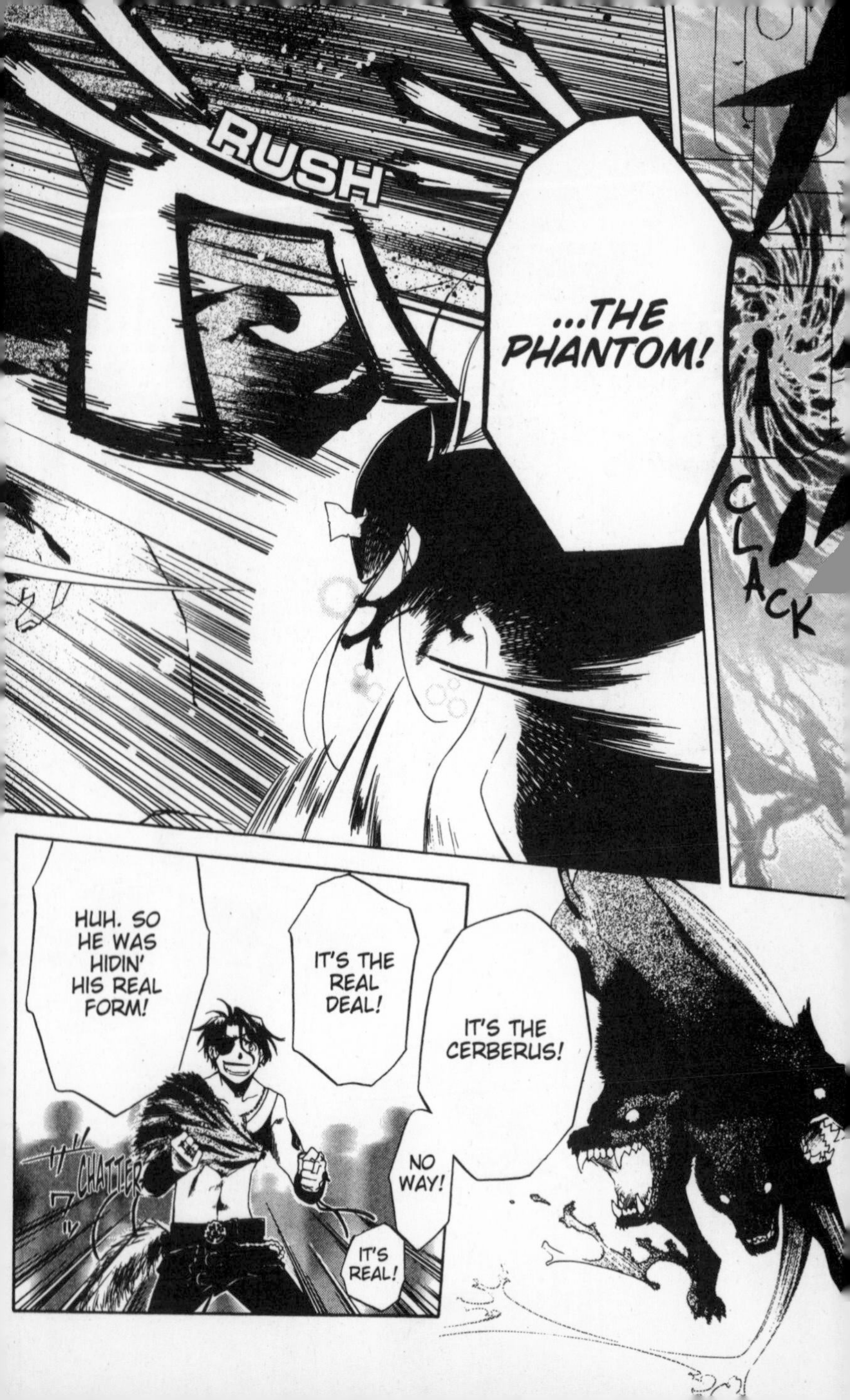
CLACK
...THE PHANTOM!
RUSH
IT'S THE CERBERUS!
IT'S THE REAL DEAL!
HUH. SO HE WAS HIDIN' HIS REAL FORM!
NO WAY!
IT'S REAL!
CHATTER

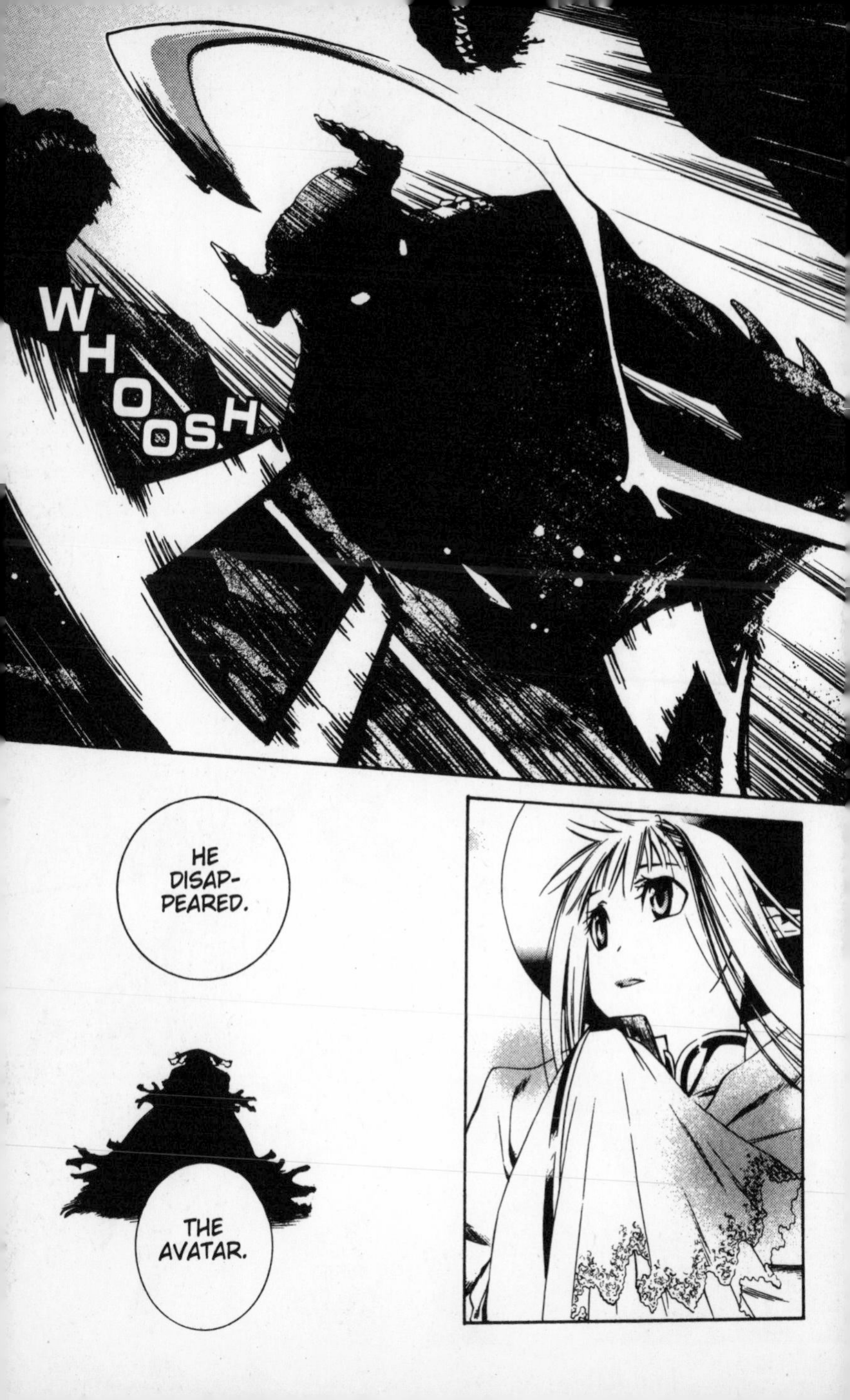
WHOOSH
HE DISAPPEARED.
THE AVATAR.

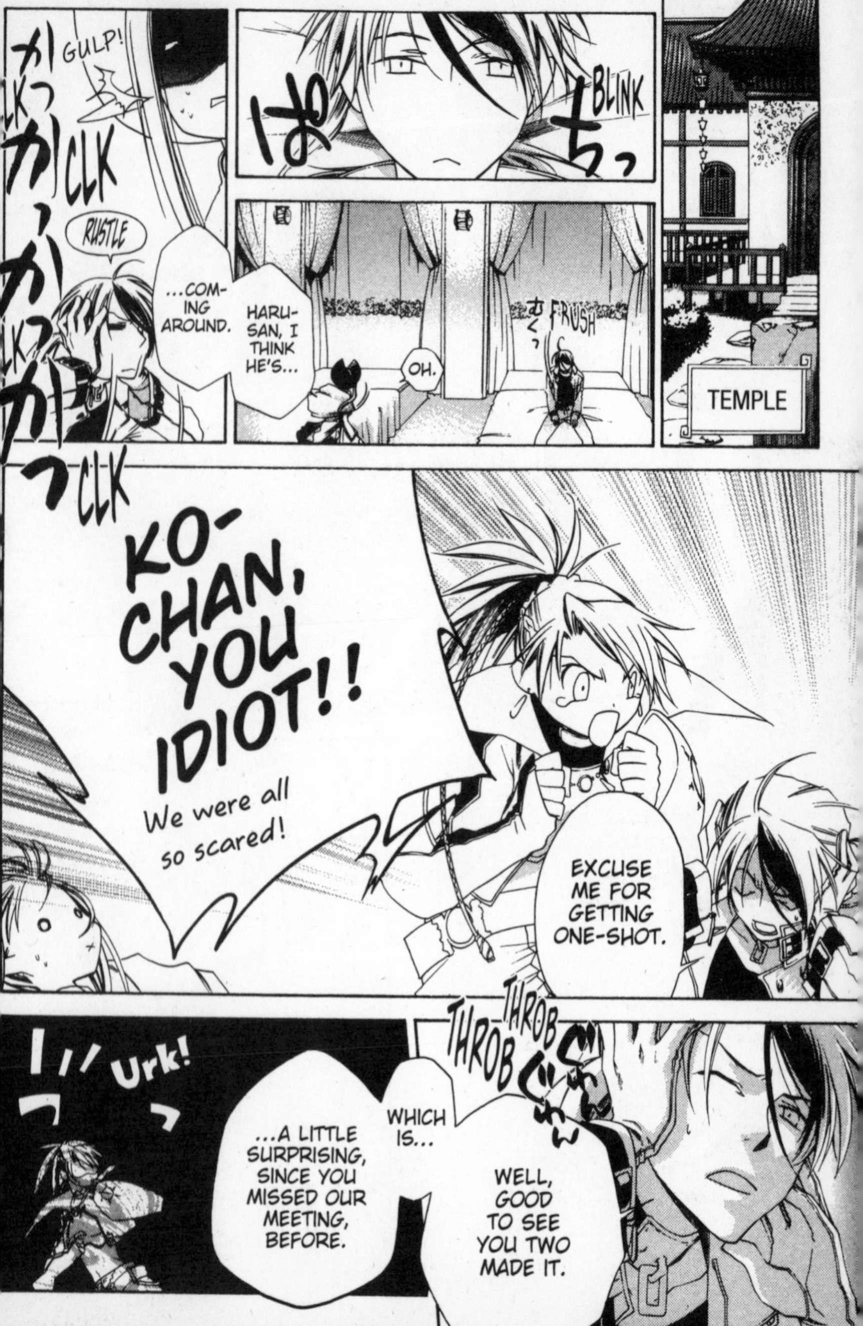
TEMPLE
BLINK
FRUSH
OH.
HARU-SAN, I THINK HE'S...
...COMING AROUND.
GULP!
CLK
RUSTLE
CLK
KO-CHAN, YOU IDIOT!!
We were all so scared!
EXCUSE ME FOR GETTING ONE-SHOT.
THROB
THROB
WELL, GOOD TO SEE YOU TWO MADE IT.
WHICH IS...
...A LITTLE SURPRISING, SINCE YOU MISSED OUR MEETING, BEFORE.
Urk!

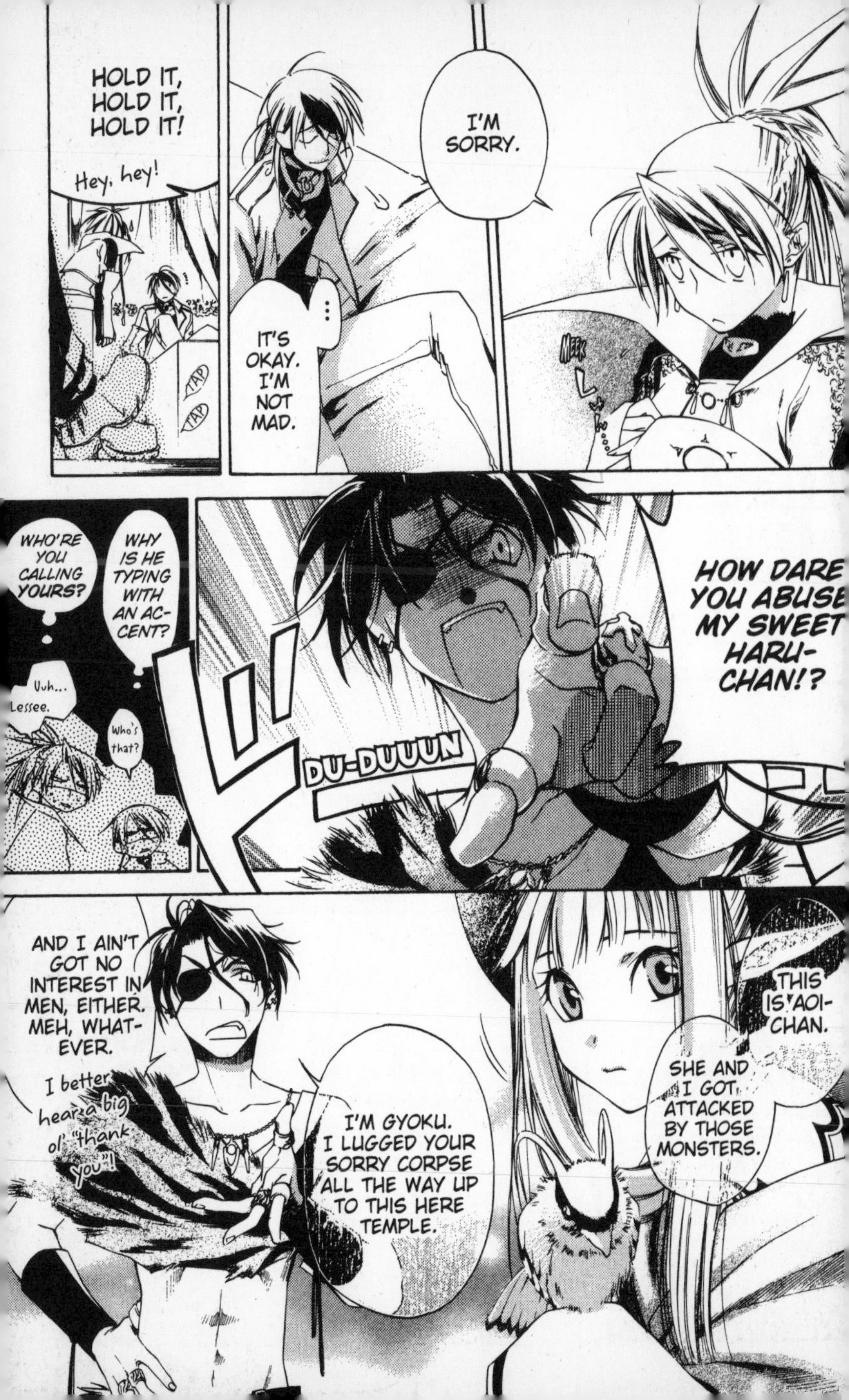
I'M SORRY.
MEEK
...
IT'S OKAY. I'M NOT MAD.
HOLD IT, HOLD IT, HOLD IT!
Hey, hey!
TAP
TAP
HOW DARE YOU ABUSE MY SWEET HARU-CHAN!?
DU-DUUUN
WHY IS HE TYPING WITH AN AC-CENT?
WHO'RE YOU CALLING YOURS?
Uuh... Lessee.
Who's that?
THIS IS AOI-CHAN.
SHE AND I GOT ATTACKED BY THOSE MONSTERS.
I'M GYOKU. I LUGGED YOUR SORRY CORPSE ALL THE WAY UP TO THIS HERE TEMPLE.
AND I AIN'T GOT NO INTEREST IN MEN, EITHER. MEH, WHAT-EVER.
I better hear a big ol' "thank you"!

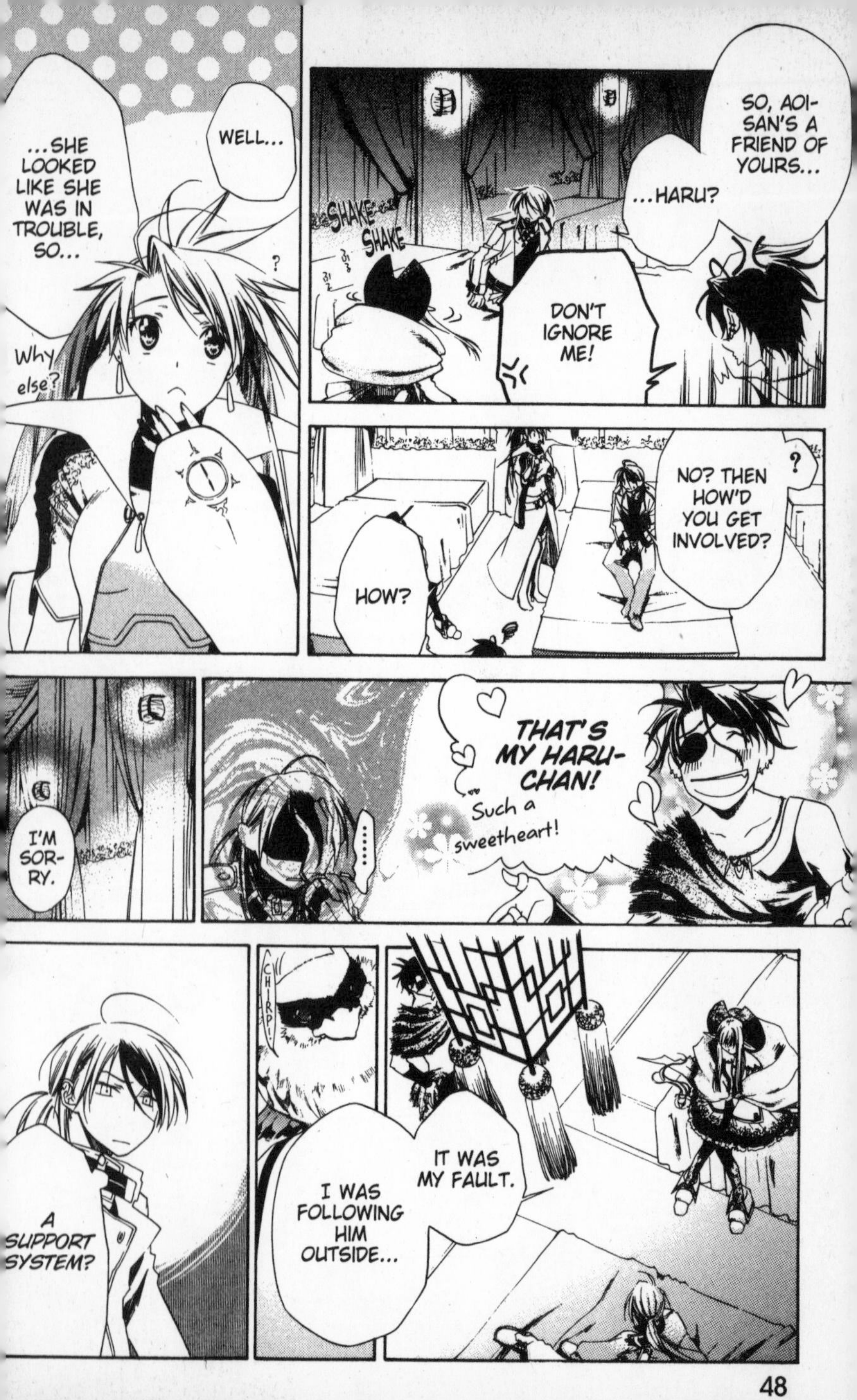
SO, AOI-SAN'S A FRIEND OF YOURS...
...HARU?
SHAKE SHAKE
DON'T IGNORE ME!
?
NO? THEN HOW'D YOU GET INVOLVED?
HOW?
WELL...
...SHE LOOKED LIKE SHE WAS IN TROUBLE, SO...
?
Why else?
THAT'S MY HARU-CHAN!
Such a sweetheart!
......
I'M SORRY.
IT WAS MY FAULT.
I WAS FOLLOWING HIM OUTSIDE...
CHIRP!
A SUPPORT SYSTEM?

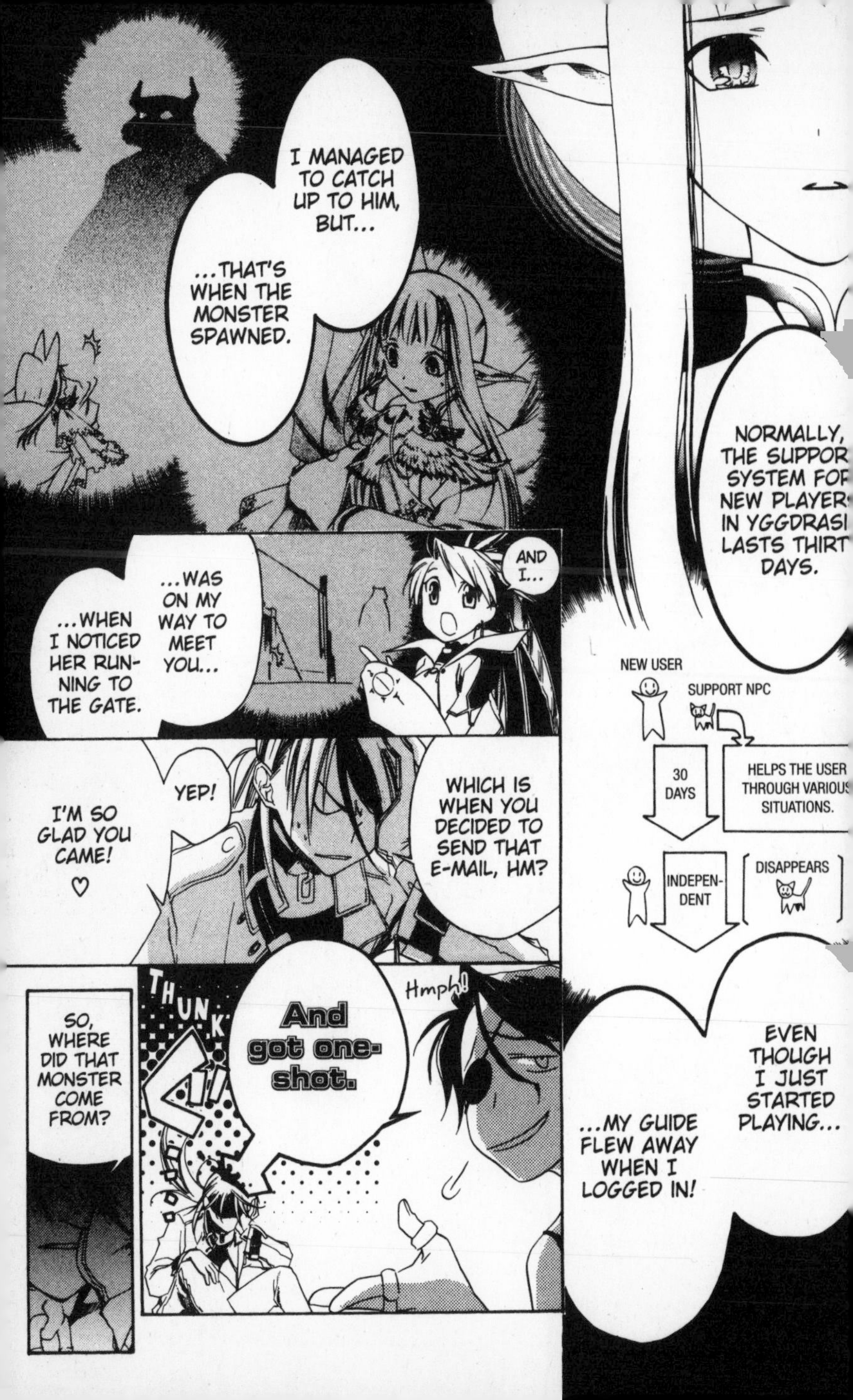
NORMALLY, THE SUPPOR SYSTEM FO NEW PLAYER IN YGGDRASI LASTS THIRT DAYS.
NEW USER
SUPPORT NPC
30 DAYS
HELPS THE USER THROUGH VARIOU SITUATIONS.
INDEPEN-DENT
DISAPPEARS
EVEN THOUGH I JUST STARTED PLAYING...
...MY GUIDE FLEW AWAY WHEN I LOGGED IN!
I MANAGED TO CATCH UP TO HIM, BUT...
...THAT'S WHEN THE MONSTER SPAWNED.
AND I...
...WAS ON MY WAY TO MEET YOU...
...WHEN I NOTICED HER RUN-NING TO THE GATE.
WHICH IS WHEN YOU DECIDED TO SEND THAT E-MAIL, HM?
YEP!
I'M SO GLAD YOU CAME! ♡
Hmph!
And got one-shot.
THUNK
SO, WHERE DID THAT MONSTER COME FROM?

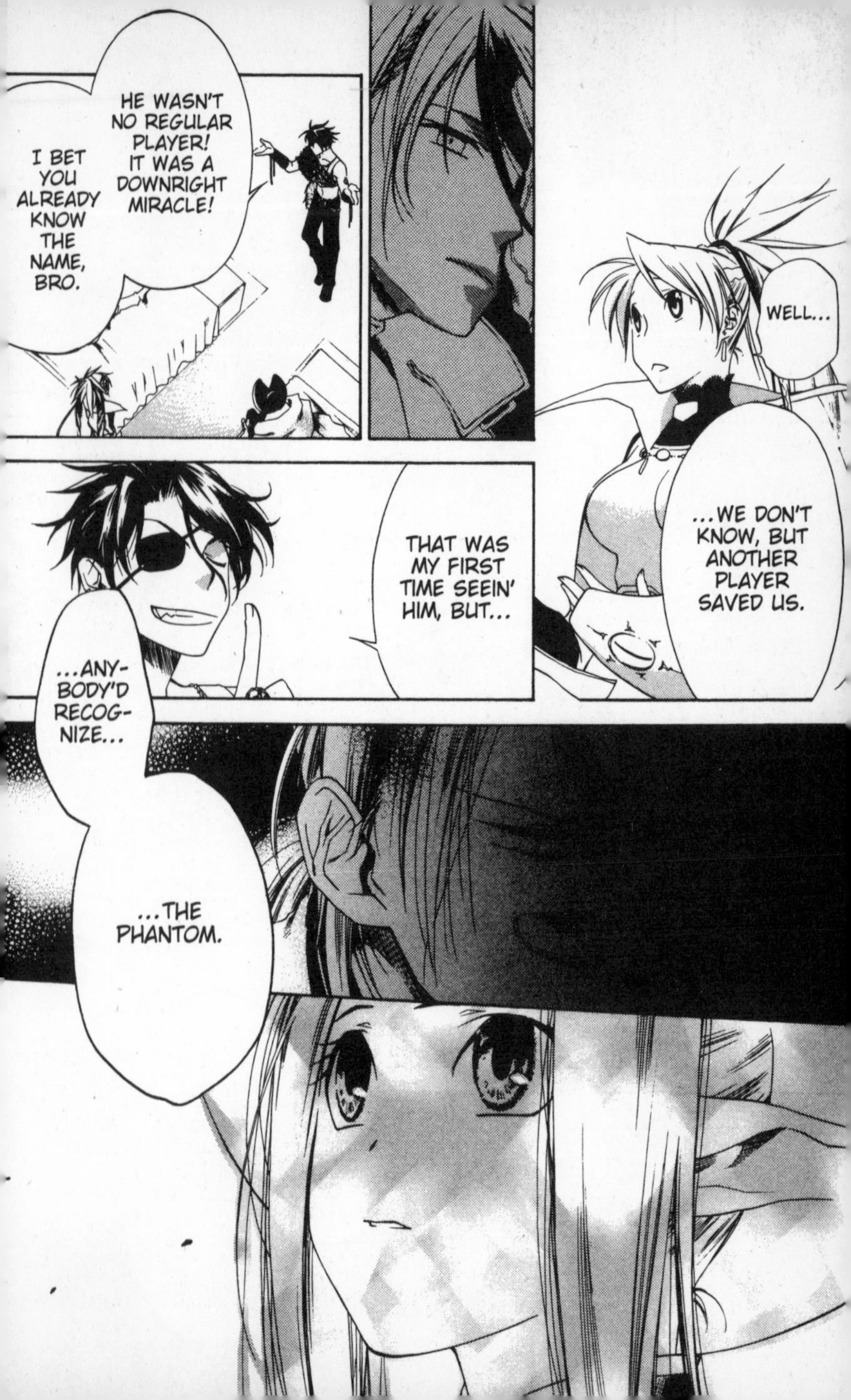
WELL...
...WE DON'T KNOW, BUT ANOTHER PLAYER SAVED US.
HE WASN'T NO REGULAR PLAYER! IT WAS A DOWNRIGHT MIRACLE!
I BET YOU ALREADY KNOW THE NAME, BRO.
THAT WAS MY FIRST TIME SEEIN' HIM, BUT...
...ANY-BODY'D RECOG-NIZE...
...THE PHANTOM.

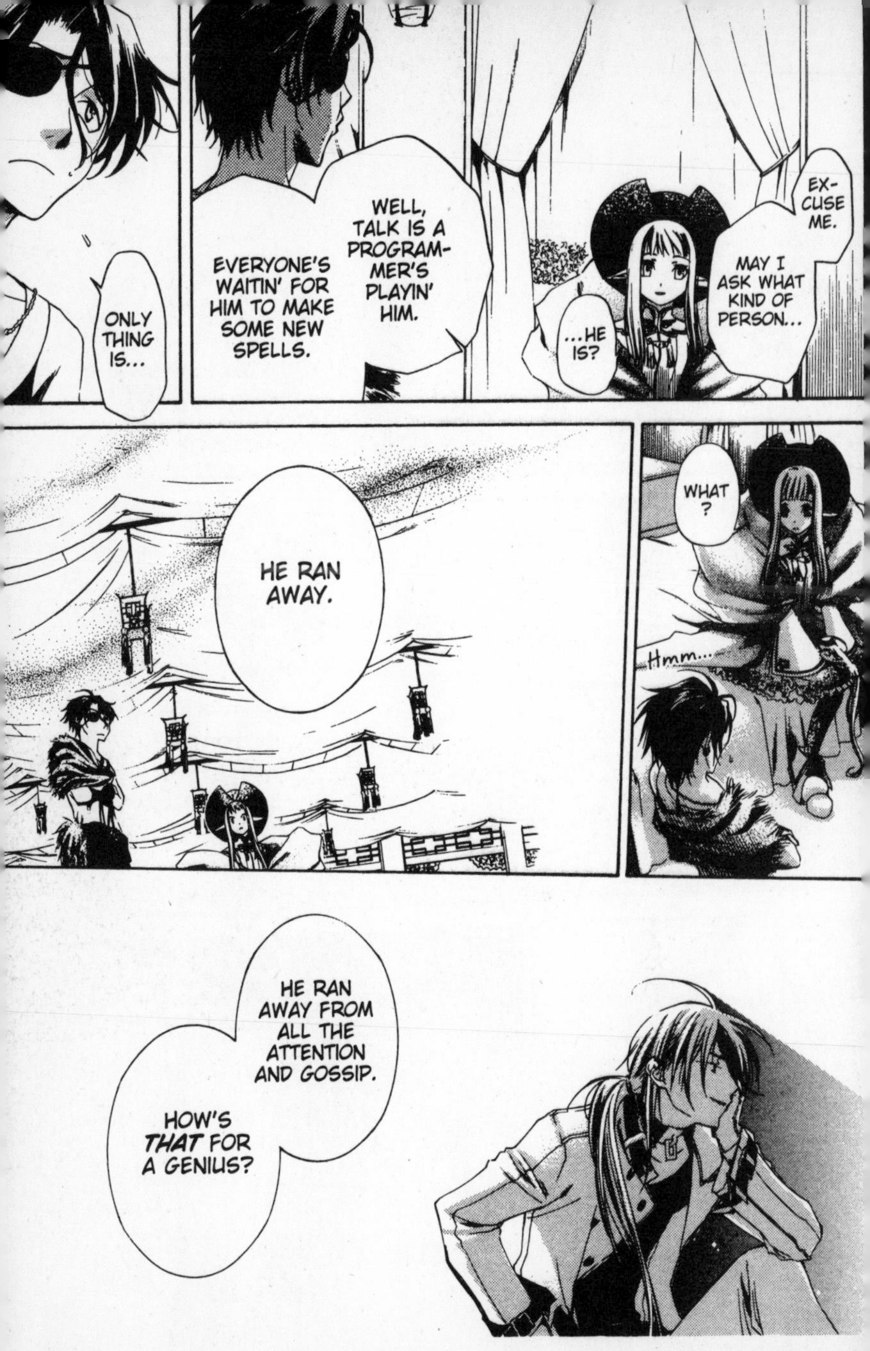
EX-CUSE ME.
MAY I ASK WHAT KIND OF PERSON...
...HE IS?
WELL, TALK IS A PROGRAM-MER'S PLAYIN' HIM.
EVERYONE'S WAITIN' FOR HIM TO MAKE SOME NEW SPELLS.
ONLY THING IS...
WHAT ?
Hmm...
HE RAN AWAY.
HE RAN AWAY FROM ALL THE ATTENTION AND GOSSIP.
HOW'S *THAT* FOR A GENIUS?

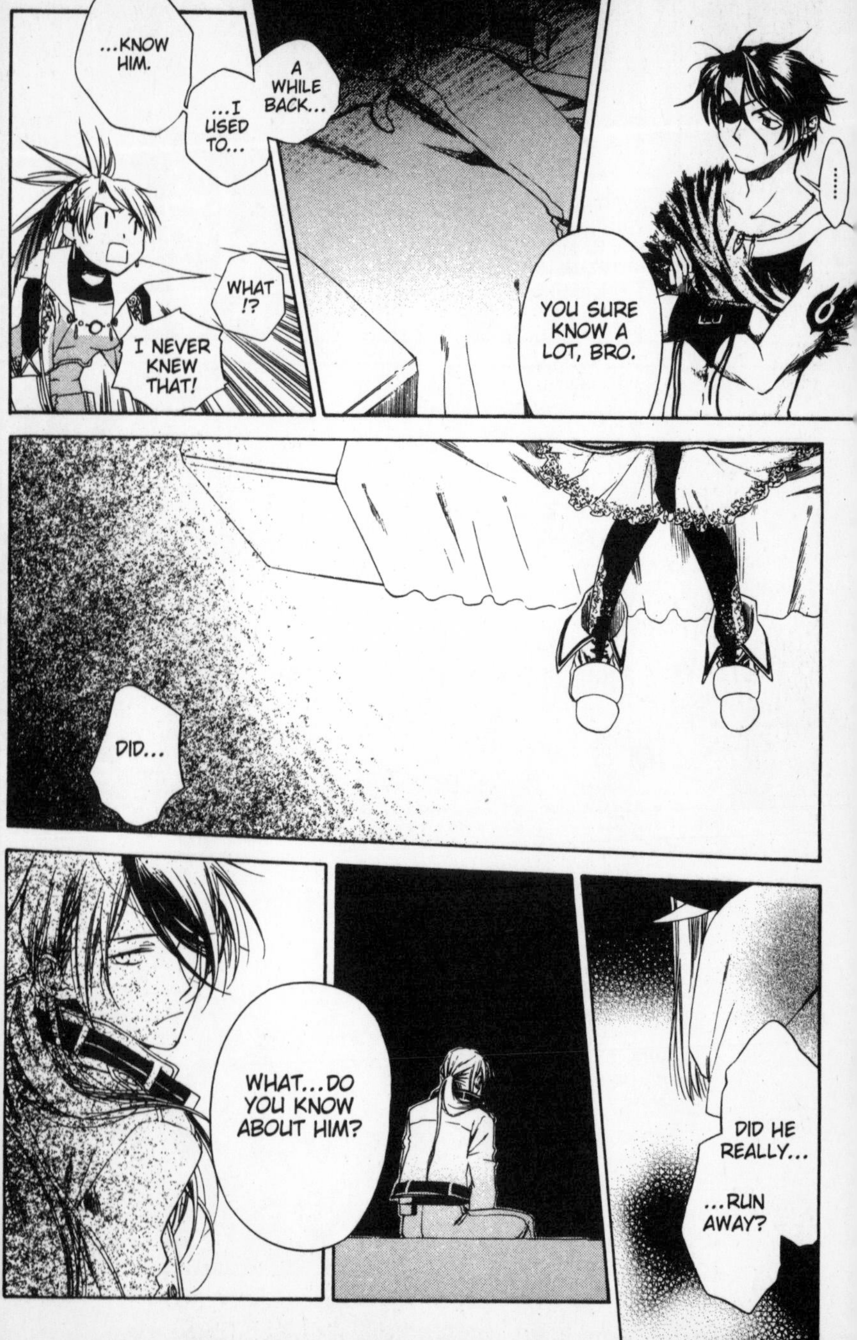
......
YOU SURE KNOW A LOT, BRO.
A WHILE BACK...
...I USED TO...
...KNOW HIM.
WHAT!?
I NEVER KNEW THAT!
DID...
DID HE REALLY...
...RUN AWAY?
WHAT...DO YOU KNOW ABOUT HIM?

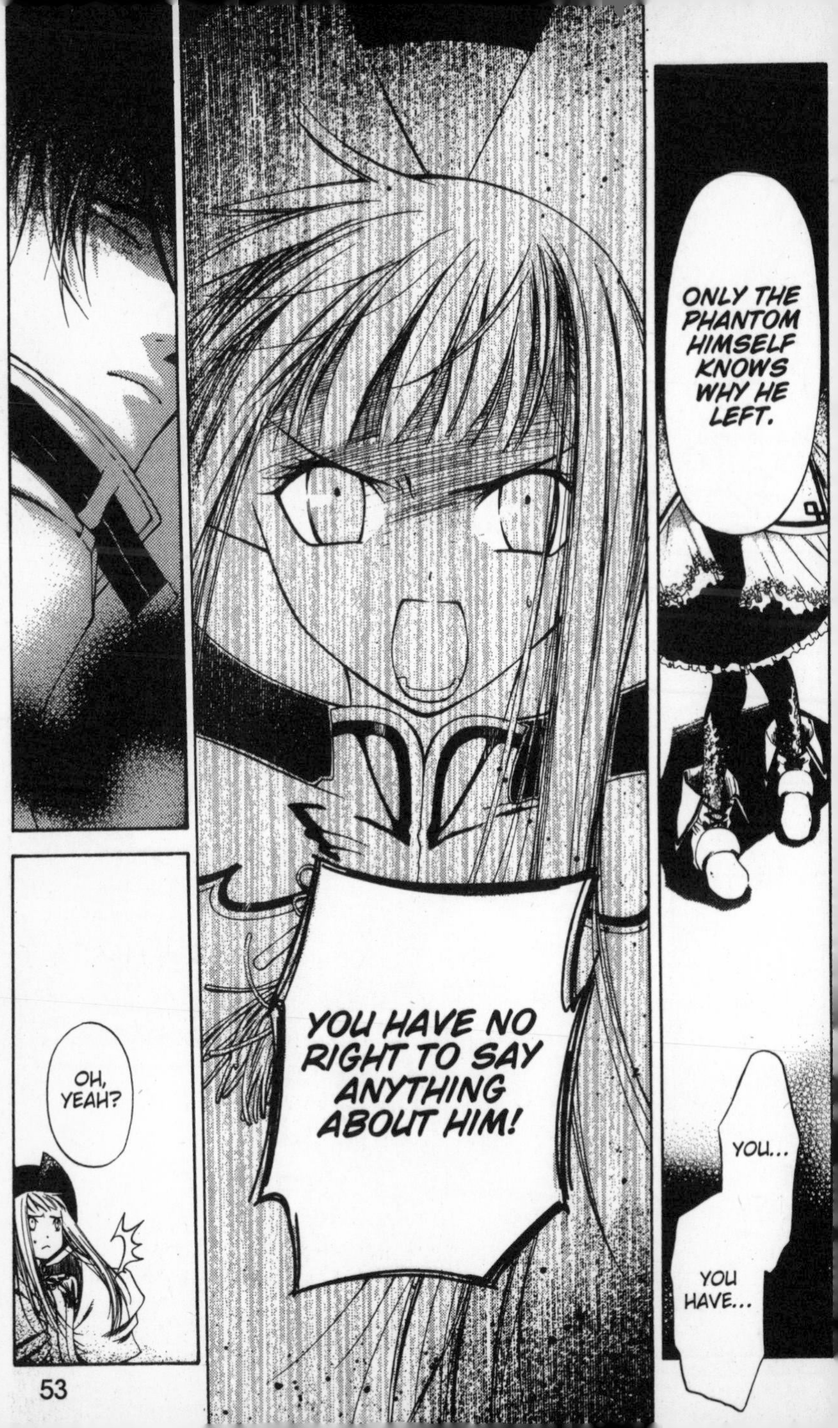
ONLY THE PHANTOM HIMSELF KNOWS WHY HE LEFT.
YOU...
YOU HAVE...
YOU HAVE NO RIGHT TO SAY ANYTHING ABOUT HIM!
OH, YEAH?

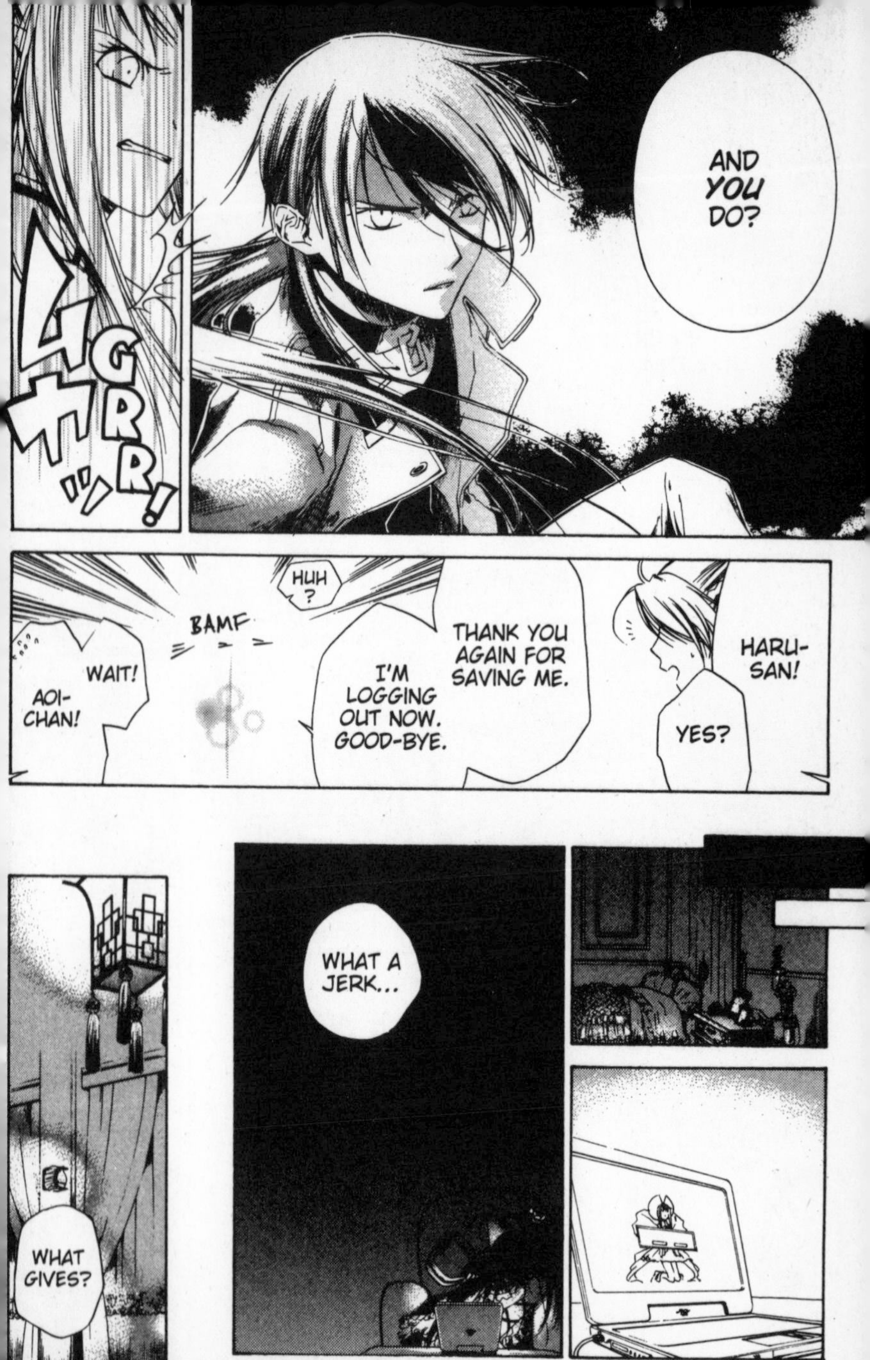
AND YOU DO?
GRRR!
HARU-SAN!
YES?
THANK YOU AGAIN FOR SAVING ME.
I'M LOGGING OUT NOW. GOOD-BYE.
HUH?
BAMF
WAIT!
AOI-CHAN!
WHAT A JERK...
WHAT GIVES?

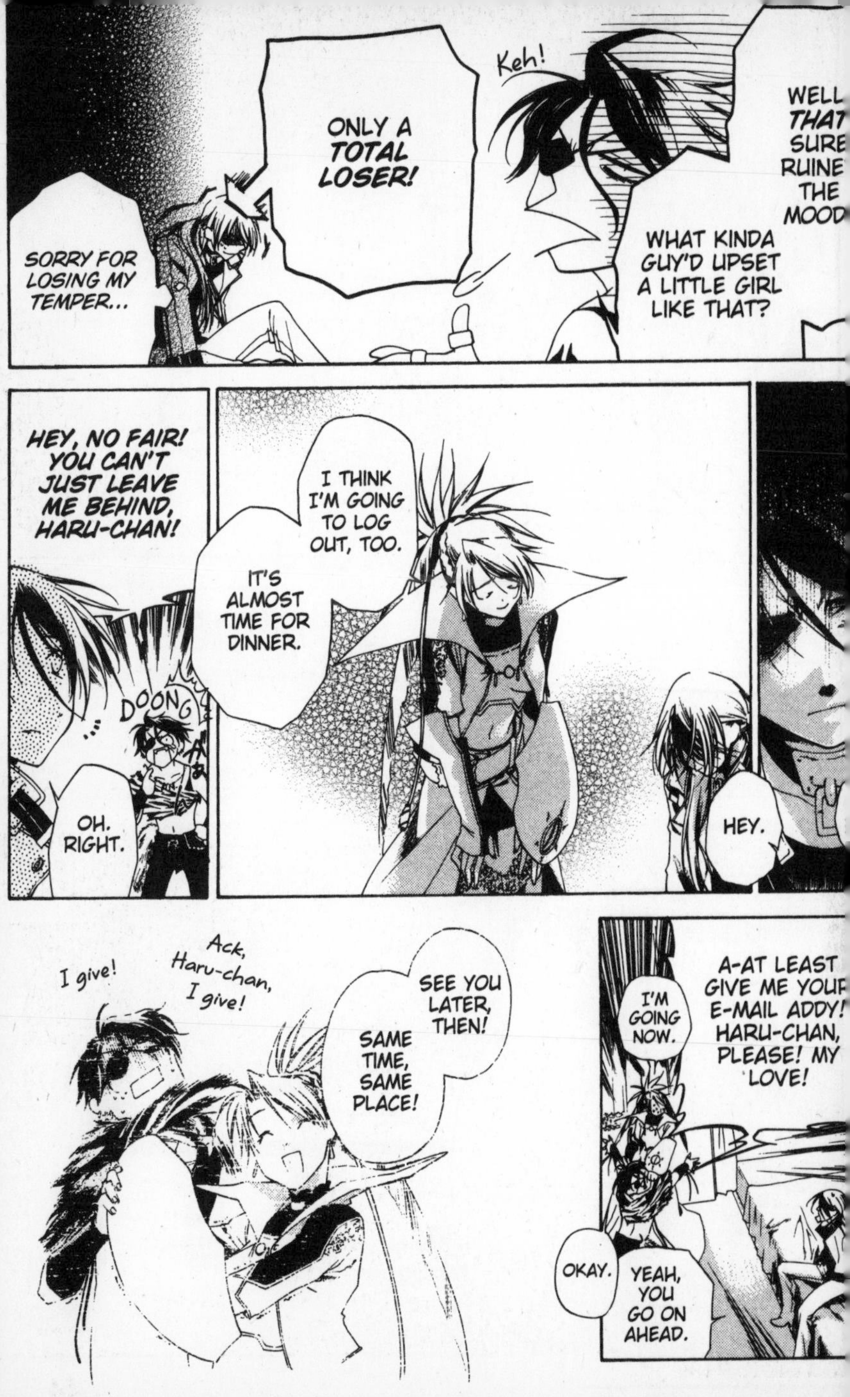
WELL THAT SURE RUINE THE MOOD
WHAT KINDA GUY'D UPSET A LITTLE GIRL LIKE THAT?
Keh!
ONLY A TOTAL LOSER!
SORRY FOR LOSING MY TEMPER...
HEY.
I THINK I'M GOING TO LOG OUT, TOO.
IT'S ALMOST TIME FOR DINNER.
HEY, NO FAIR! YOU CAN'T JUST LEAVE ME BEHIND, HARU-CHAN!
DOONG
OH. RIGHT.
A-AT LEAST GIVE ME YOUF E-MAIL ADDY! HARU-CHAN, PLEASE! MY LOVE!
I'M GOING NOW.
YEAH, YOU GO ON AHEAD.
OKAY.
SEE YOU LATER, THEN!
SAME TIME, SAME PLACE!
Ack, Haru-chan, I give!
I give!

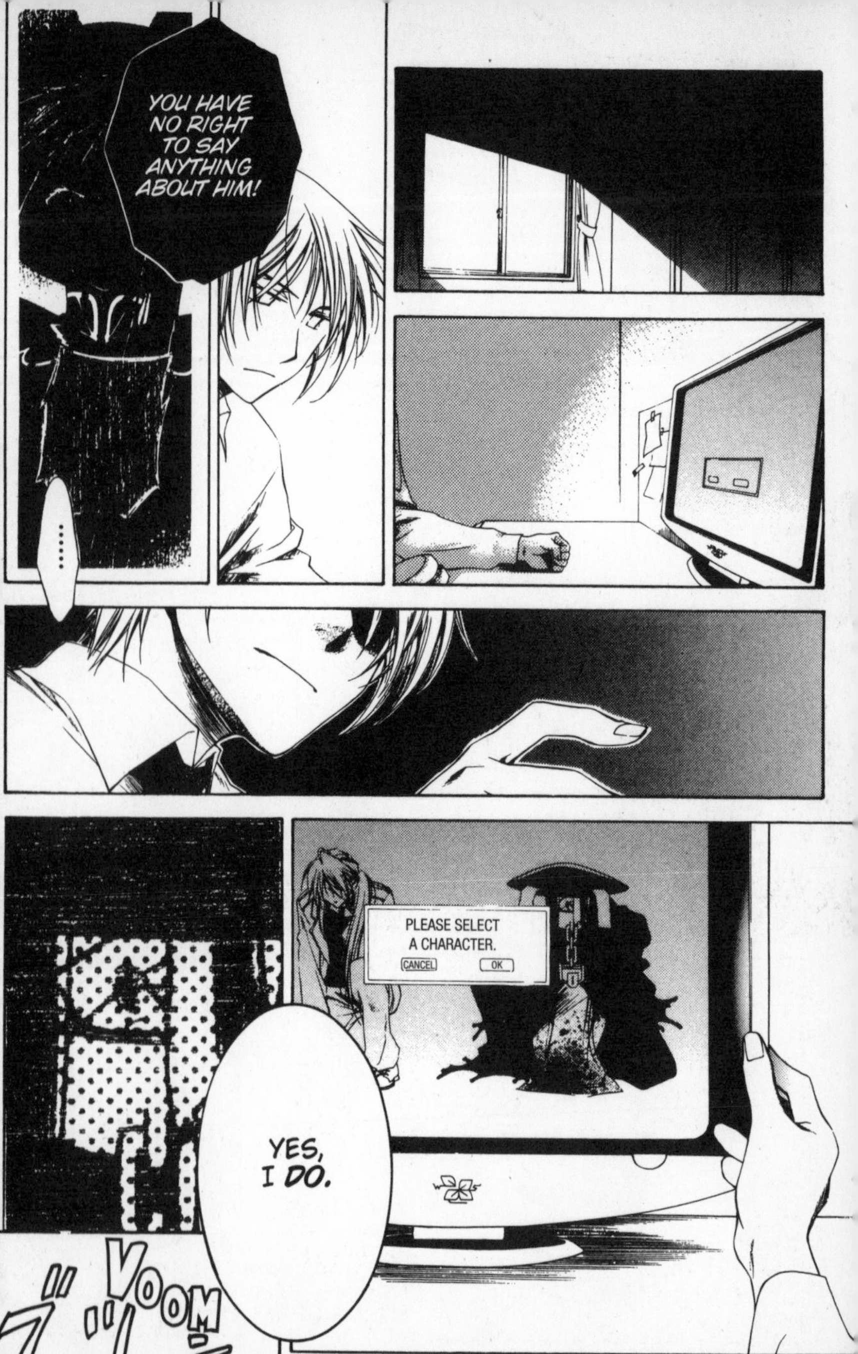
YOU HAVE NO RIGHT TO SAY ANYTHING ABOUT HIM!
......
PLEASE SELECT A CHARACTER.
CANCEL
OK
YES, I DO.
VOOM

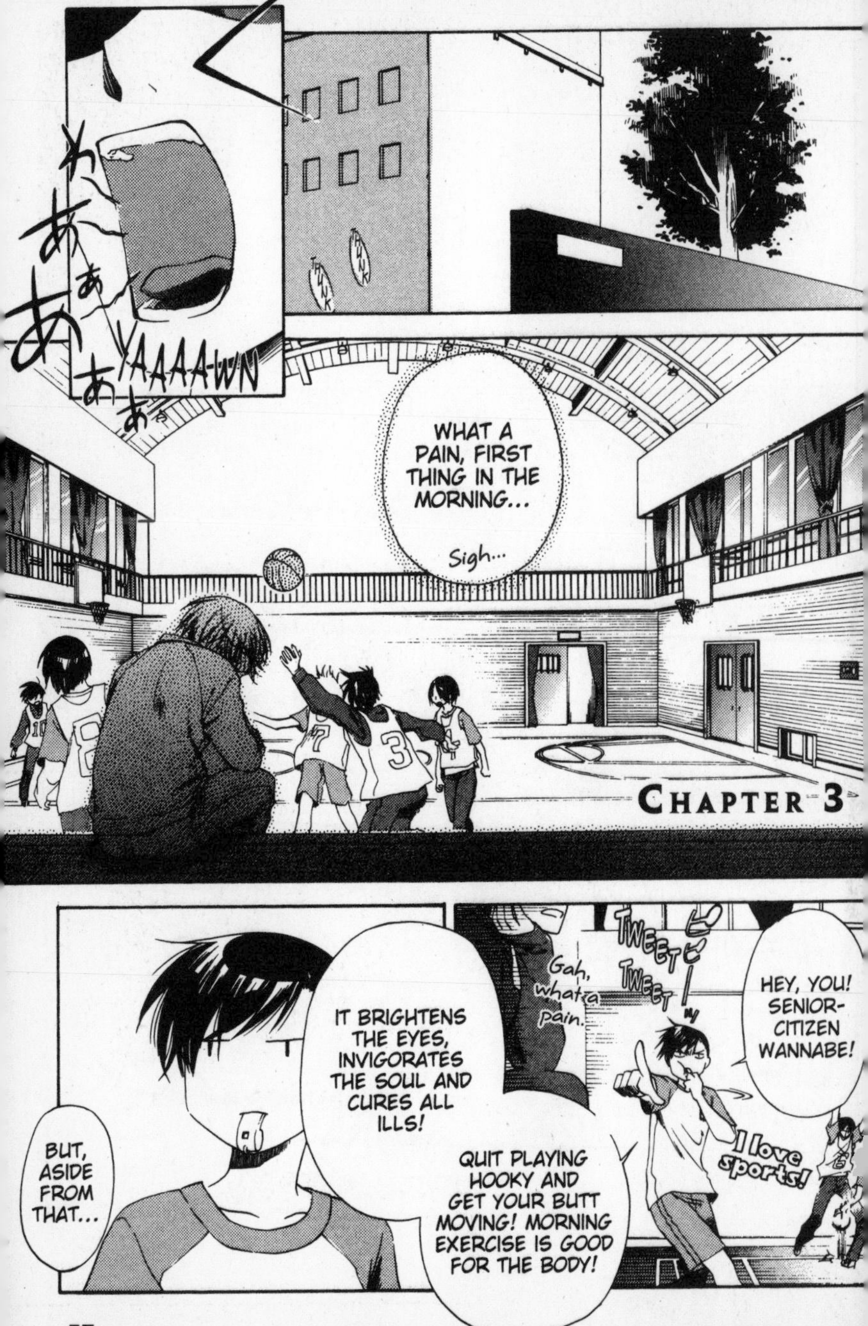
THUNK
THUNK
YAAAAWN
WHAT A PAIN, FIRST THING IN THE MORNING...
Sigh...
CHAPTER 3
HEY, YOU! SENIOR-CITIZEN WANNABE!
TWEET TWEET
Gah, what a pain.
QUIT PLAYING HOOKY AND GET YOUR BUTT MOVING! MORNING EXERCISE IS GOOD FOR THE BODY!
IT BRIGHTENS THE EYES, INVIGORATES THE SOUL AND CURES ALL ILLS!
I love sports!
BUT, ASIDE FROM THAT...

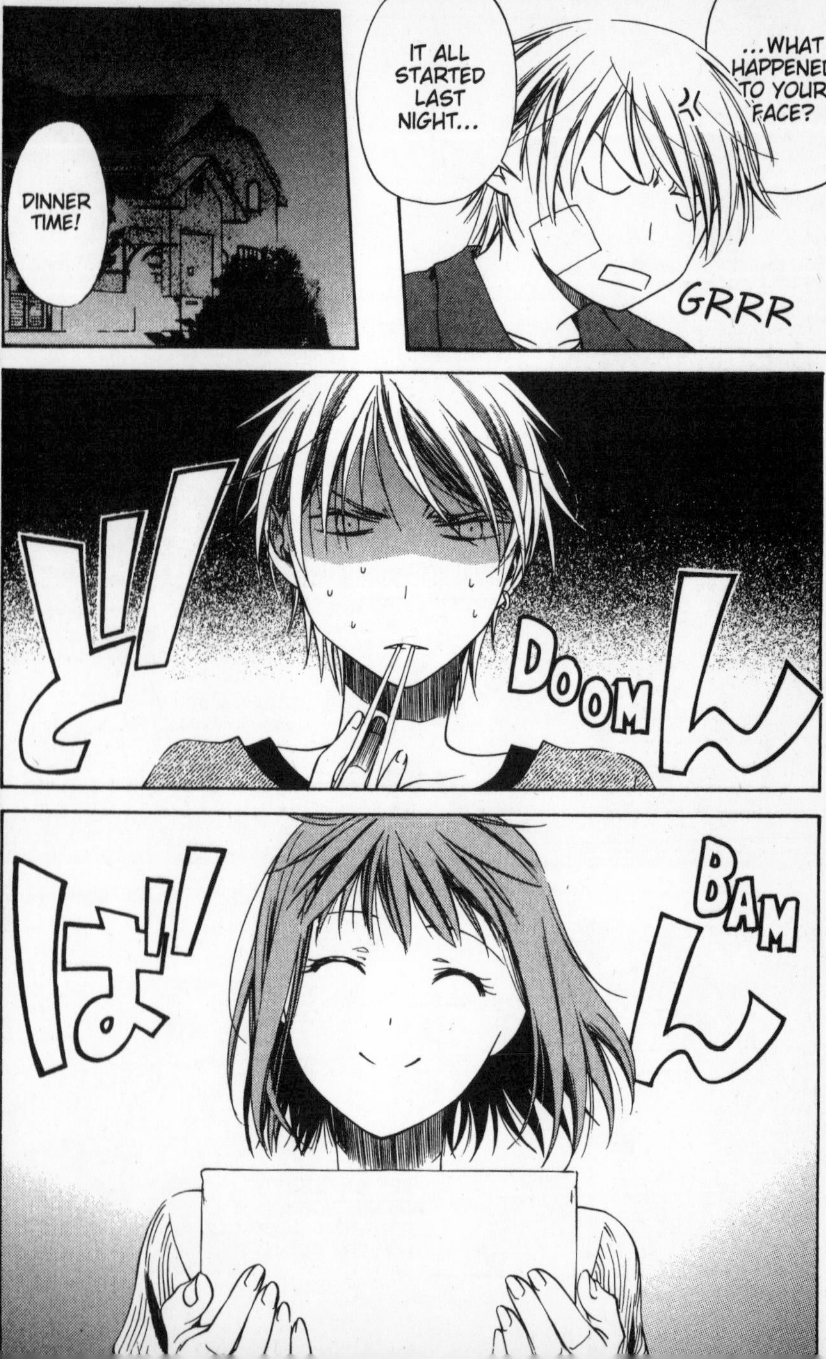
...WHAT HAPPENED TO YOUR FACE?
IT ALL STARTED LAST NIGHT...
GRRR
DINNER TIME!
ど!!
DOOM
ん
ぱ!!
BAM
ん

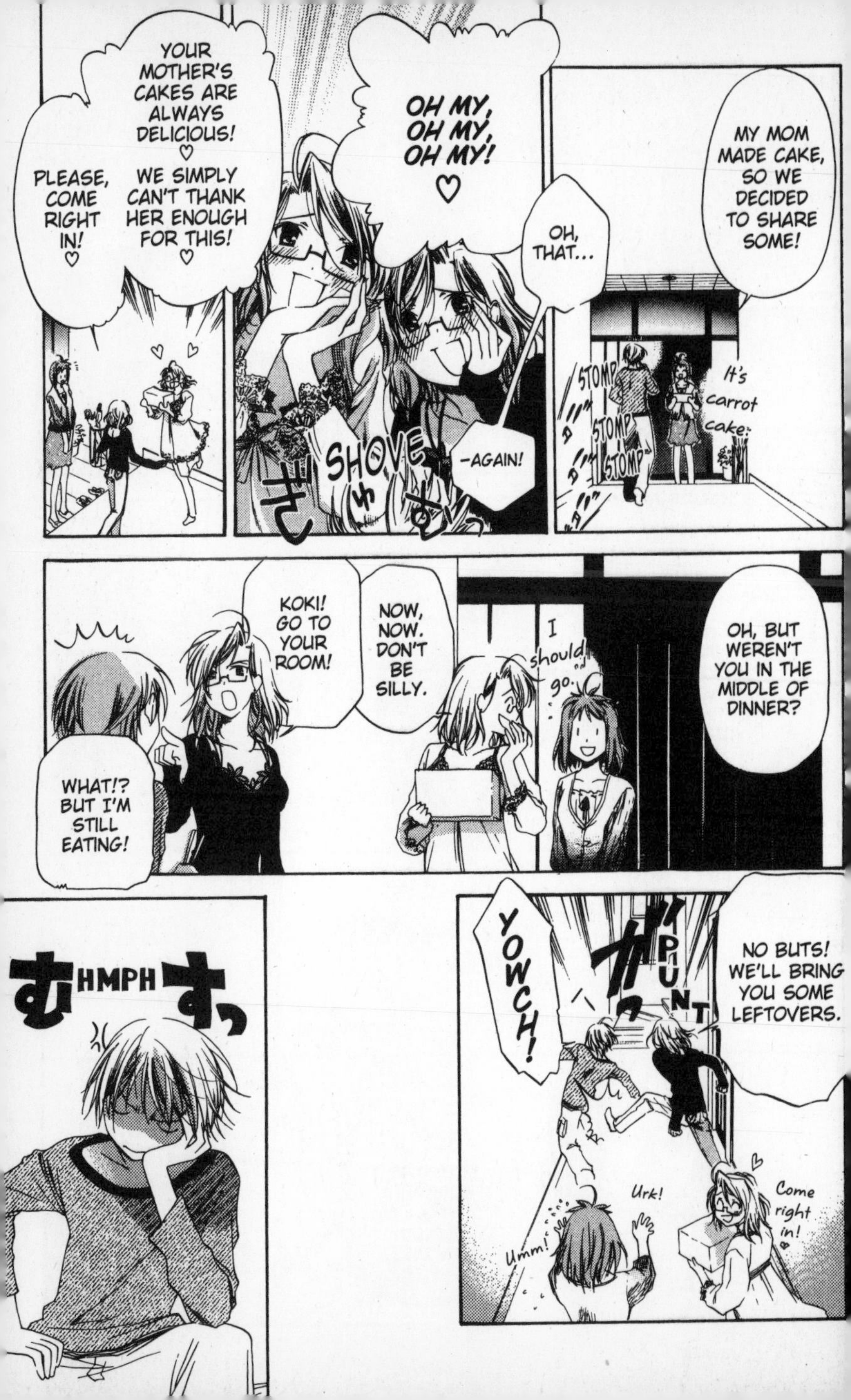
MY MOM MADE CAKE, SO WE DECIDED TO SHARE SOME!
It's carrot cake.
STOMP STOMP STOMP
OH MY, OH MY, OH MY!
OH, THAT...
SHOVE
-AGAIN!
YOUR MOTHER'S CAKES ARE ALWAYS DELICIOUS! WE SIMPLY CAN'T THANK HER ENOUGH FOR THIS!
PLEASE, COME RIGHT IN!
OH, BUT WEREN'T YOU IN THE MIDDLE OF DINNER?
I should go.
NOW, NOW. DON'T BE SILLY.
KOKI! GO TO YOUR ROOM!
WHAT!? BUT I'M STILL EATING!
NO BUTS! WE'LL BRING YOU SOME LEFTOVERS.
PUNT
YOWCH!
Come right in!
Urk!
Umm!
HMPH

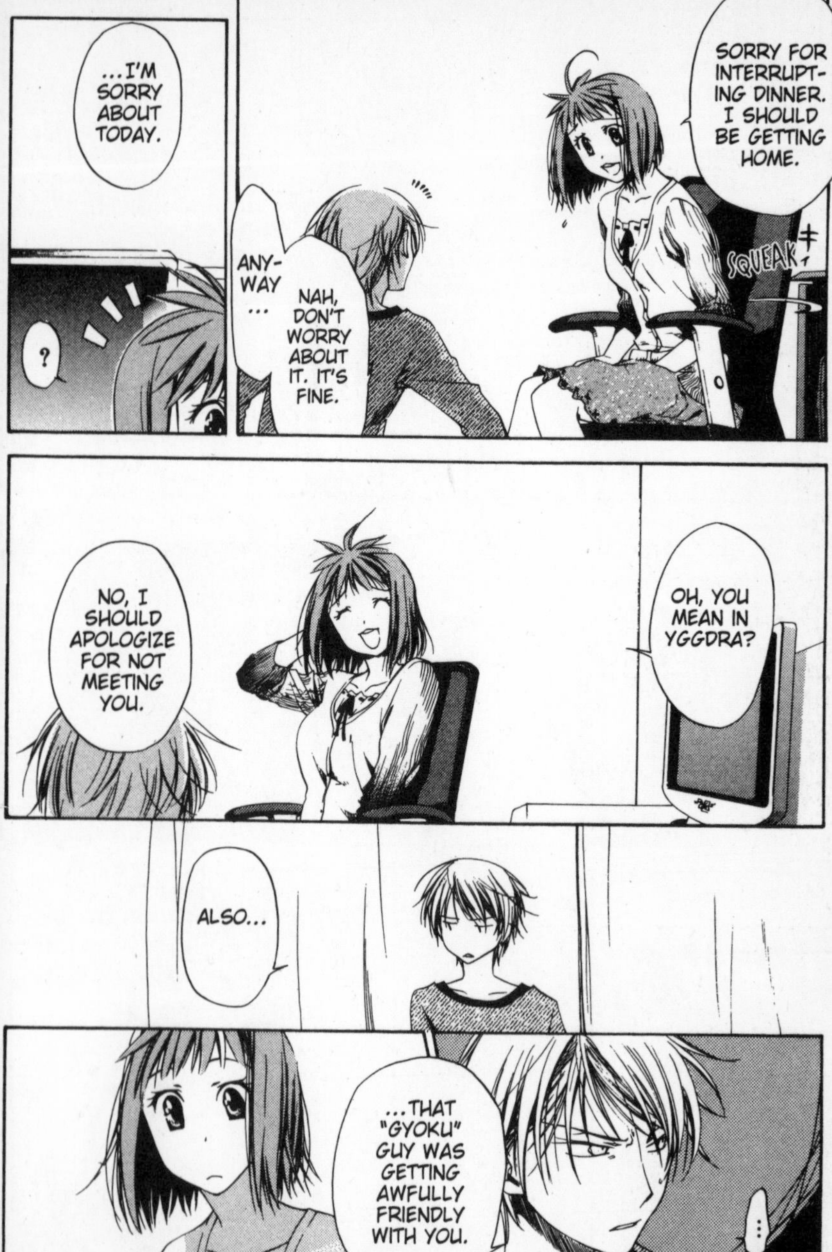
SORRY FOR INTERRUPT-ING DINNER. I SHOULD BE GETTING HOME.
SQUEAK
NAH, DON'T WORRY ABOUT IT. IT'S FINE.
ANY-WAY...
...I'M SORRY ABOUT TODAY.
?
OH, YOU MEAN IN YGGDRA?
NO, I SHOULD APOLOGIZE FOR NOT MEETING YOU.
ALSO...
...THAT "GYOKU" GUY WAS GETTING AWFULLY FRIENDLY WITH YOU.
...

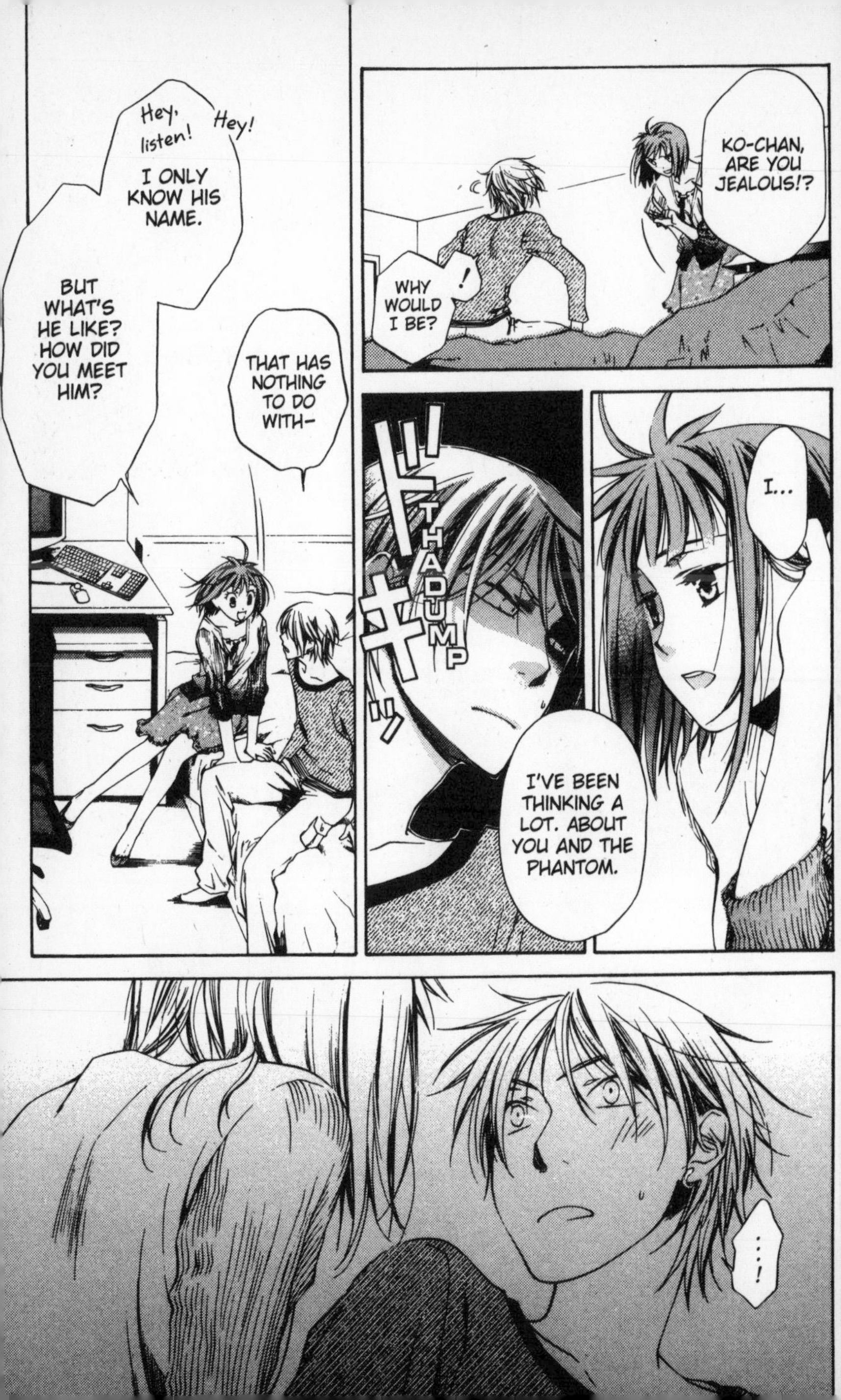

KO-CHAN, ARE YOU JEALOUS!?
!
WHY WOULD I BE?
I...
THADUMP
I'VE BEEN THINKING A LOT. ABOUT YOU AND THE PHANTOM.
Hey, listen! Hey!
I ONLY KNOW HIS NAME.
BUT WHAT'S HE LIKE? HOW DID YOU MEET HIM?
THAT HAS NOTHING TO DO WITH-
...!

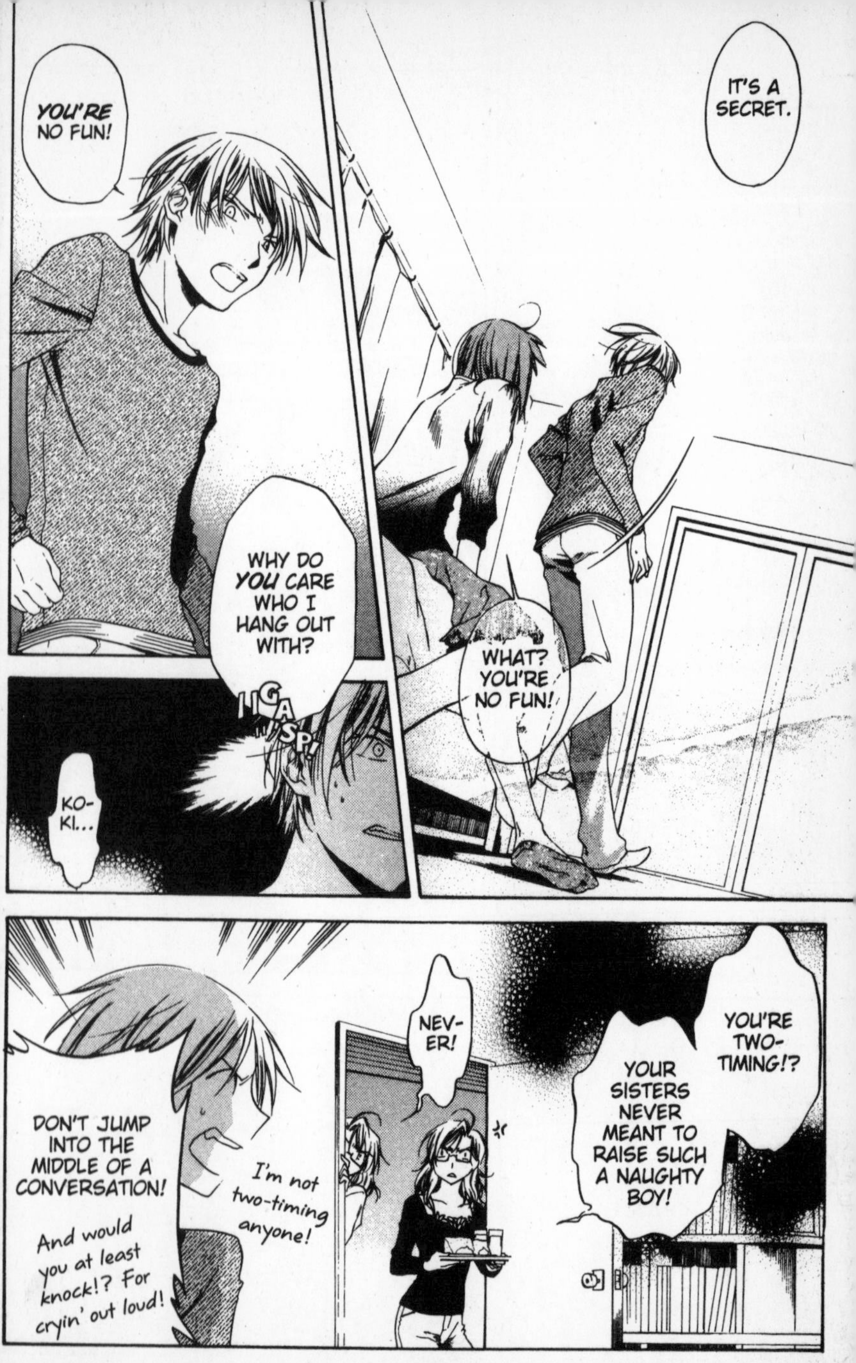
IT'S A SECRET.
WHAT? YOU'RE NO FUN!
YOU'RE NO FUN!
WHY DO YOU CARE WHO I HANG OUT WITH?
GASP!
KO-KI...
YOU'RE TWO-TIMING!?
YOUR SISTERS NEVER MEANT TO RAISE SUCH A NAUGHTY BOY!
NEVER!
I'm not two-timing anyone!
DON'T JUMP INTO THE MIDDLE OF A CONVERSATION!
And would you at least knock!? For cryin' out loud!

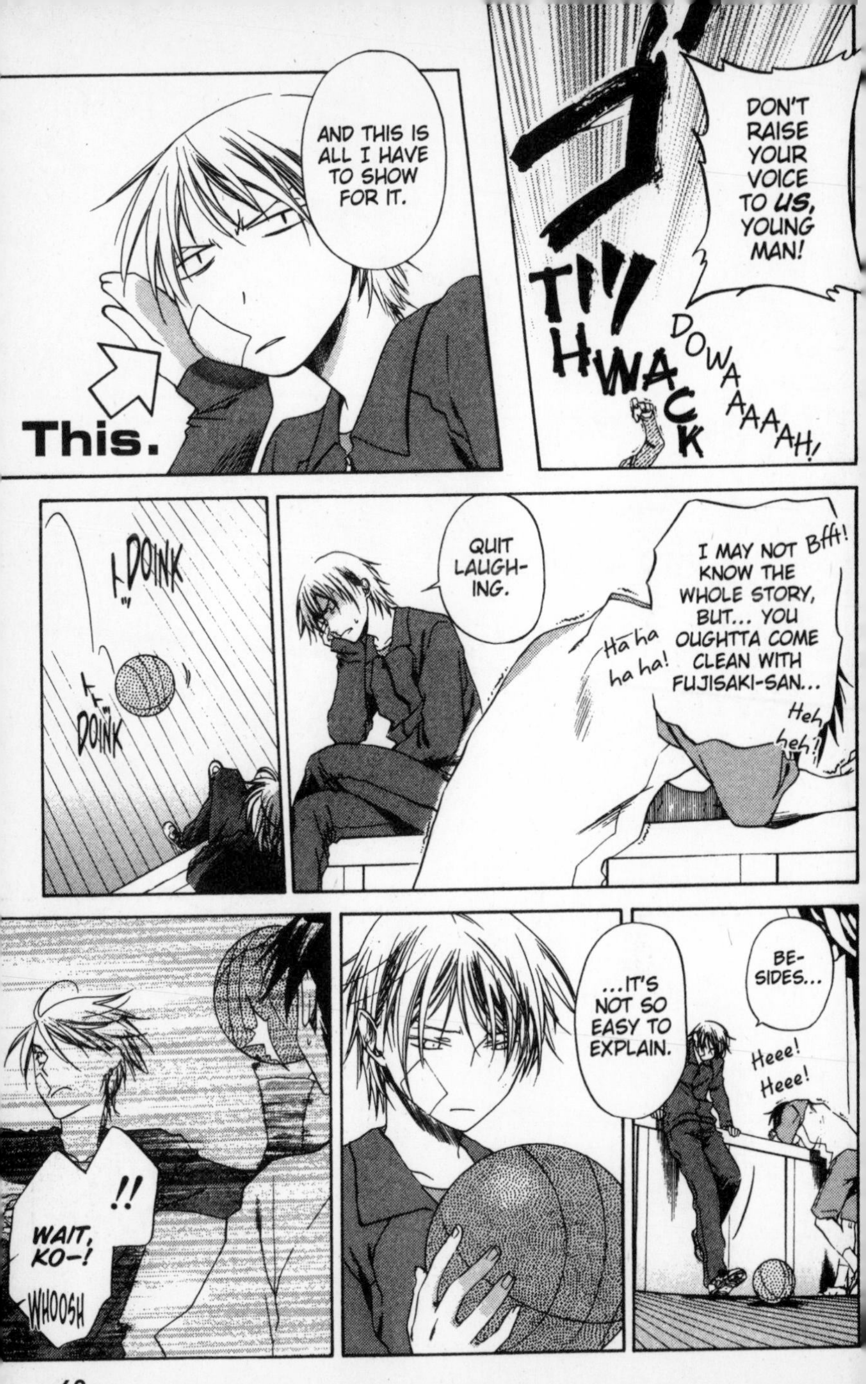
DON'T RAISE YOUR VOICE TO *US*, YOUNG MAN!
TH
HWACK
DOWAAAAAAH!
AND THIS IS ALL I HAVE TO SHOW FOR IT.
This.
Bfft!
I MAY NOT KNOW THE WHOLE STORY, BUT... YOU OUGHTTA COME CLEAN WITH FUJISAKI-SAN...
Ha ha ha ha!
Heh heh!
QUIT LAUGH-ING.
DOINK
DOINK
BE-SIDES...
Heee! Heee!
...IT'S NOT SO EASY TO EXPLAIN.
!!
WAIT, KO-!
WHOOSH

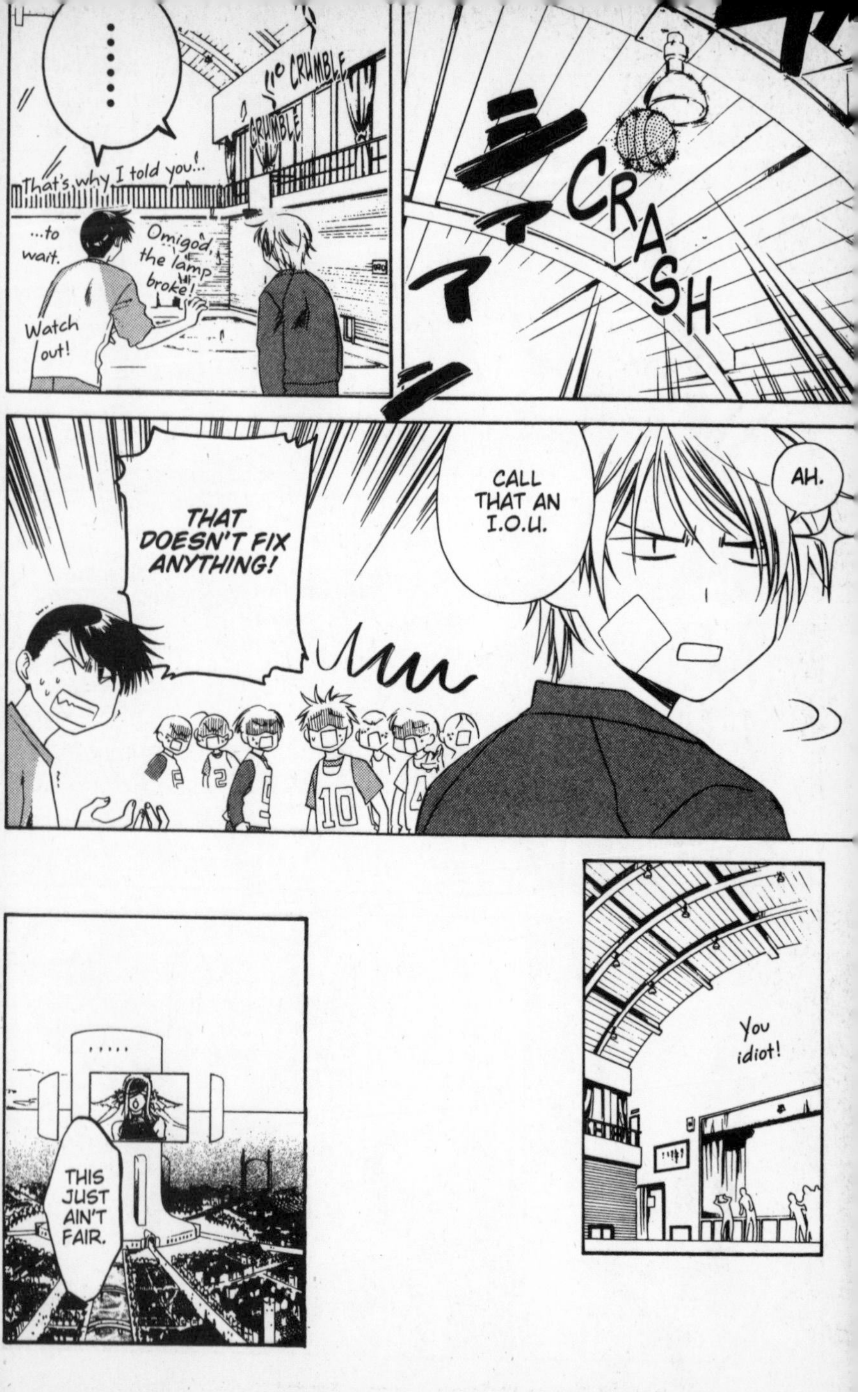
CRASH
CRUMBLE
CRUMBLE
......
That's why I told you...
...to wait.
Omigod, the lamp broke!
Watch out!
AH.
CALL THAT AN I.O.U.
THAT DOESN'T FIX ANYTHING!
You idiot!
.....
THIS JUST AIN'T FAIR.

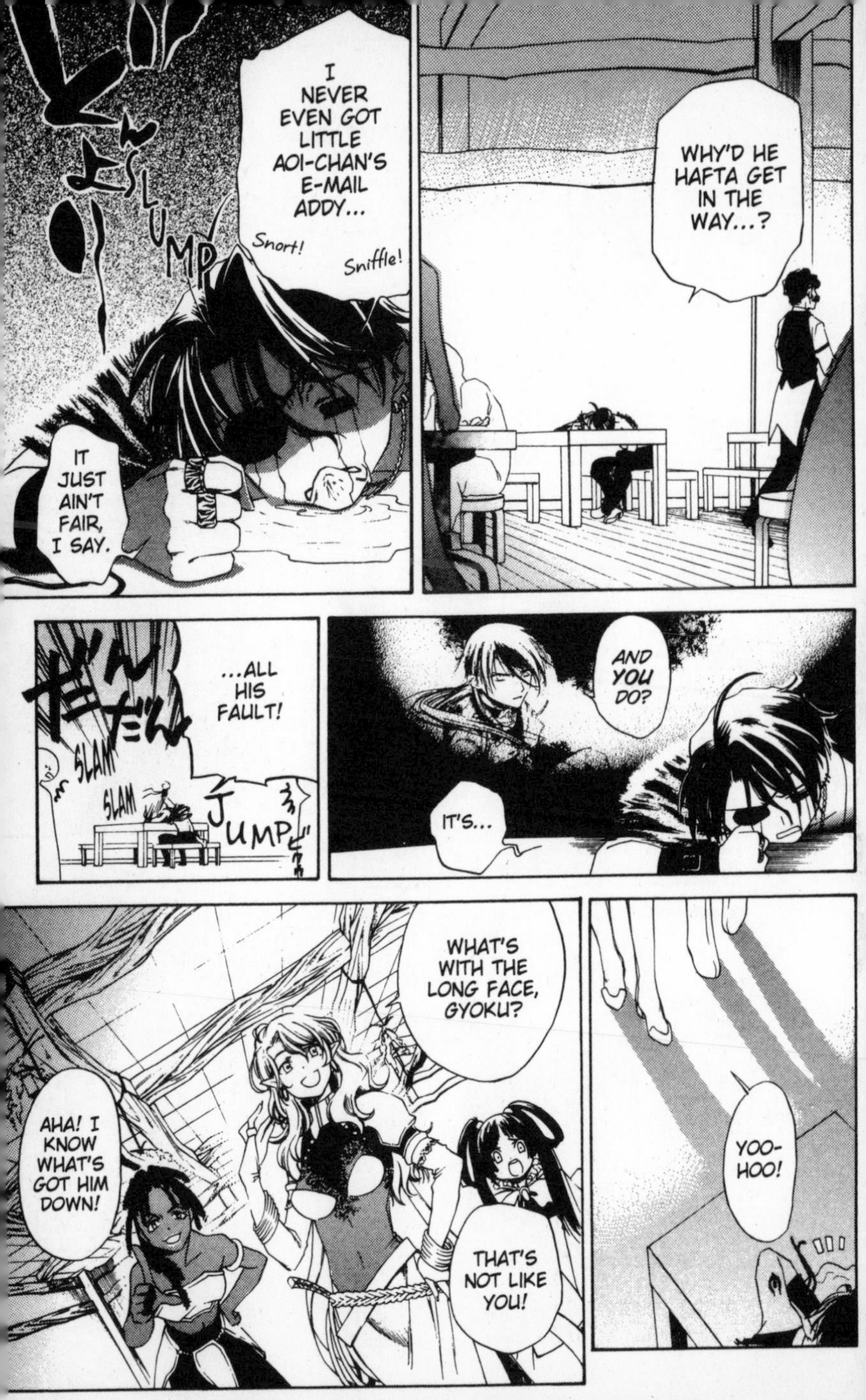
WHY'D HE HAFTA GET IN THE WAY...?
I NEVER EVEN GOT LITTLE AOI-CHAN'S E-MAIL ADDY...
SLUMP
Snort!
Sniffle!
IT JUST AIN'T FAIR, I SAY.
AND YOU DO?
IT'S...
...ALL HIS FAULT!
SLAM
SLAM
JUMP
YOO-HOO!
WHAT'S WITH THE LONG FACE, GYOKU?
THAT'S NOT LIKE YOU!
AHA! I KNOW WHAT'S GOT HIM DOWN!

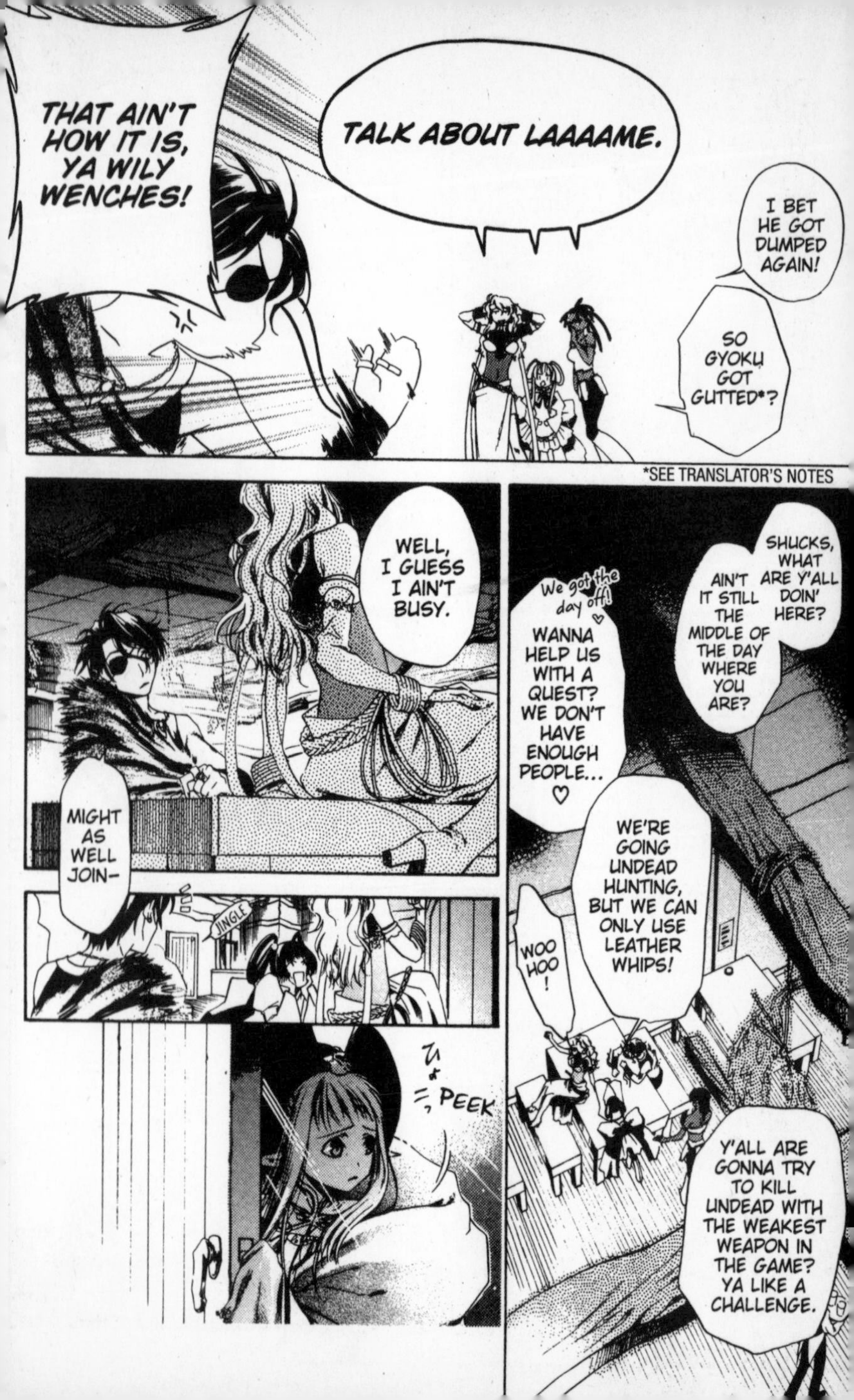
TALK ABOUT LAAAAME.
I BET HE GOT DUMPED AGAIN!
SO GYOKU GOT GUTTED*?
THAT AIN'T HOW IT IS, YA WILY WENCHES!
SHUCKS, WHAT ARE Y'ALL DOIN' HERE?
AIN'T IT STILL THE MIDDLE OF THE DAY WHERE YOU ARE?
We got the day off! ♡
WANNA HELP US WITH A QUEST? WE DON'T HAVE ENOUGH PEOPLE... ♡
WE'RE GOING UNDEAD HUNTING, BUT WE CAN ONLY USE LEATHER WHIPS!
WOO HOO!
Y'ALL ARE GONNA TRY TO KILL UNDEAD WITH THE WEAKEST WEAPON IN THE GAME? YA LIKE A CHALLENGE.
WELL, I GUESS I AIN'T BUSY.
MIGHT AS WELL JOIN-
JINGLE
PEEK

*SEE TRANSLATOR'S NOTES

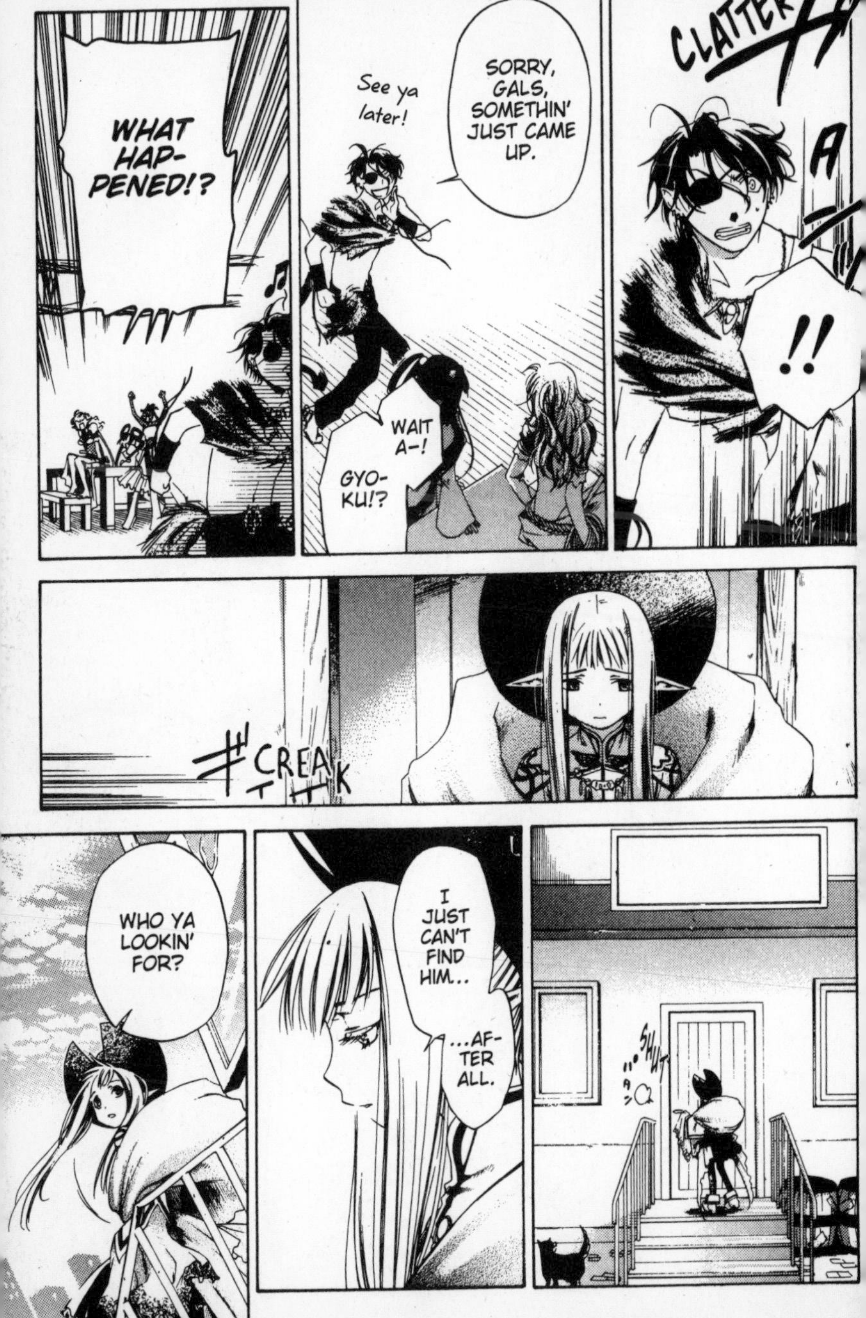
CLATTER
A-
!!
SORRY, GALS, SOMETHIN' JUST CAME UP.
See ya later!
WAIT A-!
GYO-KU!?
WHAT HAP-PENED!?
CREAK
SHUT
I JUST CAN'T FIND HIM...
...AF-TER ALL.
WHO YA LOOKIN' FOR?

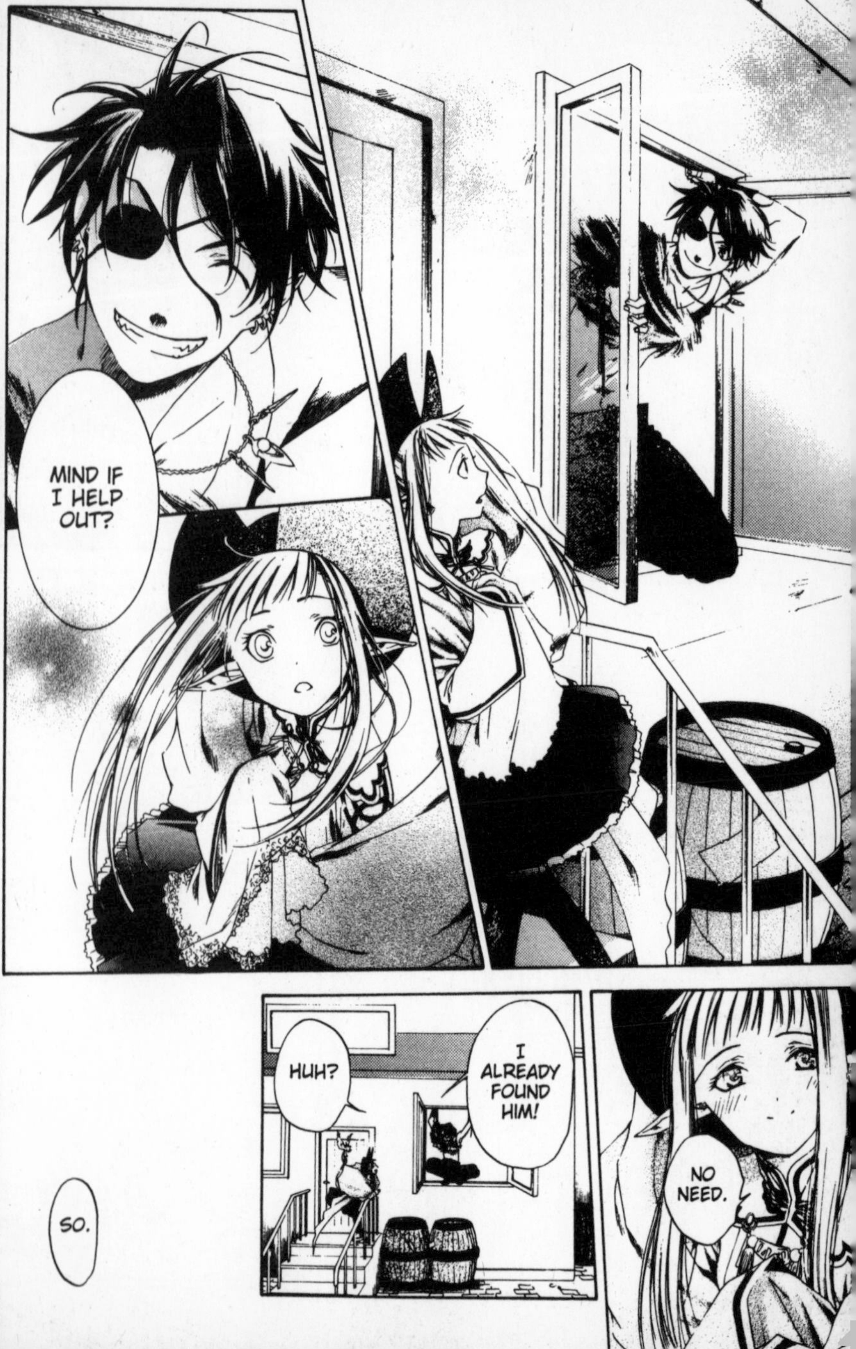
MIND IF I HELP OUT?
NO NEED.
I ALREADY FOUND HIM!
HUH?
SO.

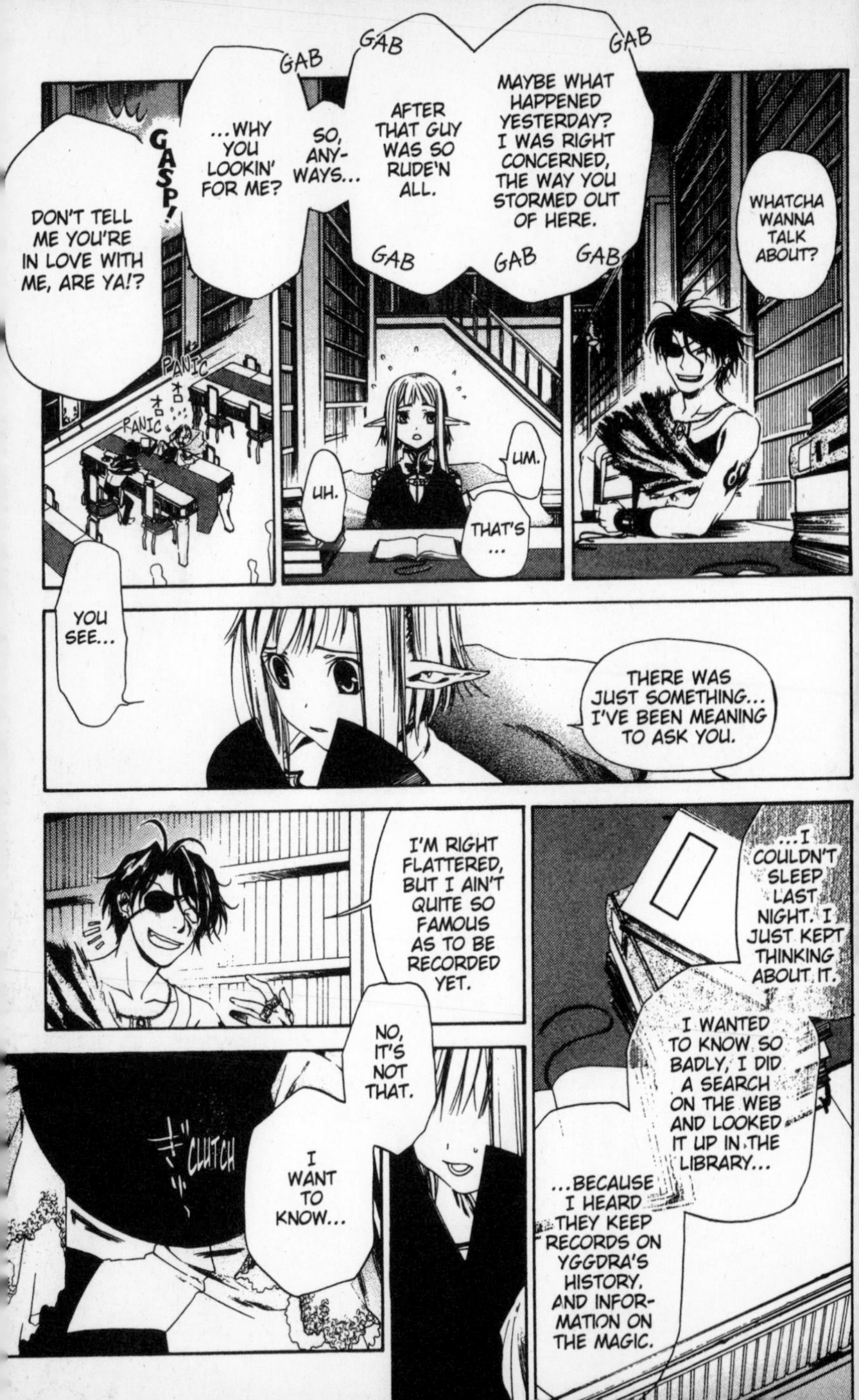
WHATCHA WANNA TALK ABOUT?
GAB
GAB
MAYBE WHAT HAPPENED YESTERDAY? I WAS RIGHT CONCERNED, THE WAY YOU STORMED OUT OF HERE.
AFTER THAT GUY WAS SO RUDE'N ALL.
SO, ANY-WAYS...
...WHY YOU LOOKIN' FOR ME?
GAB
GAB
GAB
GAB
UM.
UH.
THAT'S ...
GASP!
DON'T TELL ME YOU'RE IN LOVE WITH ME, ARE YA!?
PANIC
PANIC
YOU SEE...
THERE WAS JUST SOMETHING... I'VE BEEN MEANING TO ASK YOU.
...I COULDN'T SLEEP LAST NIGHT. I JUST KEPT THINKING ABOUT IT.
I WANTED TO KNOW SO BADLY, I DID A SEARCH ON THE WEB AND LOOKED IT UP IN THE LIBRARY...
...BECAUSE I HEARD THEY KEEP RECORDS ON YGGDRA'S HISTORY, AND INFOR-MATION ON THE MAGIC.
I'M RIGHT FLATTERED, BUT I AIN'T QUITE SO FAMOUS AS TO BE RECORDED YET.
NO, IT'S NOT THAT.
CLUTCH
I WANT TO KNOW...

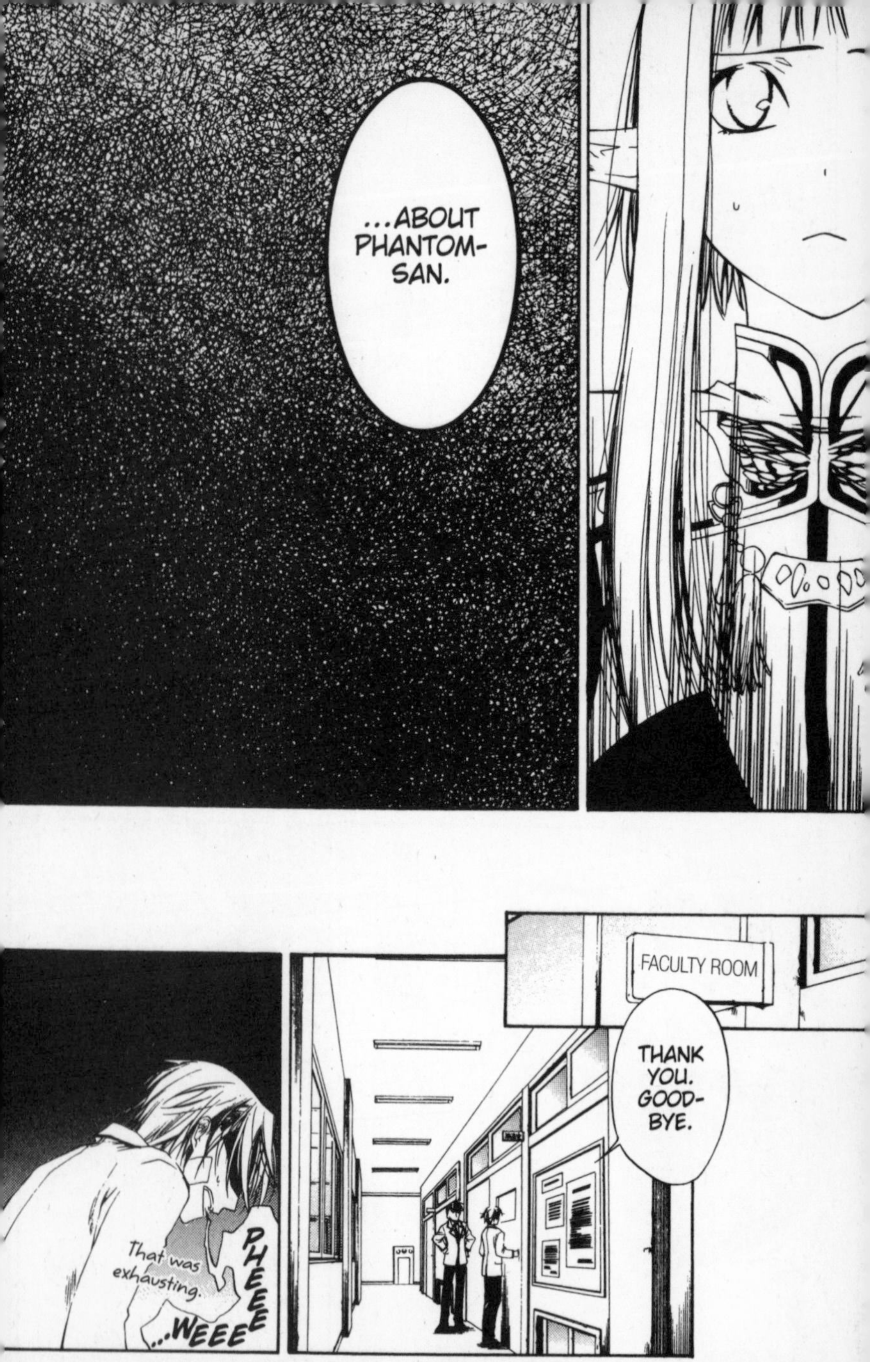
...ABOUT PHANTOM-SAN.
FACULTY ROOM
THANK YOU. GOOD-BYE.
That was exhausting.
PHEEE
...WEEE

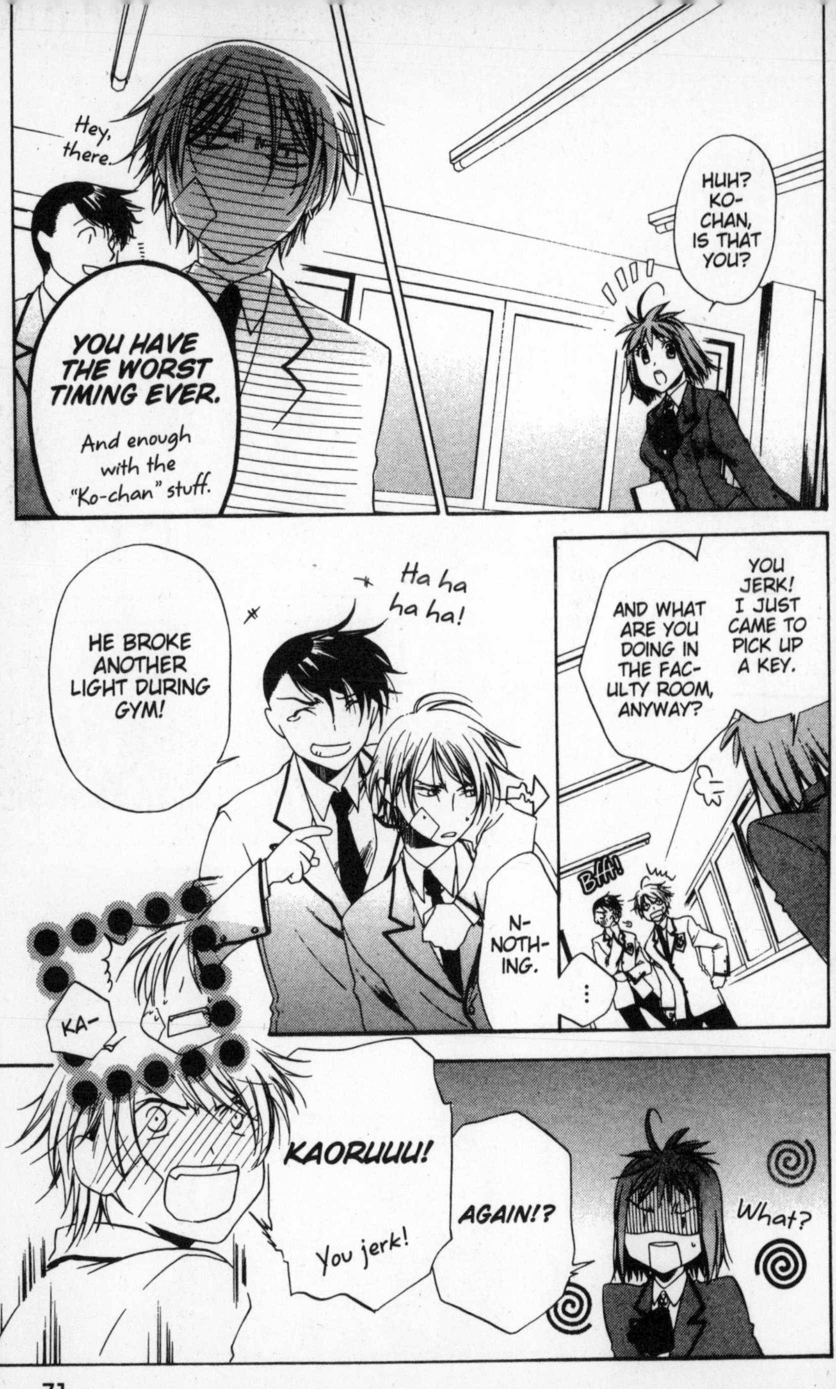
HUH? KO-CHAN, IS THAT YOU?
Hey, there.
YOU HAVE THE WORST TIMING EVER.
And enough with the "Ko-chan" stuff.
YOU JERK! I JUST CAME TO PICK UP A KEY.
AND WHAT ARE YOU DOING IN THE FAC-ULTY ROOM, ANYWAY?
...
Ha ha ha ha!
N-NOTH-ING.
HE BROKE ANOTHER LIGHT DURING GYM!
KA-
What?
AGAIN!?
KAORUUU!
You jerk!

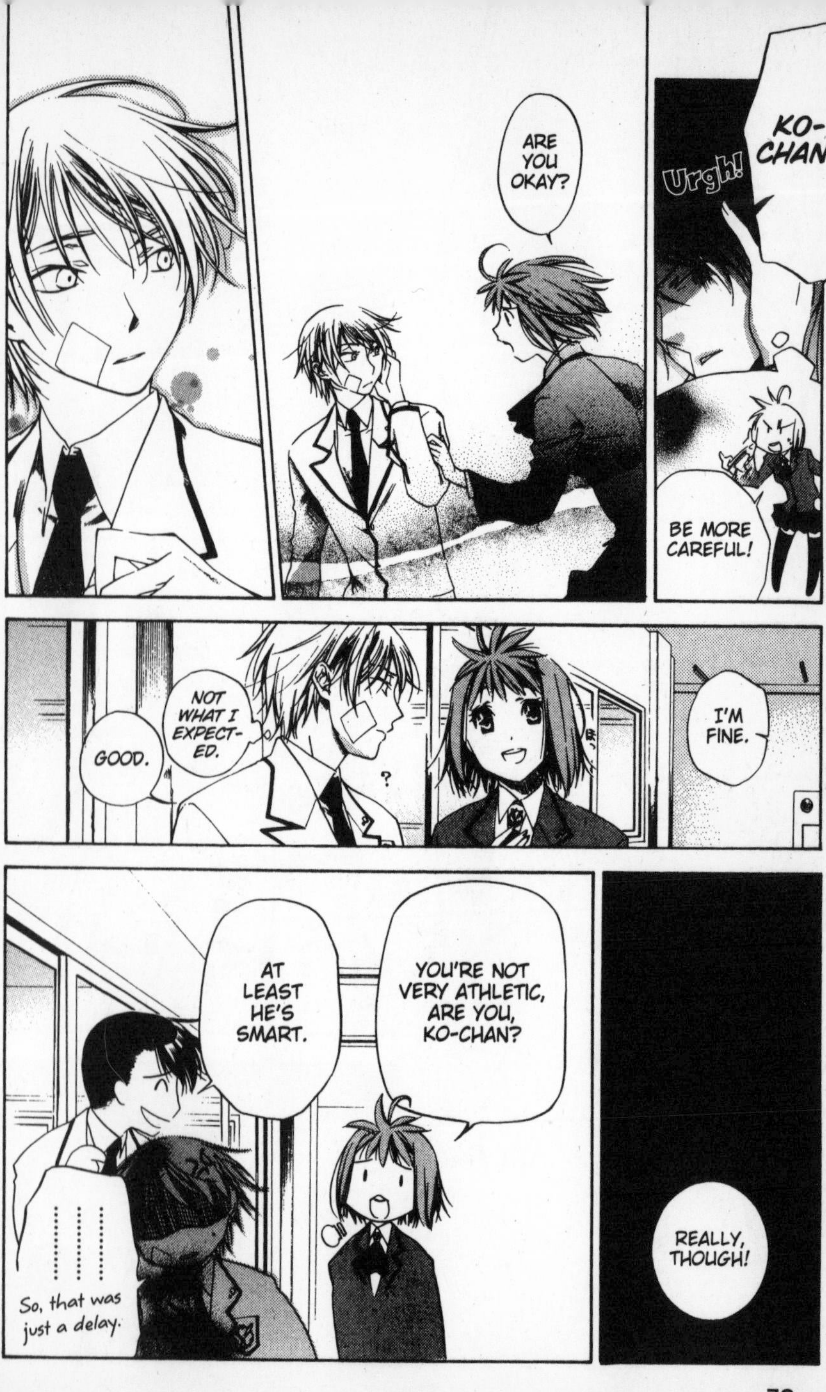
KO-CHAN!
Urgh!
BE MORE CAREFUL!
ARE YOU OKAY?
I'M FINE.
NOT WHAT I EXPECT-ED.
GOOD.
REALLY, THOUGH!
YOU'RE NOT VERY ATHLETIC, ARE YOU, KO-CHAN?
AT LEAST HE'S SMART.
......
So, that was just a delay.

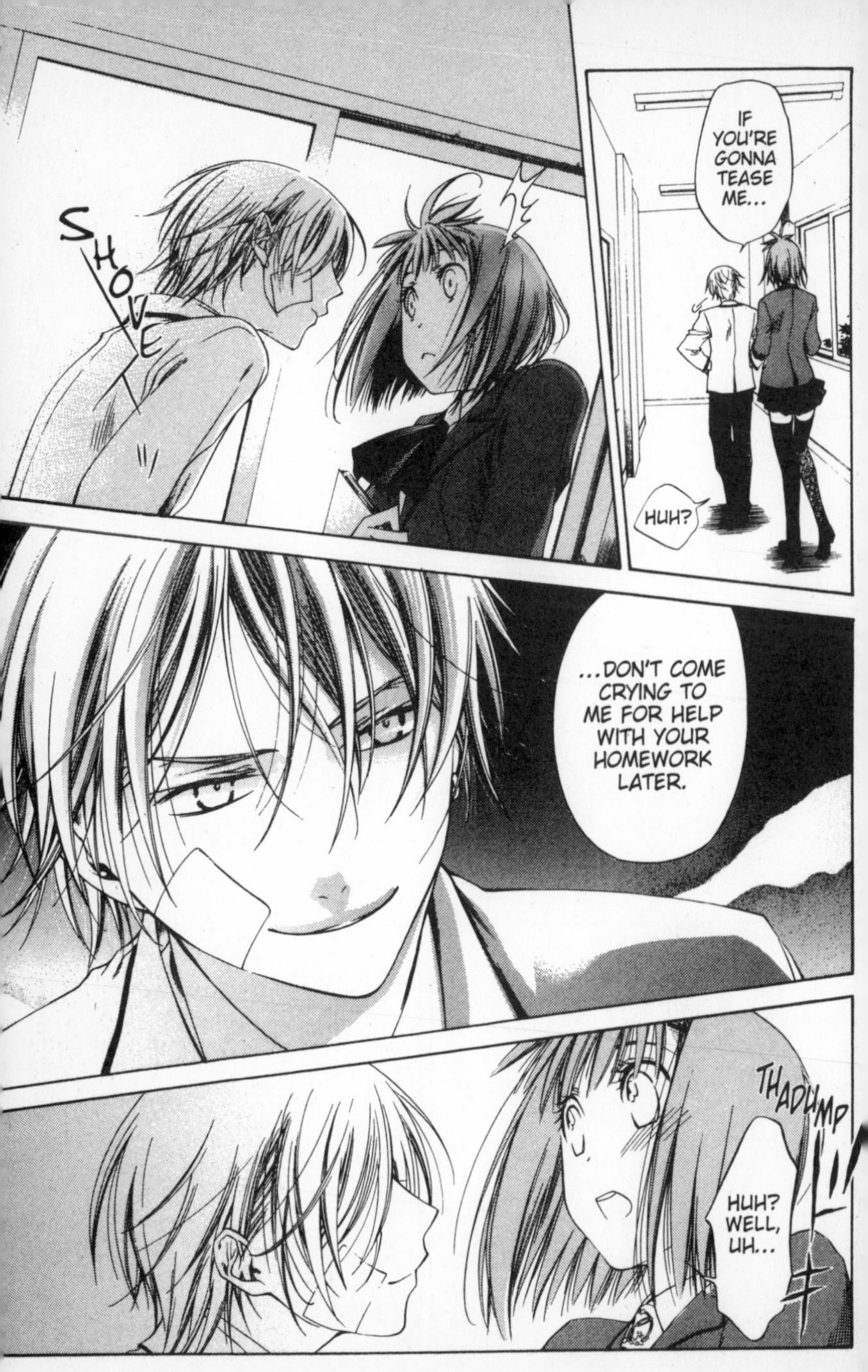
IF YOU'RE GONNA TEASE ME...
HUH?
SHOVE
...DON'T COME CRYING TO ME FOR HELP WITH YOUR HOMEWORK LATER.
THADUMP
HUH? WELL, UH...

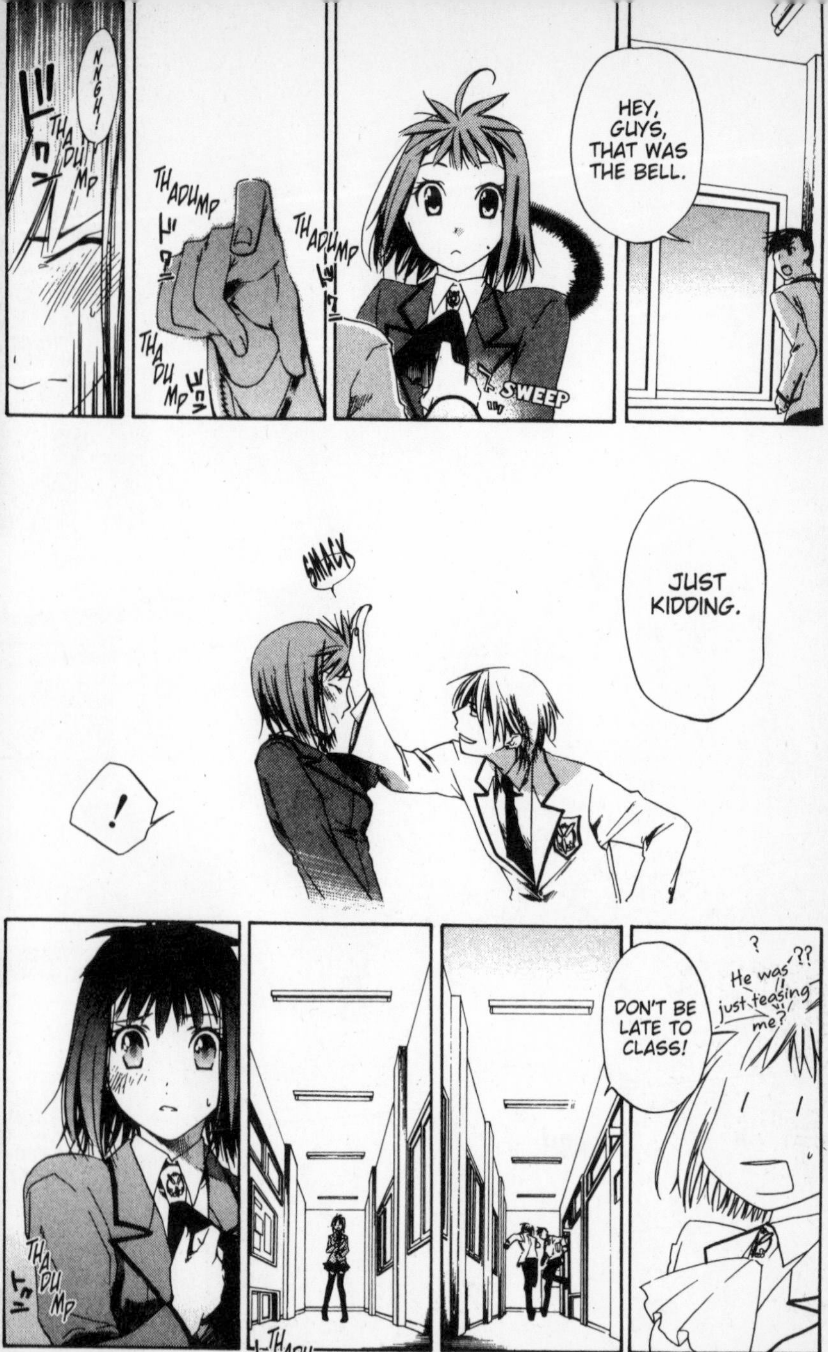
HEY, GUYS, THAT WAS THE BELL.
SWEEP
THADUMP
THADUMP
THADUMP
NNGH!
THADUMP
JUST KIDDING.
SMACK
!
DON'T BE LATE TO CLASS!
? ?? He was just teasing me?
THADUMP
THADUMP

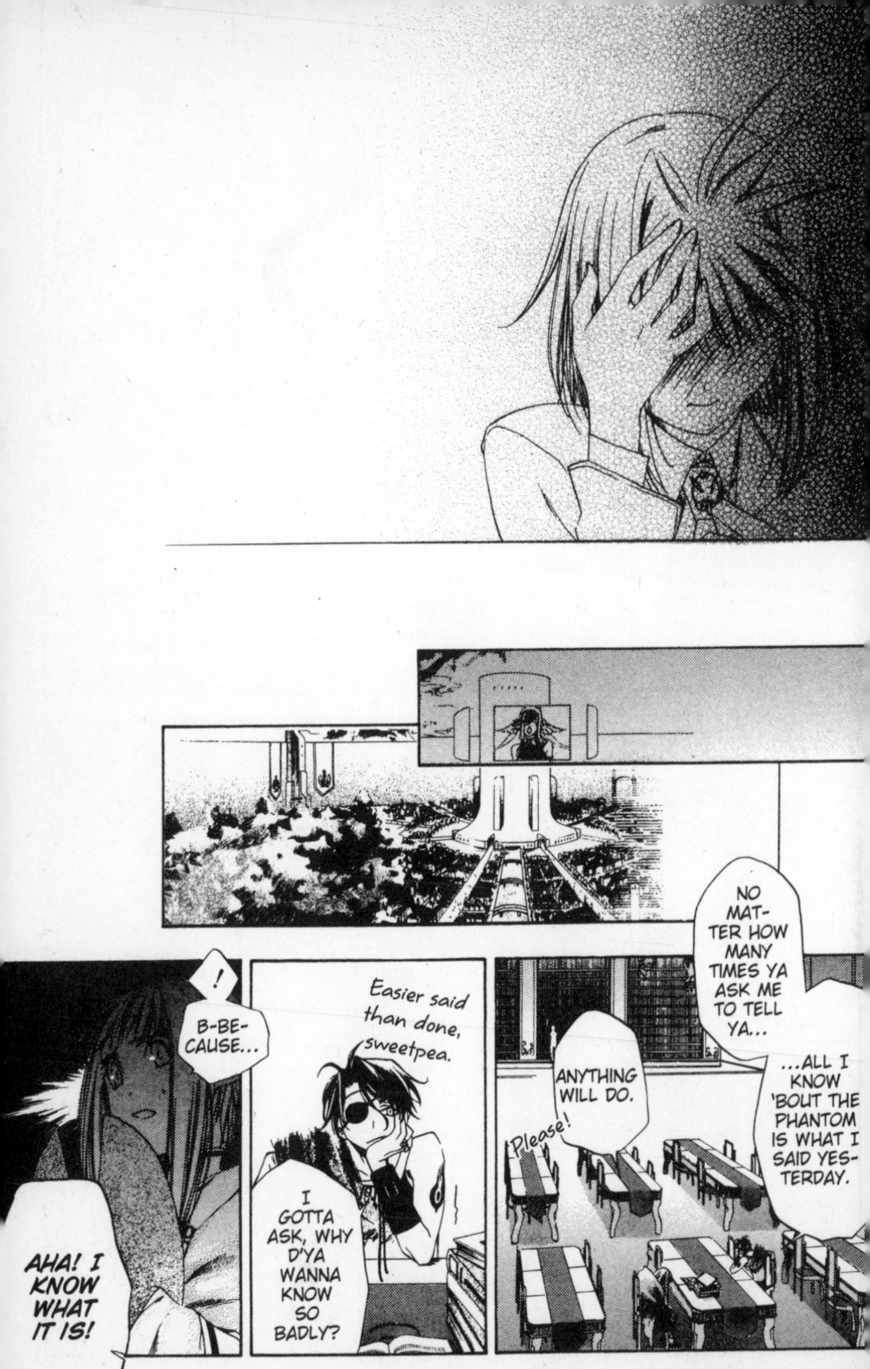
NO MAT-TER HOW MANY TIMES YA ASK ME TO TELL YA...
...ALL I KNOW 'BOUT THE PHANTOM IS WHAT I SAID YES-TERDAY.
ANYTHING WILL DO.
Please!
Easier said than done, sweetpea.
I GOTTA ASK, WHY D'YA WANNA KNOW SO BADLY?
!
B-BE-CAUSE...
AHA! I KNOW WHAT IT IS!

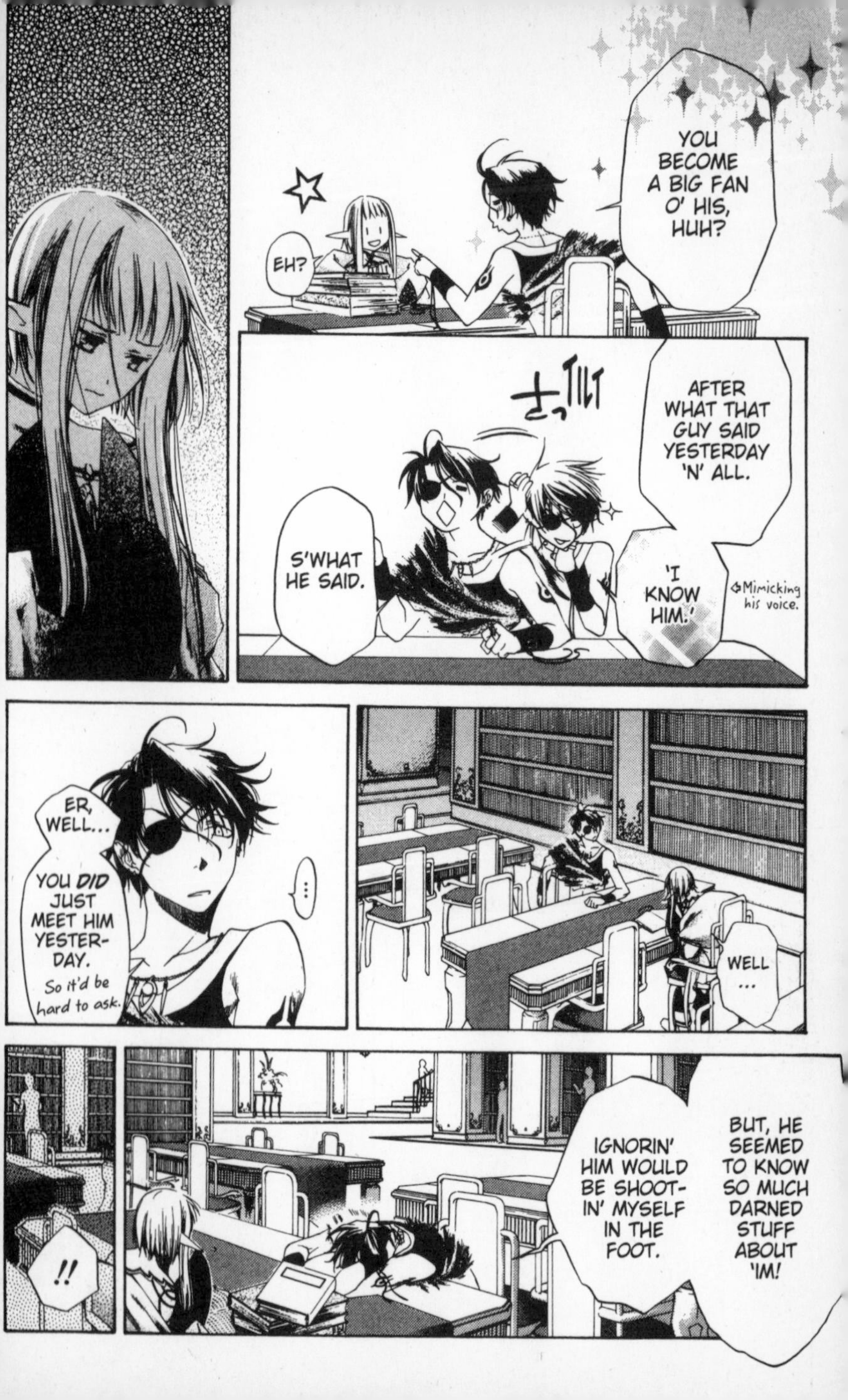
YOU BECOME A BIG FAN O' HIS, HUH?
EH?
AFTER WHAT THAT GUY SAID YESTERDAY 'N' ALL.
さっ TILT
'I KNOW HIM.'
Mimicking his voice.
S'WHAT HE SAID.
WELL ...
ER, WELL...
YOU *DID* JUST MEET HIM YESTER-DAY.
So it'd be hard to ask.
...
BUT, HE SEEMED TO KNOW SO MUCH DARNED STUFF ABOUT 'IM!
IGNORIN' HIM WOULD BE SHOOT-IN' MYSELF IN THE FOOT.
!!

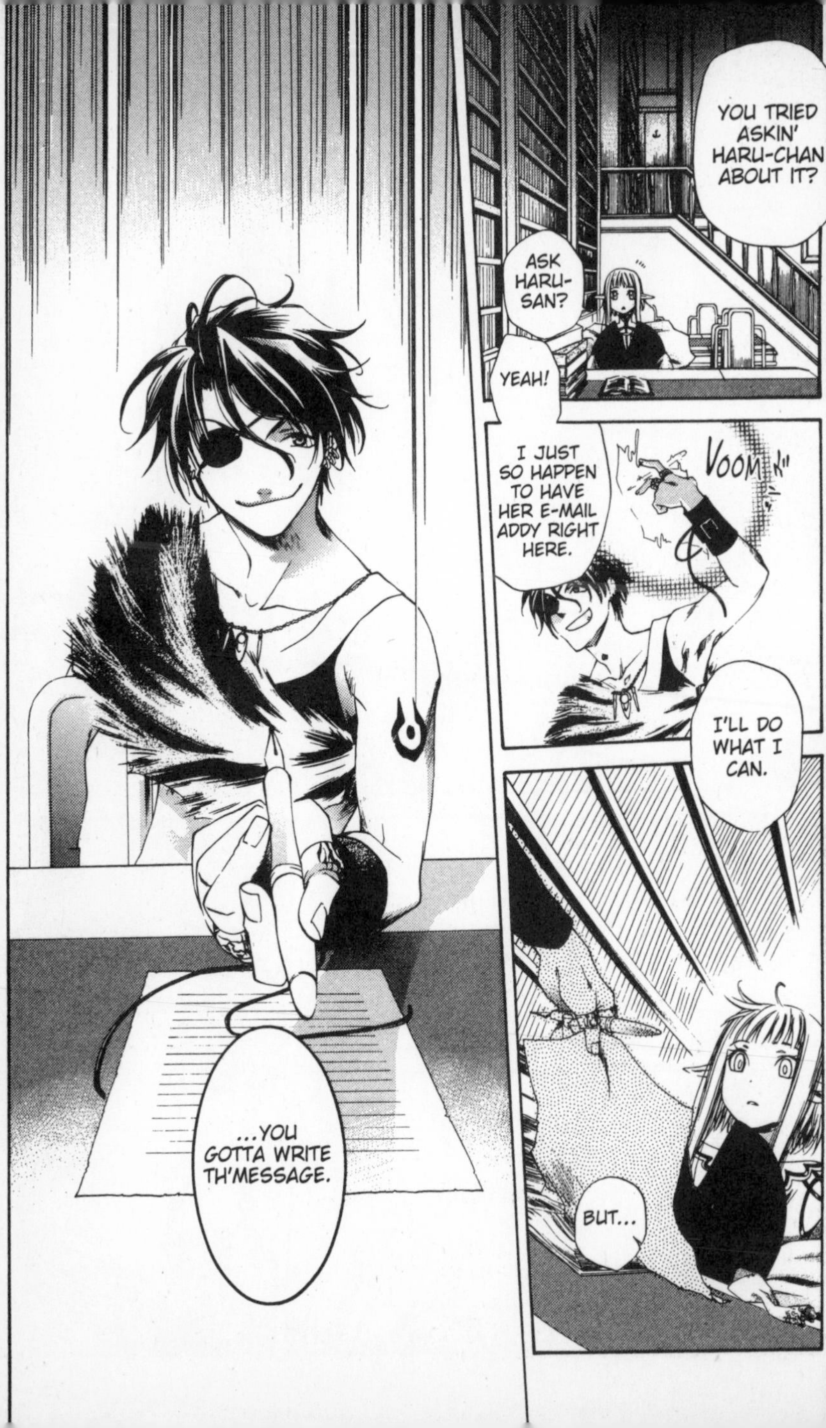
YOU TRIED ASKIN' HARU-CHAN ABOUT IT?
ASK HARU-SAN?
YEAH!
I JUST SO HAPPEN TO HAVE HER E-MAIL ADDY RIGHT HERE.
VOOM
I'LL DO WHAT I CAN.
BUT...
...YOU GOTTA WRITE TH'MESSAGE.

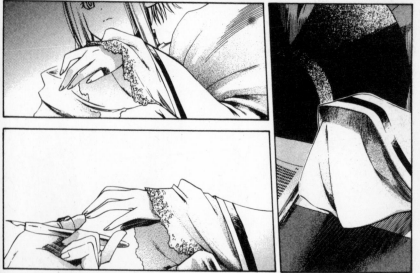

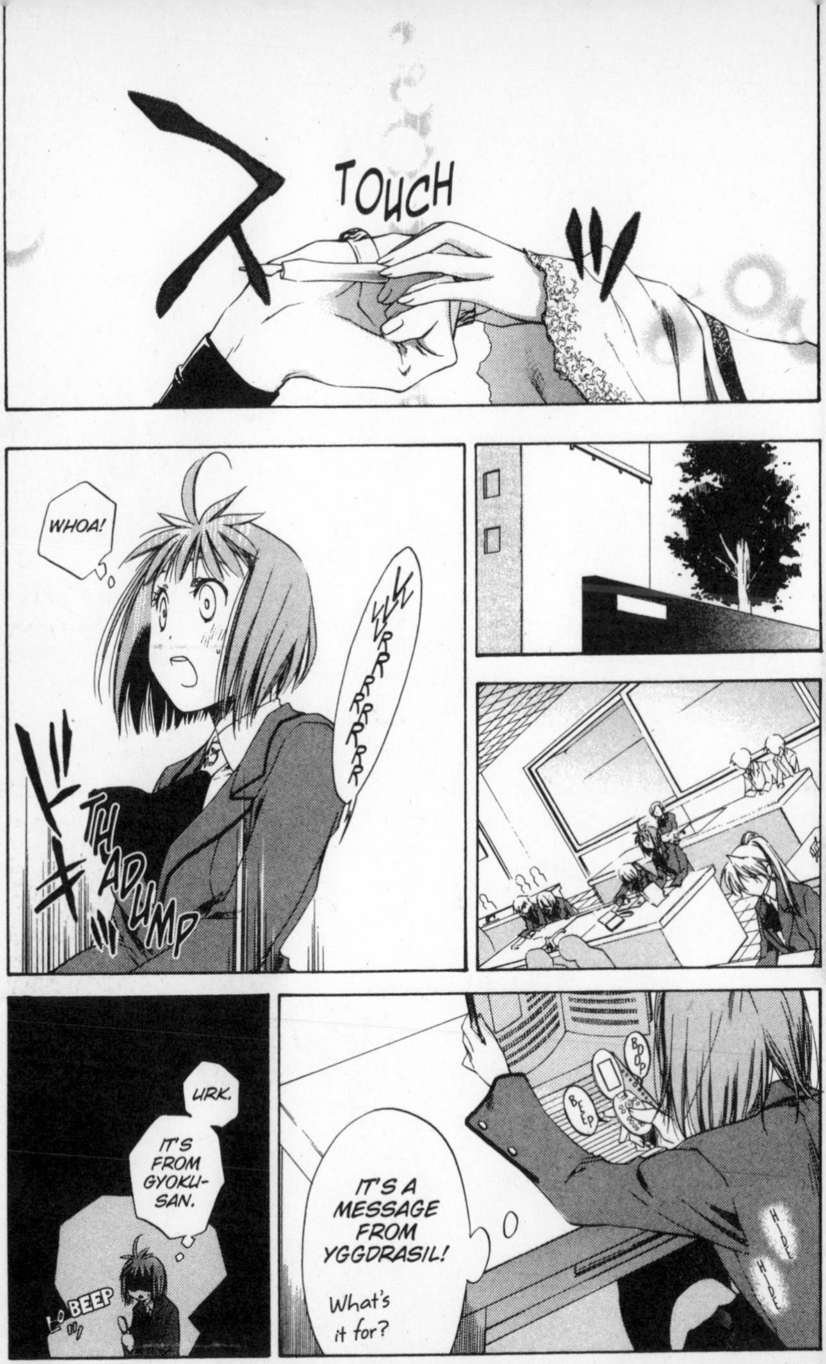
TOUCH
WHOA!
VVVVRRRRRRRRRR
THADUMP
IT'S A MESSAGE FROM YGGDRASIL!
What's it for?
BOOP
BEEP
HIDE
HIDE
URK.
IT'S FROM GYOKU-SAN.
BEEP

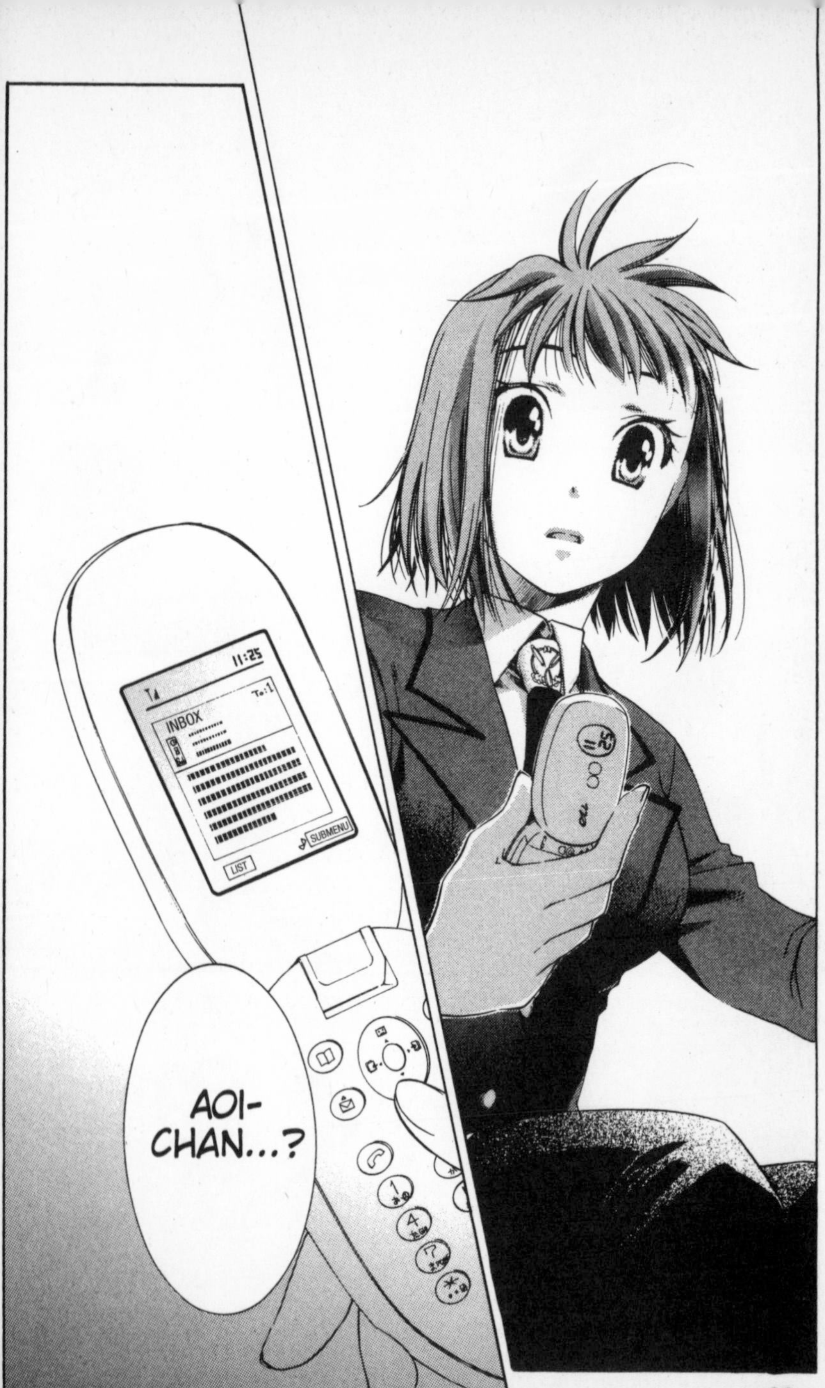
AOI-CHAN...?
11:25
INBOX
SUBMENU
LIST

A fruit of Yggdrasil

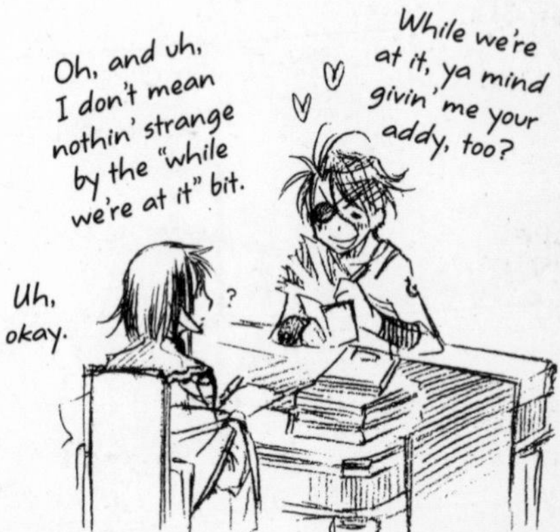
While we're at it, ya mind givin' me your addy, too?
Oh, and uh, I don't mean nothin' strange by the "while we're at it" bit.
?
Uh, okay.

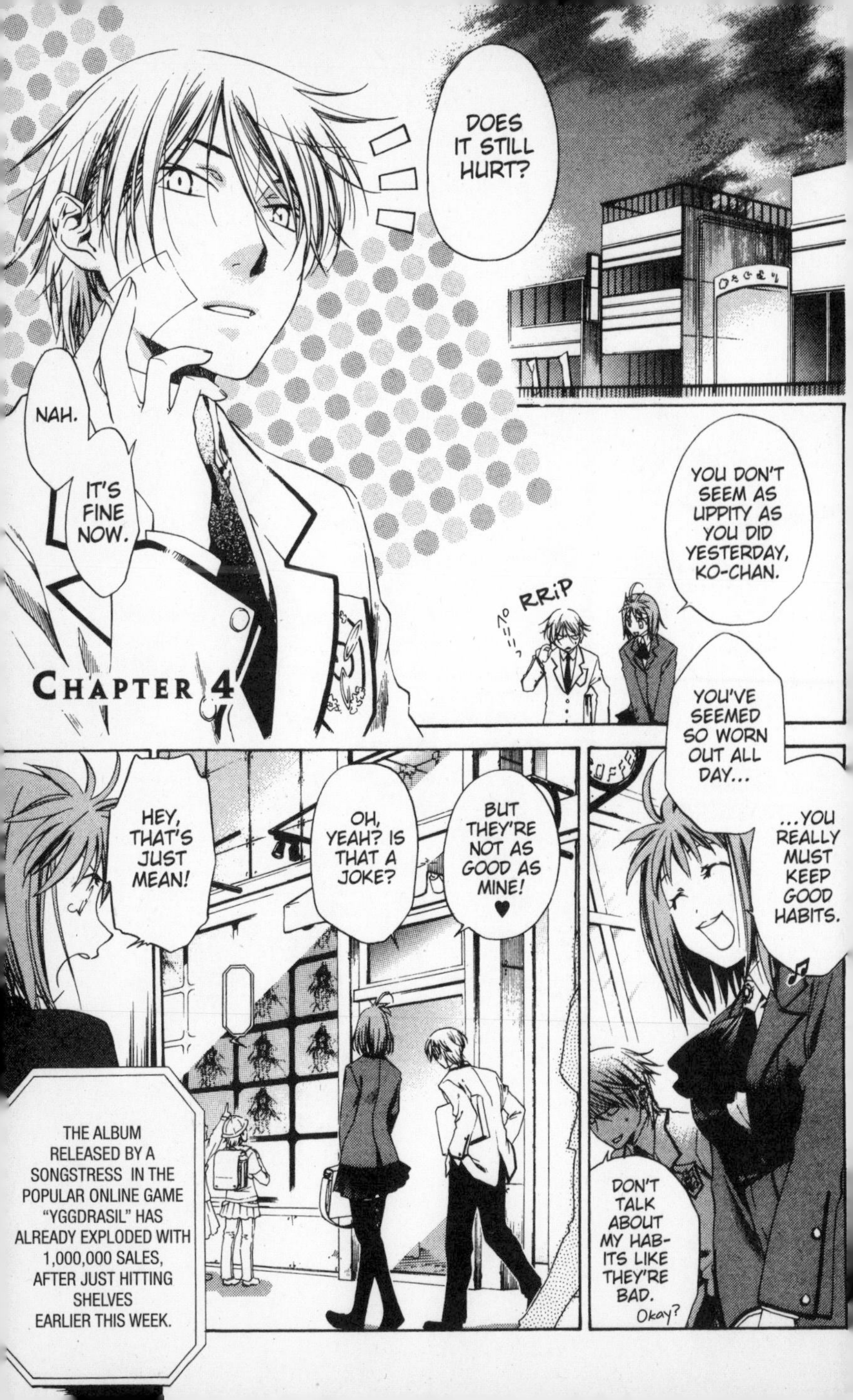
DOES IT STILL HURT?
RRiP
YOU DON'T SEEM AS UPPITY AS YOU DID YESTERDAY, KO-CHAN.
NAH.
IT'S FINE NOW.
CHAPTER 4
YOU'VE SEEMED SO WORN OUT ALL DAY...
...YOU REALLY MUST KEEP GOOD HABITS.
DON'T TALK ABOUT MY HAB-ITS LIKE THEY'RE BAD.
Okay?
BUT THEY'RE NOT AS GOOD AS MINE! ♥
OH, YEAH? IS THAT A JOKE?
HEY, THAT'S JUST MEAN!
THE ALBUM RELEASED BY A SONGSTRESS IN THE POPULAR ONLINE GAME "YGGDRASIL" HAS ALREADY EXPLODED WITH 1,000,000 SALES, AFTER JUST HITTING SHELVES EARLIER THIS WEEK.

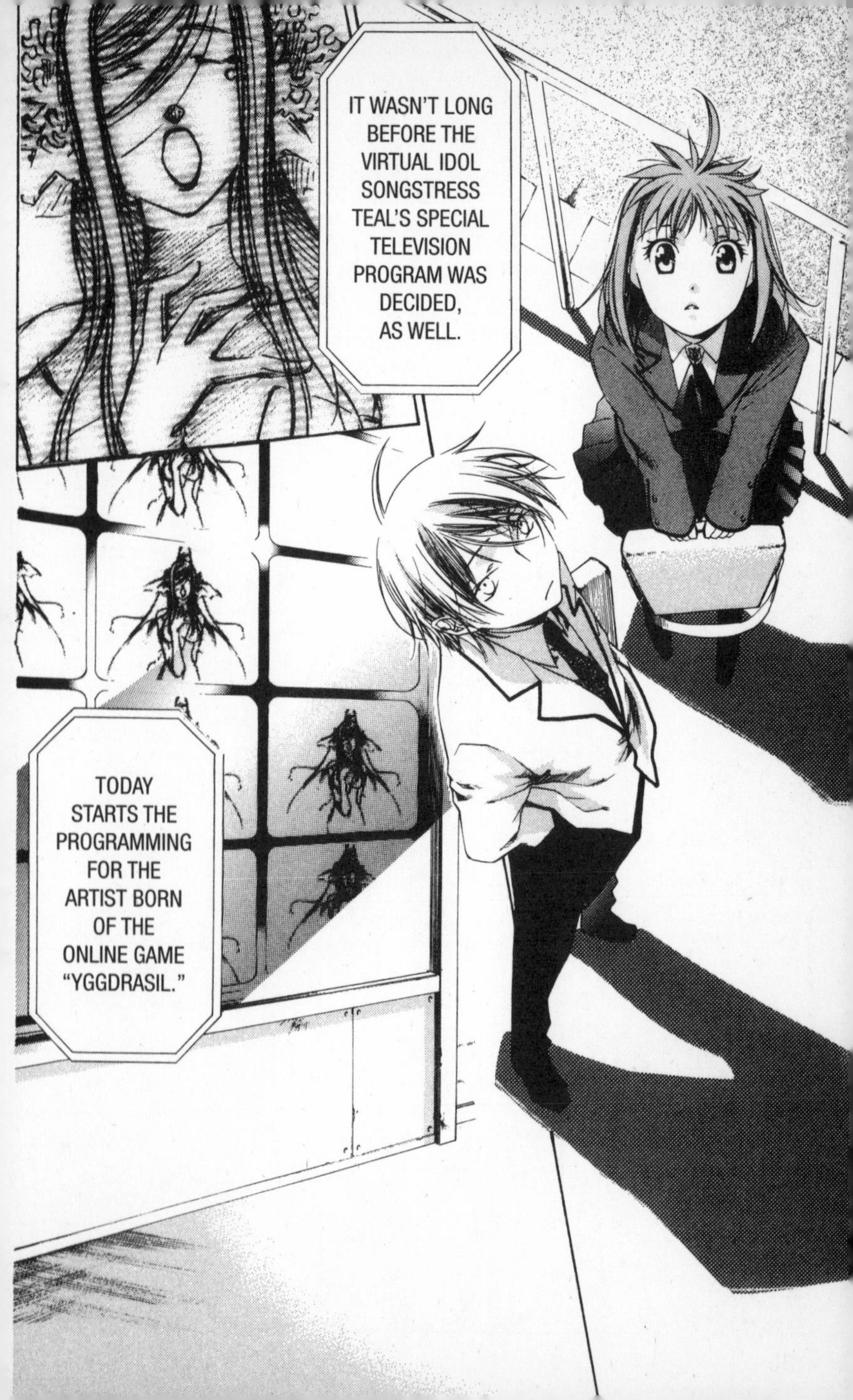
IT WASN'T LONG BEFORE THE VIRTUAL IDOL SONGSTRESS TEAL'S SPECIAL TELEVISION PROGRAM WAS DECIDED, AS WELL.
TODAY STARTS THE PROGRAMMING FOR THE ARTIST BORN OF THE ONLINE GAME "YGGDRASIL."

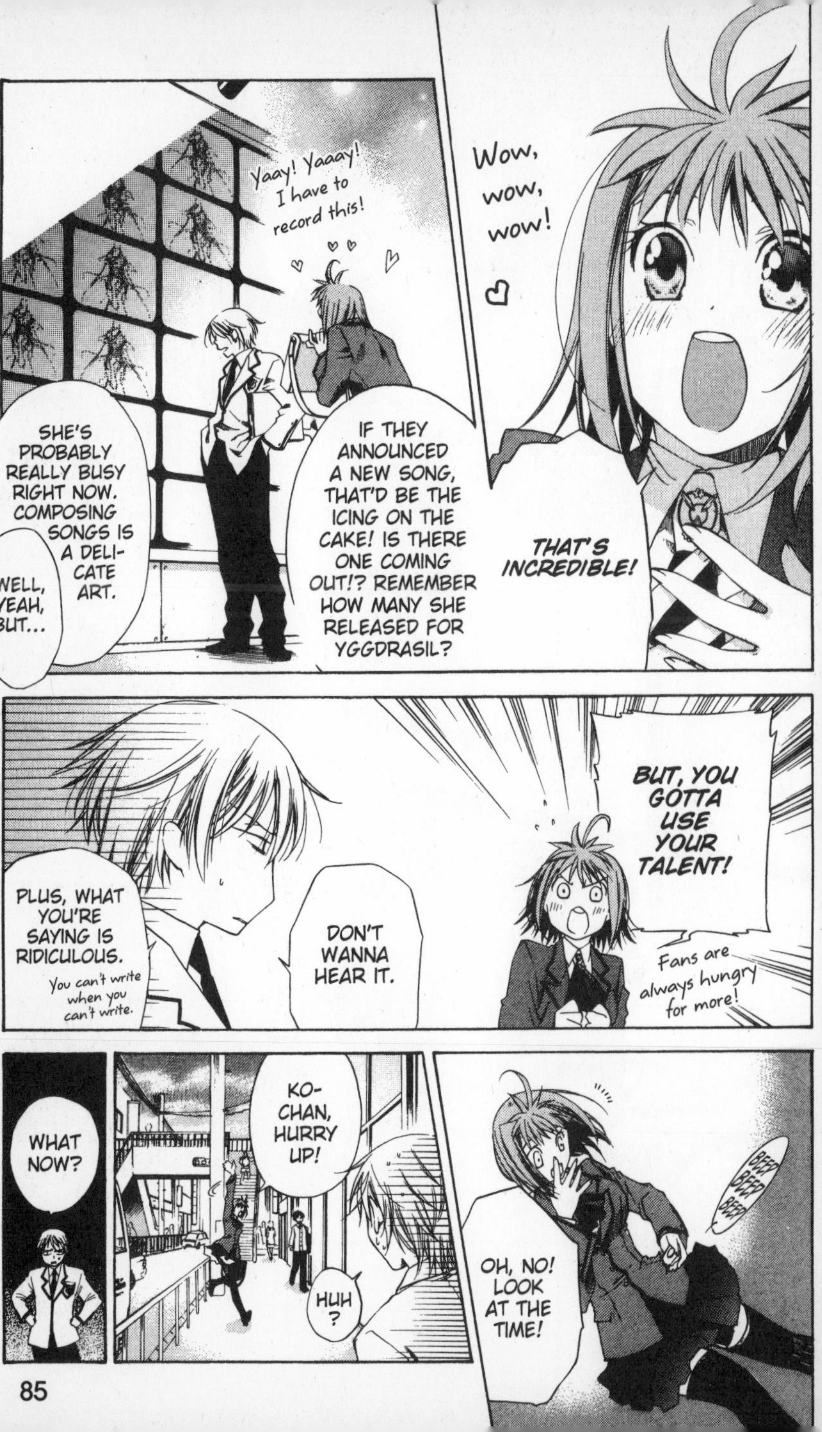
Wow, wow, wow! ♡
THAT'S INCREDIBLE!
Yaay! Yaaay! I have to record this!
IF THEY ANNOUNCED A NEW SONG, THAT'D BE THE ICING ON THE CAKE! IS THERE ONE COMING OUT!? REMEMBER HOW MANY SHE RELEASED FOR YGGDRASIL?
SHE'S PROBABLY REALLY BUSY RIGHT NOW. COMPOSING SONGS IS A DELICATE ART.
WELL, YEAH, BUT...
BUT, YOU GOTTA USE YOUR TALENT!
Fans are always hungry for more!
DON'T WANNA HEAR IT.
PLUS, WHAT YOU'RE SAYING IS RIDICULOUS.
You can't write when you can't write.
BEEP BEEP BEEP
OH, NO! LOOK AT THE TIME!
KO-CHAN, HURRY UP!
HUH?
WHAT NOW?

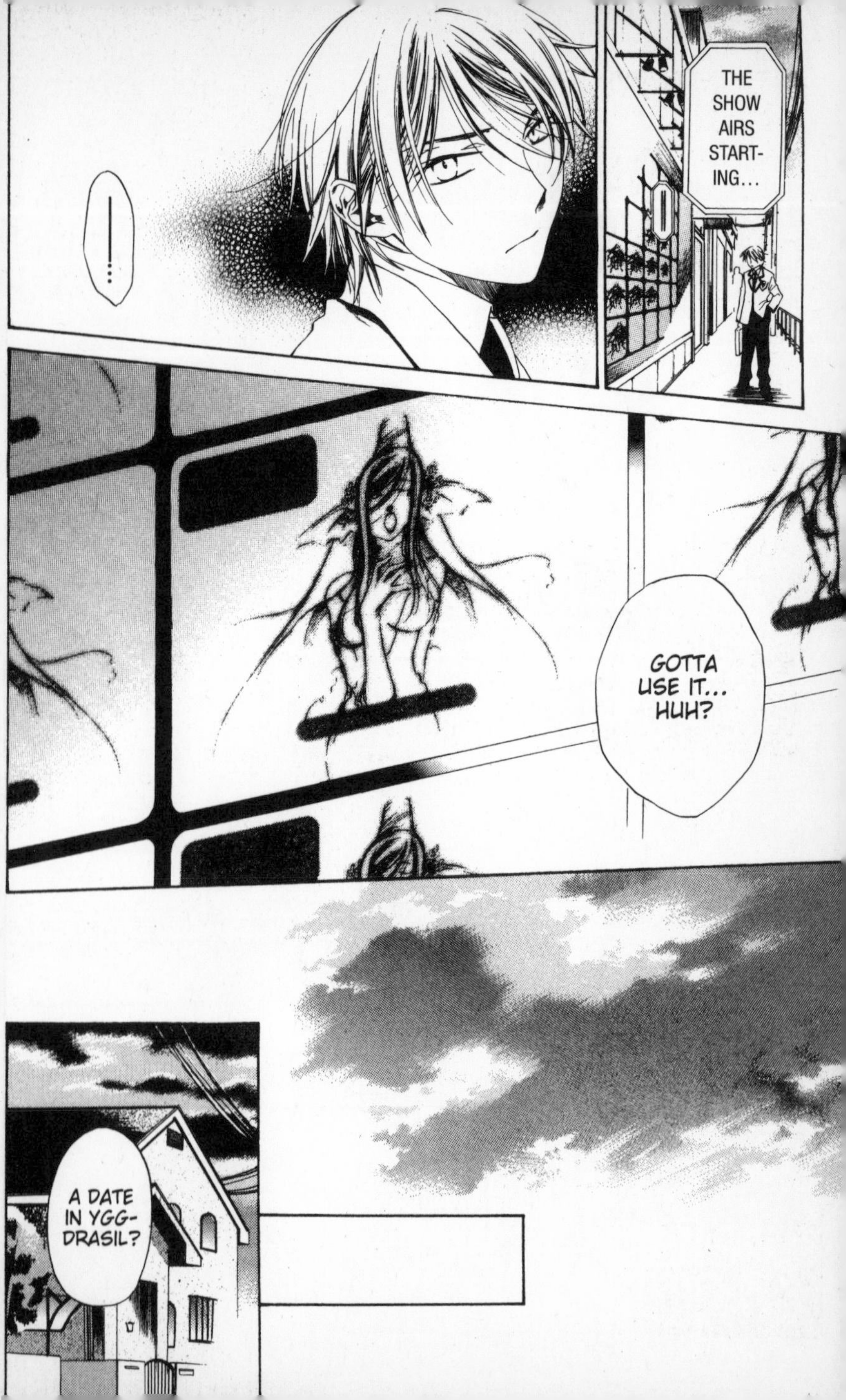
THE SHOW AIRS START- ING...
...!
GOTTA USE IT... HUH?
A DATE IN YGG- DRASIL?

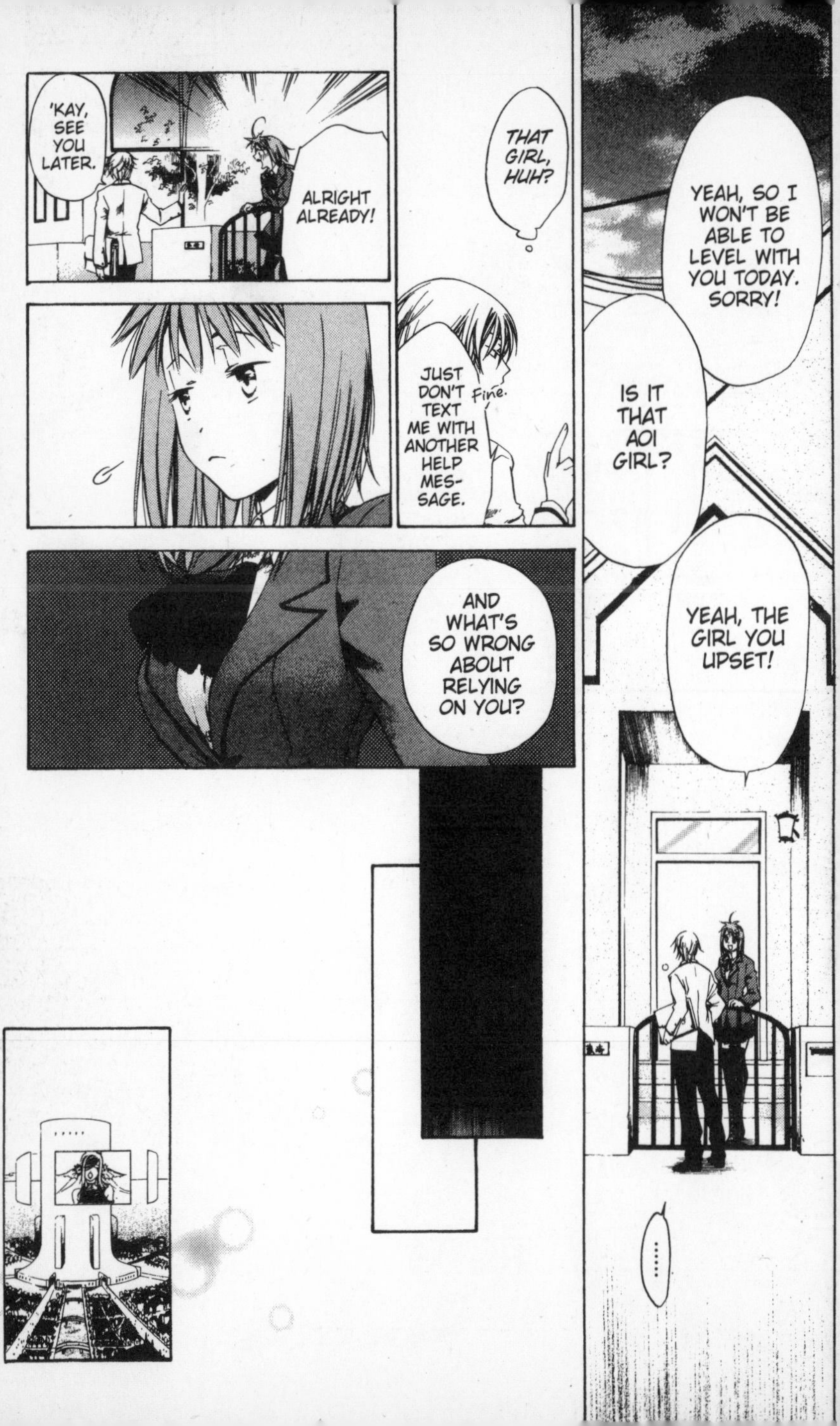
YEAH, SO I WON'T BE ABLE TO LEVEL WITH YOU TODAY. SORRY!
IS IT THAT AOI GIRL?
YEAH, THE GIRL YOU UPSET!
......
THAT GIRL, HUH?
JUST DON'T TEXT ME WITH ANOTHER HELP MES-SAGE.
Fine.
ALRIGHT ALREADY!
'KAY, SEE YOU LATER.
AND WHAT'S SO WRONG ABOUT RELYING ON YOU?
.....

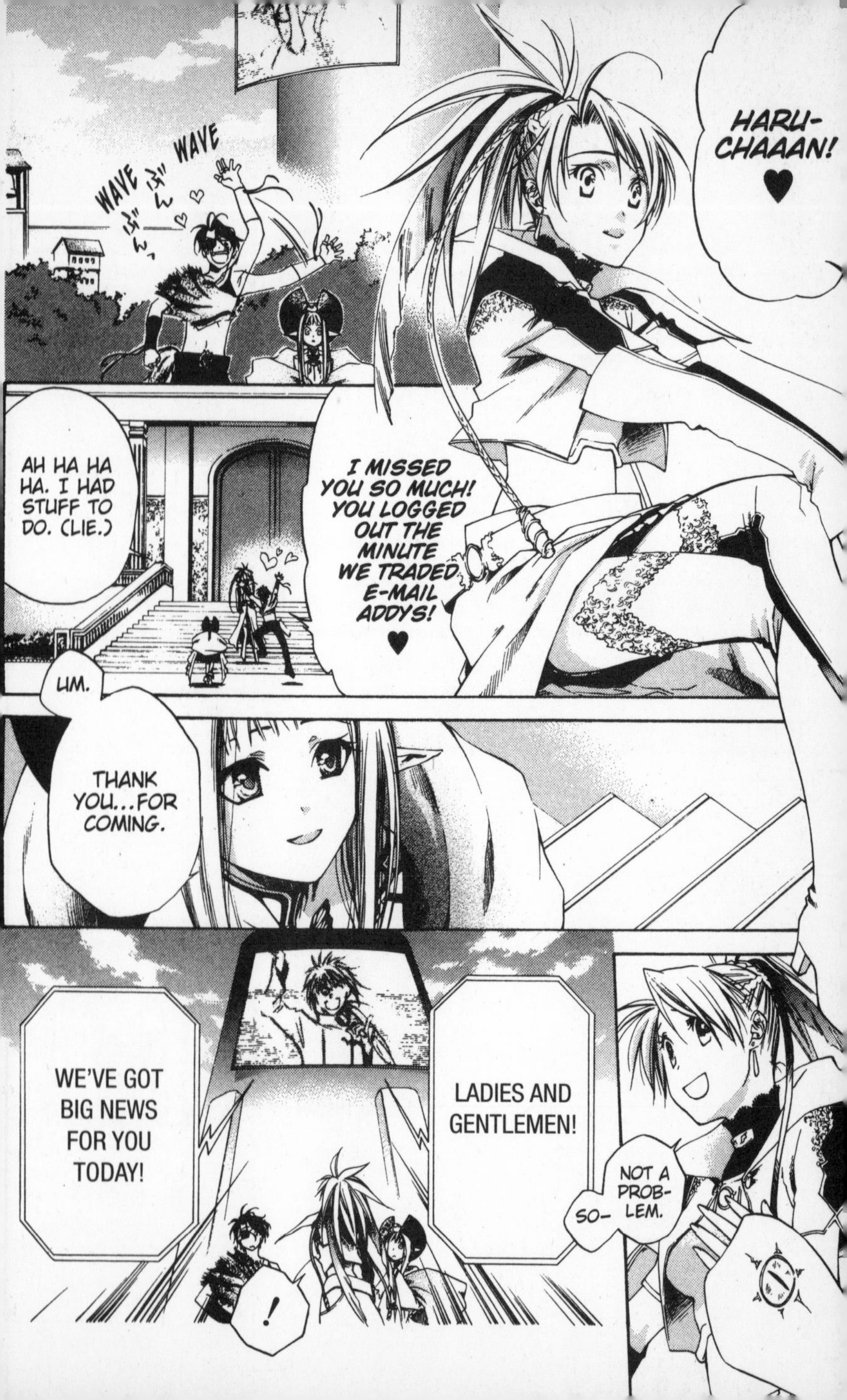
HARU-CHAAAN! ♥
WAVE WAVE
ぶんぶん
I MISSED YOU SO MUCH! YOU LOGGED OUT THE MINUTE WE TRADED E-MAIL ADDYS! ♥
AH HA HA HA. I HAD STUFF TO DO. (LIE.)
UM.
THANK YOU...FOR COMING.
NOT A PROB-LEM.
SO-
LADIES AND GENTLEMEN!
WE'VE GOT BIG NEWS FOR YOU TODAY!
!

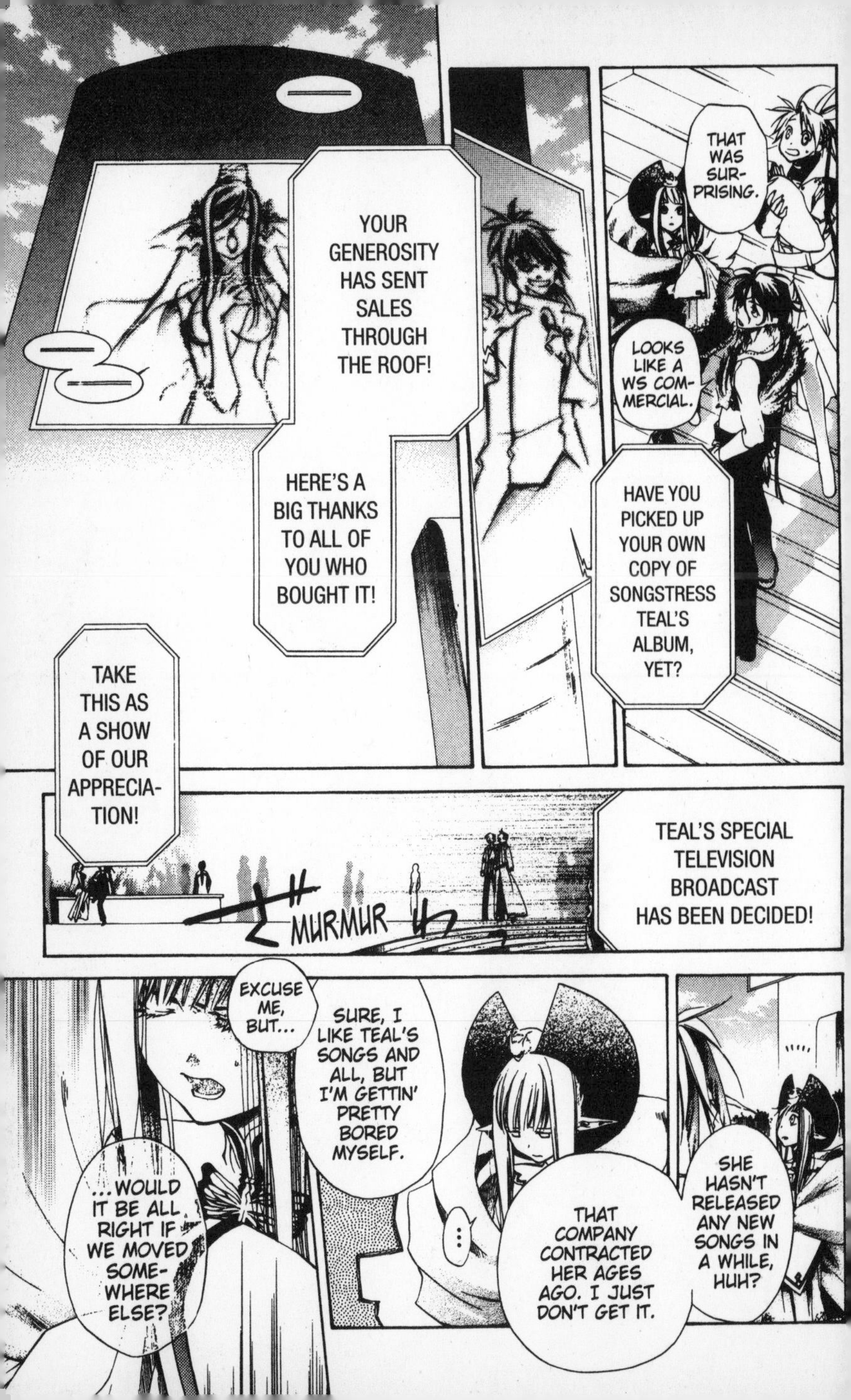
THAT WAS SUR-PRISING.
LOOKS LIKE A WS COM-MERCIAL.
HAVE YOU PICKED UP YOUR OWN COPY OF SONGSTRESS TEAL'S ALBUM, YET?
YOUR GENEROSITY HAS SENT SALES THROUGH THE ROOF!
HERE'S A BIG THANKS TO ALL OF YOU WHO BOUGHT IT!
TAKE THIS AS A SHOW OF OUR APPRECIA-TION!
TEAL'S SPECIAL TELEVISION BROADCAST HAS BEEN DECIDED!
MURMUR
SHE HASN'T RELEASED ANY NEW SONGS IN A WHILE, HUH?
THAT COMPANY CONTRACTED HER AGES AGO. I JUST DON'T GET IT.
SURE, I LIKE TEAL'S SONGS AND ALL, BUT I'M GETTIN' PRETTY BORED MYSELF.
...
EXCUSE ME, BUT...
...WOULD IT BE ALL RIGHT IF WE MOVED SOME-WHERE ELSE?

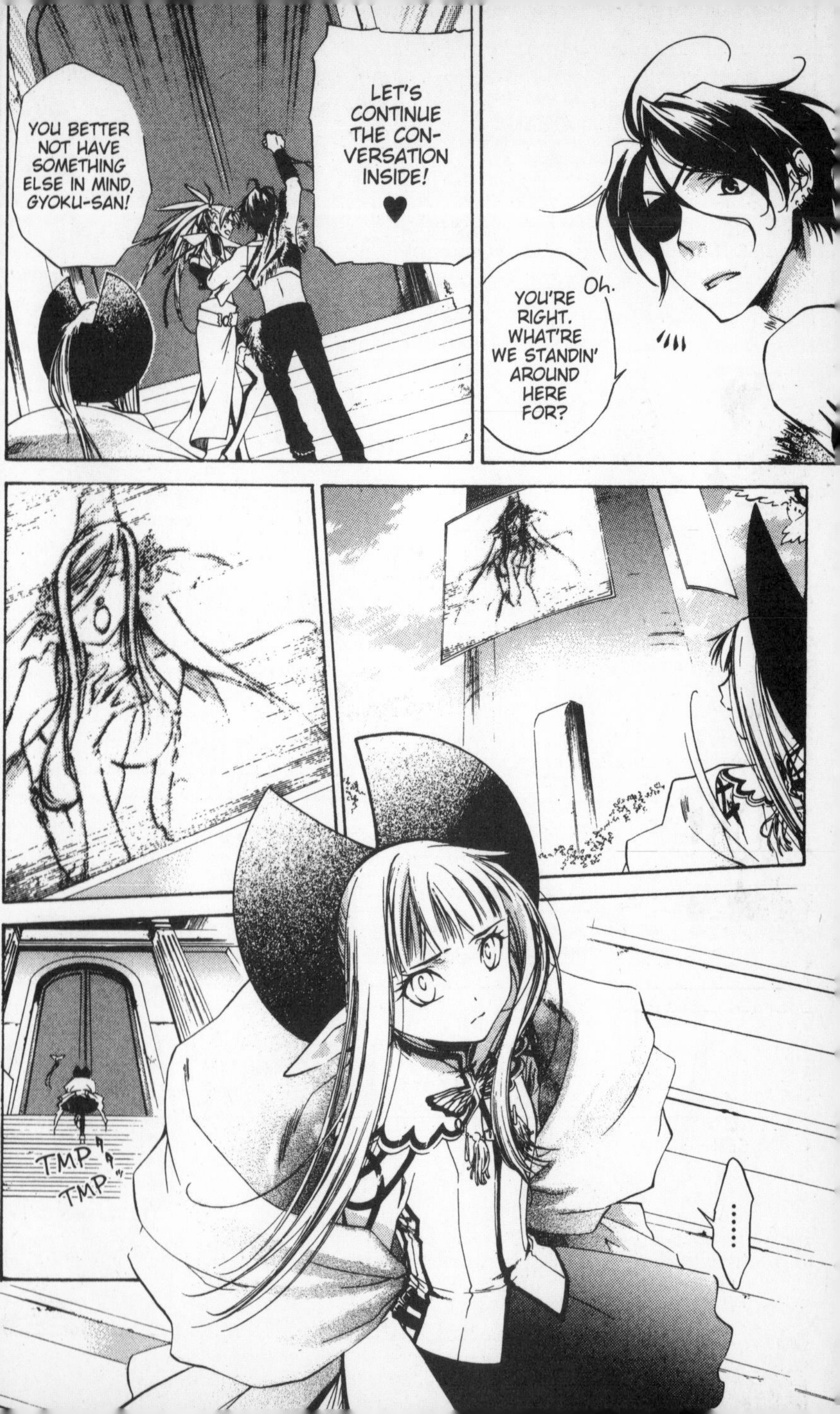
Oh.
YOU'RE RIGHT. WHAT'RE WE STANDIN' AROUND HERE FOR?
LET'S CONTINUE THE CON-VERSATION INSIDE! ♥
YOU BETTER NOT HAVE SOMETHING ELSE IN MIND, GYOKU-SAN!
......
TMP TMP

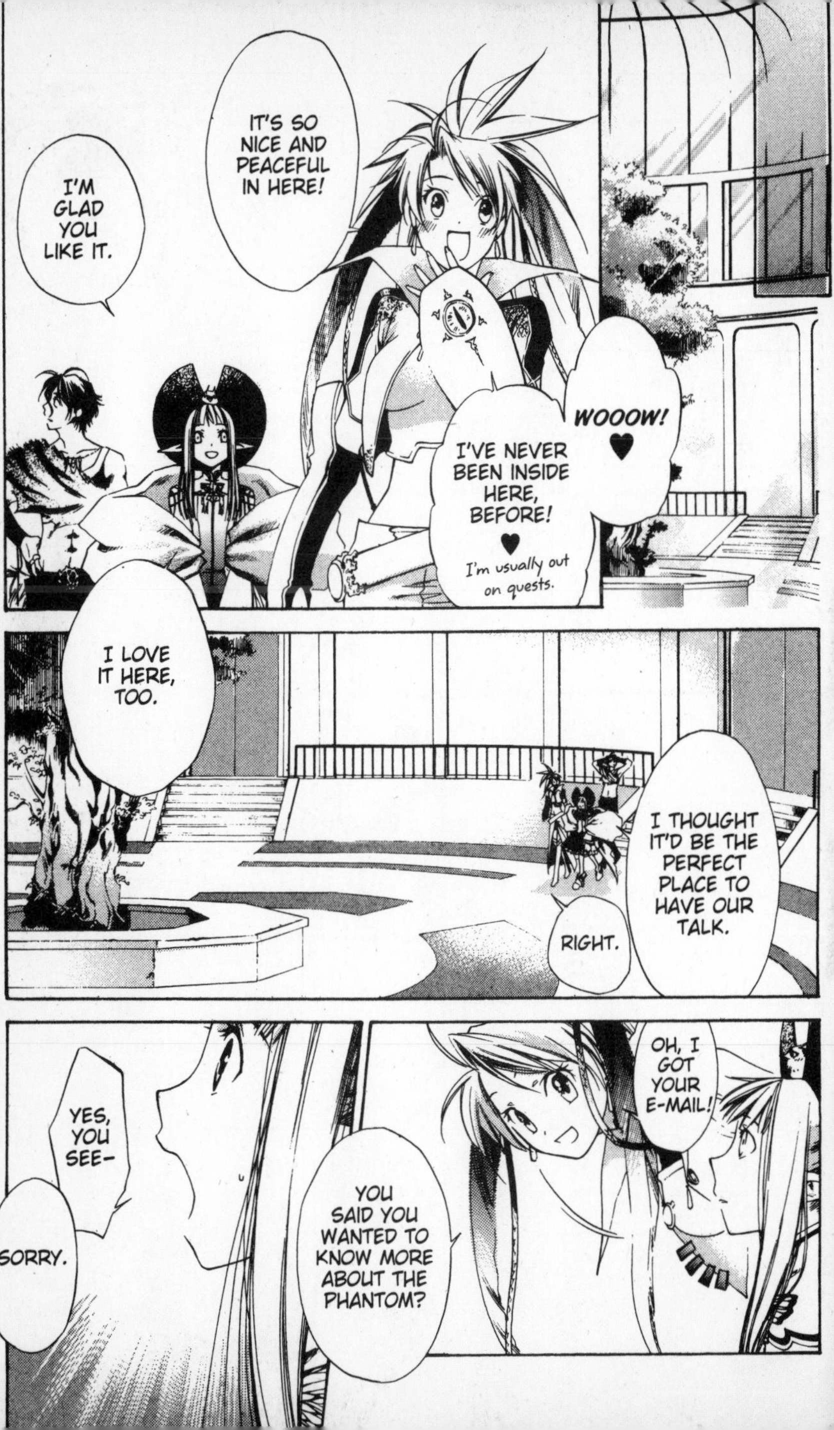
WOOOW! ♥
I'VE NEVER BEEN INSIDE HERE, BEFORE! ♥
I'm usually out on quests.
IT'S SO NICE AND PEACEFUL IN HERE!
I'M GLAD YOU LIKE IT.
I THOUGHT IT'D BE THE PERFECT PLACE TO HAVE OUR TALK.
RIGHT.
I LOVE IT HERE, TOO.
OH, I GOT YOUR E-MAIL!
YOU SAID YOU WANTED TO KNOW MORE ABOUT THE PHANTOM?
YES, YOU SEE-
SORRY.

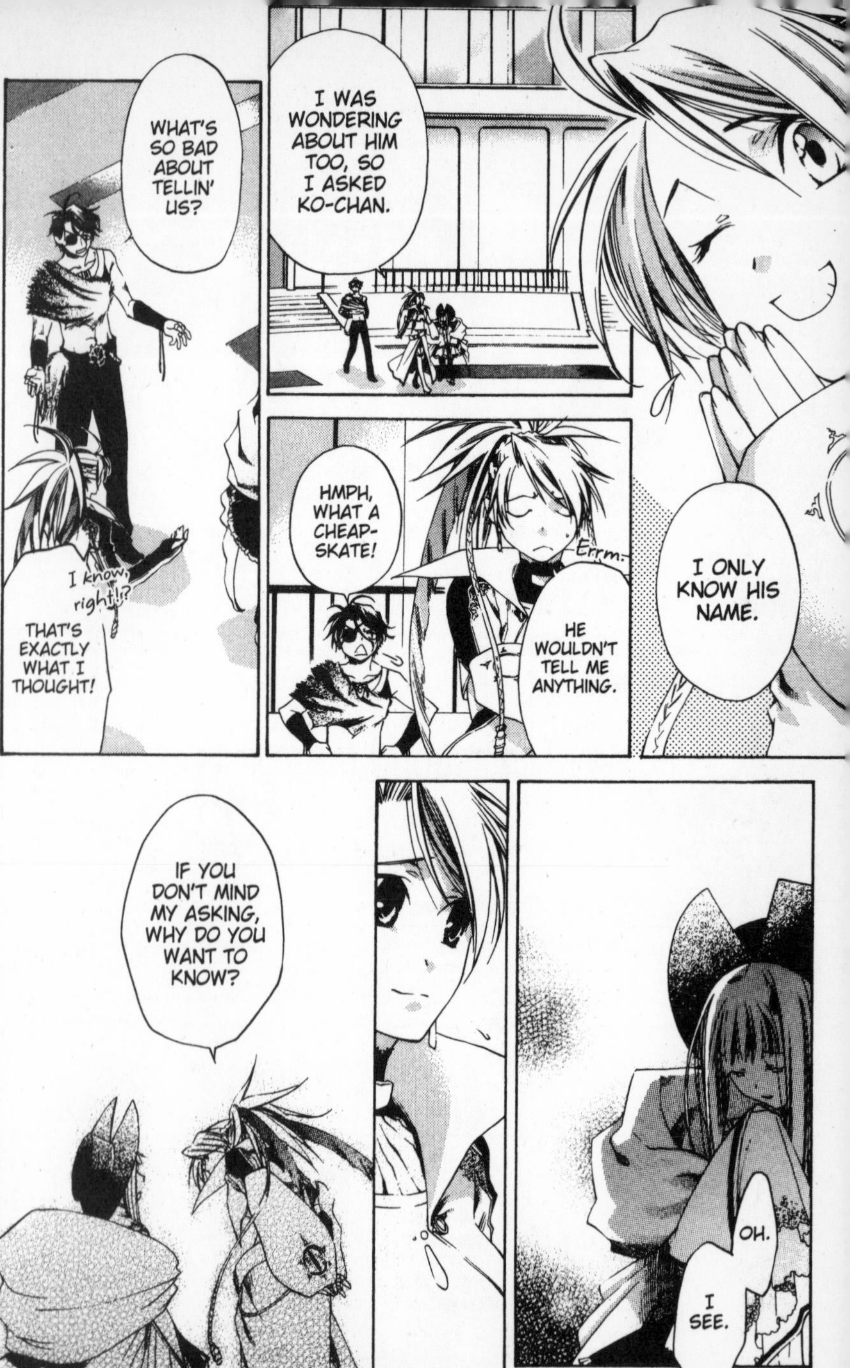
I ONLY KNOW HIS NAME.
I WAS WONDERING ABOUT HIM TOO, SO I ASKED KO-CHAN.
Errrm.
HE WOULDN'T TELL ME ANYTHING.
HMPH, WHAT A CHEAP-SKATE!
WHAT'S SO BAD ABOUT TELLIN' US?
I know, right!?
THAT'S EXACTLY WHAT I THOUGHT!
OH.
I SEE.
IF YOU DON'T MIND MY ASKING, WHY DO YOU WANT TO KNOW?

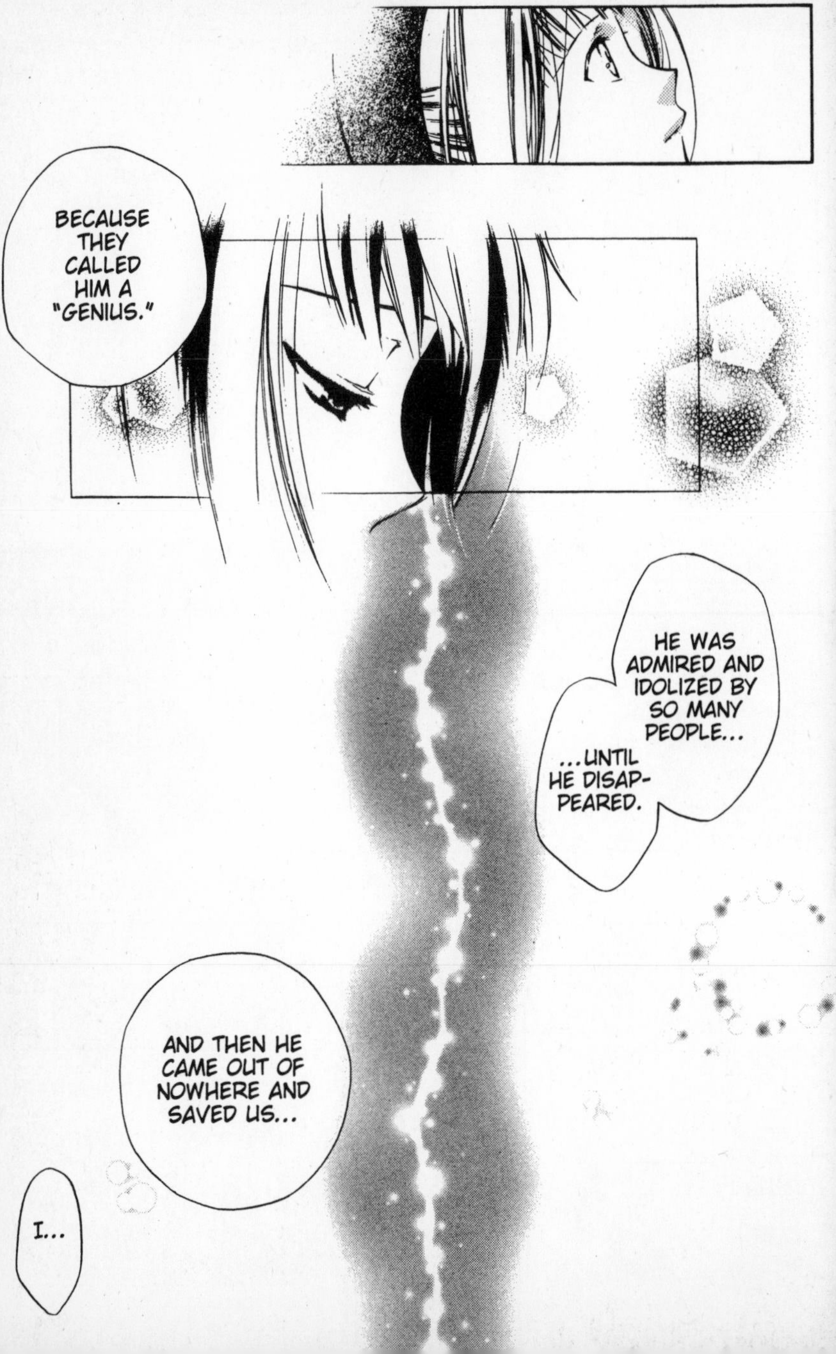
BECAUSE THEY CALLED HIM A "GENIUS."
HE WAS ADMIRED AND IDOLIZED BY SO MANY PEOPLE...
...UNTIL HE DISAP-PEARED.
AND THEN HE CAME OUT OF NOWHERE AND SAVED US...
I...

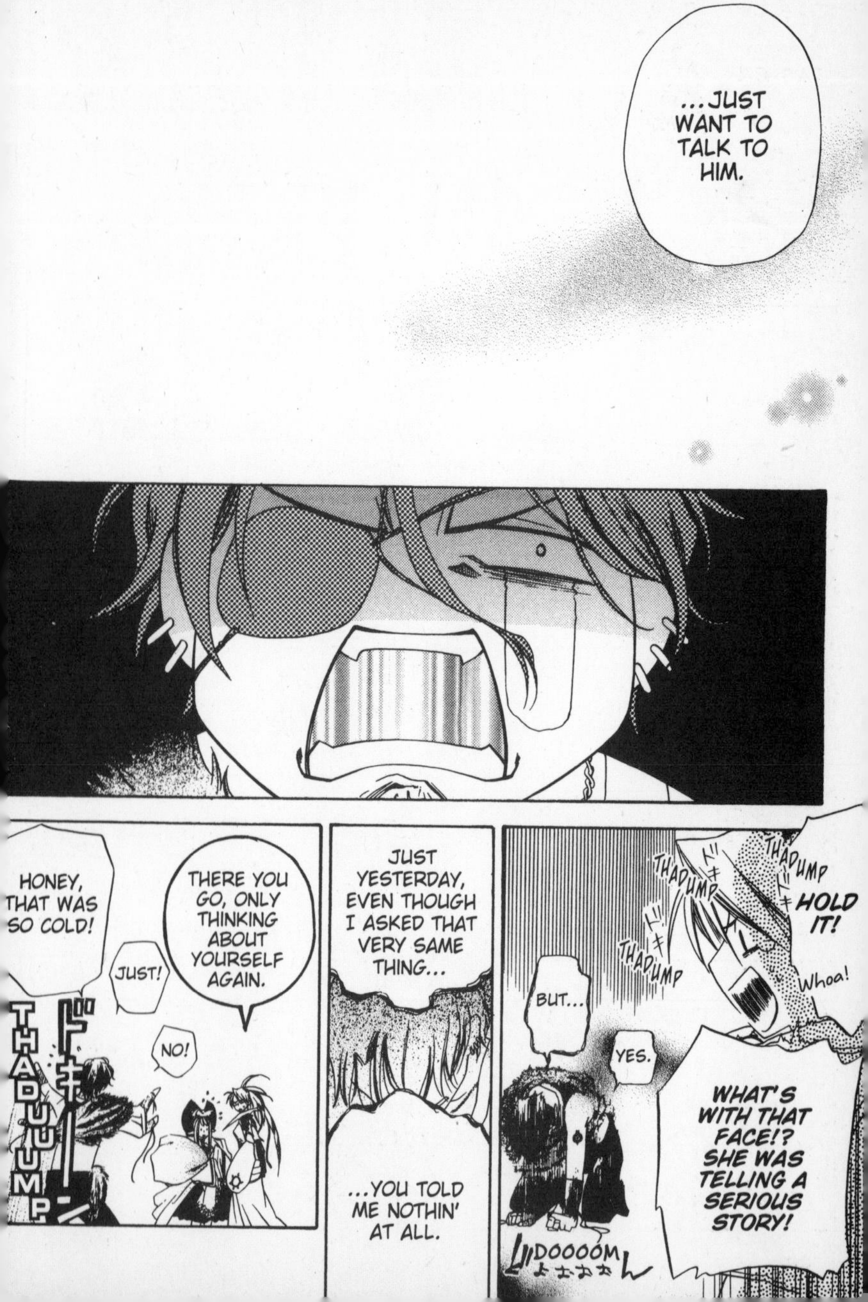
...JUST WANT TO TALK TO HIM.
THADUMP
THADUMP
THADUMP
HOLD IT!
Whoa!
WHAT'S WITH THAT FACE!? SHE WAS TELLING A SERIOUS STORY!
BUT...
YES.
DOOOOOM
JUST YESTERDAY, EVEN THOUGH I ASKED THAT VERY SAME THING...
...YOU TOLD ME NOTHIN' AT ALL.
THERE YOU GO, ONLY THINKING ABOUT YOURSELF AGAIN.
HONEY, THAT WAS SO COLD!
JUST!
NO!
THADUUUMP

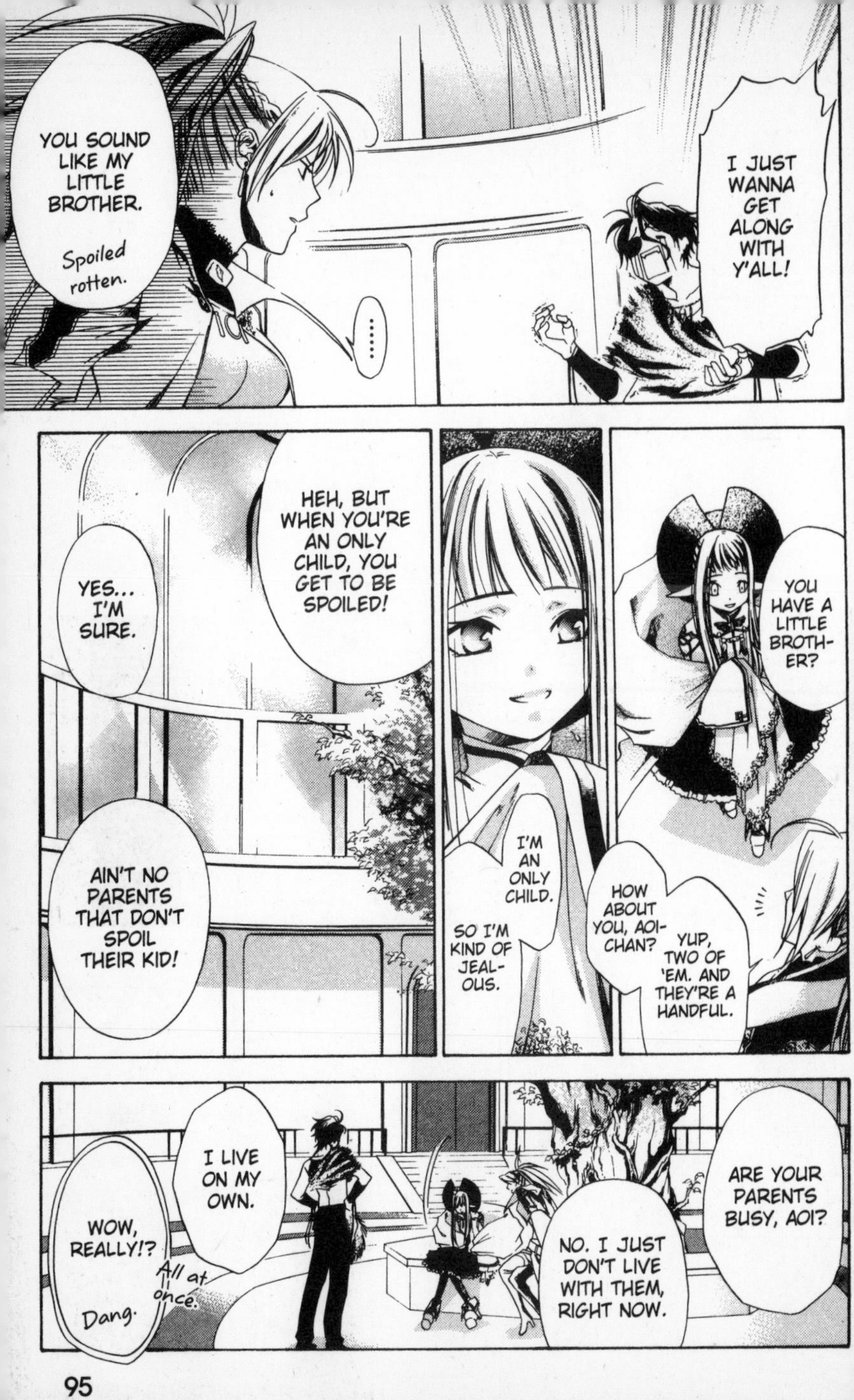
I JUST WANNA GET ALONG WITH Y'ALL!
......
YOU SOUND LIKE MY LITTLE BROTHER.
Spoiled rotten.
YOU HAVE A LITTLE BROTH-ER?
YUP, TWO OF 'EM. AND THEY'RE A HANDFUL.
HOW ABOUT YOU, AOI-CHAN?
I'M AN ONLY CHILD.
SO I'M KIND OF JEAL-OUS.
HEH, BUT WHEN YOU'RE AN ONLY CHILD, YOU GET TO BE SPOILED!
YES... I'M SURE.
AIN'T NO PARENTS THAT DON'T SPOIL THEIR KID!
ARE YOUR PARENTS BUSY, AOI?
NO. I JUST DON'T LIVE WITH THEM, RIGHT NOW.
I LIVE ON MY OWN.
WOW, REALLY!?
All at once.
Dang.

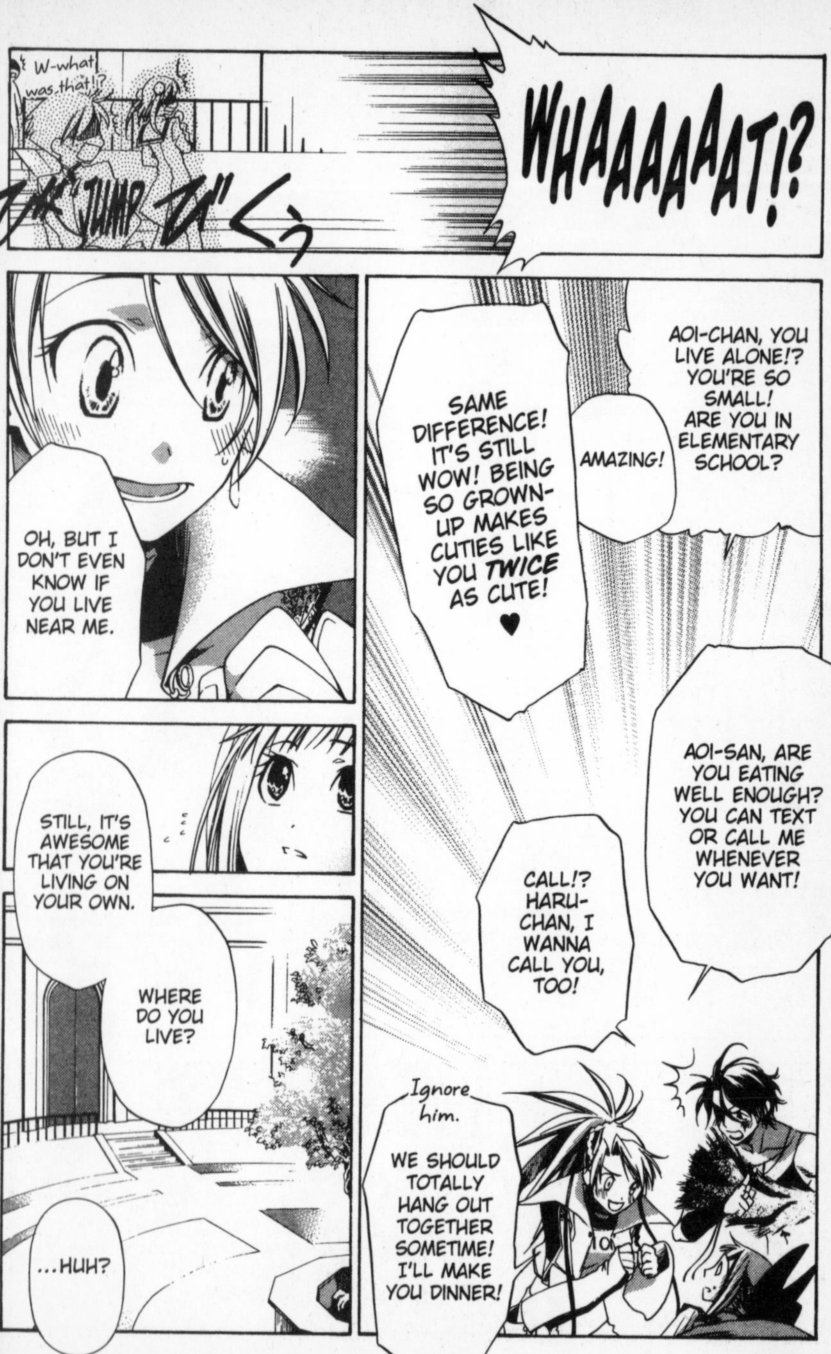
WHAAAAAAAT!?
W-what was that!?
JUMP
AOI-CHAN, YOU LIVE ALONE!? YOU'RE SO SMALL! ARE YOU IN ELEMENTARY SCHOOL?
AMAZING!
SAME DIFFERENCE! IT'S STILL WOW! BEING SO GROWN-UP MAKES CUTIES LIKE YOU *TWICE* AS CUTE! ♥
AOI-SAN, ARE YOU EATING WELL ENOUGH? YOU CAN TEXT OR CALL ME WHENEVER YOU WANT!
CALL!? HARU-CHAN, I WANNA CALL YOU, TOO!
Ignore him.
WE SHOULD TOTALLY HANG OUT TOGETHER SOMETIME! I'LL MAKE YOU DINNER!
OH, BUT I DON'T EVEN KNOW IF YOU LIVE NEAR ME.
STILL, IT'S AWESOME THAT YOU'RE LIVING ON YOUR OWN.
WHERE DO YOU LIVE?
...HUH?

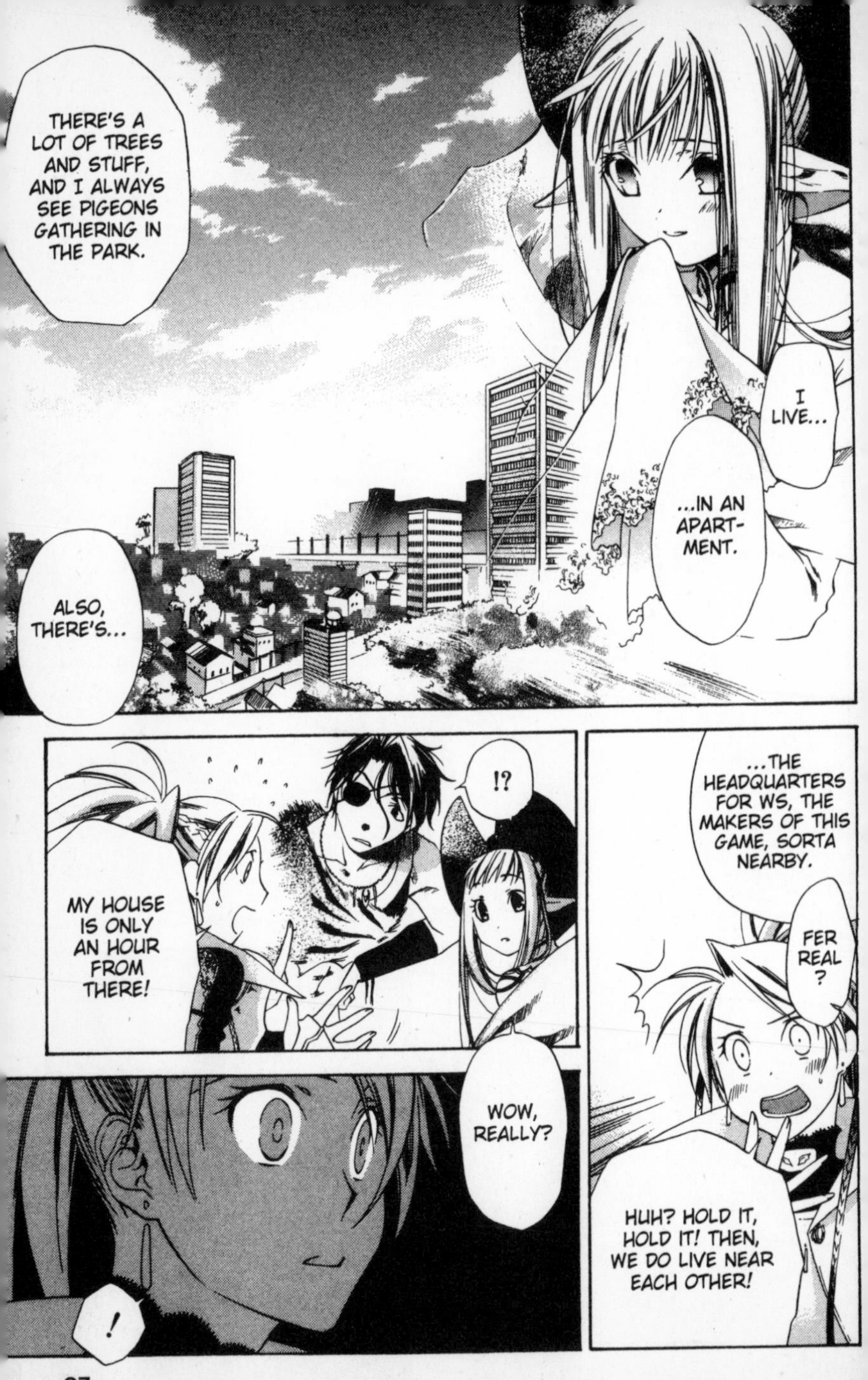
I LIVE...
...IN AN APARTMENT.
THERE'S A LOT OF TREES AND STUFF, AND I ALWAYS SEE PIGEONS GATHERING IN THE PARK.
ALSO, THERE'S...
...THE HEADQUARTERS FOR WS, THE MAKERS OF THIS GAME, SORTA NEARBY.
FER REAL?
HUH? HOLD IT, HOLD IT! THEN, WE DO LIVE NEAR EACH OTHER!
!?
MY HOUSE IS ONLY AN HOUR FROM THERE!
WOW, REALLY?
!

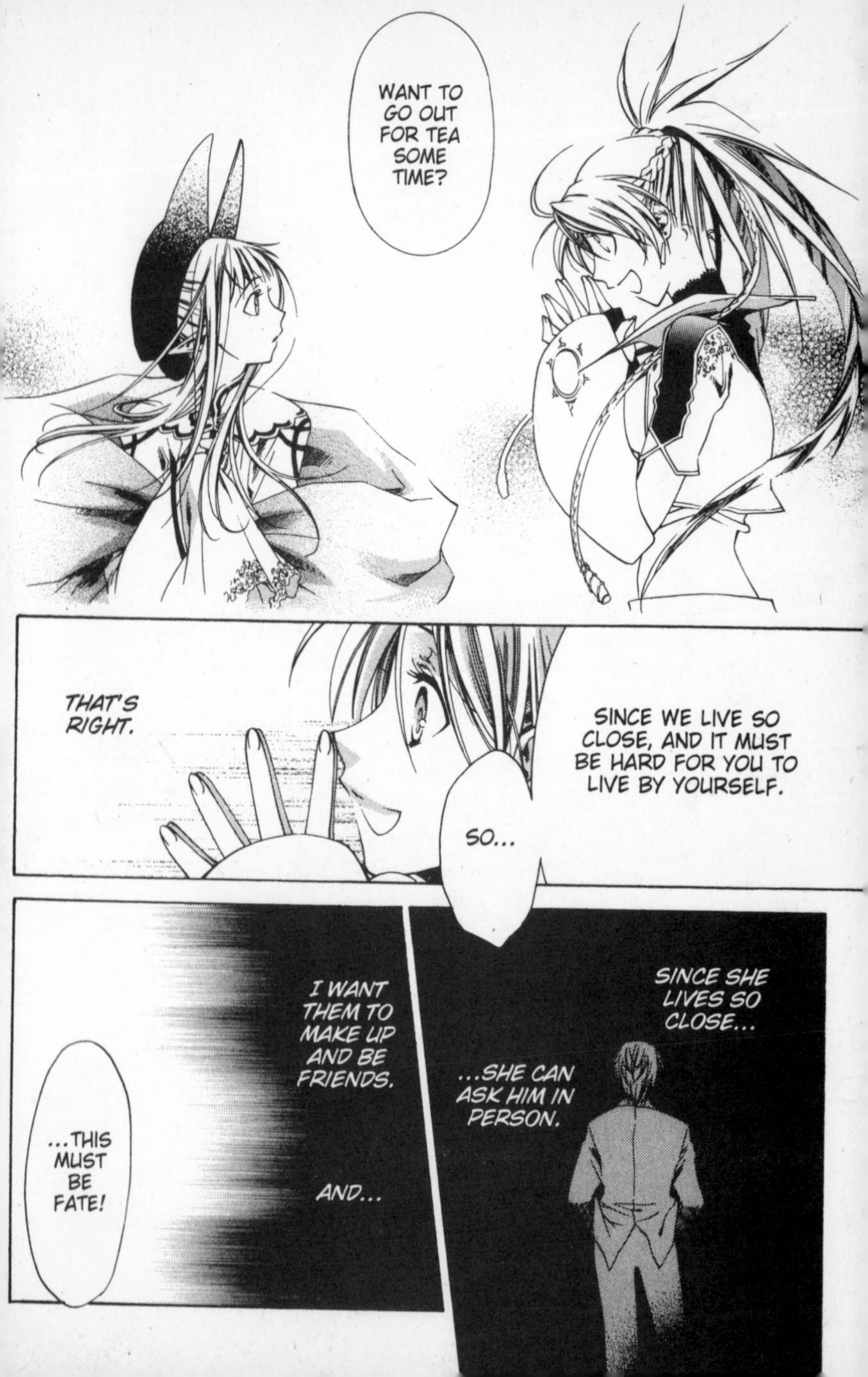
WANT TO GO OUT FOR TEA SOME TIME?
SINCE WE LIVE SO CLOSE, AND IT MUST BE HARD FOR YOU TO LIVE BY YOURSELF.
SO...
THAT'S RIGHT.
SINCE SHE LIVES SO CLOSE...
...SHE CAN ASK HIM IN PERSON.
I WANT THEM TO MAKE UP AND BE FRIENDS.
AND...
...THIS MUST BE FATE!

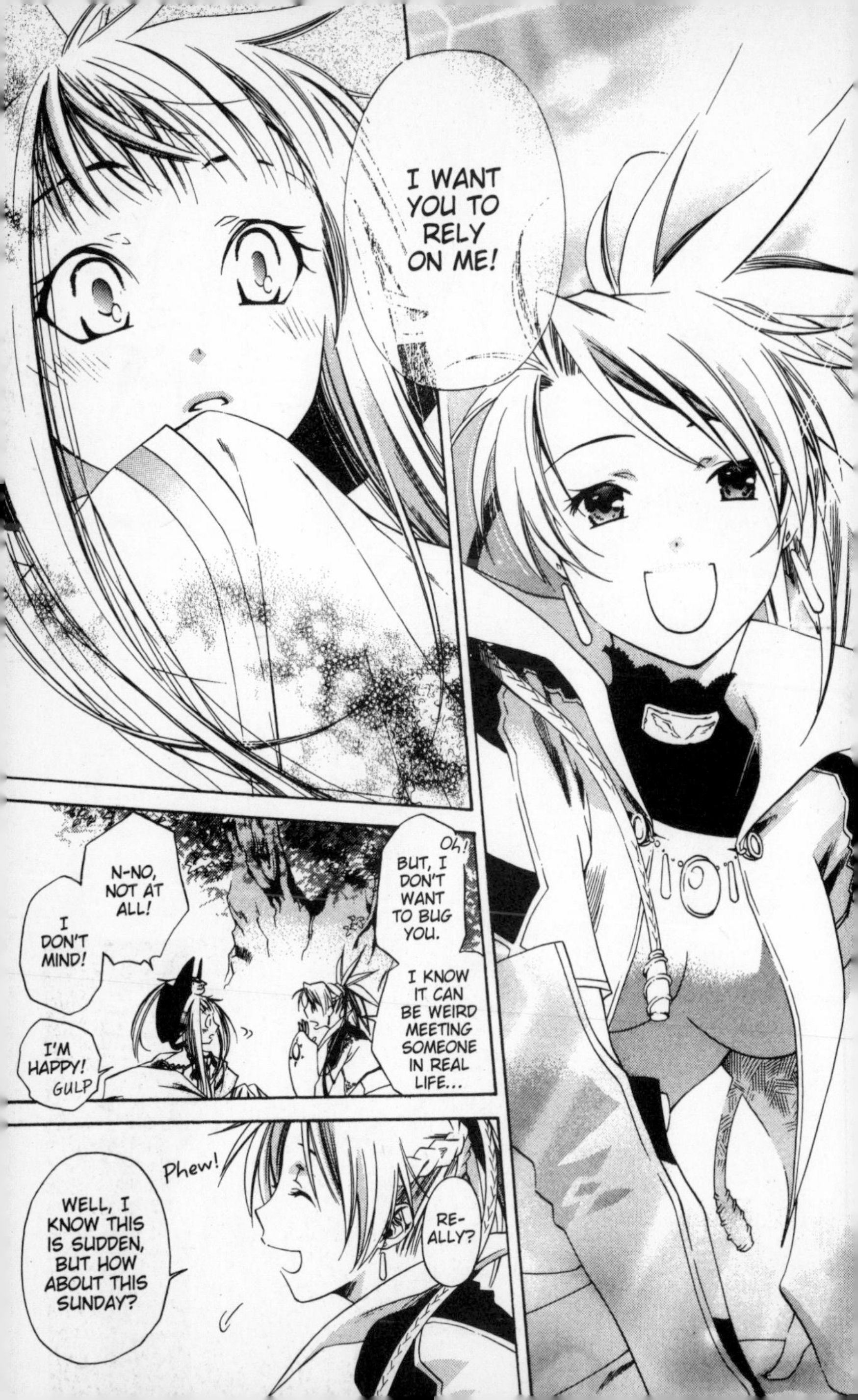
I WANT YOU TO RELY ON ME!
Oh!
BUT, I DON'T WANT TO BUG YOU.
I KNOW IT CAN BE WEIRD MEETING SOMEONE IN REAL LIFE...
N-NO, NOT AT ALL!
I DON'T MIND!
I'M HAPPY!
GULP
RE-ALLY?
Phew!
WELL, I KNOW THIS IS SUDDEN, BUT HOW ABOUT THIS SUNDAY?

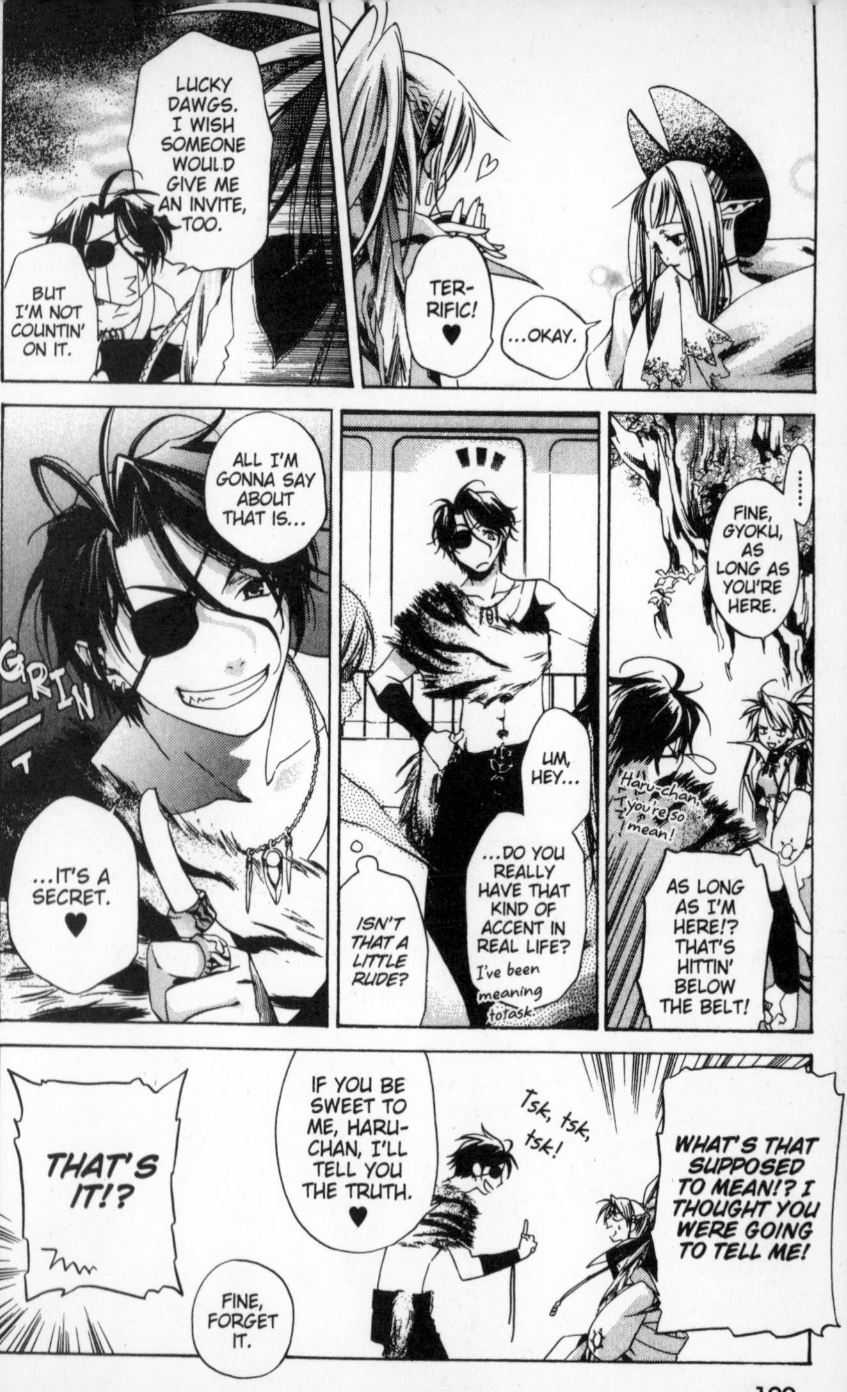
...OKAY.
TER-RIFIC! ♥
LUCKY DAWGS. I WISH SOMEONE WOULD GIVE ME AN INVITE, TOO.
BUT I'M NOT COUNTIN' ON IT.
......
FINE, GYOKU, AS LONG AS YOU'RE HERE.
Haru-chan, you're so mean!
AS LONG AS I'M HERE!? THAT'S HITTIN' BELOW THE BELT!
UM, HEY...
...DO YOU REALLY HAVE THAT KIND OF ACCENT IN REAL LIFE?
I've been meaning to ask.
ISN'T THAT A LITTLE RUDE?
ALL I'M GONNA SAY ABOUT THAT IS...
GRIN
...IT'S A SECRET. ♥
WHAT'S THAT SUPPOSED TO MEAN!? I THOUGHT YOU WERE GOING TO TELL ME!
Tsk, tsk, tsk!
IF YOU BE SWEET TO ME, HARU-CHAN, I'LL TELL YOU THE TRUTH. ♥
FINE, FORGET IT.
THAT'S IT!?

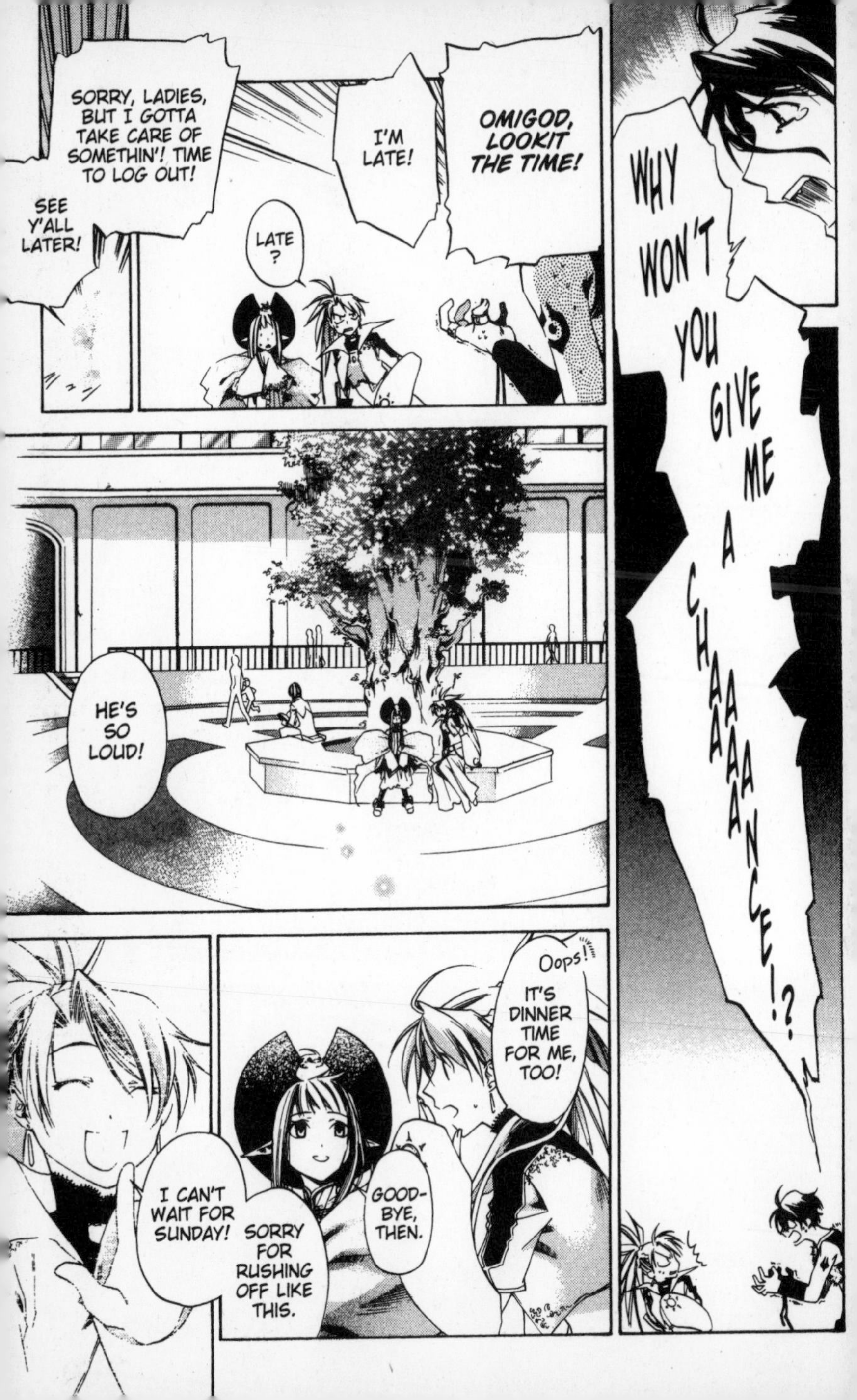
WHY WON'T YOU GIVE ME A CHAAAAAANCE!?
OMIGOD, LOOKIT THE TIME!
I'M LATE!
LATE?
SORRY, LADIES, BUT I GOTTA TAKE CARE OF SOMETHIN'! TIME TO LOG OUT!
SEE Y'ALL LATER!
HE'S SO LOUD!
Oops!
IT'S DINNER TIME FOR ME, TOO!
GOOD-BYE, THEN.
I CAN'T WAIT FOR SUNDAY!
SORRY FOR RUSHING OFF LIKE THIS.

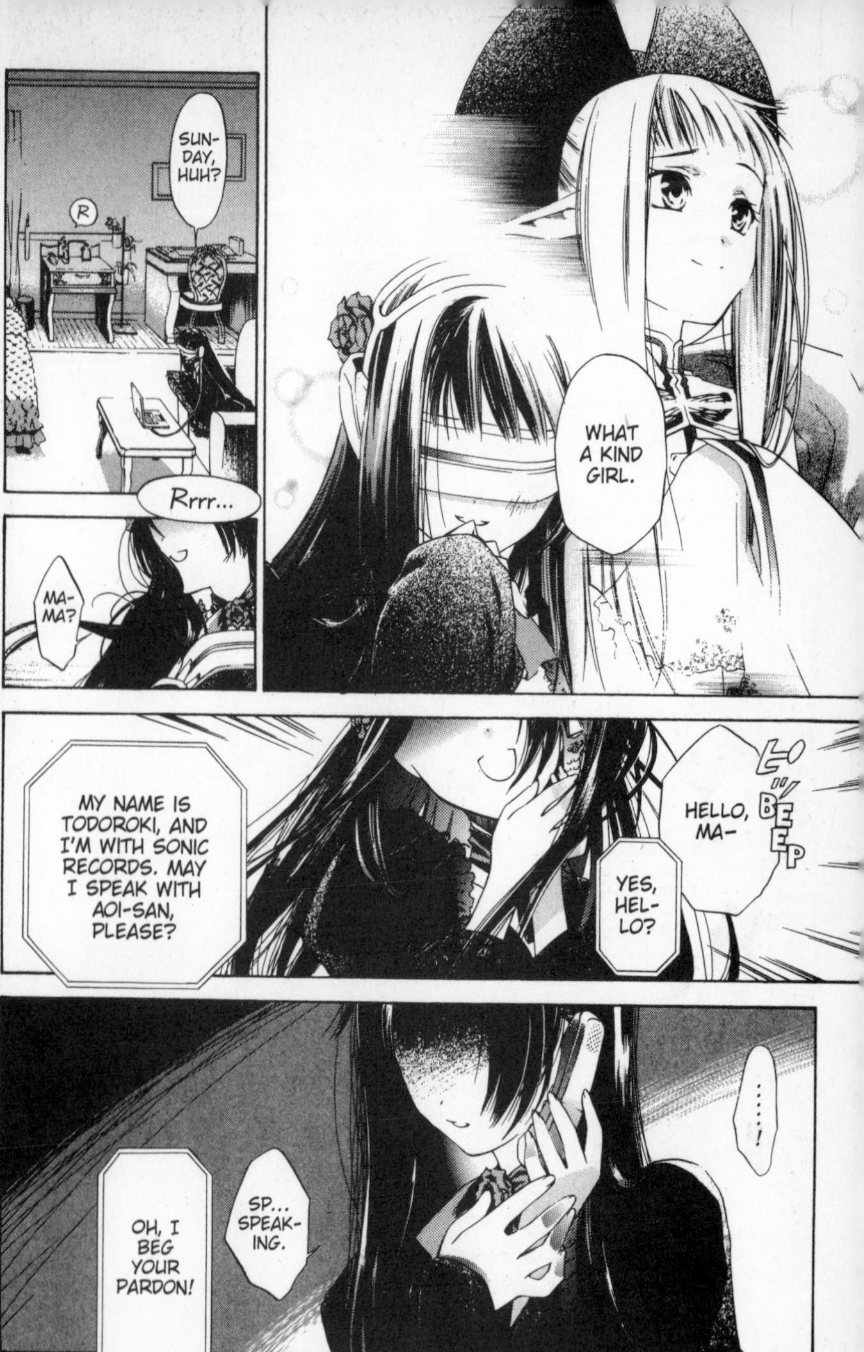
WHAT A KIND GIRL.
SUN-DAY, HUH?
R
Rrrr...
MA-MA?
BEEP
HELLO, MA-
YES, HEL-LO?
MY NAME IS TODOROKI, AND I'M WITH SONIC RECORDS. MAY I SPEAK WITH AOI-SAN, PLEASE?
......!
SP... SPEAK-ING.
OH, I BEG YOUR PARDON!

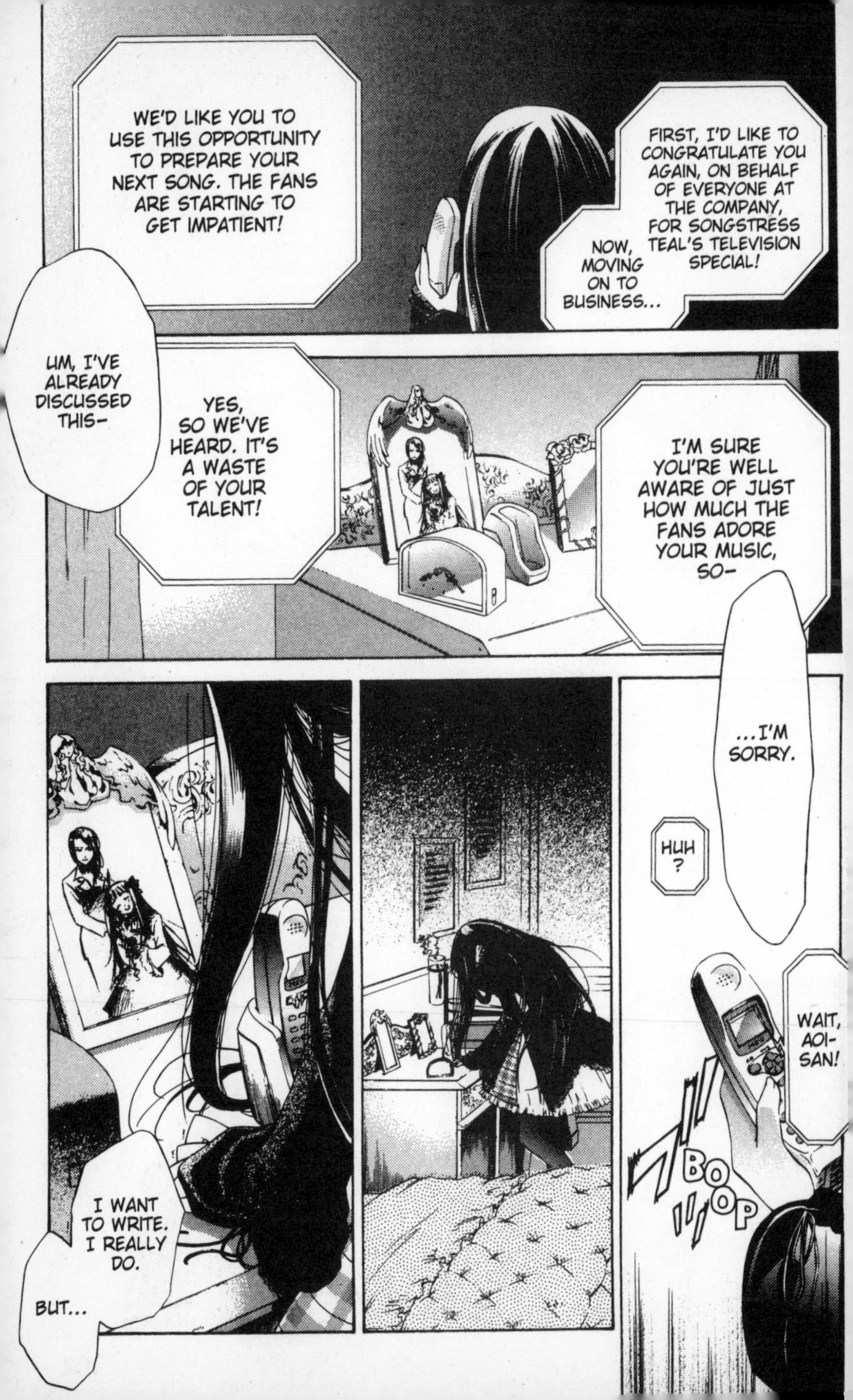

FIRST, I'D LIKE TO CONGRATULATE YOU AGAIN, ON BEHALF OF EVERYONE AT THE COMPANY, FOR SONGSTRESS TEAL'S TELEVISION SPECIAL!
NOW, MOVING ON TO BUSINESS...
WE'D LIKE YOU TO USE THIS OPPORTUNITY TO PREPARE YOUR NEXT SONG. THE FANS ARE STARTING TO GET IMPATIENT!
UM, I'VE ALREADY DISCUSSED THIS-
YES, SO WE'VE HEARD. IT'S A WASTE OF YOUR TALENT!
I'M SURE YOU'RE WELL AWARE OF JUST HOW MUCH THE FANS ADORE YOUR MUSIC, SO-
...I'M SORRY.
HUH?
WAIT, AOI-SAN!
BOOP
I WANT TO WRITE. I REALLY DO.
BUT...

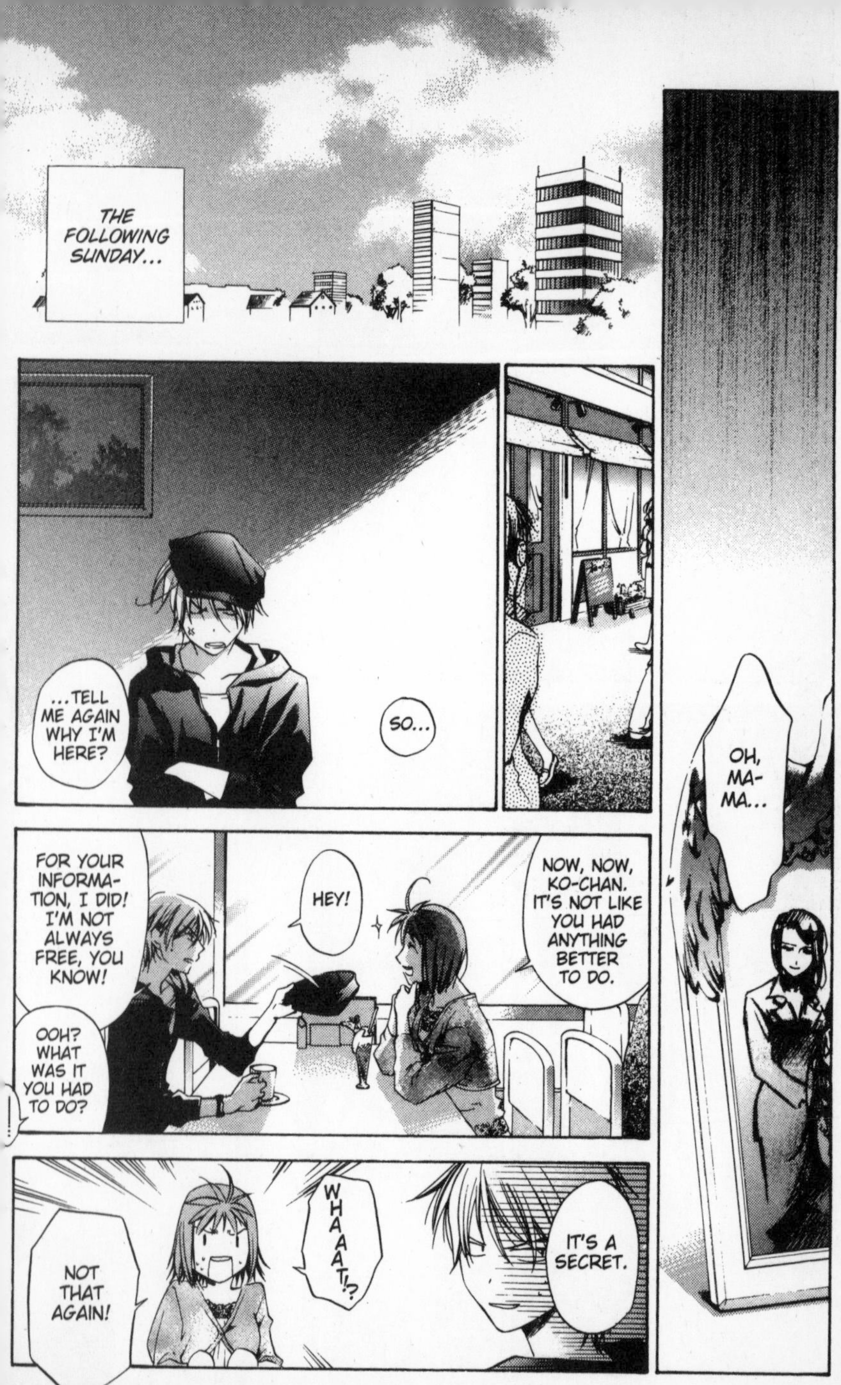
THE FOLLOWING SUNDAY...
OH, MAMA...
SO...
...TELL ME AGAIN WHY I'M HERE?
NOW, NOW, KO-CHAN. IT'S NOT LIKE YOU HAD ANYTHING BETTER TO DO.
HEY!
FOR YOUR INFORMATION, I DID! I'M NOT ALWAYS FREE, YOU KNOW!
OOH? WHAT WAS IT YOU HAD TO DO?
!
IT'S A SECRET.
WHAAAT!?
NOT THAT AGAIN!

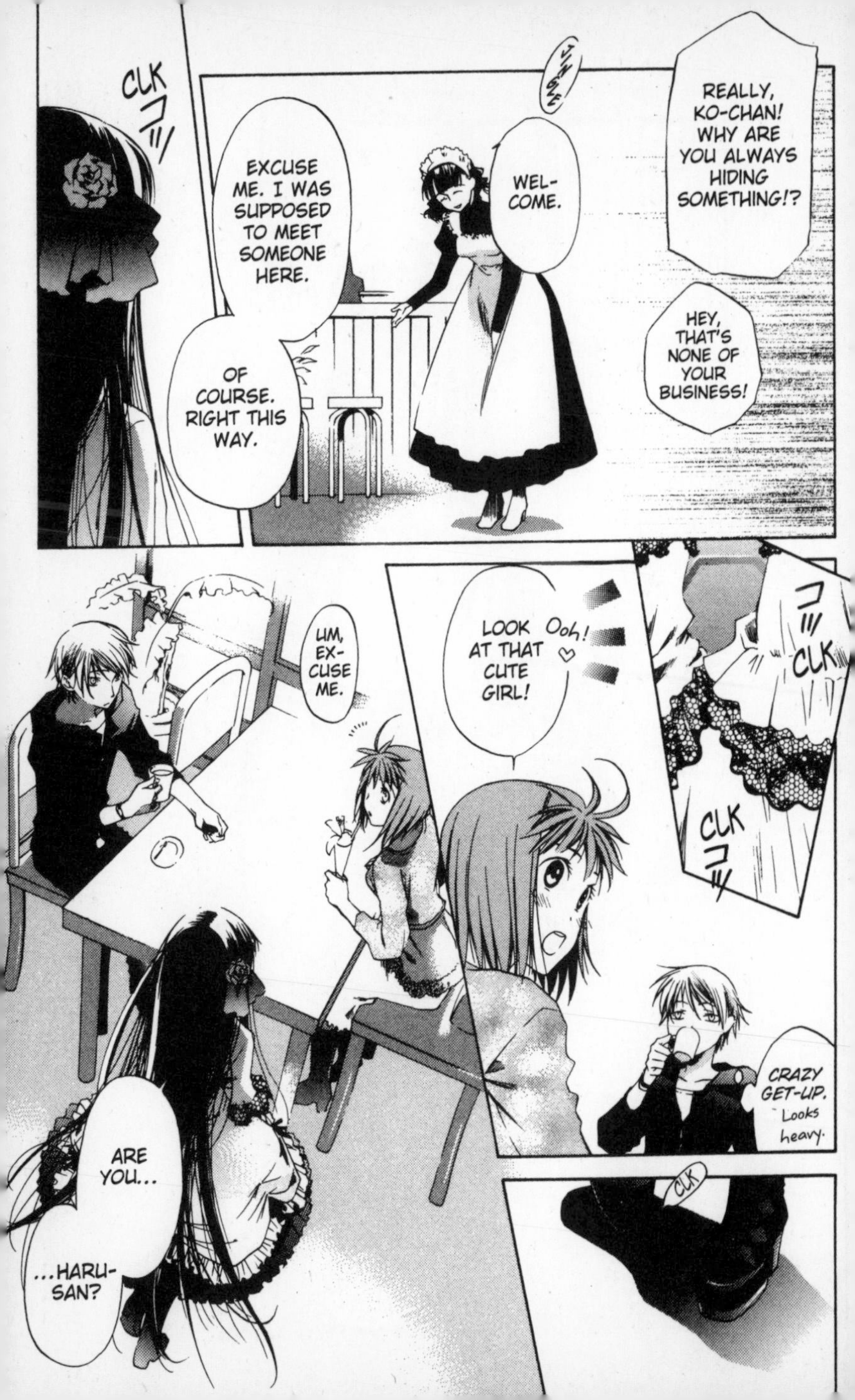
REALLY, KO-CHAN! WHY ARE YOU ALWAYS HIDING SOMETHING!?
HEY, THAT'S NONE OF YOUR BUSINESS!
JINGLE
WEL-COME.
CLK
EXCUSE ME. I WAS SUPPOSED TO MEET SOMEONE HERE.
OF COURSE. RIGHT THIS WAY.
CLK
CLK
LOOK AT THAT CUTE GIRL!
Ooh!
CRAZY GET-UP.
Looks heavy.
CLK
UM, EXCUSE ME.
ARE YOU...
...HARU-SAN?

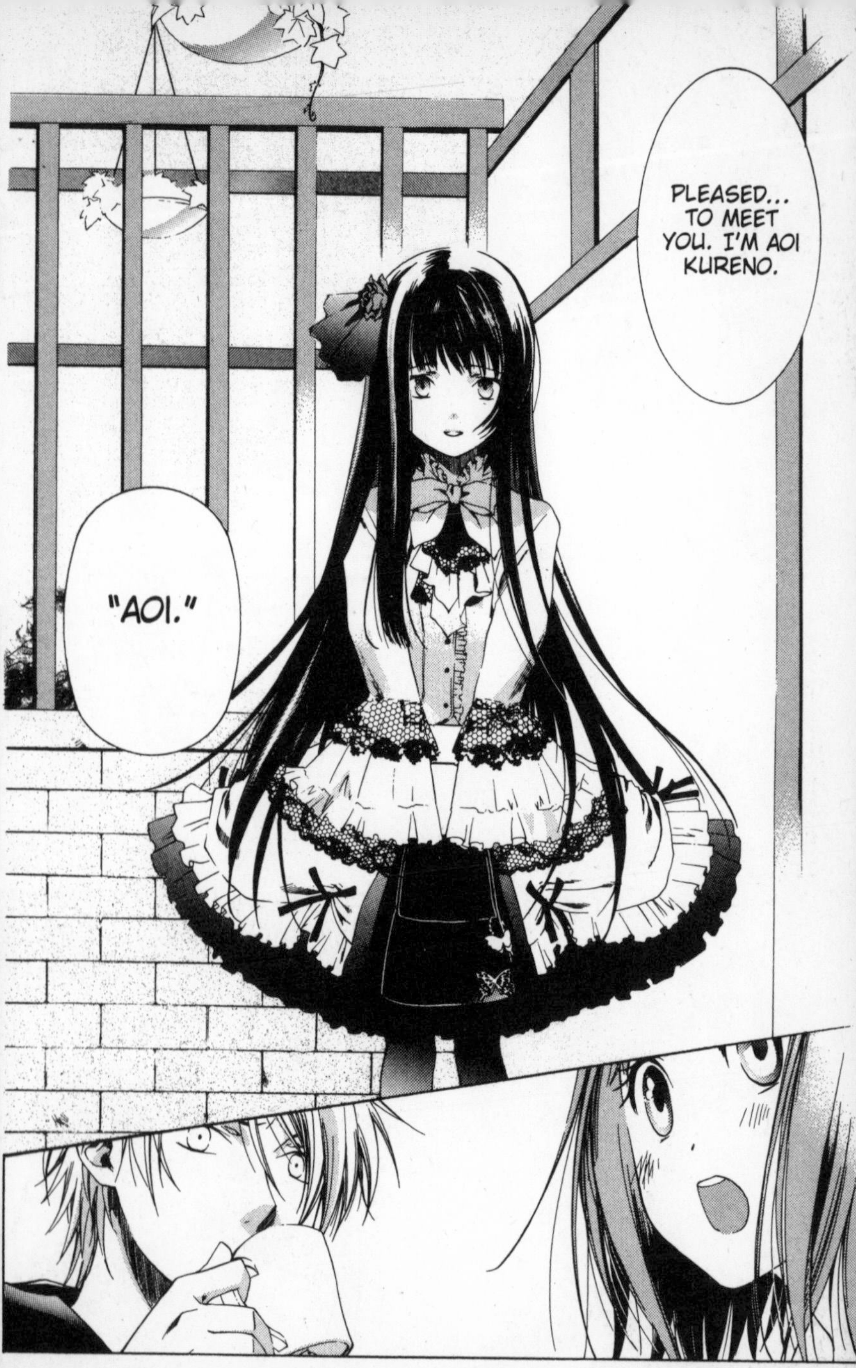
PLEASED... TO MEET YOU. I'M AOI KURENO.
"AOI."

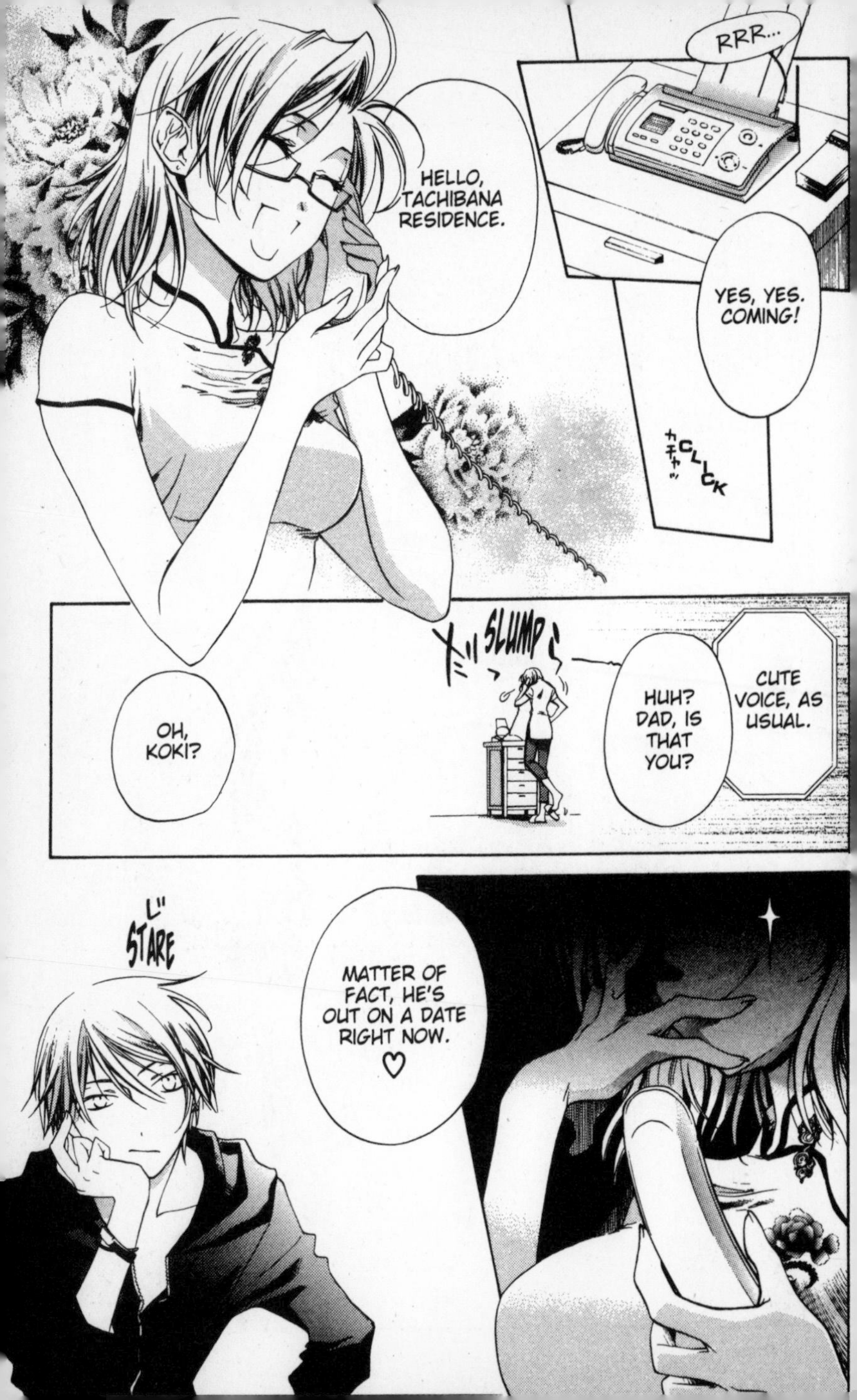
RRR...
YES, YES. COMING!
CLICK
HELLO, TACHIBANA RESIDENCE.
CUTE VOICE, AS USUAL.
HUH? DAD, IS THAT YOU?
SLUMP
OH, KOKI?
MATTER OF FACT, HE'S OUT ON A DATE RIGHT NOW. ♡
STARE

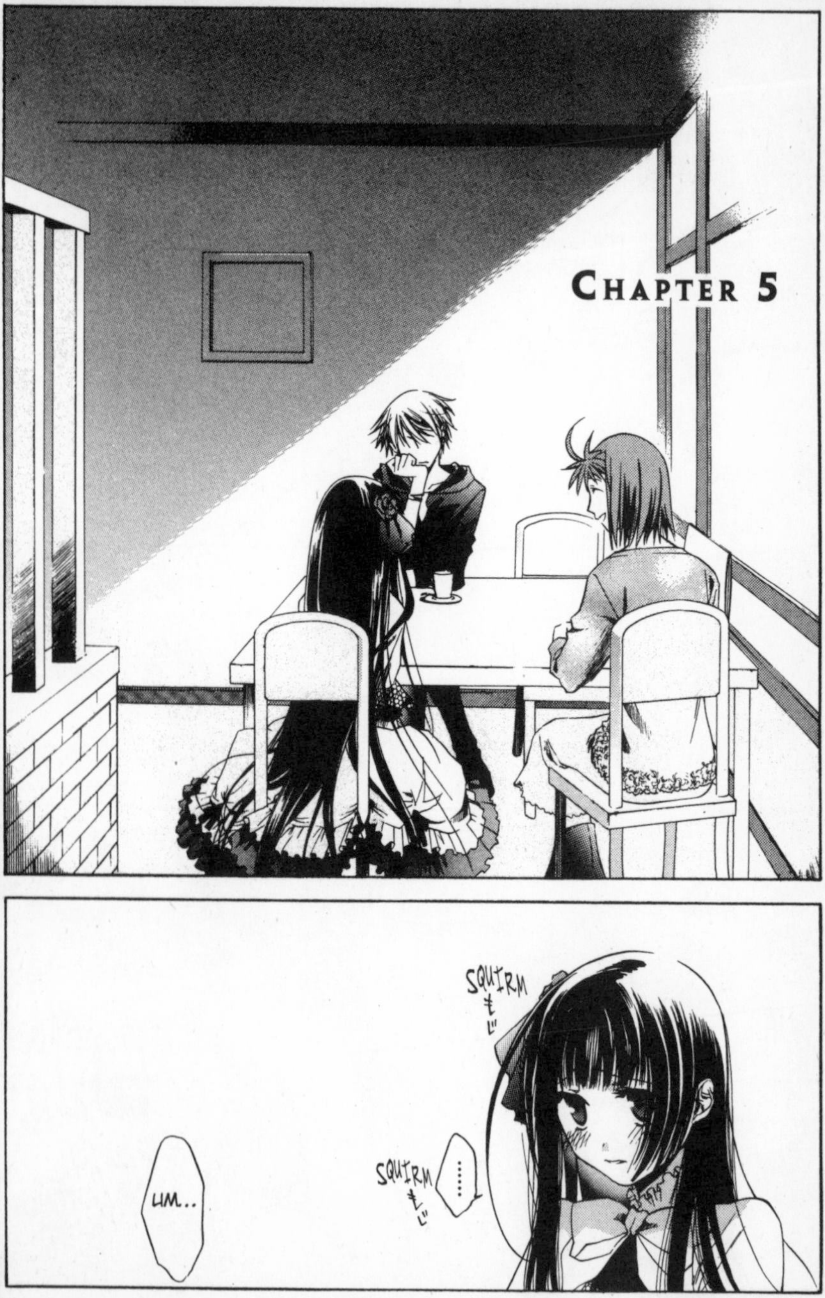
CHAPTER 5
SQUIRM もじ
......
SQUIRM もじ
UM..

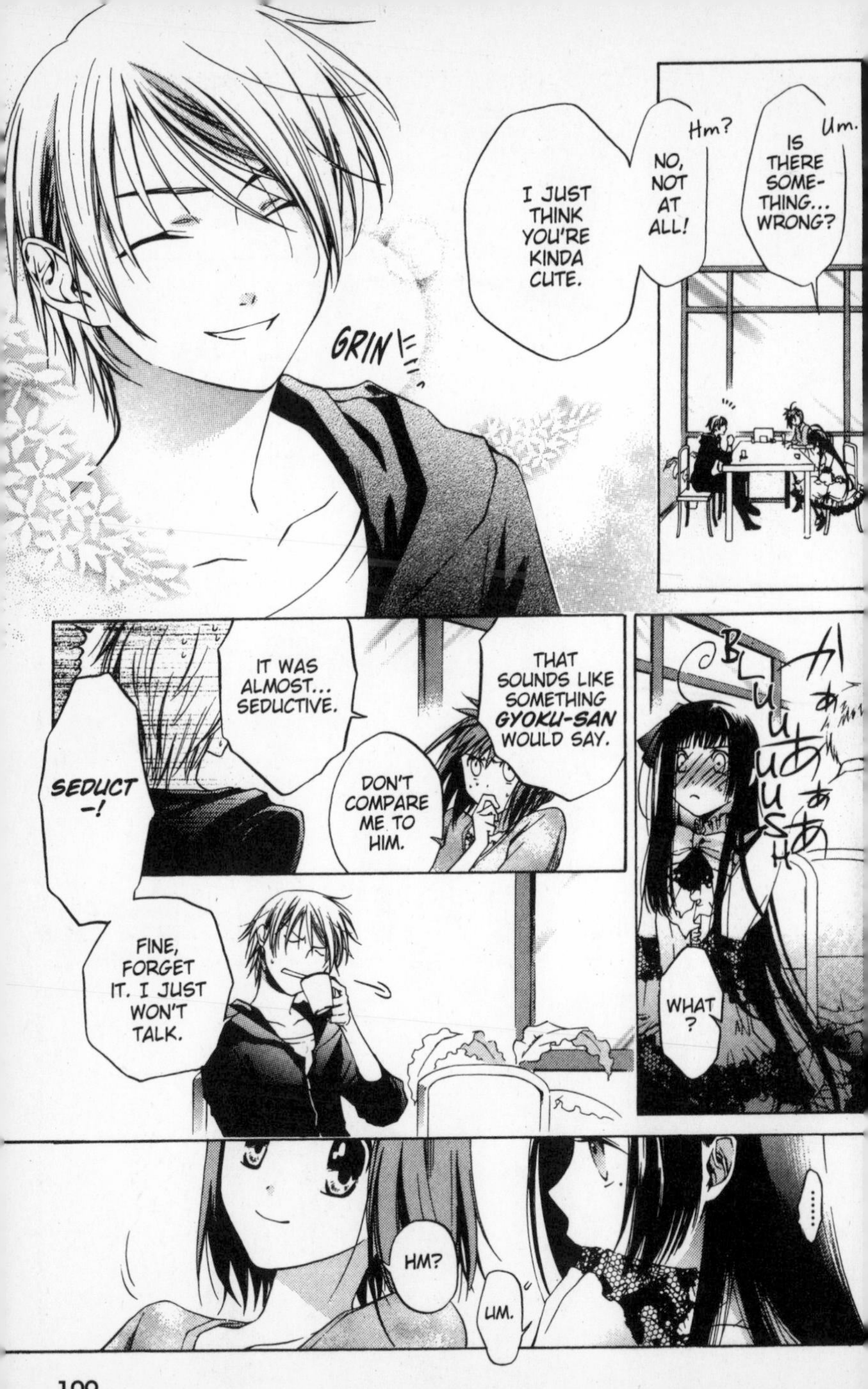
Um.
IS THERE SOME-THING... WRONG?
Hm?
NO, NOT AT ALL!
I JUST THINK YOU'RE KINDA CUTE.
GRIN
かあああ
BLUUUUUSH
WHAT?
THAT SOUNDS LIKE SOMETHING GYOKU-SAN WOULD SAY.
DON'T COMPARE ME TO HIM.
IT WAS ALMOST... SEDUCTIVE.
SEDUCT-!
FINE, FORGET IT. I JUST WON'T TALK.
......
HM?
UM.

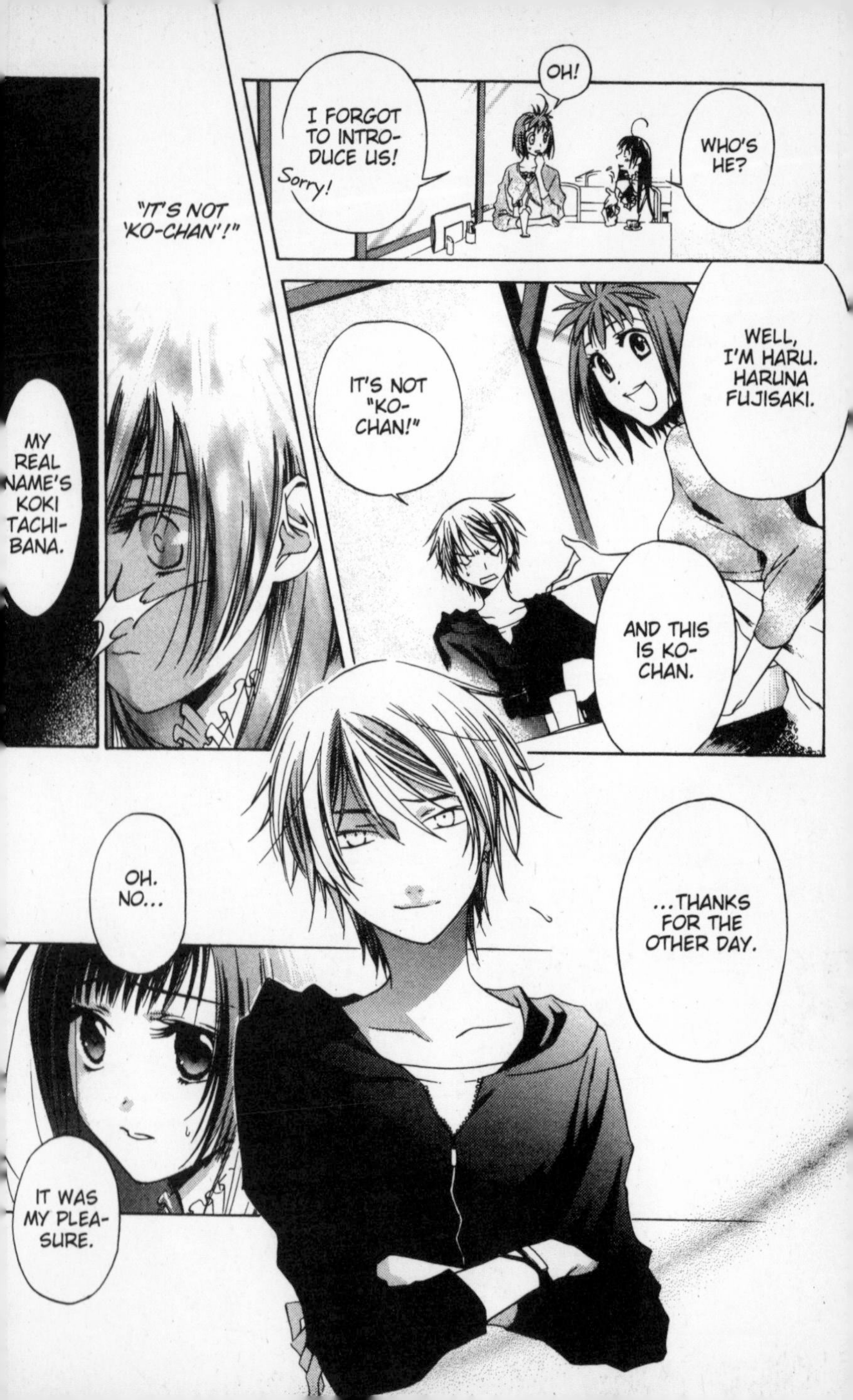
WHO'S HE?
OH!
I FORGOT TO INTRODUCE US!
Sorry!
WELL, I'M HARU. HARUNA FUJISAKI.
AND THIS IS KO-CHAN.
IT'S NOT "KO-CHAN!"
"IT'S NOT 'KO-CHAN'!"
MY REAL NAME'S KOKI TACHIBANA.
...THANKS FOR THE OTHER DAY.
OH. NO...
IT WAS MY PLEASURE.

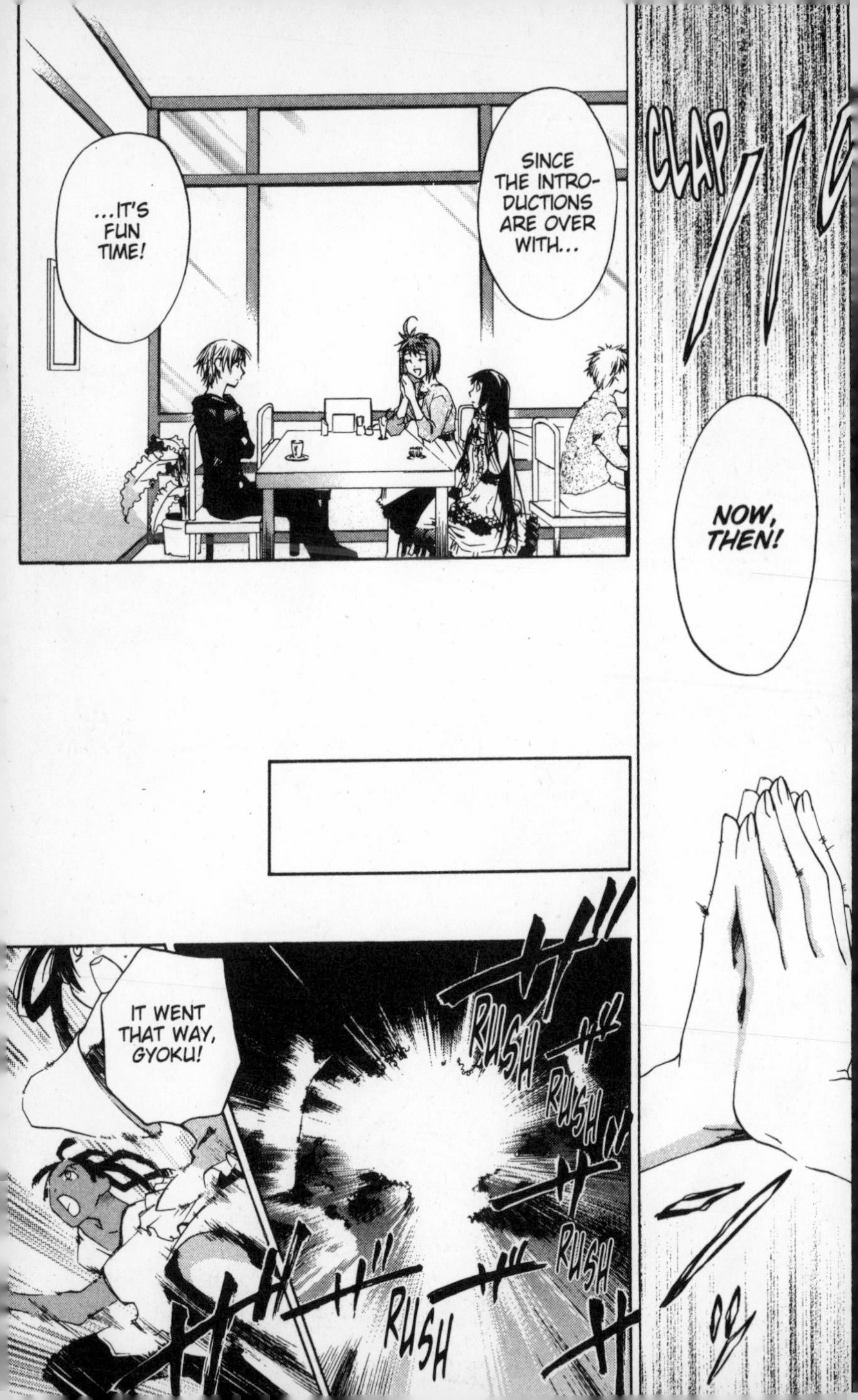
CLAP
NOW, THEN!
SINCE THE INTRO-DUCTIONS ARE OVER WITH...
...IT'S FUN TIME!
RUSH
RUSH
RUSH
IT WENT THAT WAY, GYOKU!
RUSH

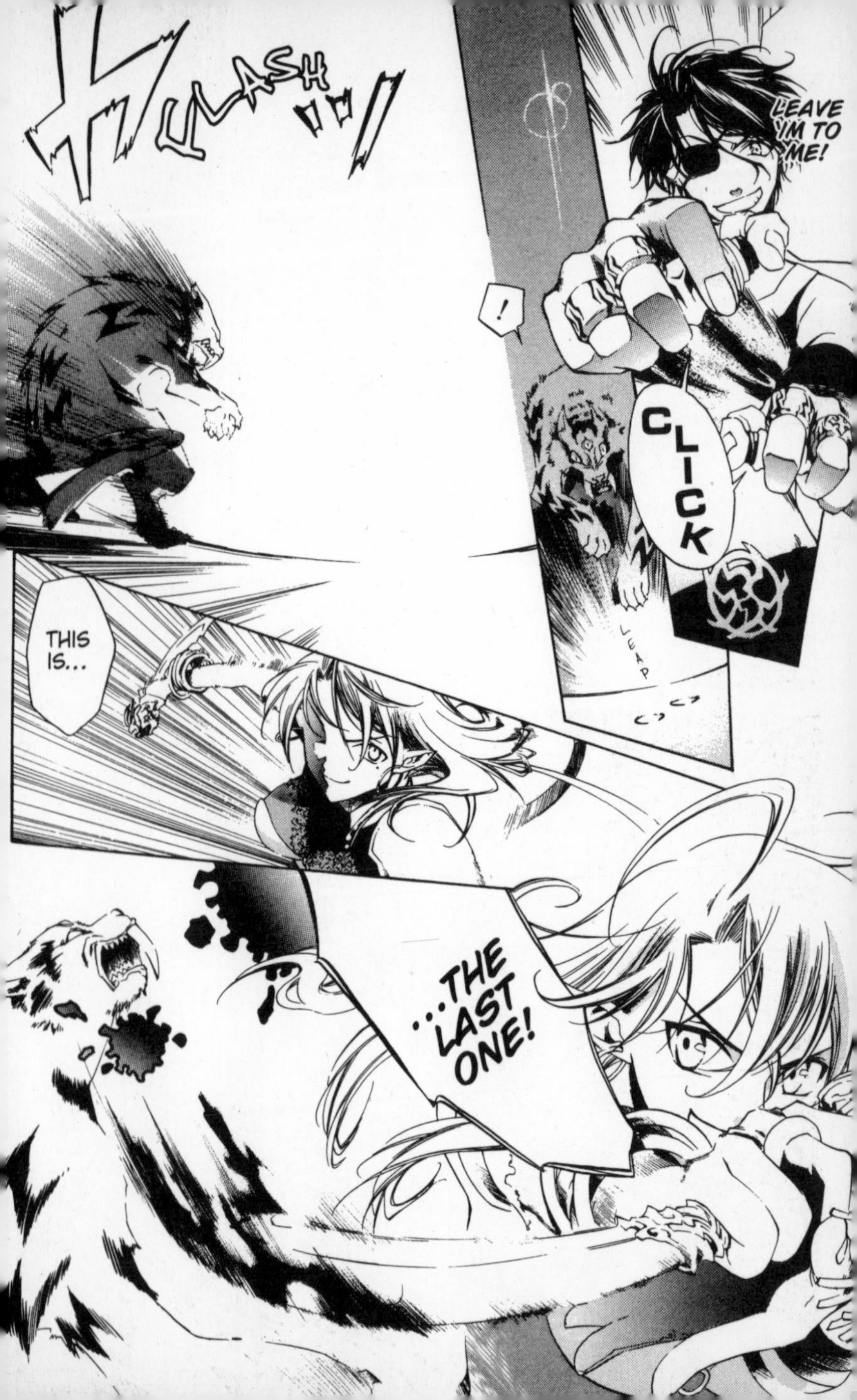
LEAVE 'IM TO ME!
!
CLICK
LEAP
THIS IS...
...THE LAST ONE!

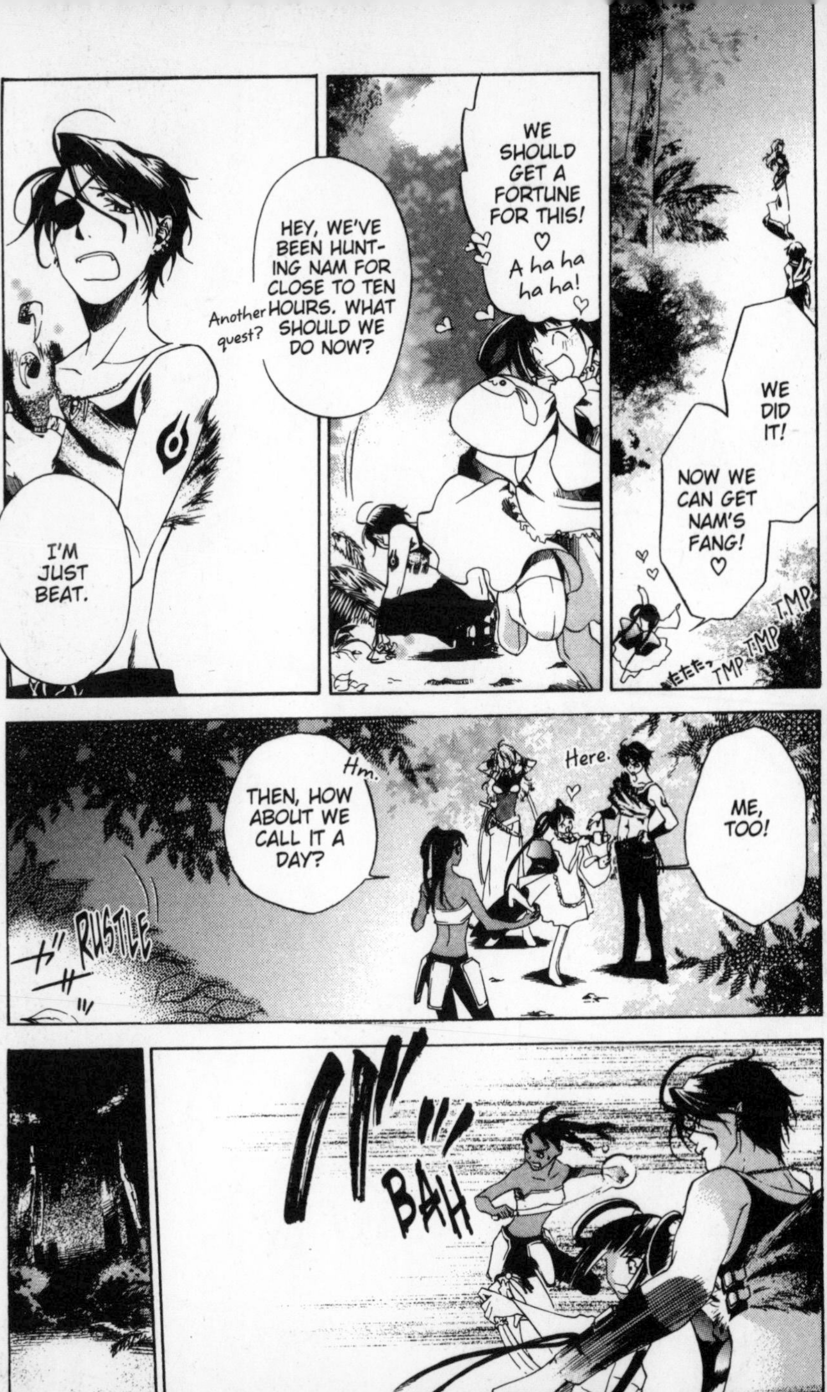
WE DID IT!
NOW WE CAN GET NAM'S FANG! ♡
TMP TMP TMP
WE SHOULD GET A FORTUNE FOR THIS! ♡
A ha ha ha ha!
HEY, WE'VE BEEN HUNTING NAM FOR CLOSE TO TEN HOURS. WHAT SHOULD WE DO NOW?
Another quest?
I'M JUST BEAT.
ME, TOO!
Here.
Hm.
THEN, HOW ABOUT WE CALL IT A DAY?
RUSTLE
BAH

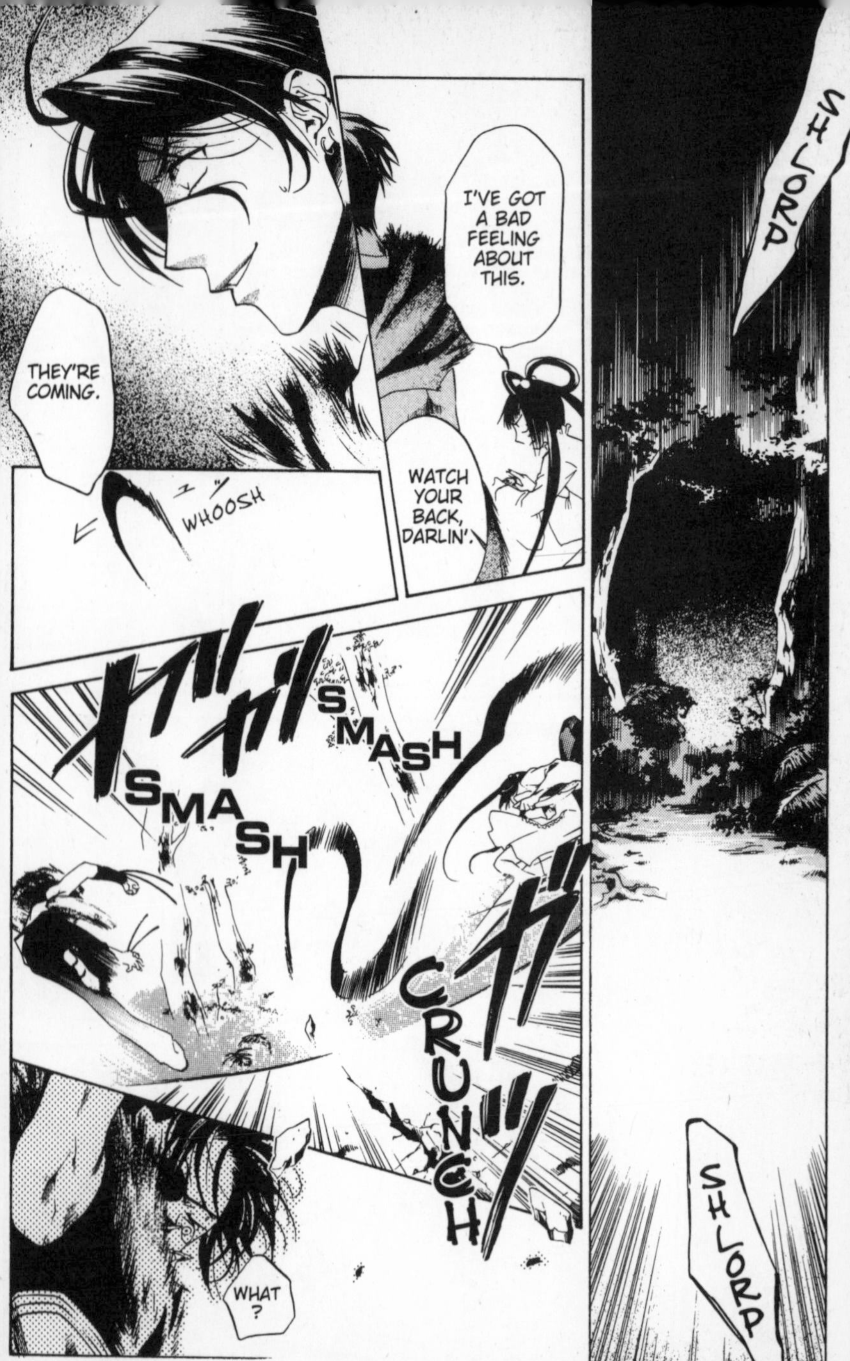
SHLORP
SHLORP
I'VE GOT A BAD FEELING ABOUT THIS.
THEY'RE COMING.
WATCH YOUR BACK, DARLIN'.
WHOOSH
SMASH
SMASH
CRUNCH
WHAT?

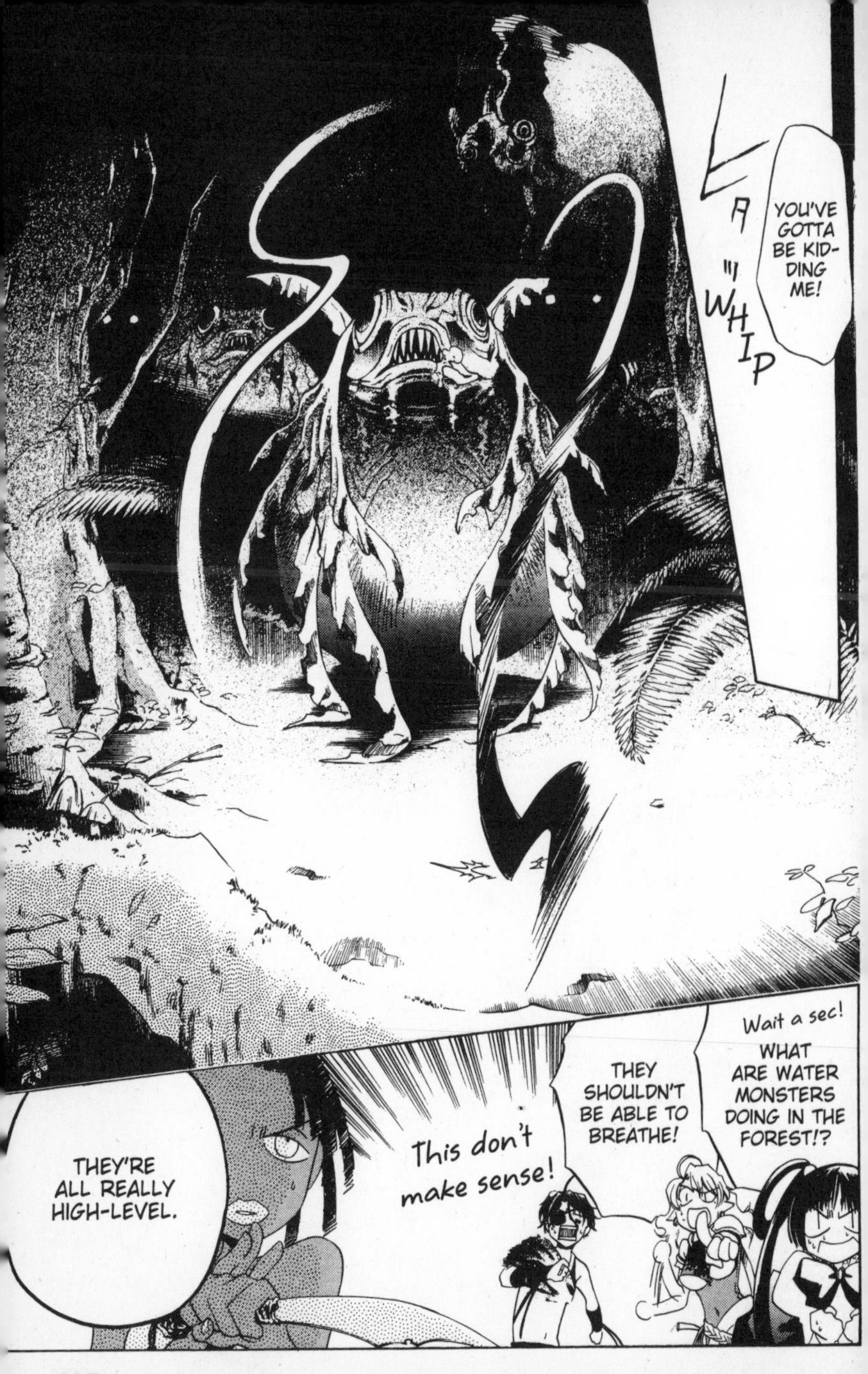
YOU'VE GOTTA BE KID-DING ME!
WHIP
Wait a sec! WHAT ARE WATER MONSTERS DOING IN THE FOREST!?
THEY SHOULDN'T BE ABLE TO BREATHE!
This don't make sense!
THEY'RE ALL REALLY HIGH-LEVEL.

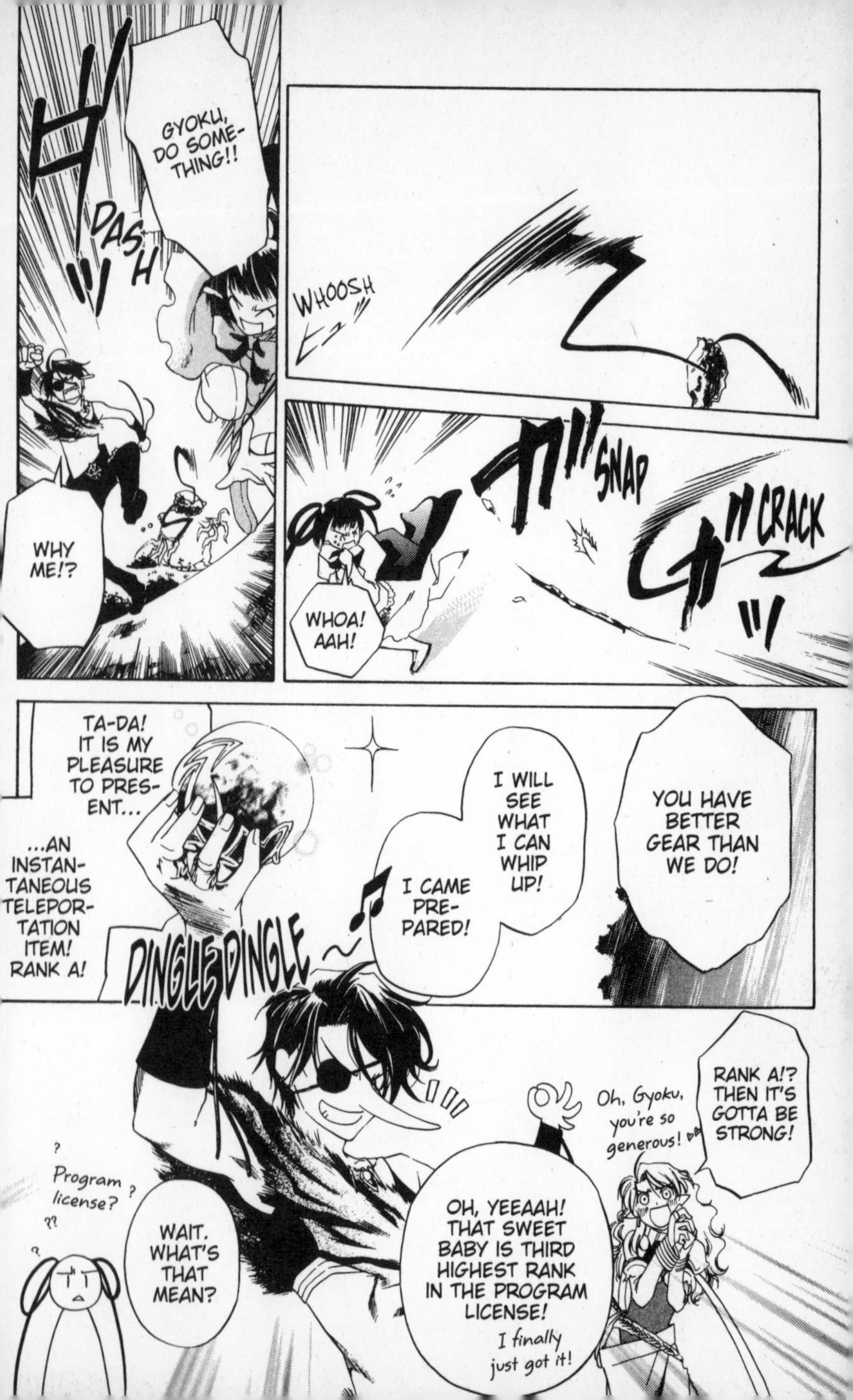
WHOOSH
SNAP
CRACK
WHOA! AAH!
GYOKU, DO SOME-THING!!
DASH
WHY ME!?
YOU HAVE BETTER GEAR THAN WE DO!
I WILL SEE WHAT I CAN WHIP UP!
I CAME PRE-PARED!
DINGLE DINGLE
TA-DA! IT IS MY PLEASURE TO PRES-ENT...
...AN INSTAN-TANEOUS TELEPOR-TATION ITEM! RANK A!
RANK A!? THEN IT'S GOTTA BE STRONG!
Oh, Gyoku, you're so generous!
OH, YEEAAH! THAT SWEET BABY IS THIRD HIGHEST RANK IN THE PROGRAM LICENSE!
I finally just got it!
WAIT. WHAT'S THAT MEAN?
Program license?

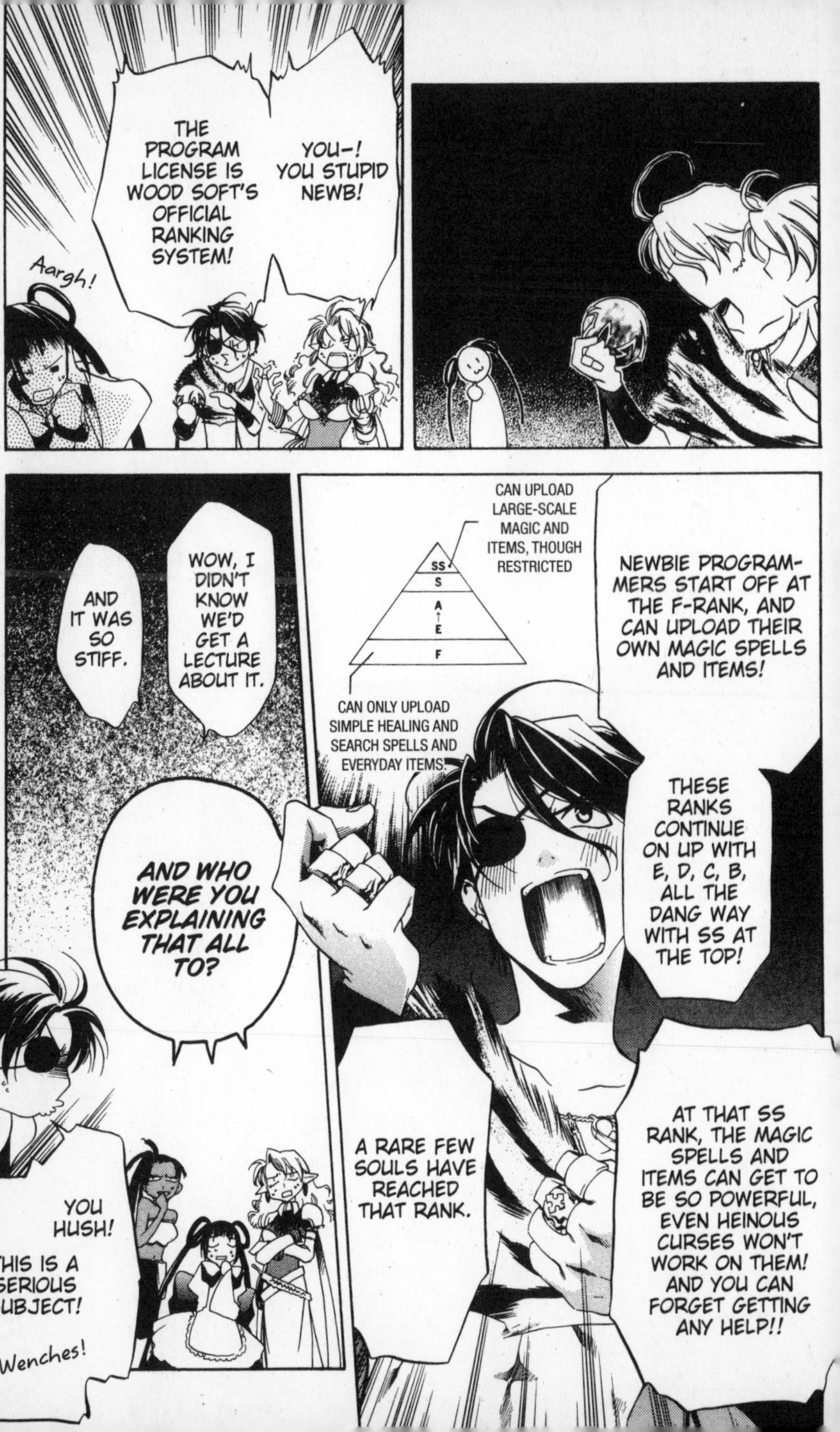
YOU-! YOU STUPID NEWB!
THE PROGRAM LICENSE IS WOOD SOFT'S OFFICIAL RANKING SYSTEM!
Aargh!
NEWBIE PROGRAM-MERS START OFF AT THE F-RANK, AND CAN UPLOAD THEIR OWN MAGIC SPELLS AND ITEMS!
CAN UPLOAD LARGE-SCALE MAGIC AND ITEMS, THOUGH RESTRICTED
SS
S
A
E
F
CAN ONLY UPLOAD SIMPLE HEALING AND SEARCH SPELLS AND EVERYDAY ITEMS.
THESE RANKS CONTINUE ON UP WITH E, D, C, B, ALL THE DANG WAY WITH SS AT THE TOP!
AT THAT SS RANK, THE MAGIC SPELLS AND ITEMS CAN GET TO BE SO POWERFUL, EVEN HEINOUS CURSES WON'T WORK ON THEM! AND YOU CAN FORGET GETTING ANY HELP!!
A RARE FEW SOULS HAVE REACHED THAT RANK.
WOW, I DIDN'T KNOW WE'D GET A LECTURE ABOUT IT.
AND IT WAS SO STIFF.
AND WHO WERE YOU EXPLAINING THAT ALL TO?
YOU HUSH! THIS IS A SERIOUS SUBJECT!
Wenches!

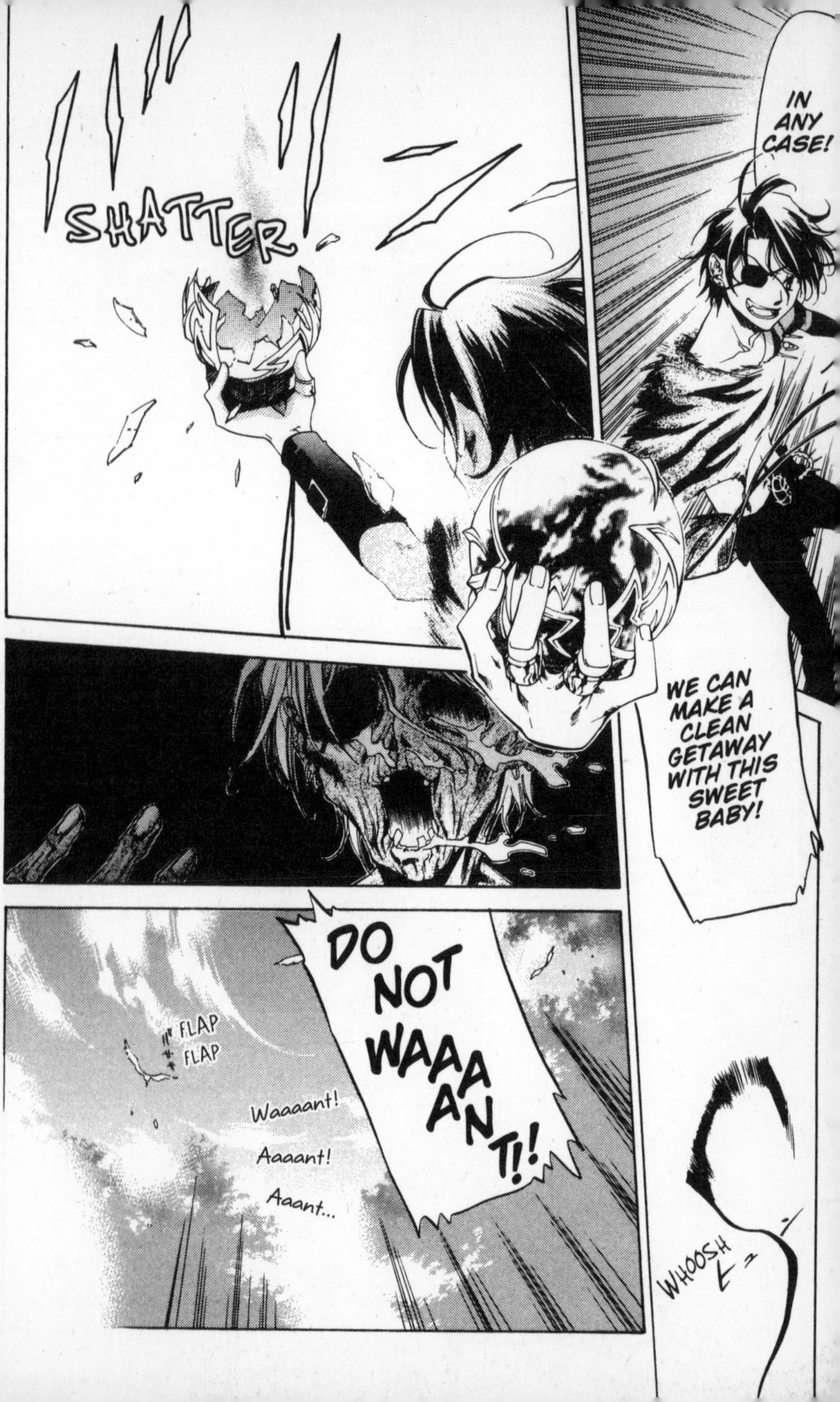
IN ANY CASE!
WE CAN MAKE A CLEAN GETAWAY WITH THIS SWEET BABY!
SHATTER
WHOOSH
DO NOT WAAAANT!!
FLAP FLAP
Waaaant!
Aaaant!
Aaant...

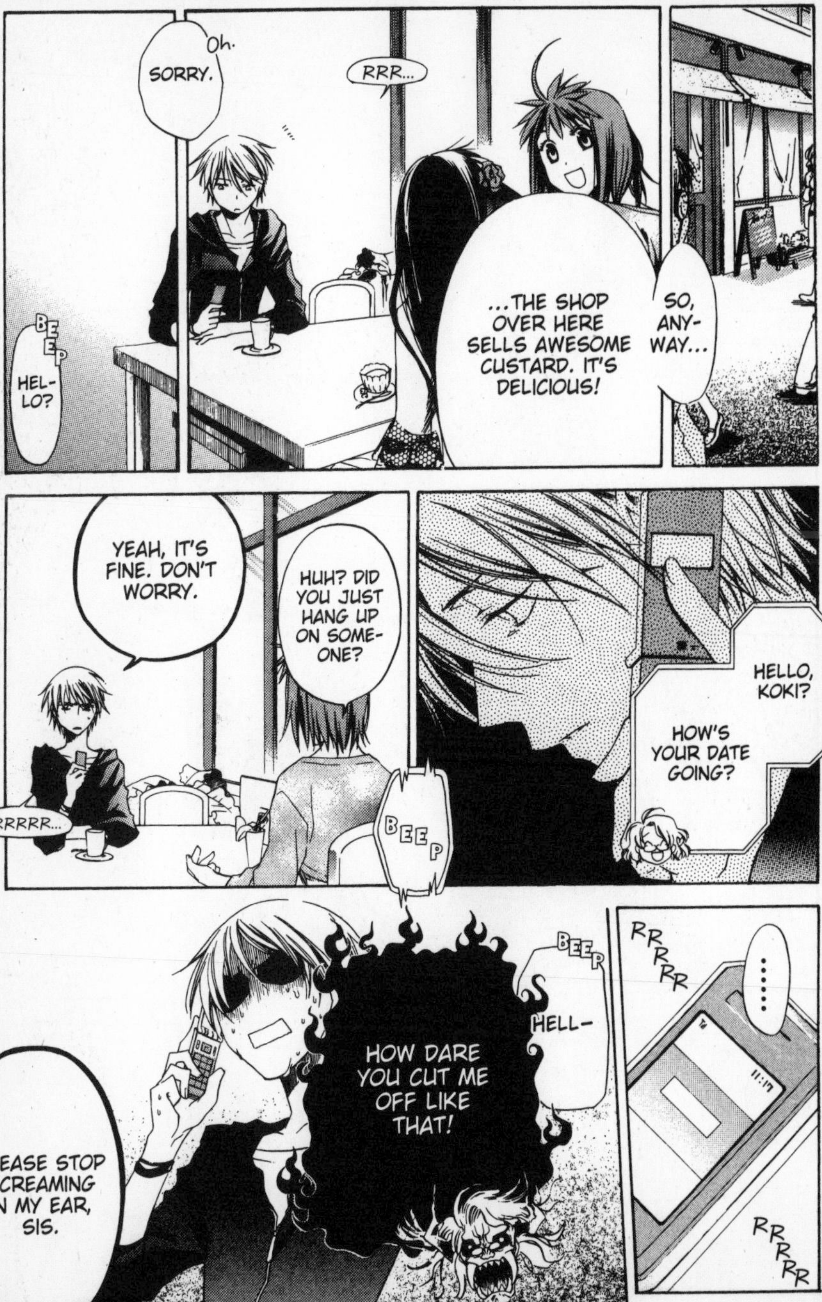

SO, ANYWAY...
...THE SHOP OVER HERE SELLS AWESOME CUSTARD. IT'S DELICIOUS!
RRR...
Oh. SORRY.
BEEP
HEL-LO?
HELLO, KOKI?
HOW'S YOUR DATE GOING?
BEEP
HUH? DID YOU JUST HANG UP ON SOME-ONE?
YEAH, IT'S FINE. DON'T WORRY.
RRRRR...
RRRRR
......
RRRRR
BEEP
HELL-
HOW DARE YOU CUT ME OFF LIKE THAT!
PLEASE STOP SCREAMING IN MY EAR, SIS.

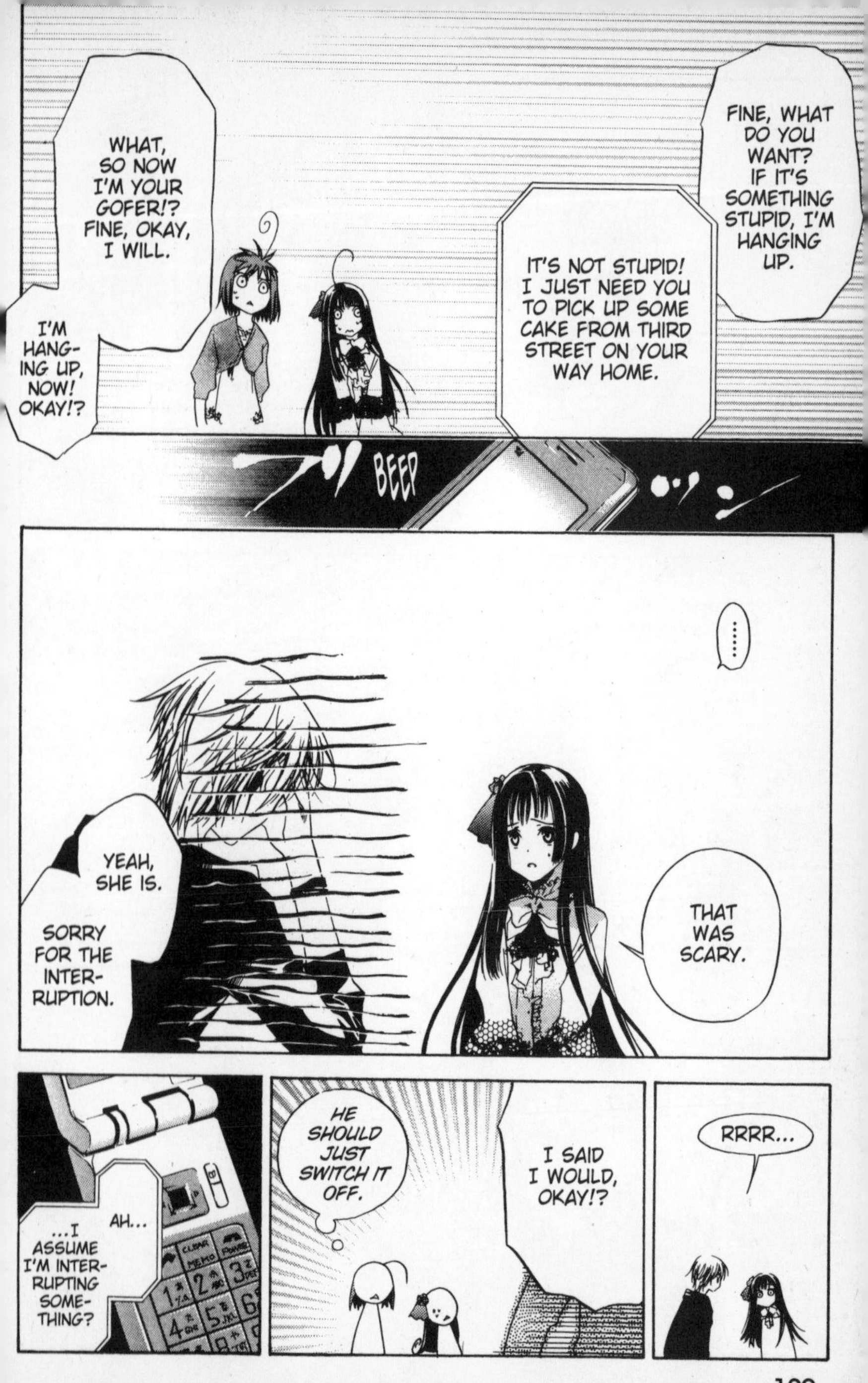
FINE, WHAT DO YOU WANT? IF IT'S SOMETHING STUPID, I'M HANGING UP.
IT'S NOT STUPID! I JUST NEED YOU TO PICK UP SOME CAKE FROM THIRD STREET ON YOUR WAY HOME.
WHAT, SO NOW I'M YOUR GOFER!? FINE, OKAY, I WILL.
I'M HANG-ING UP, NOW! OKAY!?
BEEP
......
THAT WAS SCARY.
YEAH, SHE IS.
SORRY FOR THE INTER-RUPTION.
RRRR...
I SAID I WOULD, OKAY!?
HE SHOULD JUST SWITCH IT OFF.
AH...
...I ASSUME I'M INTER-RUPTING SOME-THING?

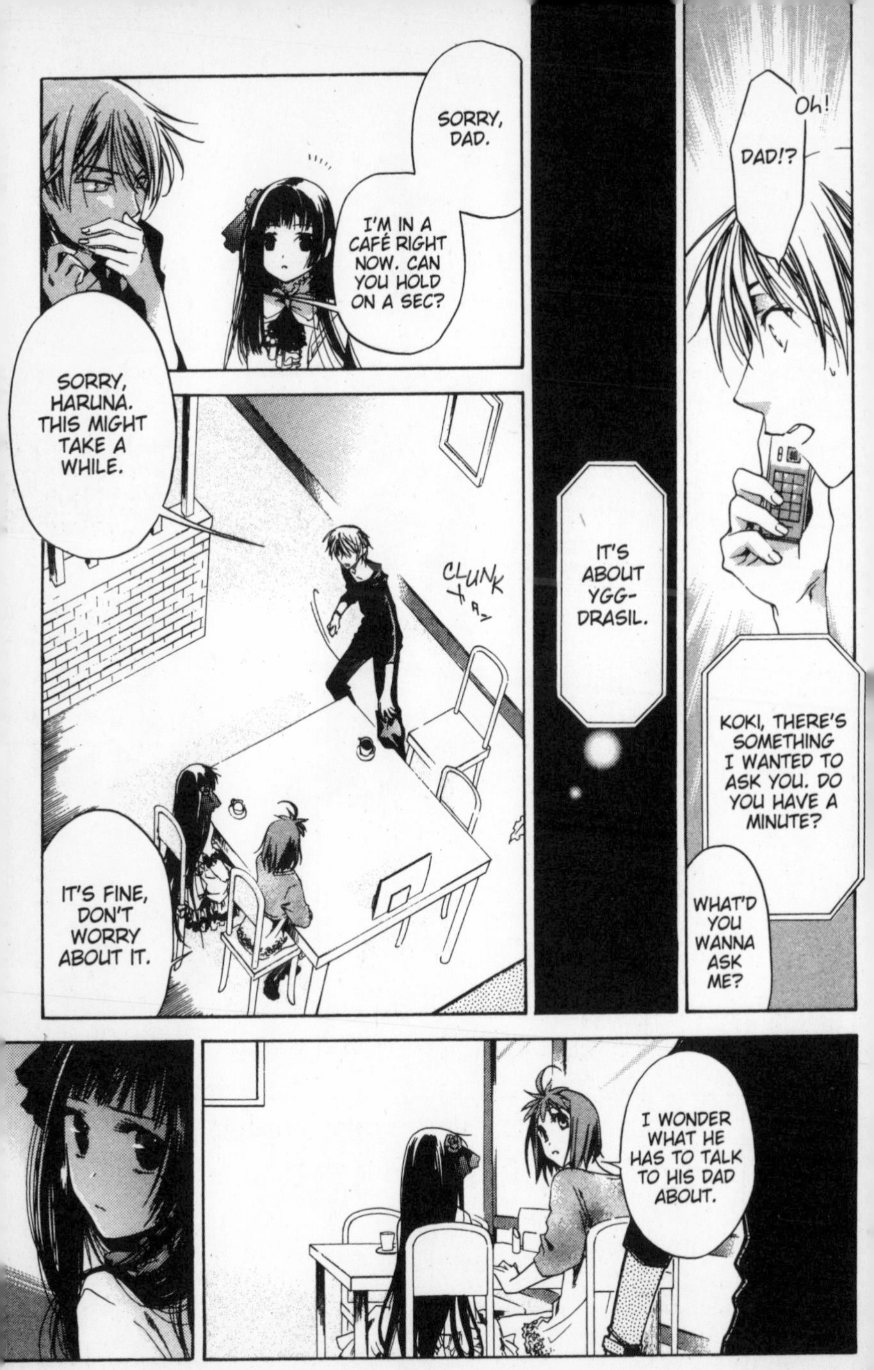

Oh! DAD!?
KOKI, THERE'S SOMETHING I WANTED TO ASK YOU. DO YOU HAVE A MINUTE?
WHAT'D YOU WANNA ASK ME?
IT'S ABOUT YGG-DRASIL.
SORRY, DAD.
I'M IN A CAFÉ RIGHT NOW. CAN YOU HOLD ON A SEC?
SORRY, HARUNA. THIS MIGHT TAKE A WHILE.
CLUNK
IT'S FINE, DON'T WORRY ABOUT IT.
I WONDER WHAT HE HAS TO TALK TO HIS DAD ABOUT.

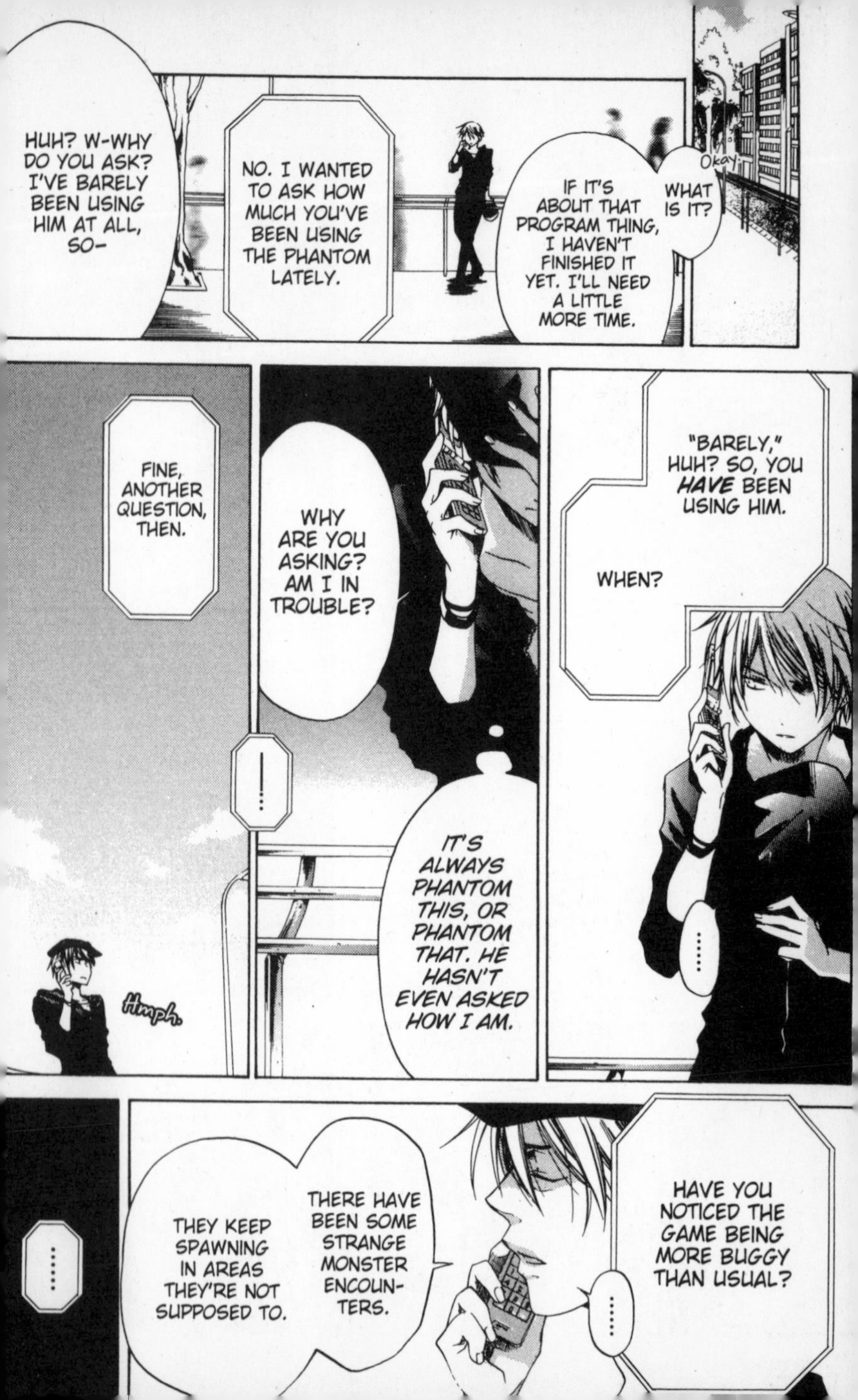
Okay.
WHAT IS IT?
IF IT'S ABOUT THAT PROGRAM THING, I HAVEN'T FINISHED IT YET. I'LL NEED A LITTLE MORE TIME.
NO. I WANTED TO ASK HOW MUCH YOU'VE BEEN USING THE PHANTOM LATELY.
HUH? W-WHY DO YOU ASK? I'VE BARELY BEEN USING HIM AT ALL, SO-
"BARELY," HUH? SO, YOU *HAVE* BEEN USING HIM.
WHEN?
......
WHY ARE YOU ASKING? AM I IN TROUBLE?
IT'S ALWAYS PHANTOM THIS, OR PHANTOM THAT. HE HASN'T EVEN ASKED HOW I AM.
FINE, ANOTHER QUESTION, THEN.
!...
Hmph.
HAVE YOU NOTICED THE GAME BEING MORE BUGGY THAN USUAL?
......
THERE HAVE BEEN SOME STRANGE MONSTER ENCOUN-TERS.
THEY KEEP SPAWNING IN AREAS THEY'RE NOT SUPPOSED TO.
......

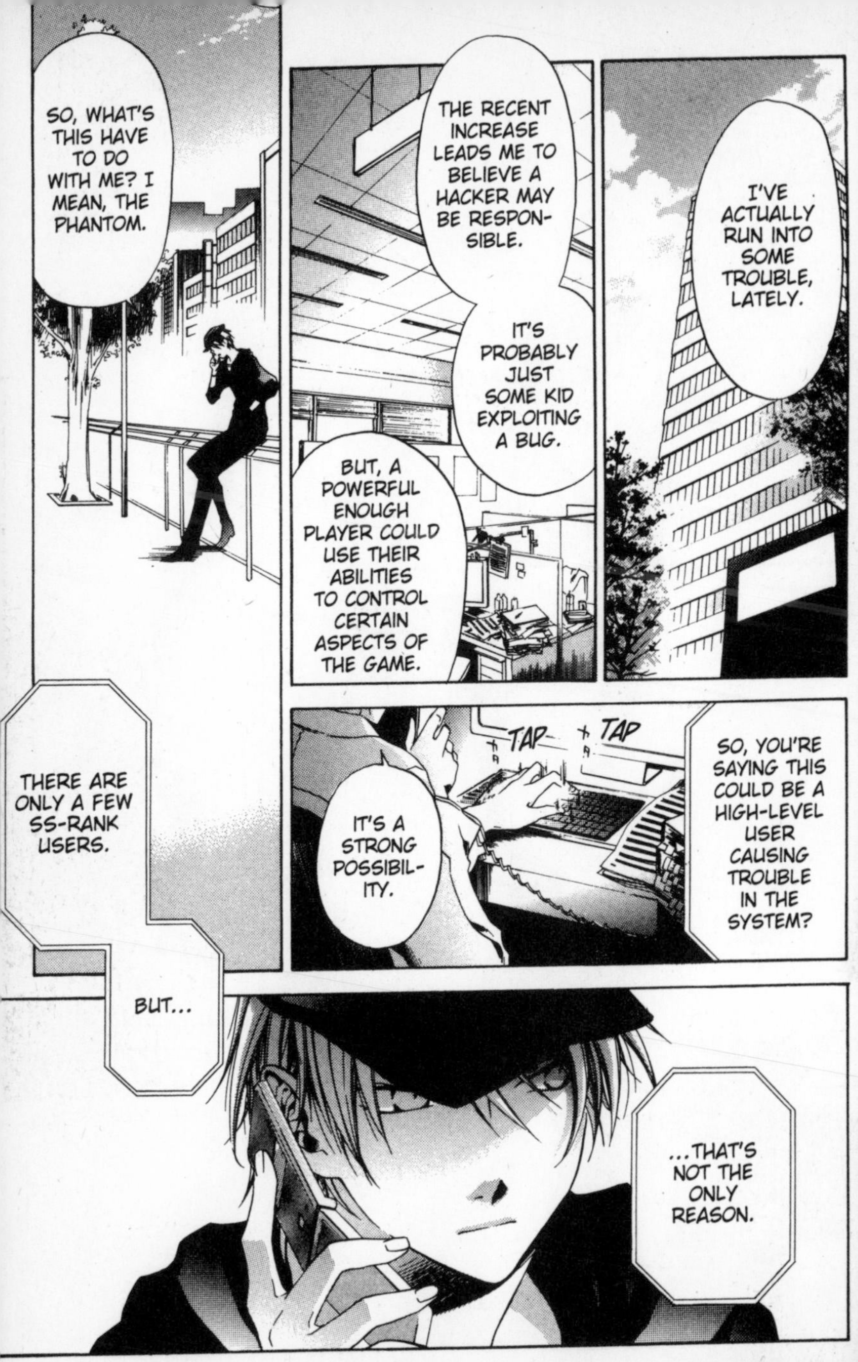
I'VE ACTUALLY RUN INTO SOME TROUBLE, LATELY.
THE RECENT INCREASE LEADS ME TO BELIEVE A HACKER MAY BE RESPON-SIBLE.
IT'S PROBABLY JUST SOME KID EXPLOITING A BUG.
BUT, A POWERFUL ENOUGH PLAYER COULD USE THEIR ABILITIES TO CONTROL CERTAIN ASPECTS OF THE GAME.
SO, YOU'RE SAYING THIS COULD BE A HIGH-LEVEL USER CAUSING TROUBLE IN THE SYSTEM?
TAP TAP
IT'S A STRONG POSSIBIL-ITY.
SO, WHAT'S THIS HAVE TO DO WITH ME? I MEAN, THE PHANTOM.
THERE ARE ONLY A FEW SS-RANK USERS.
BUT...
...THAT'S NOT THE ONLY REASON.

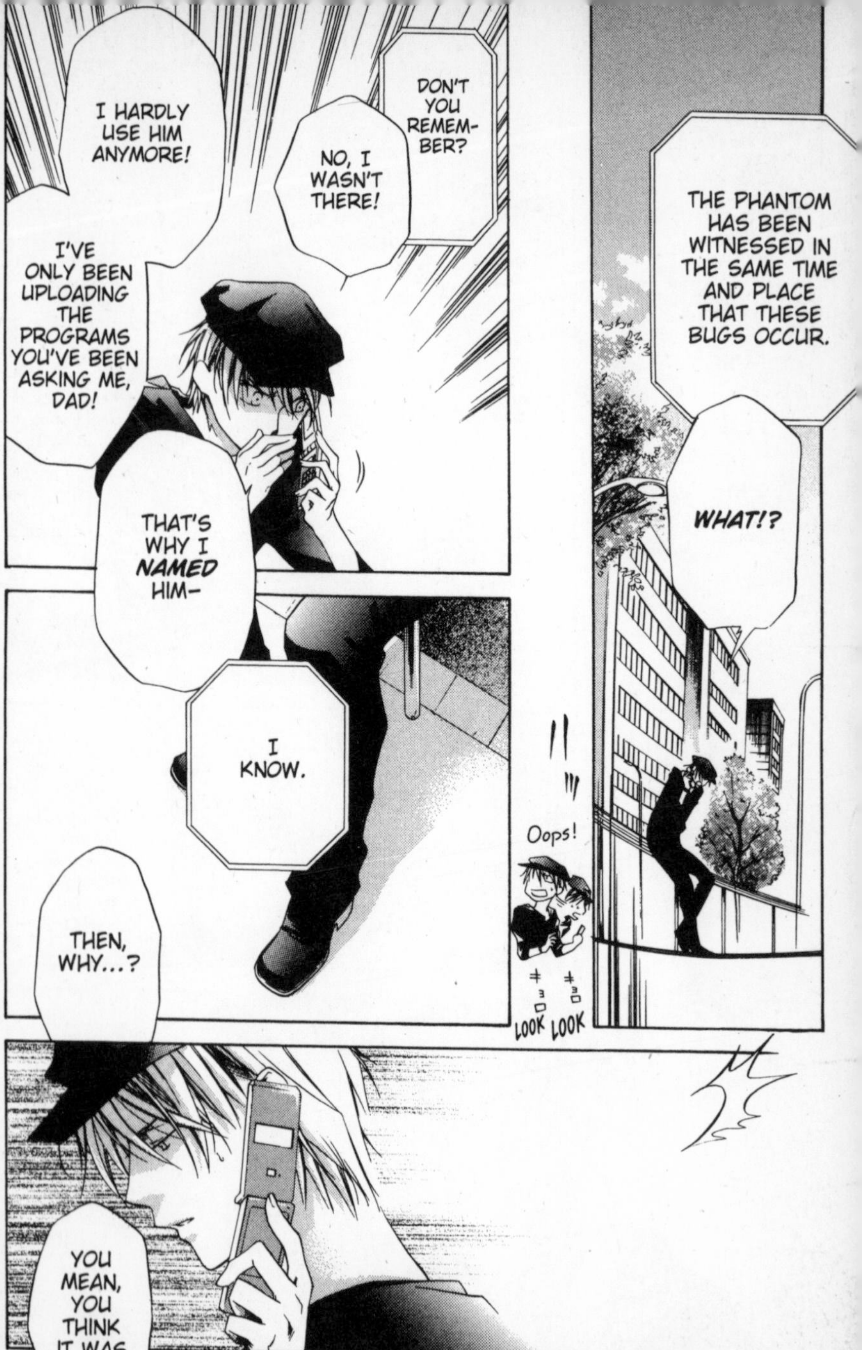
THE PHANTOM HAS BEEN WITNESSED IN THE SAME TIME AND PLACE THAT THESE BUGS OCCUR.
WHAT!?
Oops!
LOOK LOOK
DON'T YOU REMEMBER?
NO, I WASN'T THERE!
I HARDLY USE HIM ANYMORE!
I'VE ONLY BEEN UPLOADING THE PROGRAMS YOU'VE BEEN ASKING ME, DAD!
THAT'S WHY I NAMED HIM-
I KNOW.
THEN, WHY...?
YOU MEAN, YOU THINK IT WAS ME?

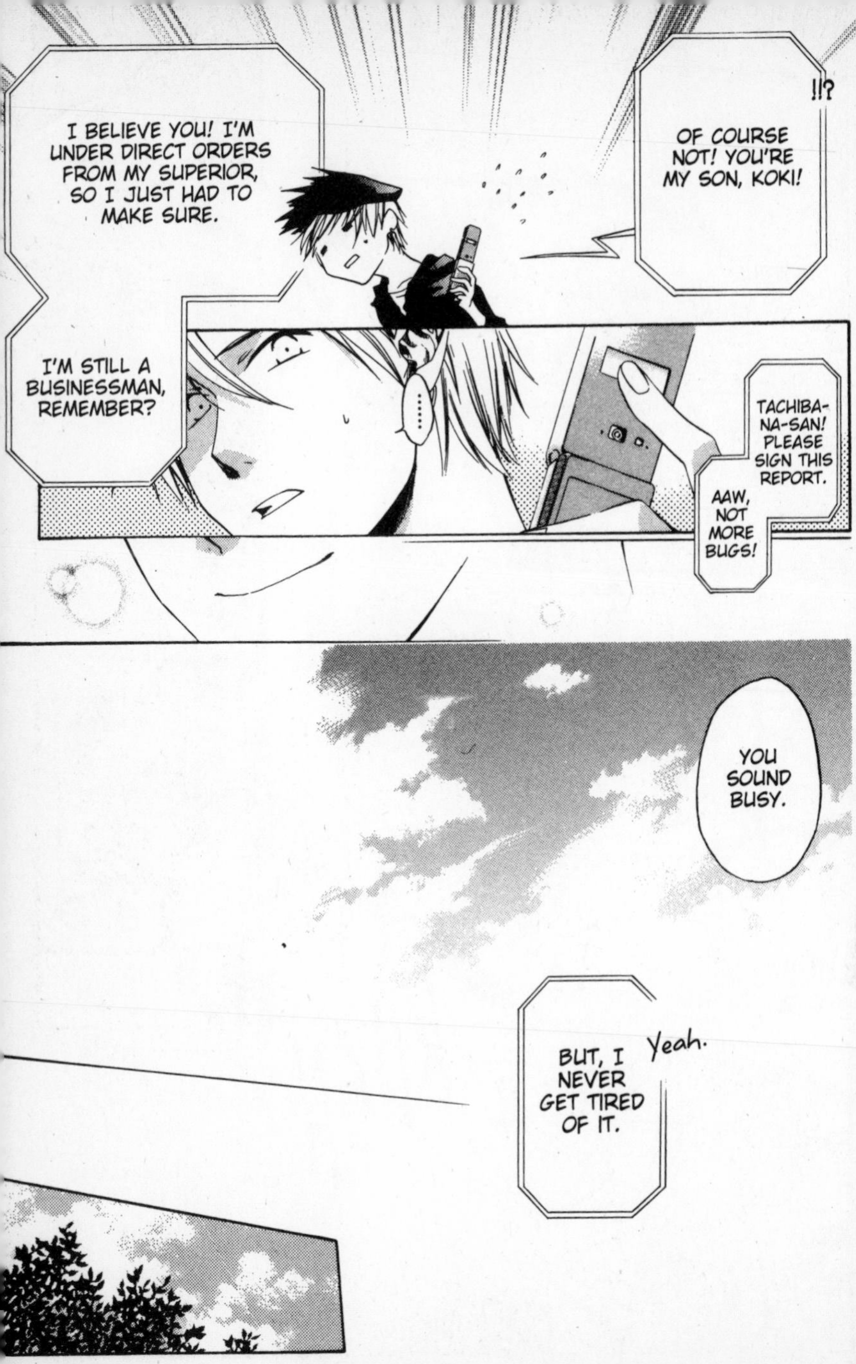
!!?
OF COURSE NOT! YOU'RE MY SON, KOKI!
I BELIEVE YOU! I'M UNDER DIRECT ORDERS FROM MY SUPERIOR, SO I JUST HAD TO MAKE SURE.
TACHIBA-NA-SAN! PLEASE SIGN THIS REPORT.
AAW, NOT MORE BUGS!
......
I'M STILL A BUSINESSMAN, REMEMBER?
YOU SOUND BUSY.
Yeah.
BUT, I NEVER GET TIRED OF IT.

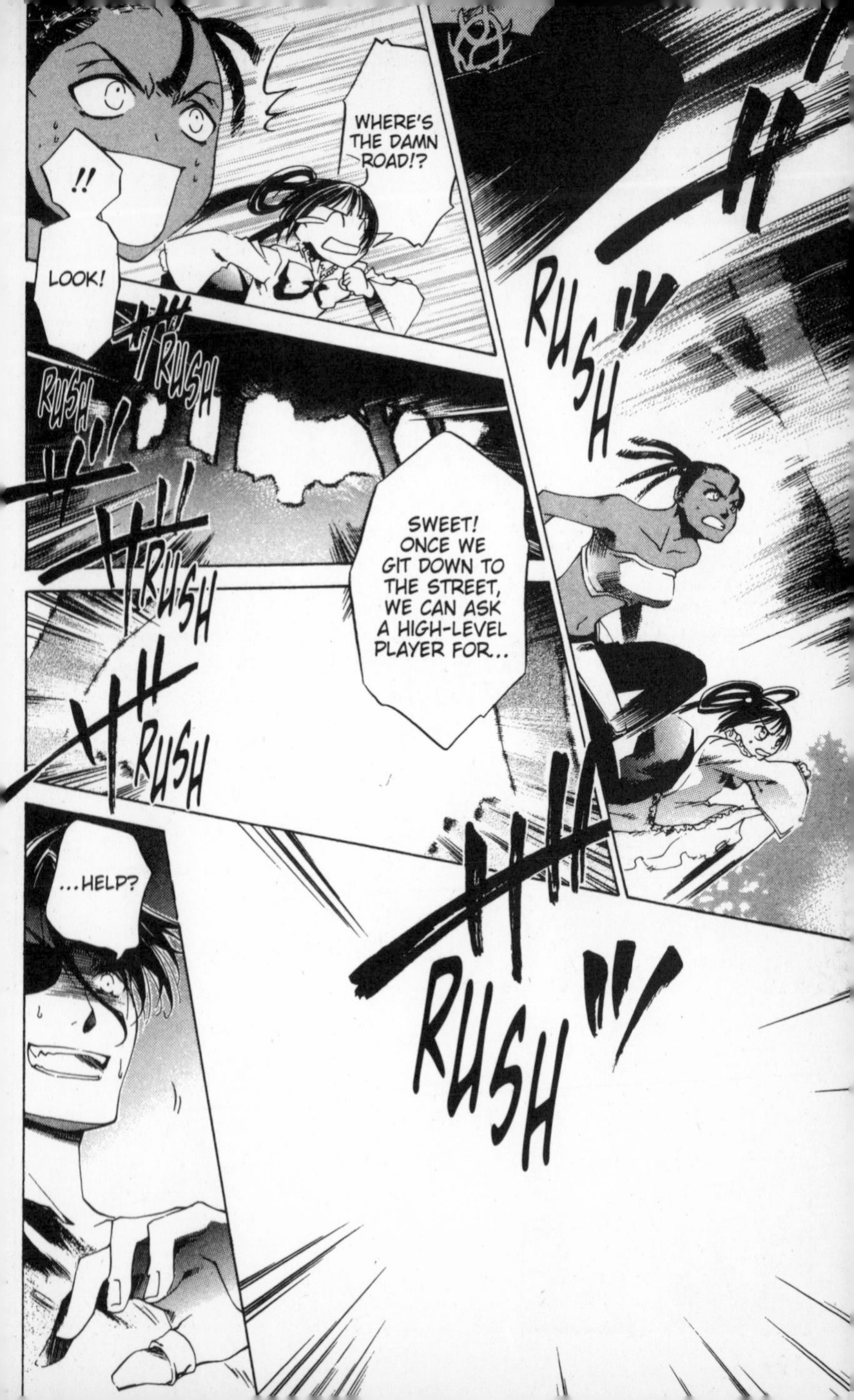
RUSH
WHERE'S THE DAMN ROAD!?
!!
LOOK!
RUSH
RUSH
RUSH
SWEET! ONCE WE GIT DOWN TO THE STREET, WE CAN ASK A HIGH-LEVEL PLAYER FOR...
RUSH
...HELP?
RUSH

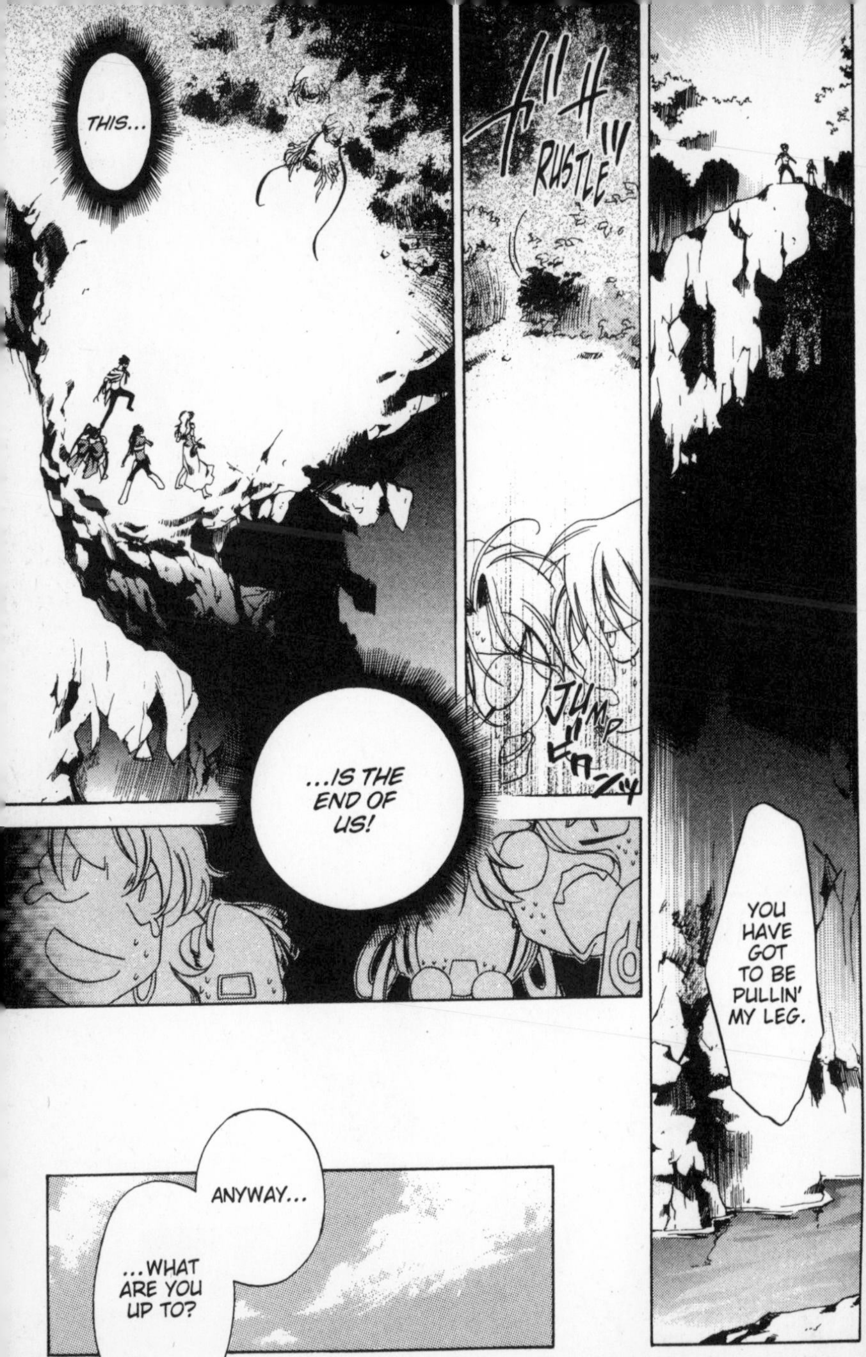
YOU HAVE GOT TO BE PULLIN' MY LEG.
RUSTLE
JUMP
THIS...
...IS THE END OF US!
ANYWAY...
...WHAT ARE YOU UP TO?

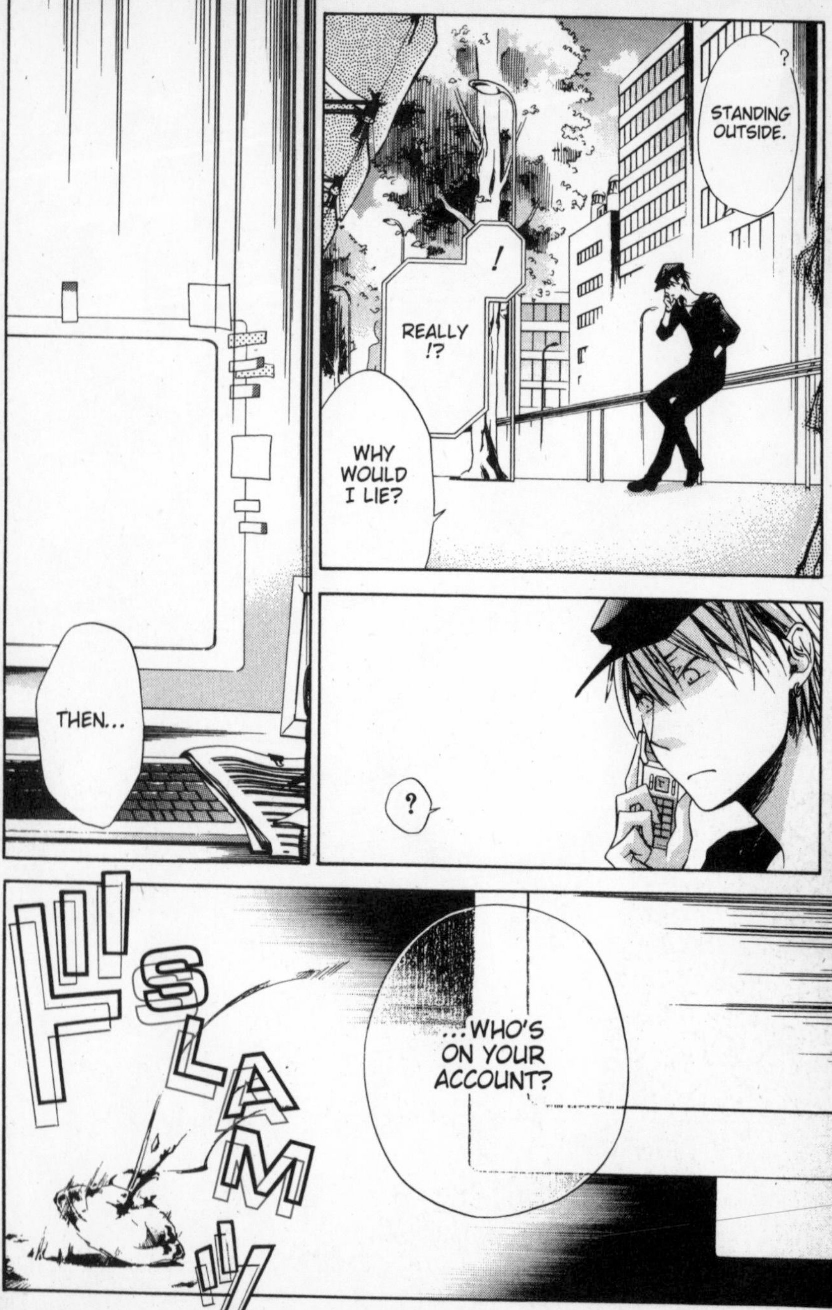
?
STANDING OUTSIDE.
!
REALLY!?
WHY WOULD I LIE?
?
THEN...
...WHO'S ON YOUR ACCOUNT?
SLAM

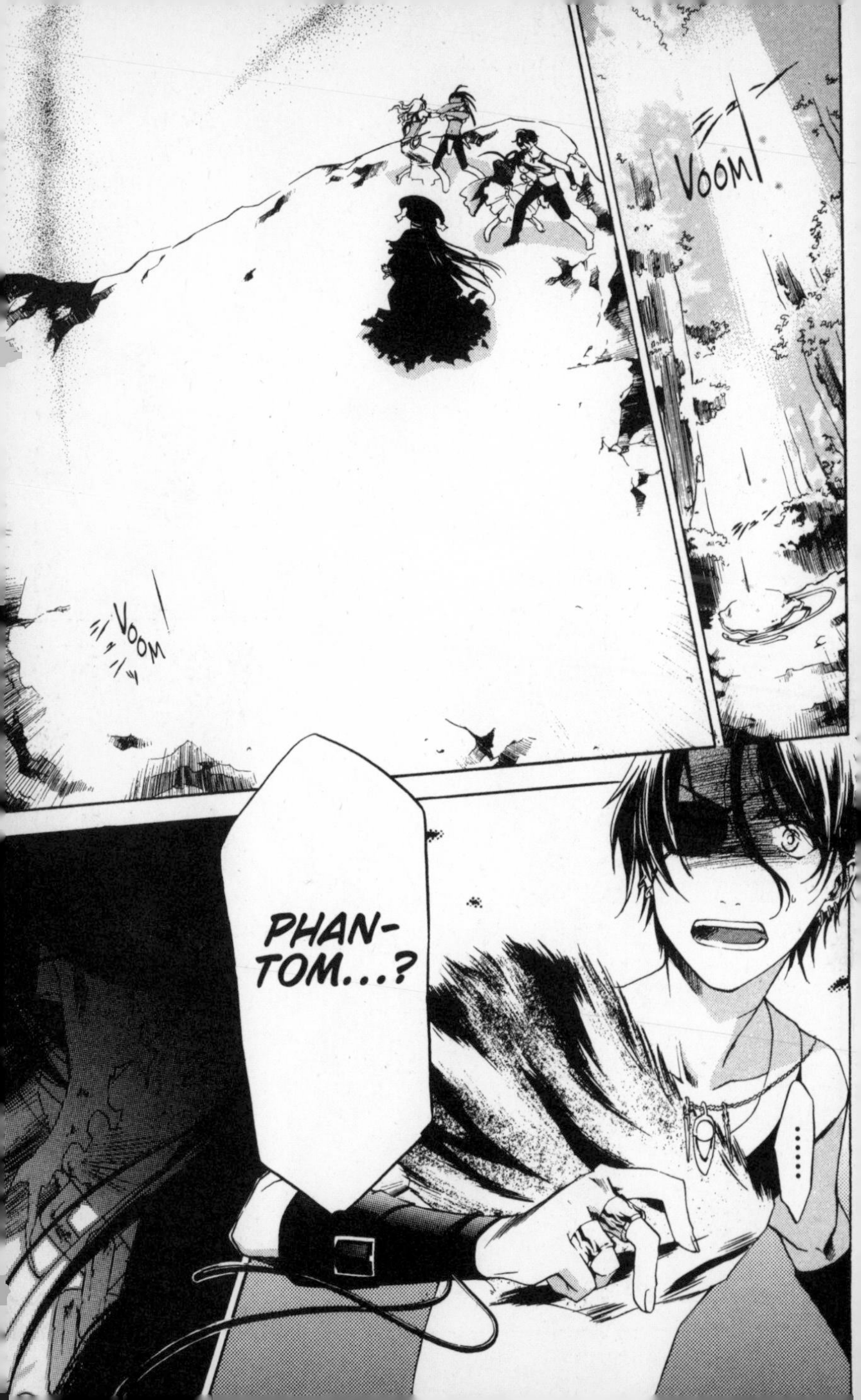
VOOM
VOOM
PHAN-TOM...?
......

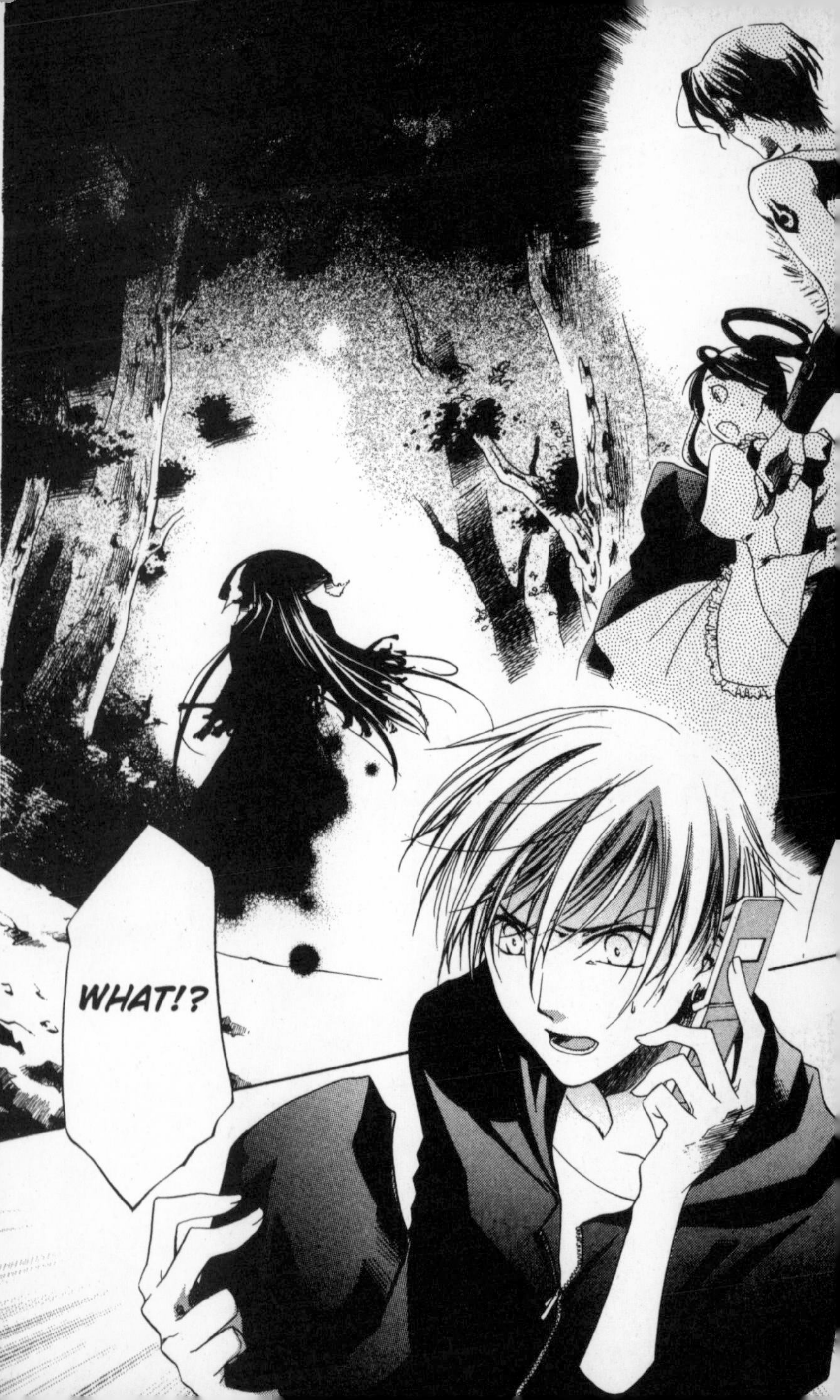
WHAT!?

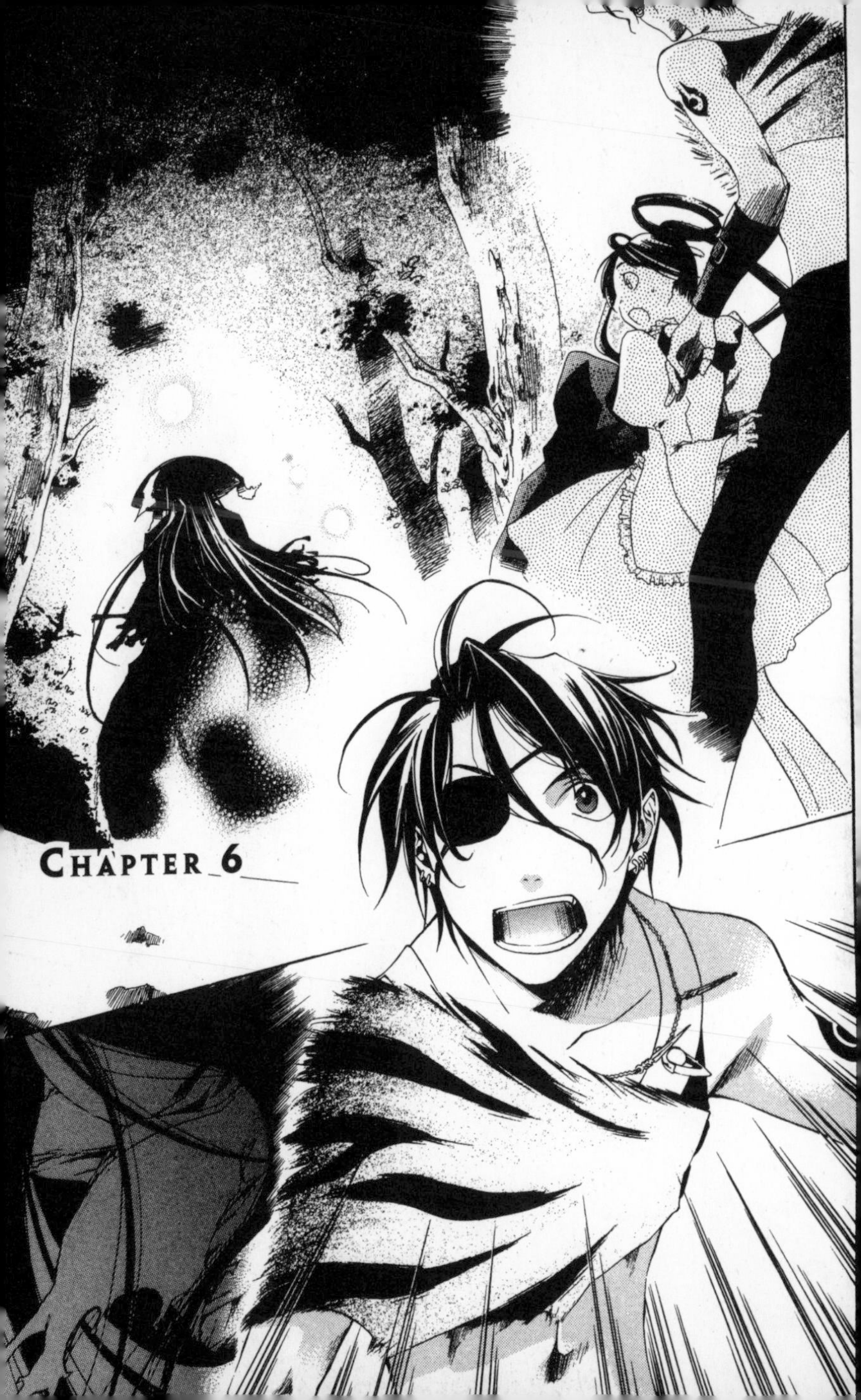
CHAPTER 6

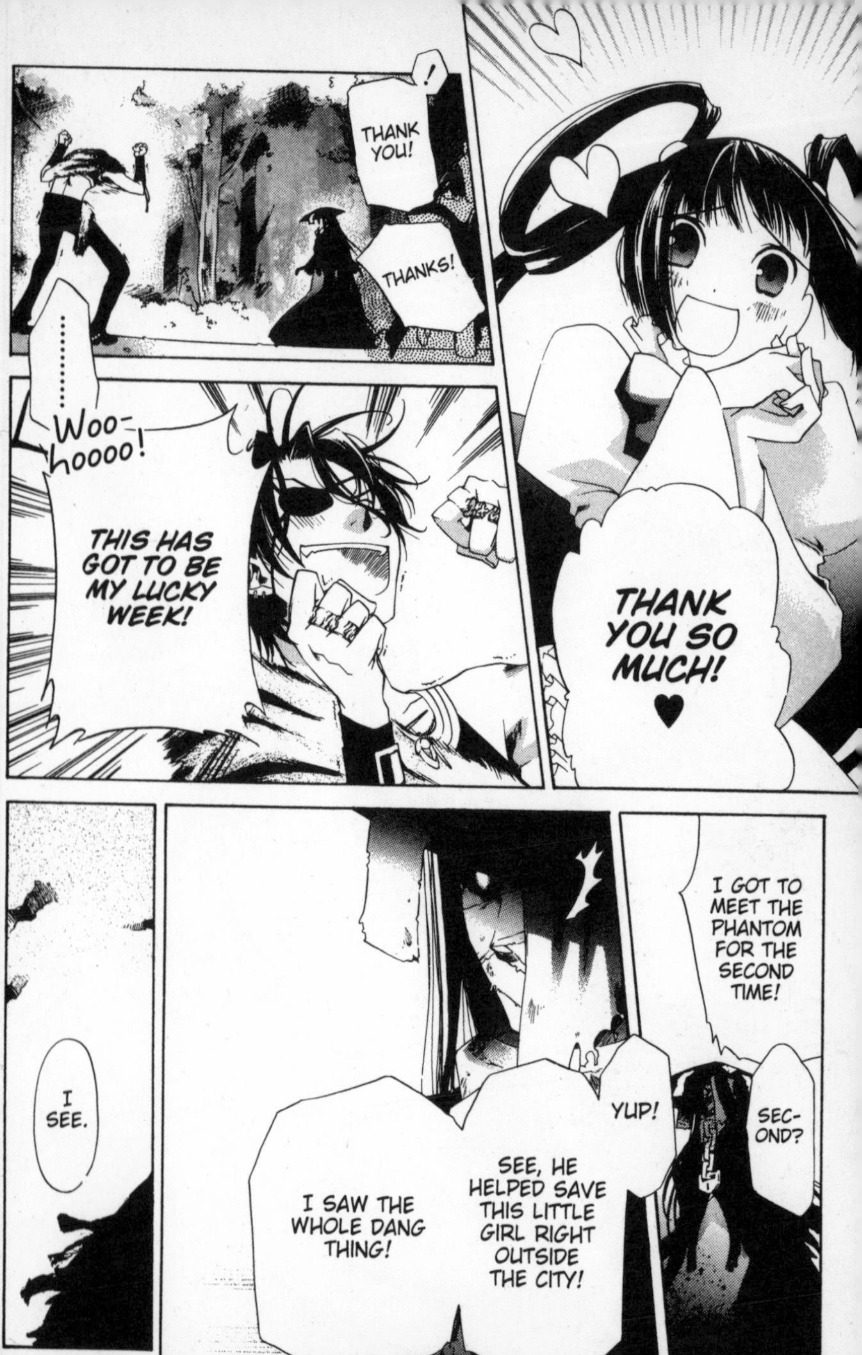

THANK YOU SO MUCH! ♥
!
THANK YOU!
THANKS!
......
Woo-hoooo!
THIS HAS GOT TO BE MY LUCKY WEEK!
I GOT TO MEET THE PHANTOM FOR THE SECOND TIME!
SEC-OND?
YUP!
SEE, HE HELPED SAVE THIS LITTLE GIRL RIGHT OUTSIDE THE CITY!
I SAW THE WHOLE DANG THING!
I SEE.

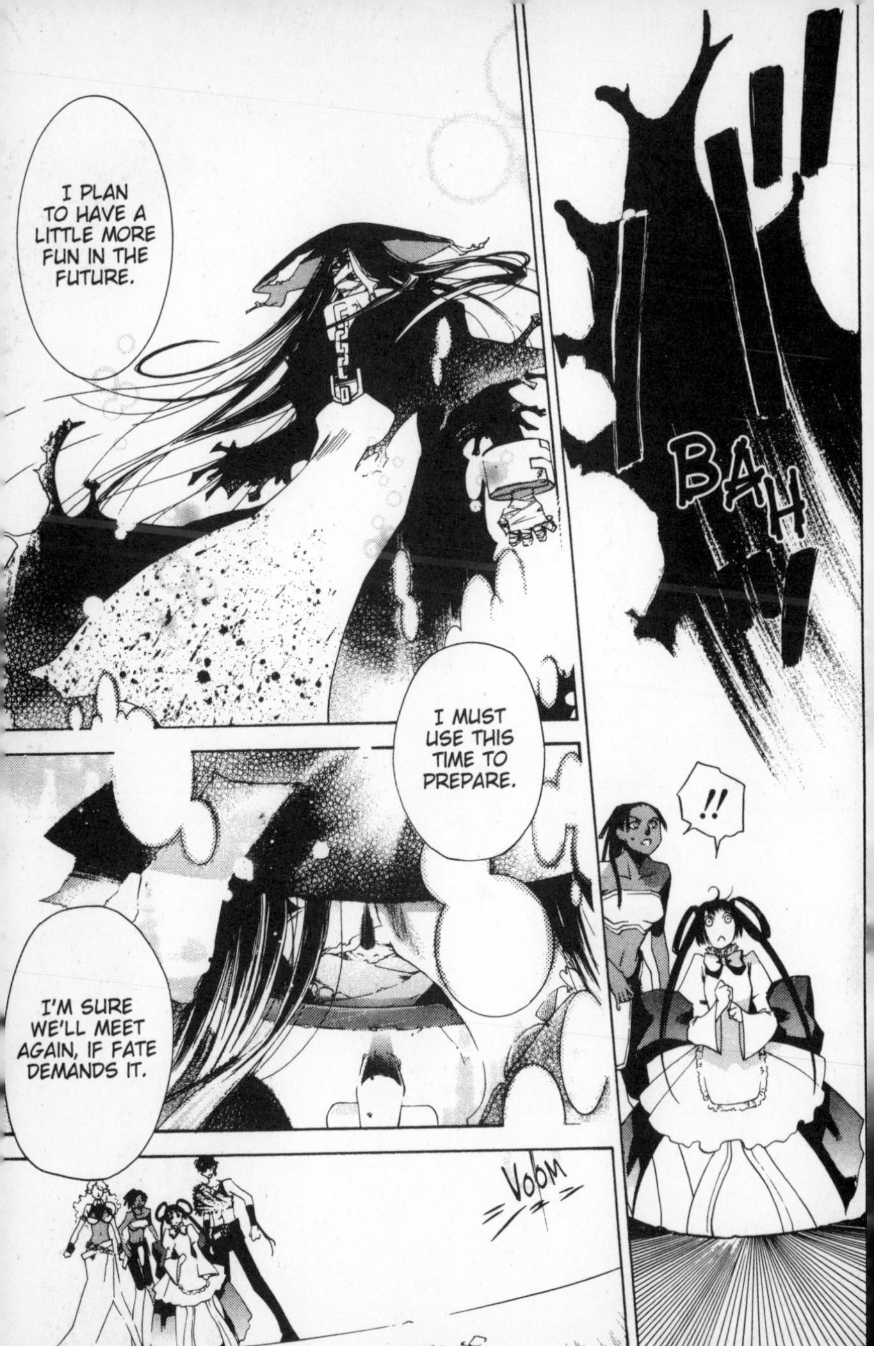
BAH
!!
I PLAN TO HAVE A LITTLE MORE FUN IN THE FUTURE.
I MUST USE THIS TIME TO PREPARE.
I'M SURE WE'LL MEET AGAIN, IF FATE DEMANDS IT.
VOOM

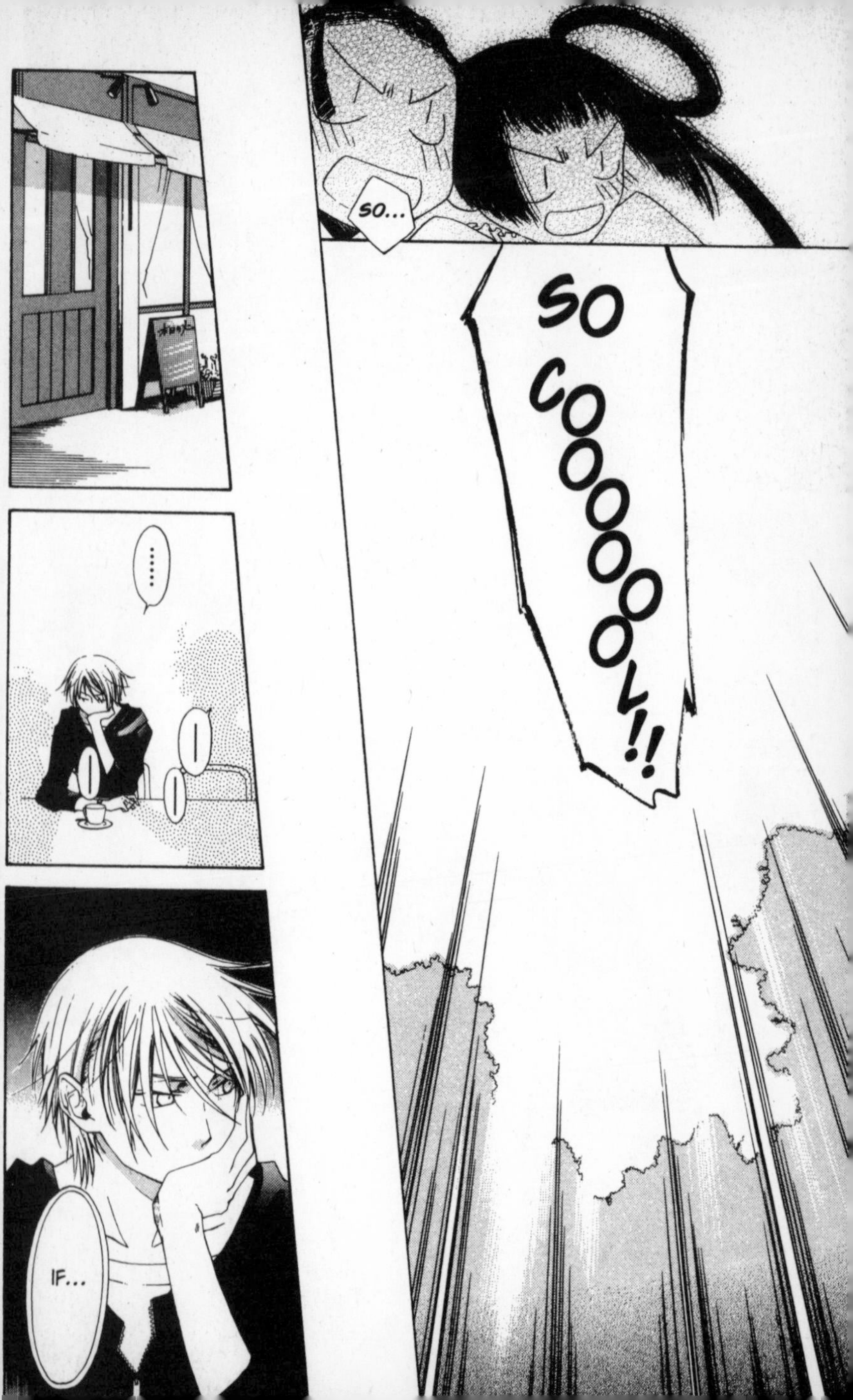
SO...
SO COOOOOOL!!
......
IF...

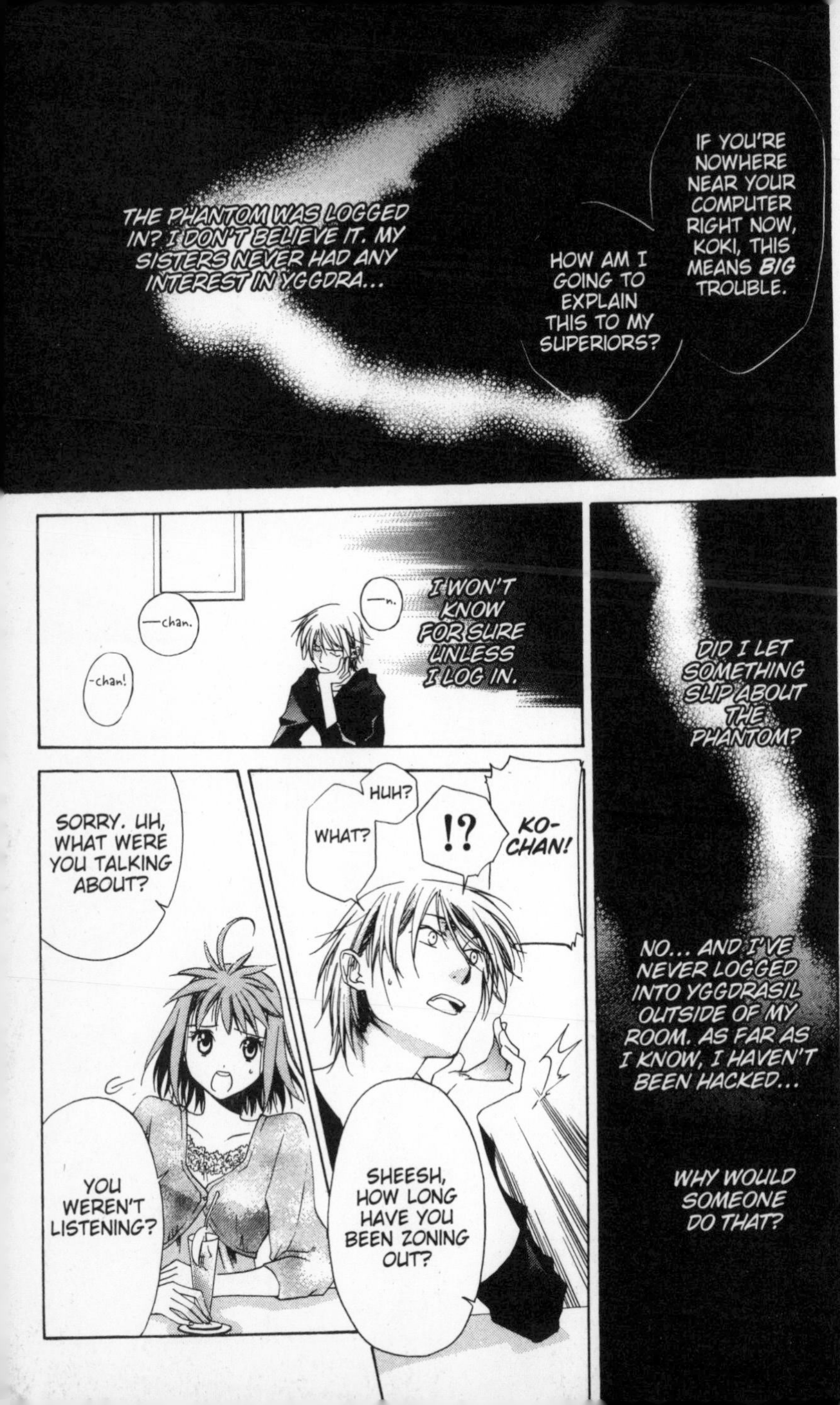
IF YOU'RE NOWHERE NEAR YOUR COMPUTER RIGHT NOW, KOKI, THIS MEANS BIG TROUBLE.
HOW AM I GOING TO EXPLAIN THIS TO MY SUPERIORS?
THE PHANTOM WAS LOGGED IN? I DON'T BELIEVE IT. MY SISTERS NEVER HAD ANY INTEREST IN YGGDRA...
DID I LET SOMETHING SLIP ABOUT THE PHANTOM?
I WON'T KNOW FOR SURE UNLESS I LOG IN.
—n.
—chan.
-chan!
NO... AND I'VE NEVER LOGGED INTO YGGDRASIL OUTSIDE OF MY ROOM. AS FAR AS I KNOW, I HAVEN'T BEEN HACKED...
WHY WOULD SOMEONE DO THAT?
KO-CHAN!
!?
HUH?
WHAT?
SORRY. UH, WHAT WERE YOU TALKING ABOUT?
SHEESH, HOW LONG HAVE YOU BEEN ZONING OUT?
YOU WEREN'T LISTENING?

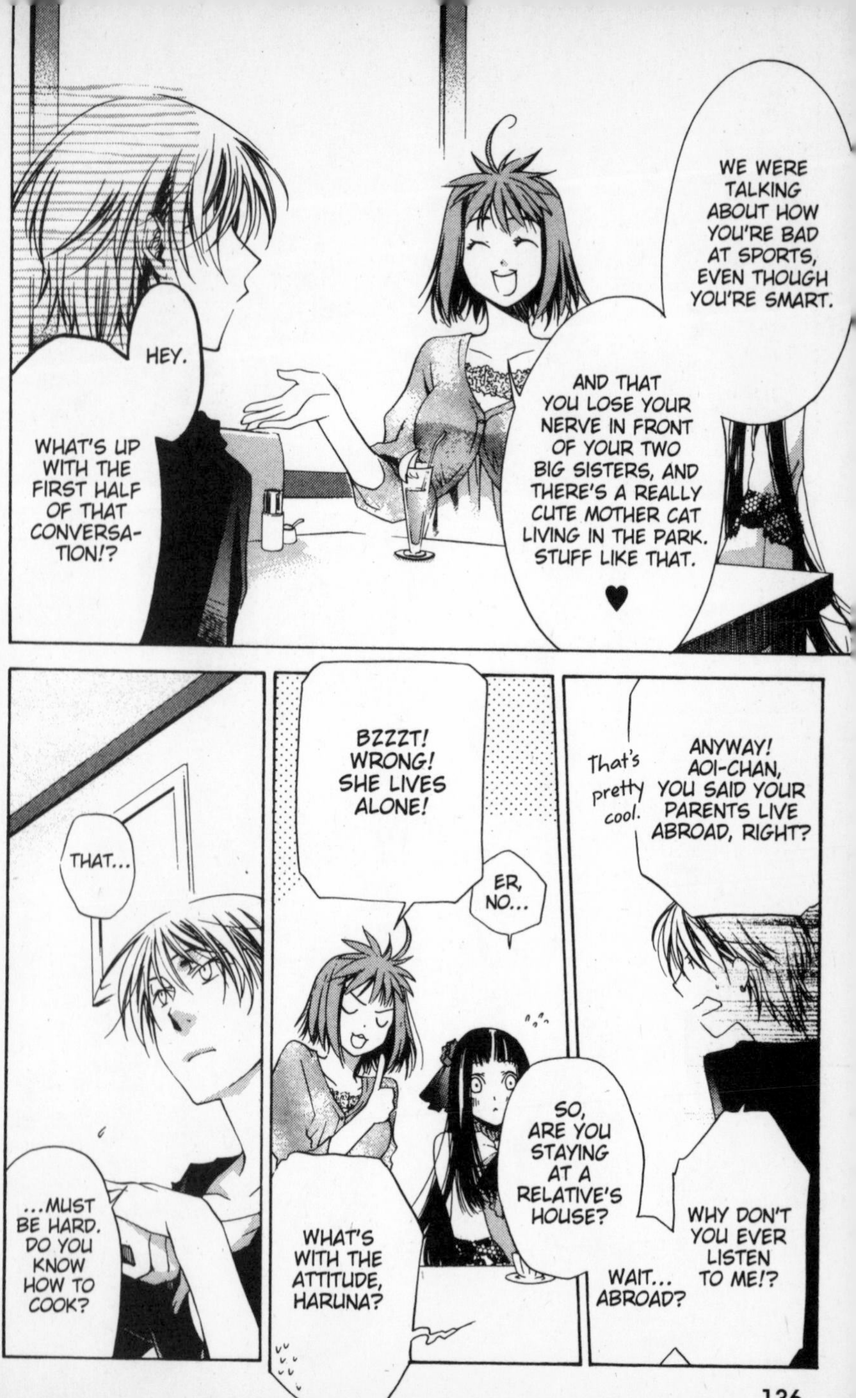
WE WERE TALKING ABOUT HOW YOU'RE BAD AT SPORTS, EVEN THOUGH YOU'RE SMART.
AND THAT YOU LOSE YOUR NERVE IN FRONT OF YOUR TWO BIG SISTERS, AND THERE'S A REALLY CUTE MOTHER CAT LIVING IN THE PARK. STUFF LIKE THAT. ♥
HEY.
WHAT'S UP WITH THE FIRST HALF OF THAT CONVERSA-TION!?
ANYWAY! AOI-CHAN, YOU SAID YOUR PARENTS LIVE ABROAD, RIGHT?
That's pretty cool.
SO, ARE YOU STAYING AT A RELATIVE'S HOUSE?
WHY DON'T YOU EVER LISTEN TO ME!?
WAIT... ABROAD?
BZZZT! WRONG! SHE LIVES ALONE!
ER, NO...
WHAT'S WITH THE ATTITUDE, HARUNA?
THAT...
...MUST BE HARD. DO YOU KNOW HOW TO COOK?

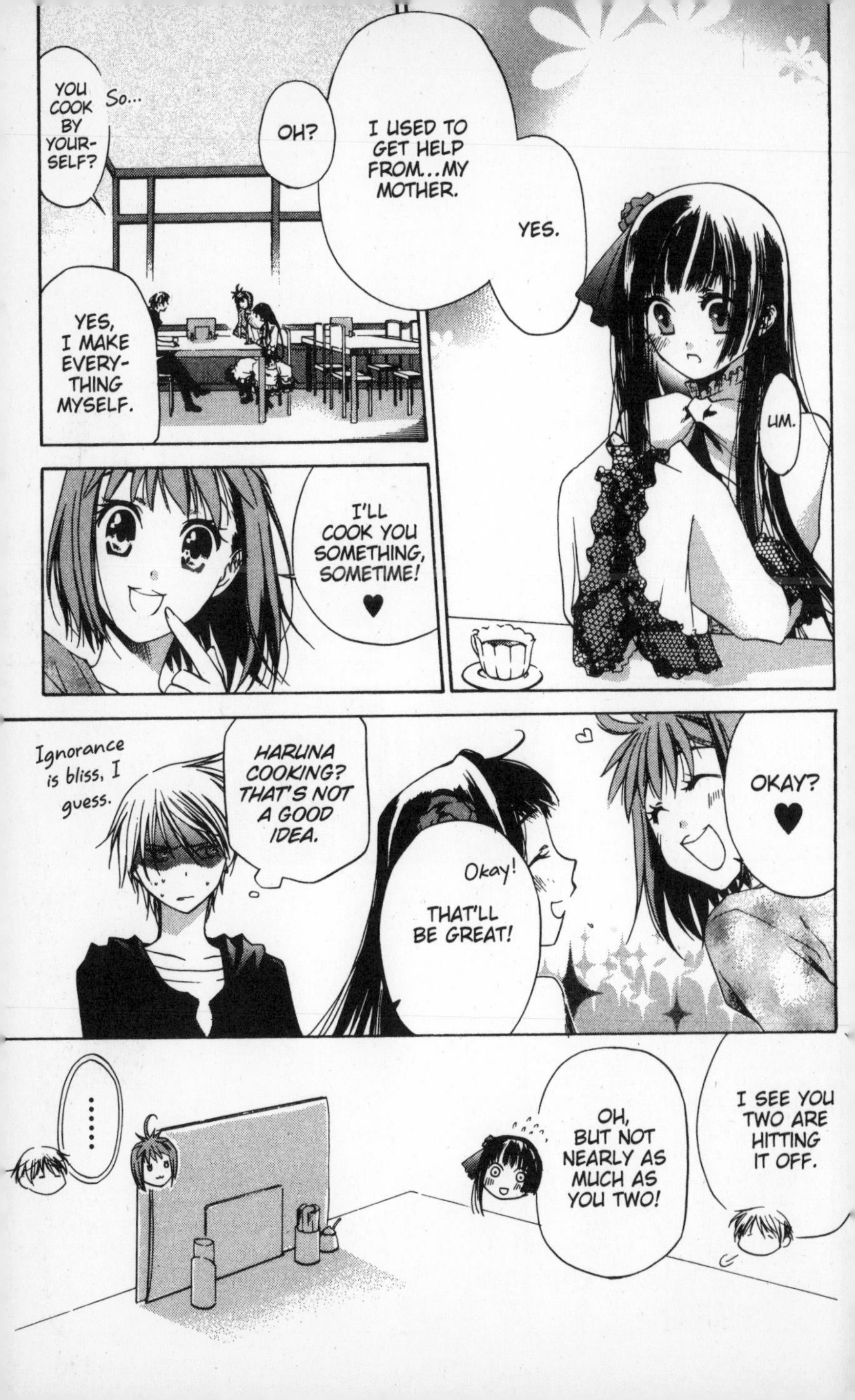
So...
YOU COOK BY YOURSELF?
YES, I MAKE EVERYTHING MYSELF.
OH?
I USED TO GET HELP FROM...MY MOTHER.
YES.
UM.
I'LL COOK YOU SOMETHING, SOMETIME! ♥
OKAY? ♥
Okay!
THAT'LL BE GREAT!
HARUNA COOKING? THAT'S NOT A GOOD IDEA.
Ignorance is bliss, I guess.
I SEE YOU TWO ARE HITTING IT OFF.
OH, BUT NOT NEARLY AS MUCH AS YOU TWO!
......

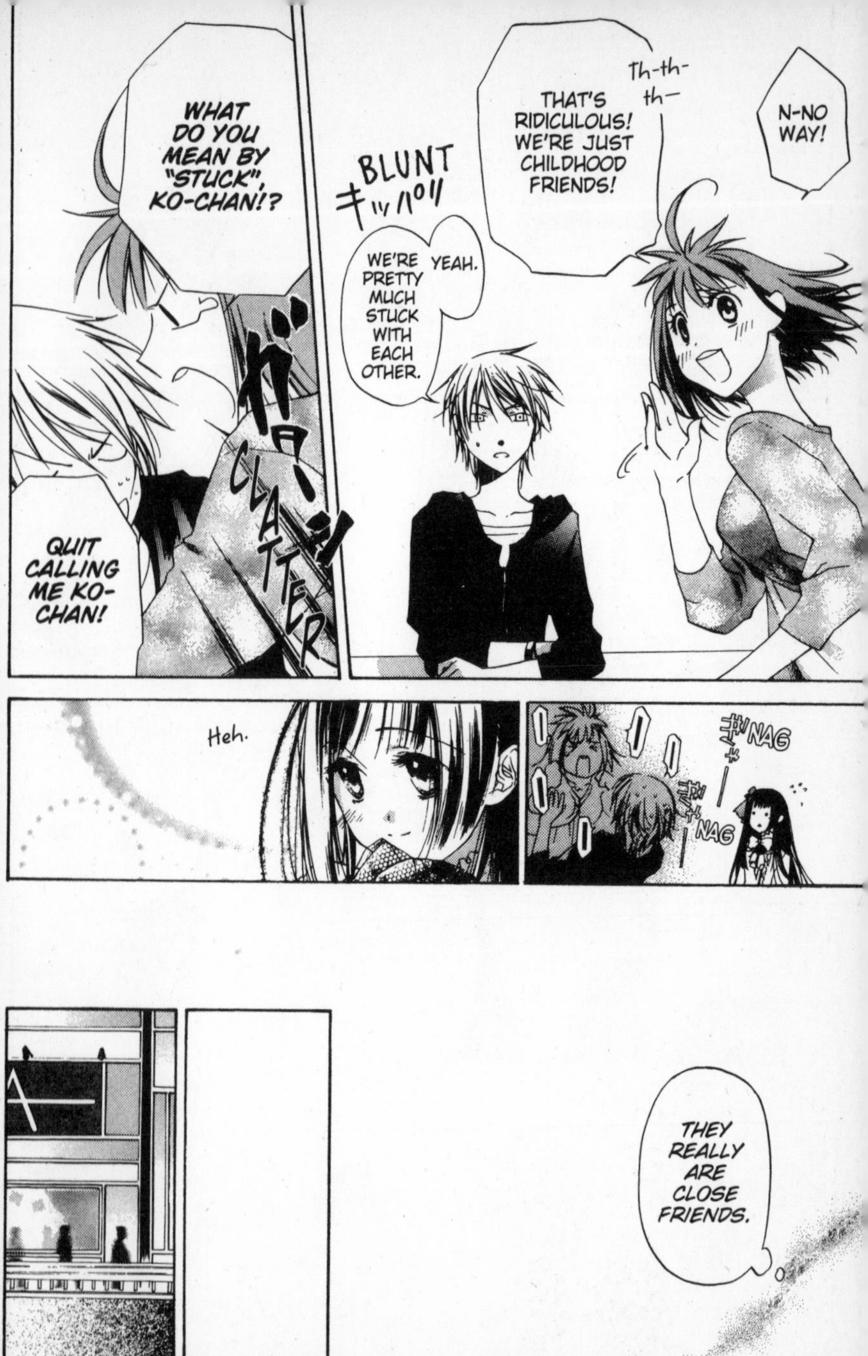
N-NO WAY!
Th-th- th-
THAT'S RIDICULOUS! WE'RE JUST CHILDHOOD FRIENDS!
BLUNT
キッパリ
YEAH.
WE'RE PRETTY MUCH STUCK WITH EACH OTHER.
WHAT DO YOU MEAN BY "STUCK", KO-CHAN!?
ガバッ
CLATTER
QUIT CALLING ME KO-CHAN!
NAG
NAG
Heh.
THEY REALLY ARE CLOSE FRIENDS.

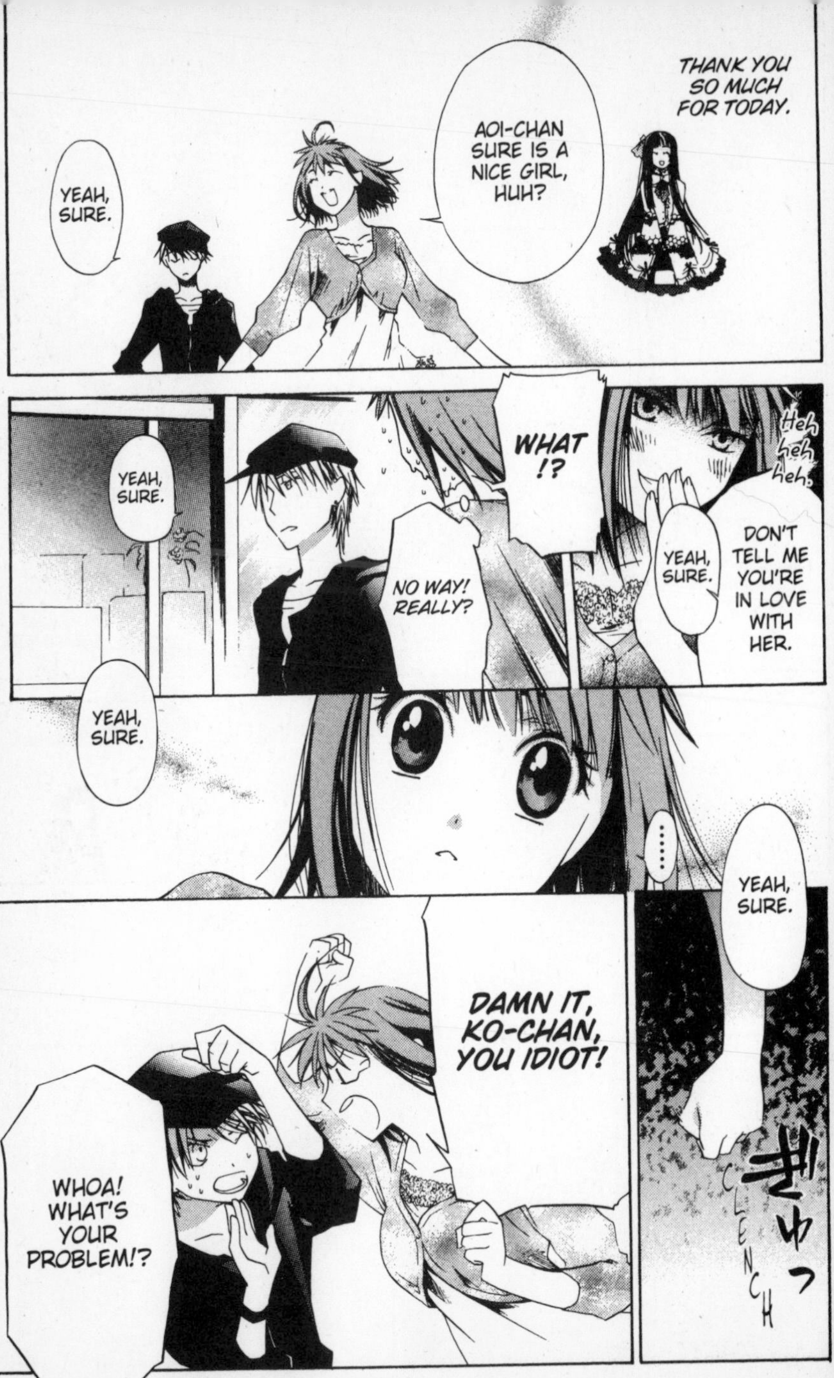
THANK YOU SO MUCH FOR TODAY.
AOI-CHAN SURE IS A NICE GIRL, HUH?
YEAH, SURE.
Heh heh heh.
DON'T TELL ME YOU'RE IN LOVE WITH HER.
YEAH, SURE.
WHAT!?
NO WAY! REALLY?
YEAH, SURE.
YEAH, SURE.
......
YEAH, SURE.
CLENCH
DAMN IT, KO-CHAN, YOU IDIOT!
WHOA! WHAT'S YOUR PROBLEM!?

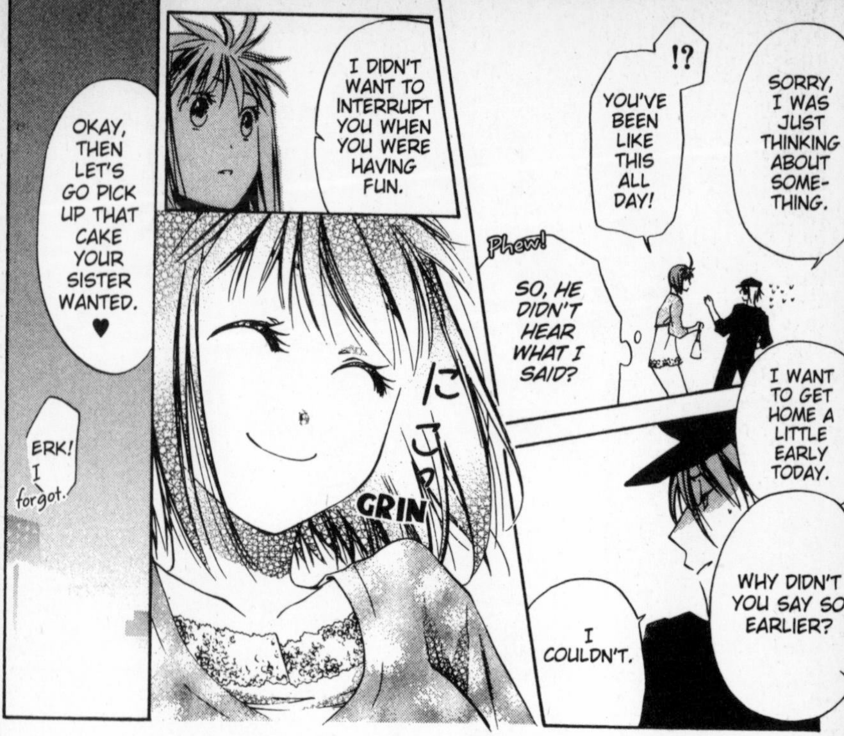
SORRY, I WAS JUST THINKING ABOUT SOME-THING.
!?
YOU'VE BEEN LIKE THIS ALL DAY!
I WANT TO GET HOME A LITTLE EARLY TODAY.
WHY DIDN'T YOU SAY SO EARLIER?
I COULDN'T.
Phew!
SO, HE DIDN'T HEAR WHAT I SAID?
I DIDN'T WANT TO INTERRUPT YOU WHEN YOU WERE HAVING FUN.
GRIN
OKAY, THEN LET'S GO PICK UP THAT CAKE YOUR SISTER WANTED. ♥
ERK! I forgot.

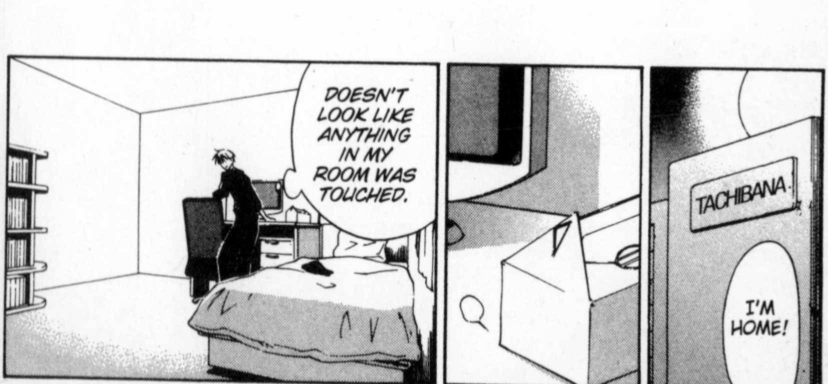
TACHIBANA
I'M HOME!
DOESN'T LOOK LIKE ANYTHING IN MY ROOM WAS TOUCHED.

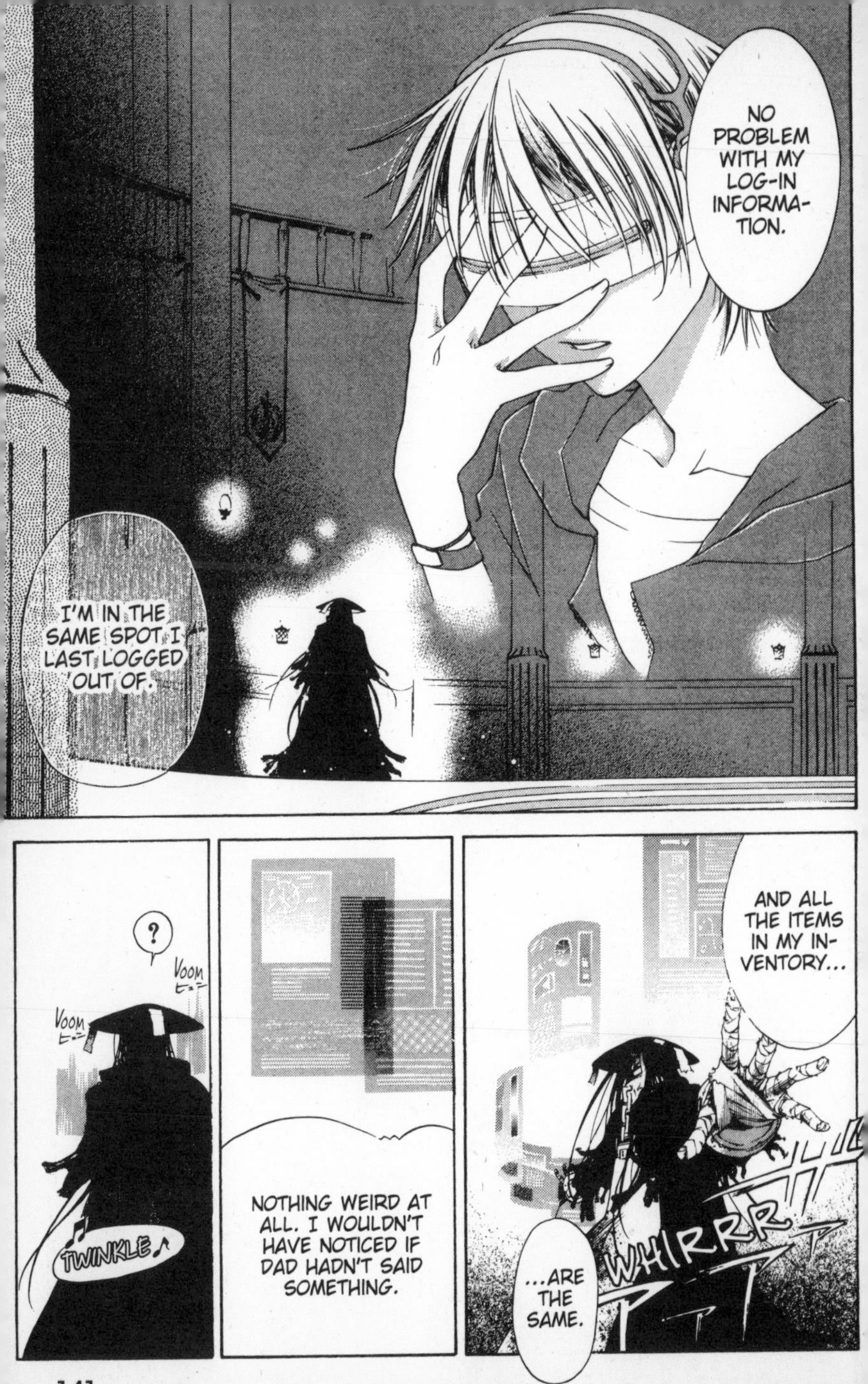
NO PROBLEM WITH MY LOG-IN INFORMA-TION.
I'M IN THE SAME SPOT I LAST LOGGED OUT OF.
AND ALL THE ITEMS IN MY IN-VENTORY...
WHIRRR
...ARE THE SAME.
NOTHING WEIRD AT ALL. I WOULDN'T HAVE NOTICED IF DAD HADN'T SAID SOMETHING.
?
VOOM
VOOM
TWINKLE♪

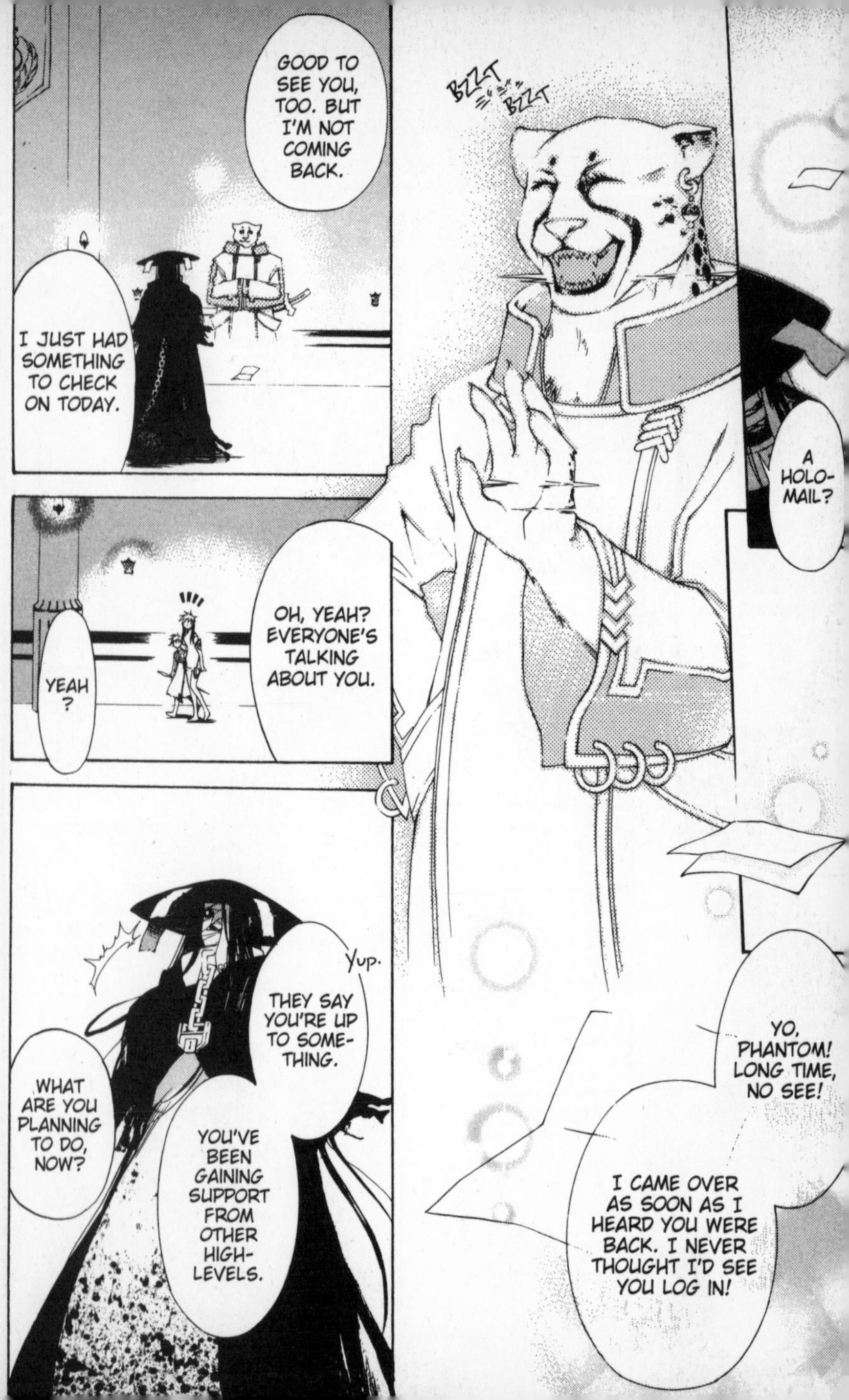
A HOLO-MAIL?
BZZ-T BZZ-T
YO, PHANTOM! LONG TIME, NO SEE!
I CAME OVER AS SOON AS I HEARD YOU WERE BACK. I NEVER THOUGHT I'D SEE YOU LOG IN!
GOOD TO SEE YOU, TOO. BUT I'M NOT COMING BACK.
I JUST HAD SOMETHING TO CHECK ON TODAY.
OH, YEAH? EVERYONE'S TALKING ABOUT YOU.
YEAH?
Yup.
THEY SAY YOU'RE UP TO SOME-THING.
YOU'VE BEEN GAINING SUPPORT FROM OTHER HIGH-LEVELS.
WHAT ARE YOU PLANNING TO DO, NOW?

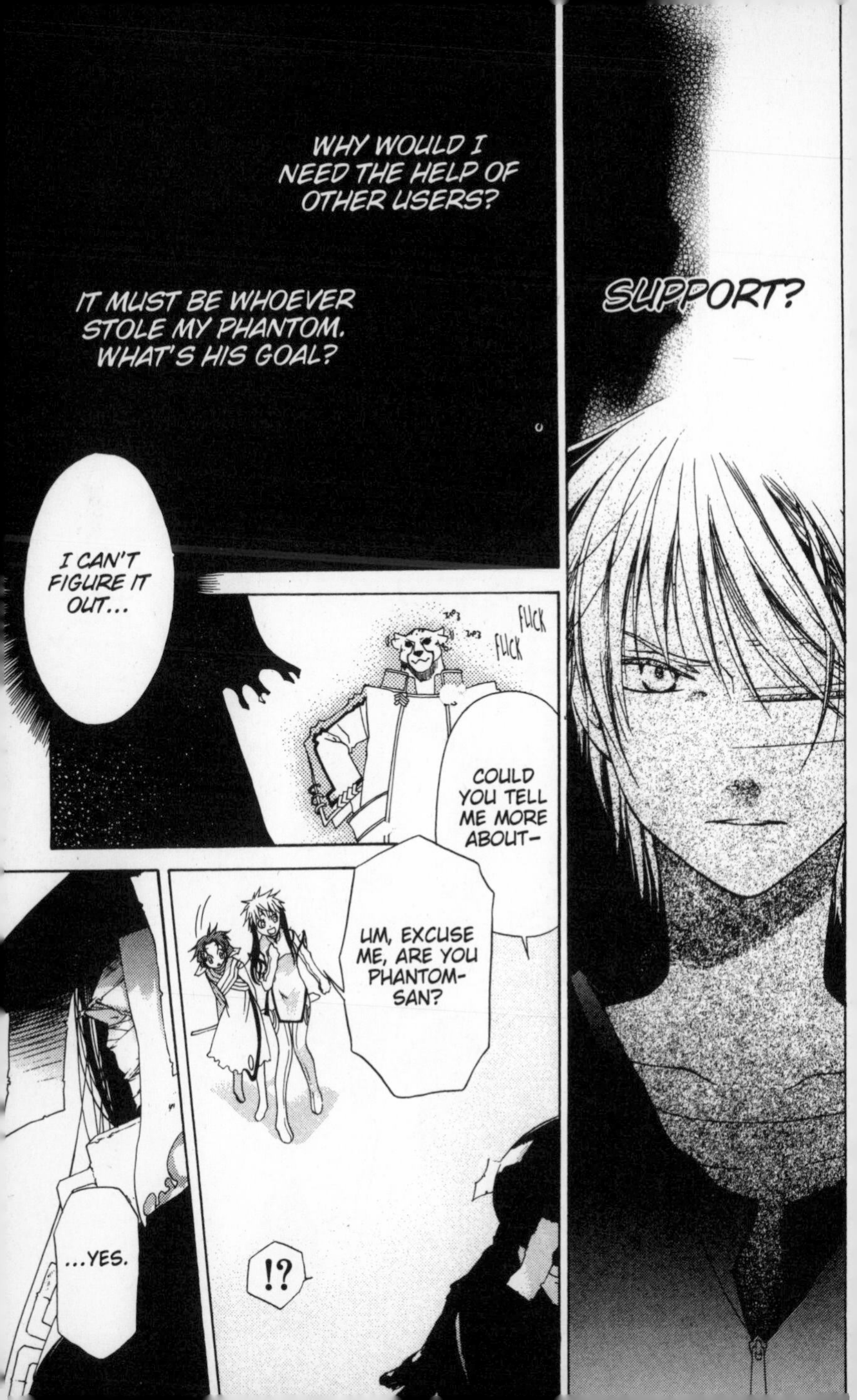
SUPPORT?
WHY WOULD I NEED THE HELP OF OTHER USERS?
IT MUST BE WHOEVER STOLE MY PHANTOM. WHAT'S HIS GOAL?
I CAN'T FIGURE IT OUT...
FLICK
FLICK
COULD YOU TELL ME MORE ABOUT-
UM, EXCUSE ME, ARE YOU PHANTOM-SAN?
!?
...YES.

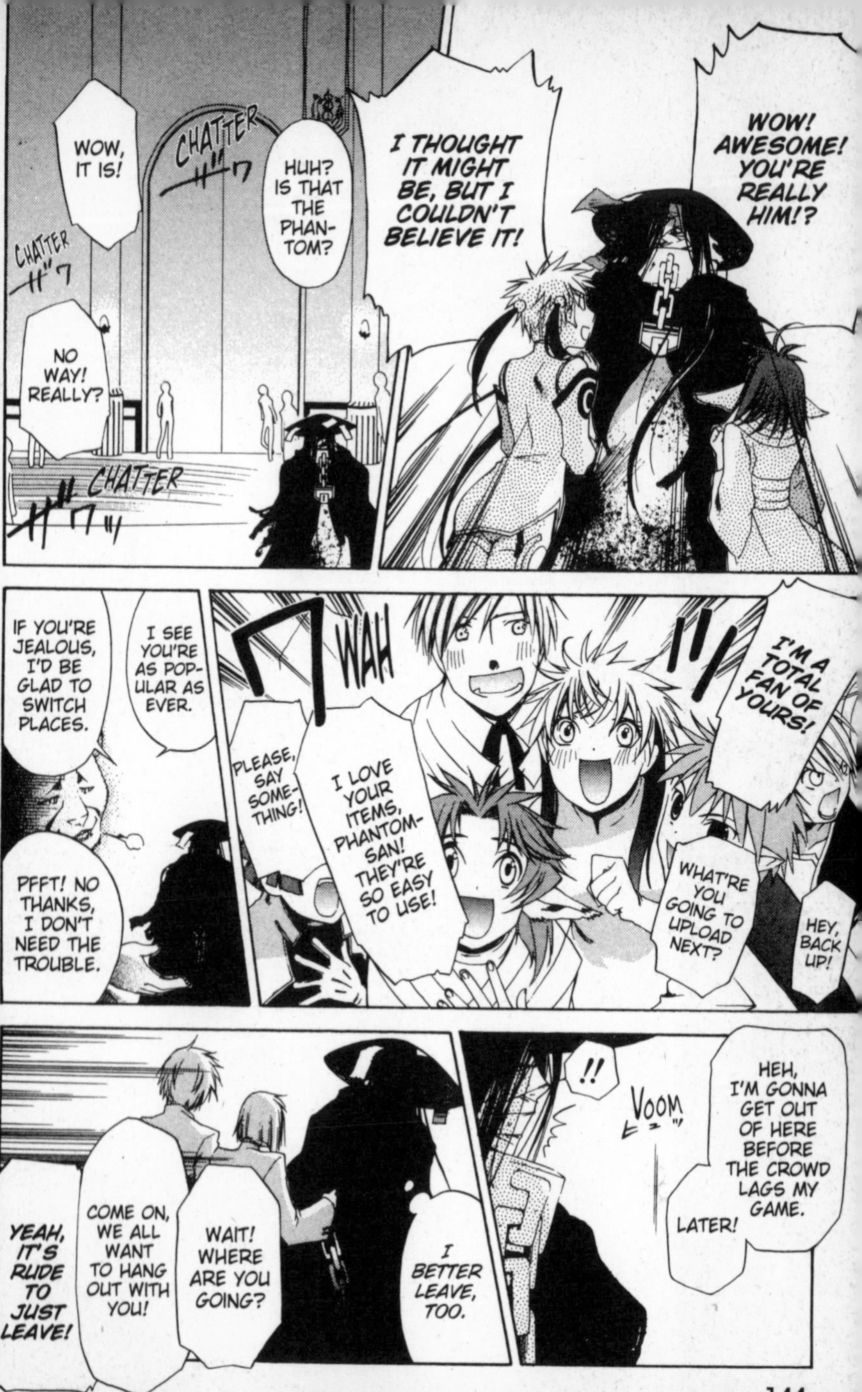
WOW! AWESOME! YOU'RE REALLY HIM!?
I THOUGHT IT MIGHT BE, BUT I COULDN'T BELIEVE IT!
HUH? IS THAT THE PHAN-TOM?
CHATTER
WOW, IT IS!
CHATTER
NO WAY! REALLY?
CHATTER
I'M A TOTAL FAN OF YOURS!
WAH
HEY, BACK UP!
WHAT'RE YOU GOING TO UPLOAD NEXT?
I LOVE YOUR ITEMS, PHANTOM-SAN! THEY'RE SO EASY TO USE!
PLEASE, SAY SOME-THING!
I SEE YOU'RE AS POP-ULAR AS EVER.
IF YOU'RE JEALOUS, I'D BE GLAD TO SWITCH PLACES.
PFFT! NO THANKS, I DON'T NEED THE TROUBLE.
HEH, I'M GONNA GET OUT OF HERE BEFORE THE CROWD LAGS MY GAME.
LATER!
!!
VOOM
I BETTER LEAVE, TOO.
WAIT! WHERE ARE YOU GOING?
COME ON, WE ALL WANT TO HANG OUT WITH YOU!
YEAH, IT'S RUDE TO JUST LEAVE!

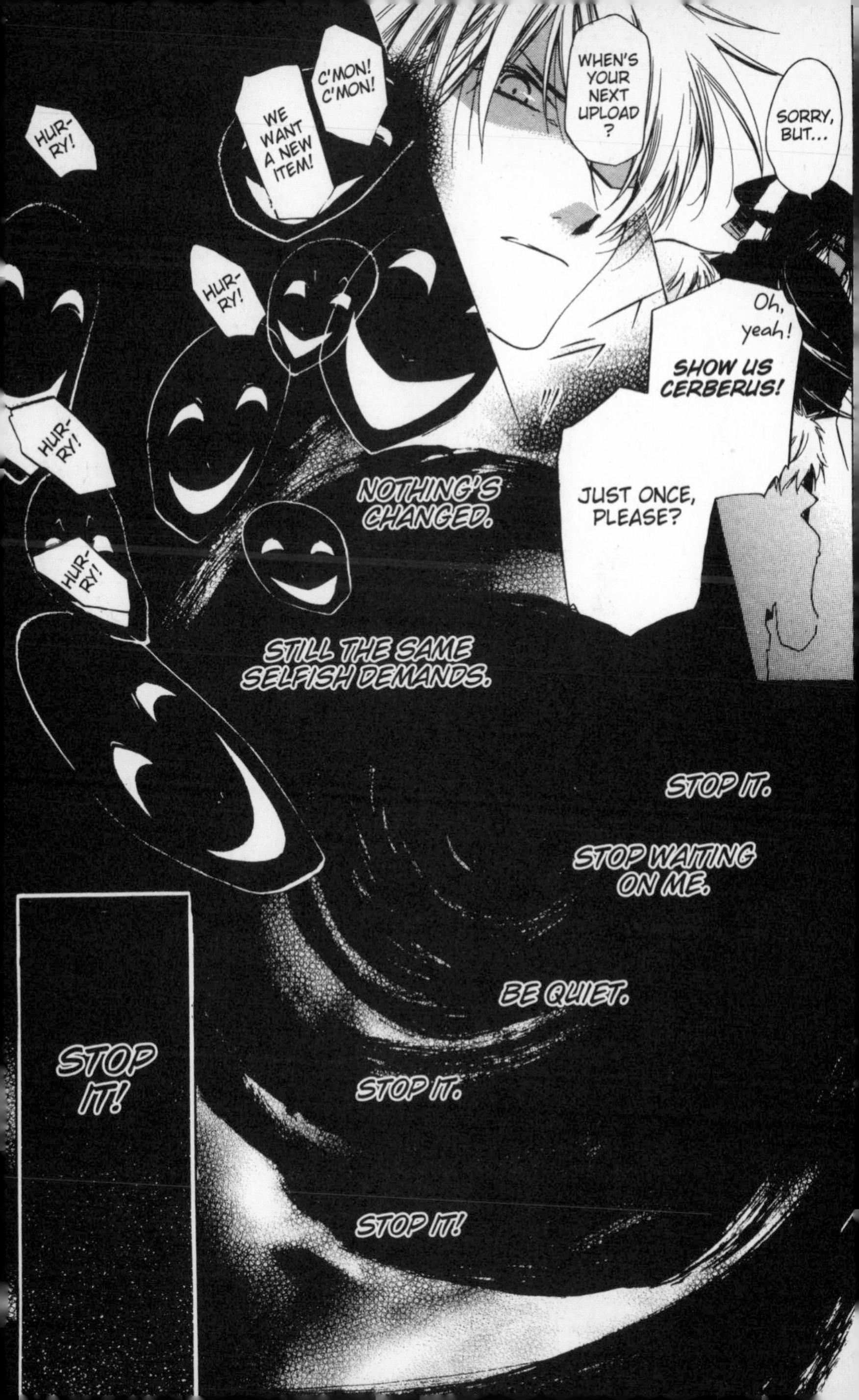
SORRY, BUT...
WHEN'S YOUR NEXT UPLOAD?
Oh, yeah! SHOW US CERBERUS!
C'MON! C'MON!
WE WANT A NEW ITEM!
HUR-RY!
HUR-RY!
JUST ONCE, PLEASE?
HUR-RY!
HUR-RY!
NOTHING'S CHANGED.
STILL THE SAME SELFISH DEMANDS.
STOP IT.
STOP WAITING ON ME.
BE QUIET.
STOP IT.
STOP IT!
STOP IT!

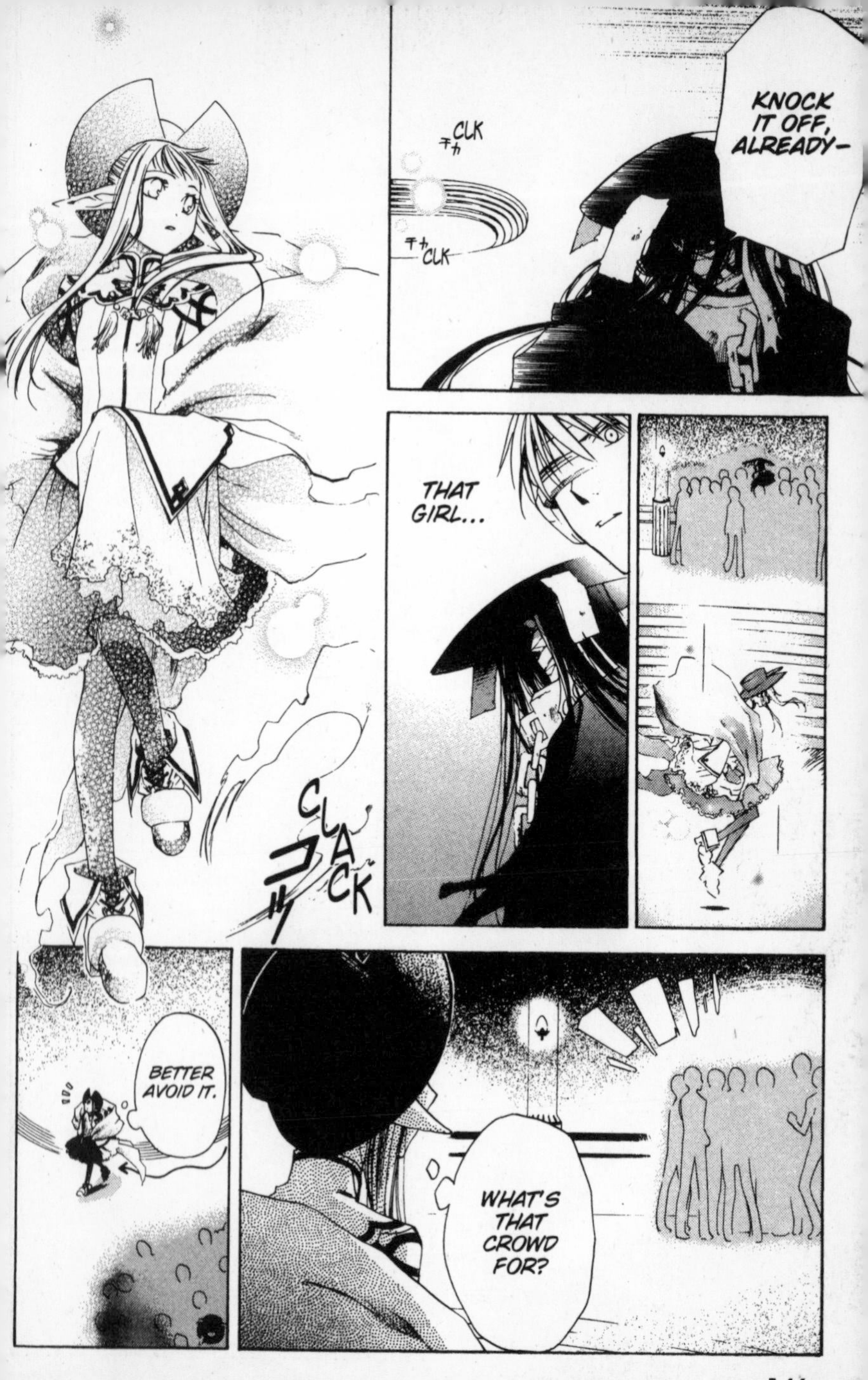
CLK
CLK
KNOCK IT OFF, ALREADY—
THAT GIRL...
CLACK
WHAT'S THAT CROWD FOR?
BETTER AVOID IT.

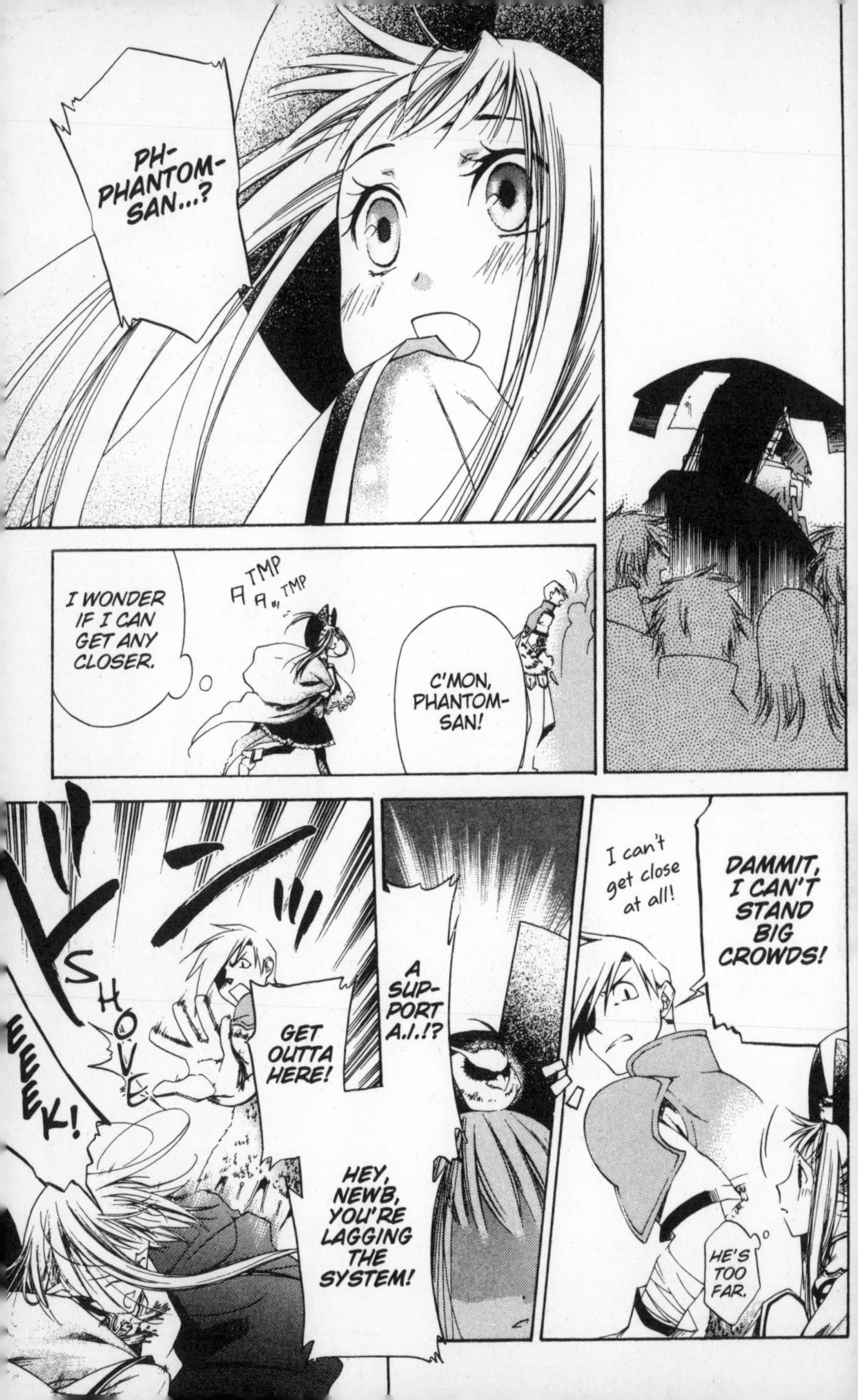
PH-PHANTOM-SAN...?
C'MON, PHANTOM-SAN!
TMP TMP
I WONDER IF I CAN GET ANY CLOSER.
DAMMIT, I CAN'T STAND BIG CROWDS!
I can't get close at all!
HE'S TOO FAR.
A SUP-PORT A.I.!?
HEY, NEWB, YOU'RE LAGGING THE SYSTEM!
GET OUTTA HERE!
SHOVE
EEEEK!

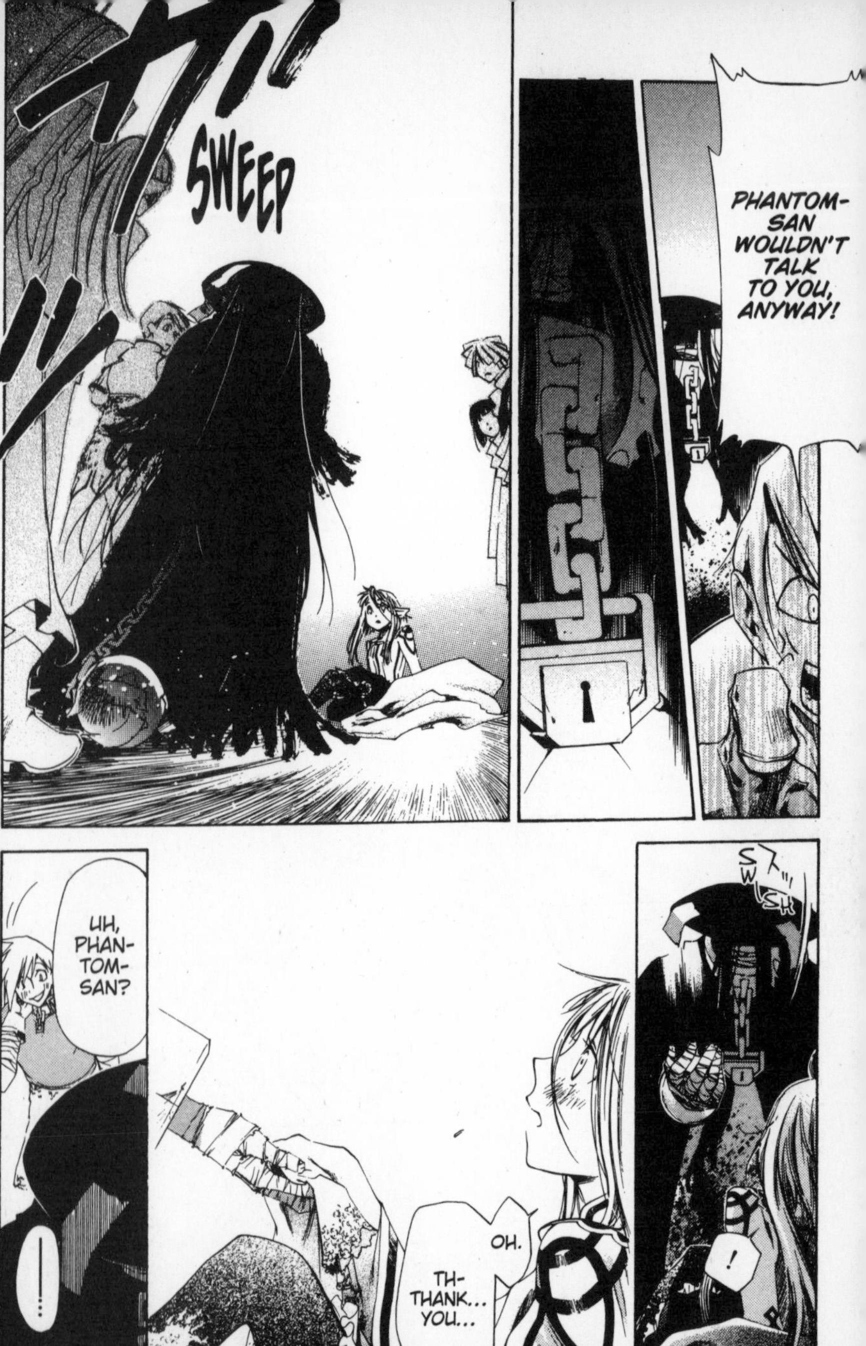
PHANTOM-SAN WOULDN'T TALK TO YOU, ANYWAY!
SWEEP
SWISH
!
OH.
TH-THANK... YOU...
UH, PHAN-TOM-SAN?
!...

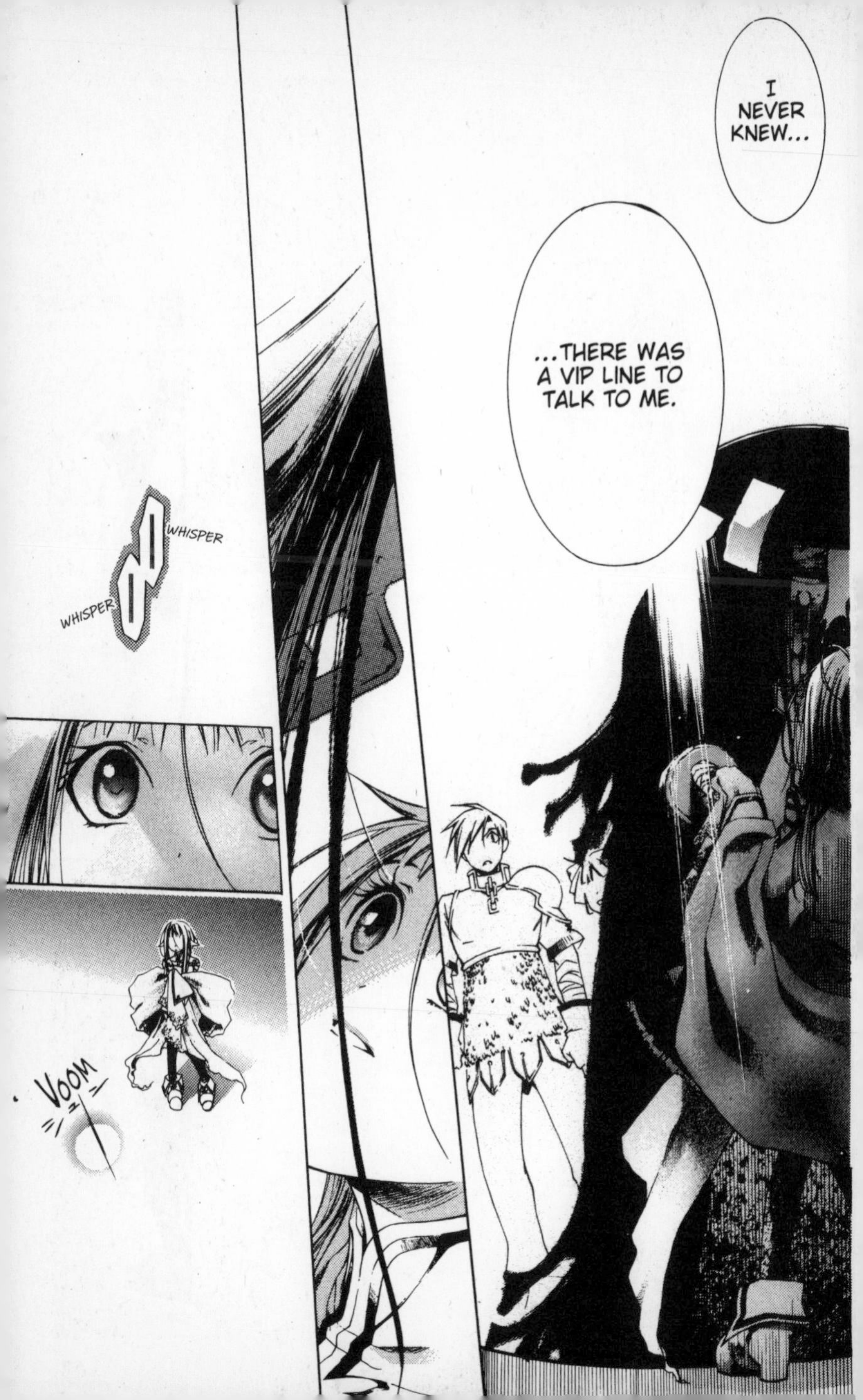
I NEVER KNEW...
...THERE WAS A VIP LINE TO TALK TO ME.
WHISPER
WHISPER
VOOM

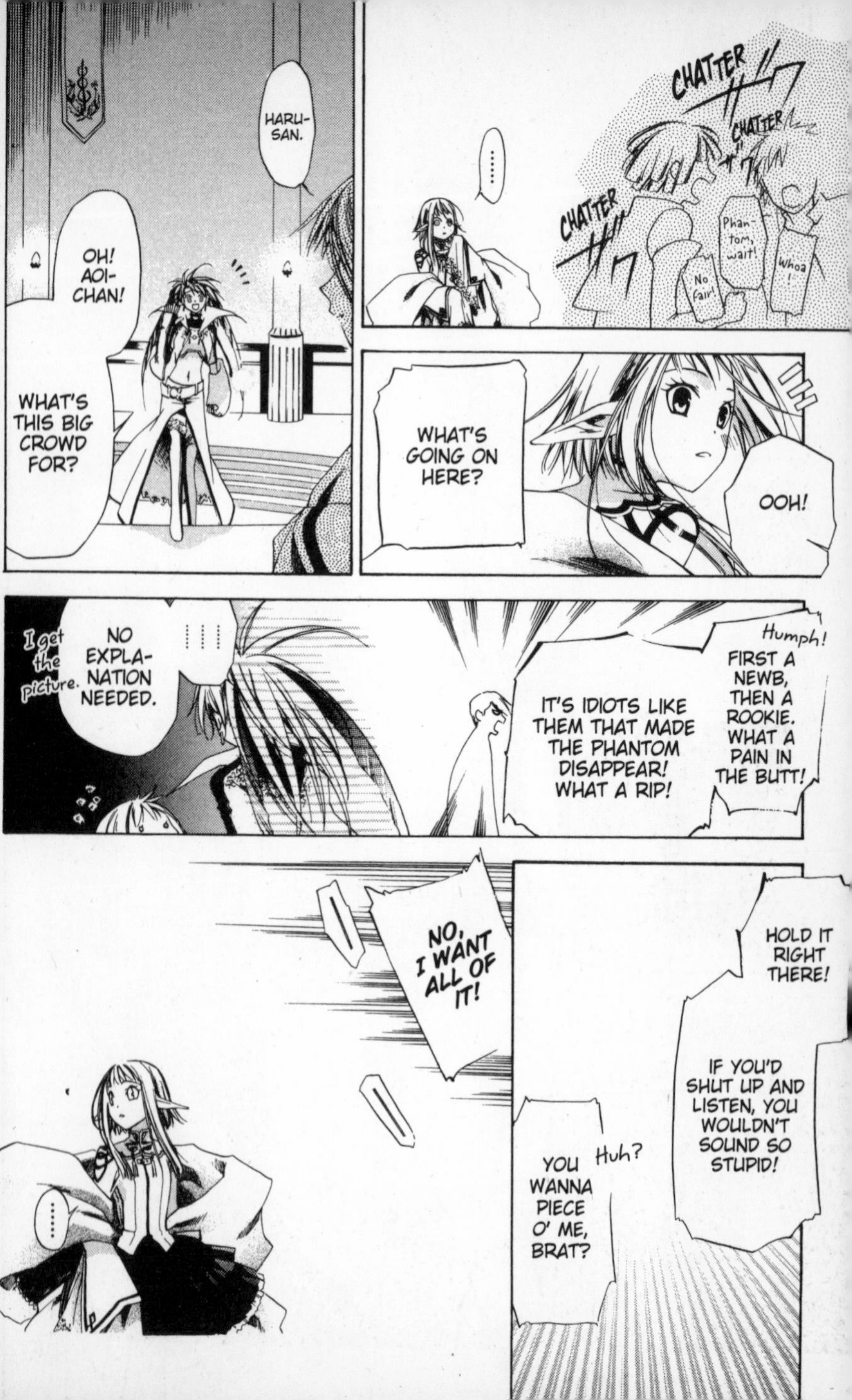
CHATTER
CHATTER
CHATTER
Phantom, wait!
Whoa!
No fair!
......
HARU-SAN.
OH! AOI-CHAN!
WHAT'S THIS BIG CROWD FOR?
OOH!
WHAT'S GOING ON HERE?
Humph!
FIRST A NEWB, THEN A ROOKIE. WHAT A PAIN IN THE BUTT!
IT'S IDIOTS LIKE THEM THAT MADE THE PHANTOM DISAPPEAR! WHAT A RIP!
....
NO EXPLANATION NEEDED.
I get the picture.
HOLD IT RIGHT THERE!
IF YOU'D SHUT UP AND LISTEN, YOU WOULDN'T SOUND SO STUPID!
NO, I WANT ALL OF IT!
Huh?
YOU WANNA PIECE O' ME, BRAT?
......

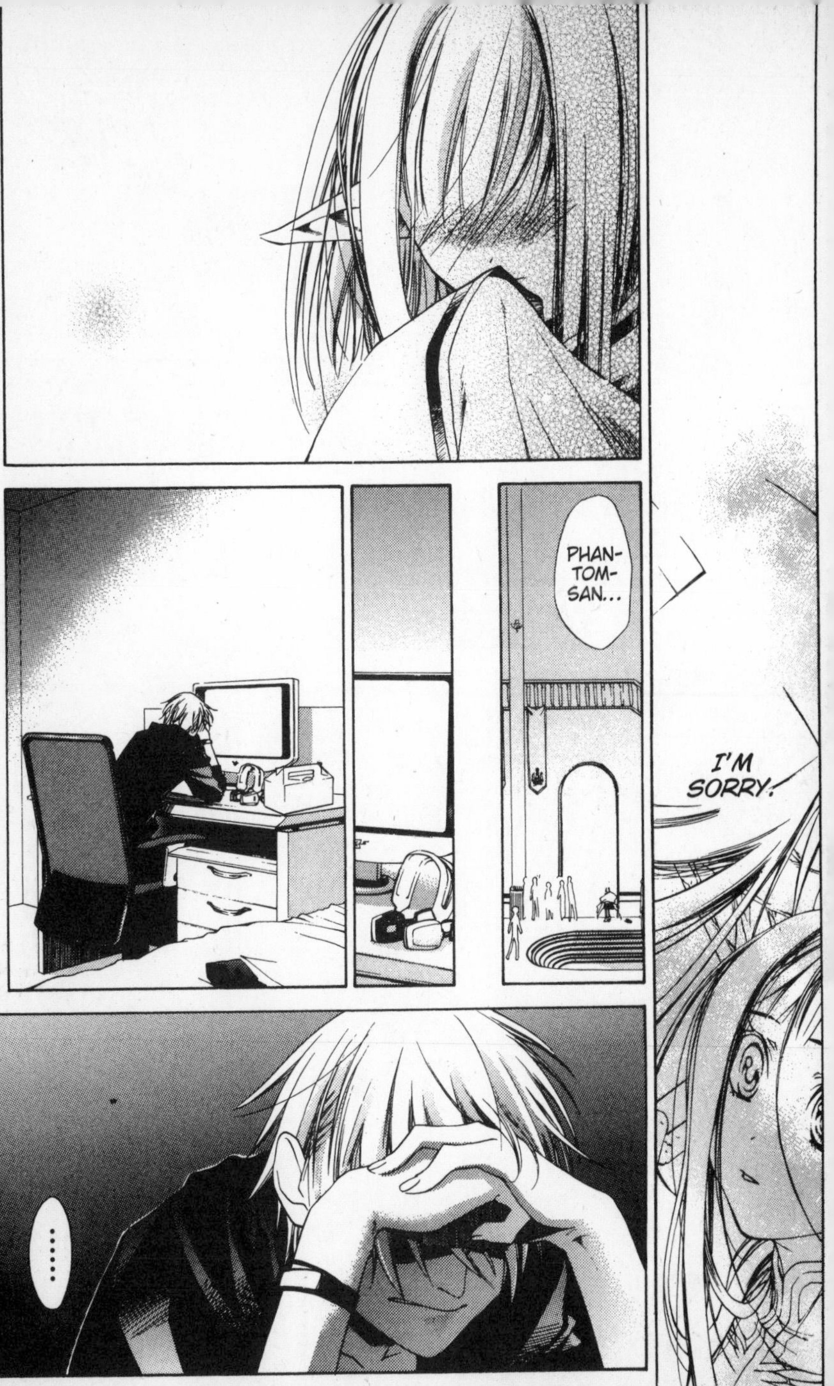
I'M SORRY!
PHAN-TOM-SAN...
......

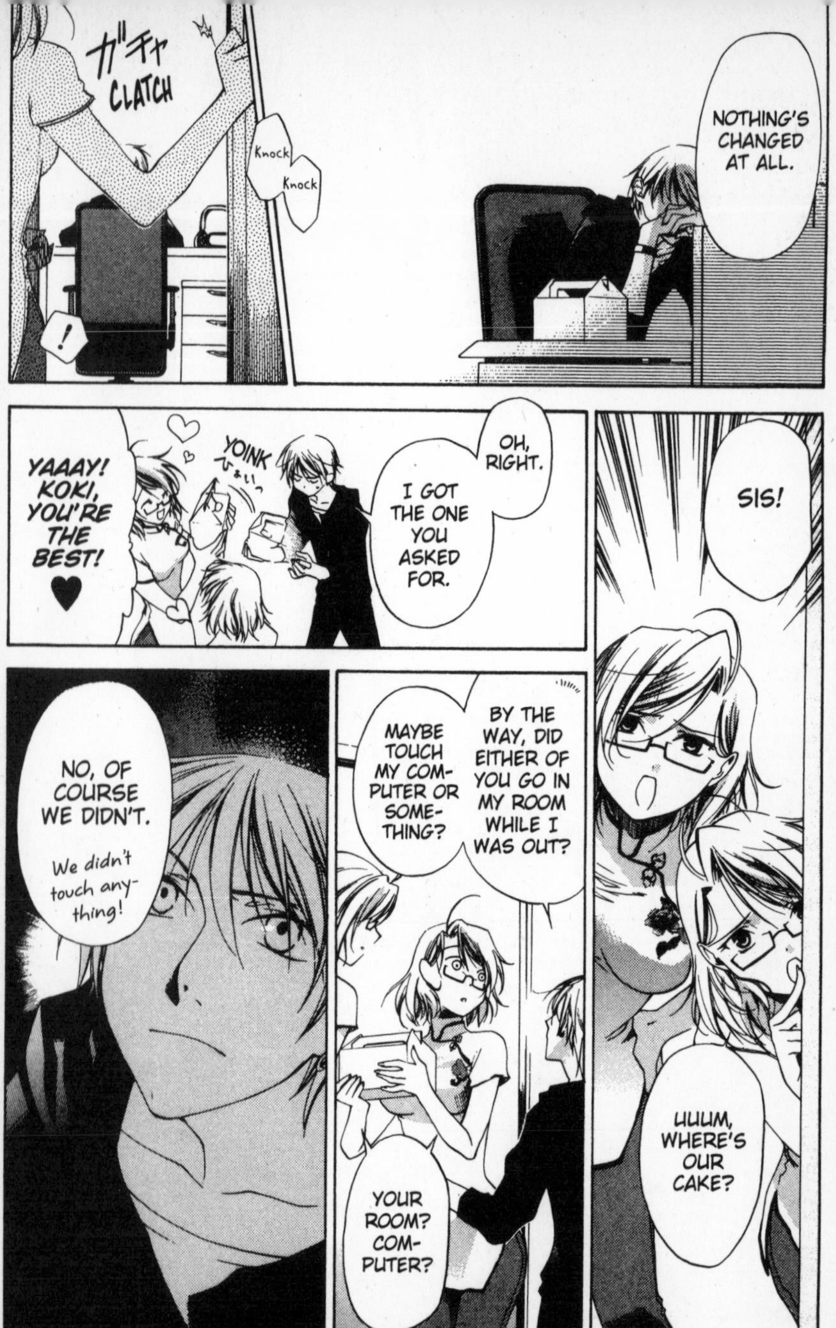
NOTHING'S CHANGED AT ALL.
ガチャ
CLATCH
Knock
Knock
!
SIS!
UUUM, WHERE'S OUR CAKE?
OH, RIGHT.
I GOT THE ONE YOU ASKED FOR.
YOINK
YAAAY! KOKI, YOU'RE THE BEST!
BY THE WAY, DID EITHER OF YOU GO IN MY ROOM WHILE I WAS OUT?
MAYBE TOUCH MY COM- PUTER OR SOME- THING?
YOUR ROOM? COM- PUTER?
NO, OF COURSE WE DIDN'T.
We didn't touch any- thing!

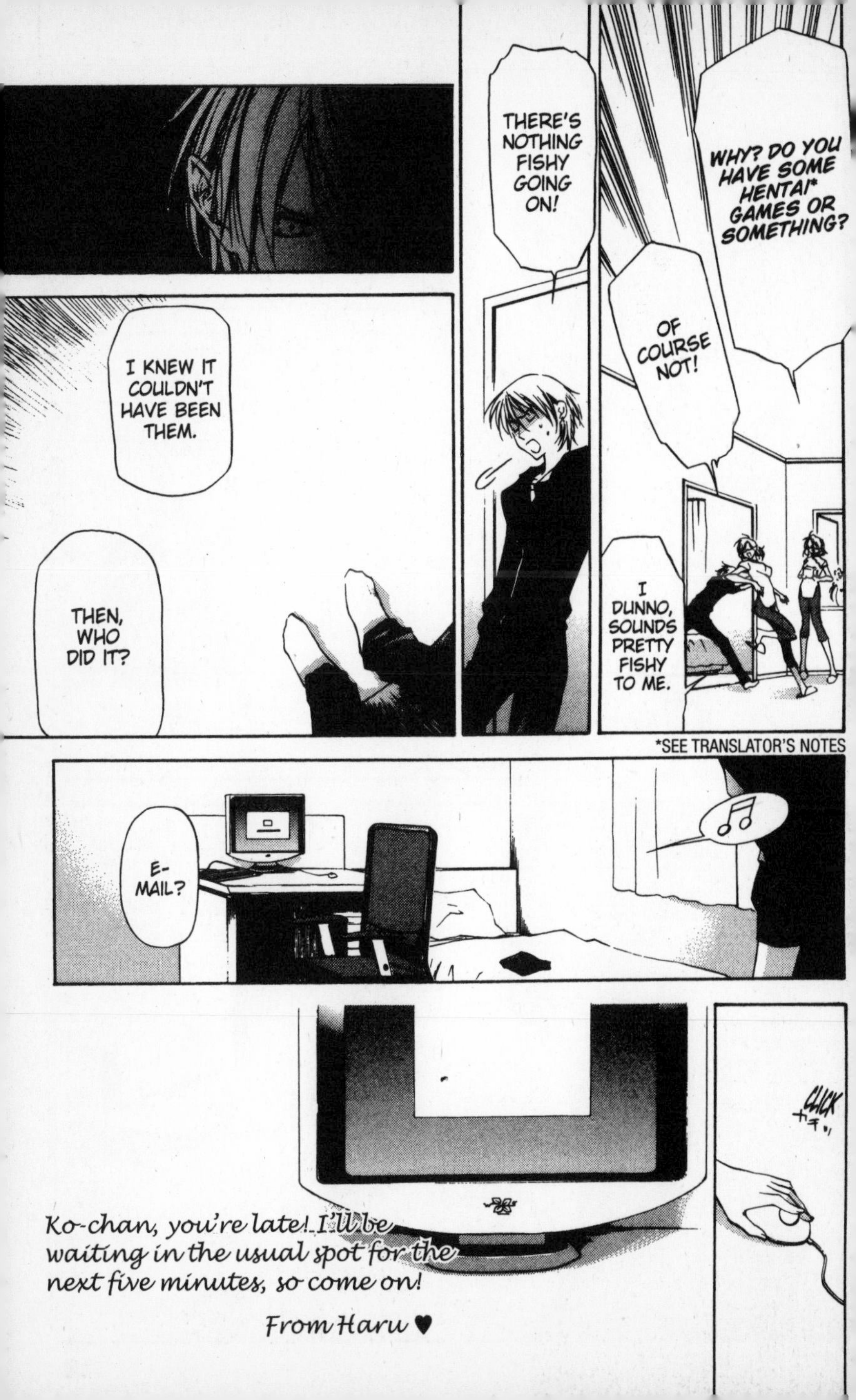
WHY? DO YOU HAVE SOME HENTAI* GAMES OR SOMETHING?
OF COURSE NOT!
I DUNNO, SOUNDS PRETTY FISHY TO ME.
THERE'S NOTHING FISHY GOING ON!
I KNEW IT COULDN'T HAVE BEEN THEM.
THEN, WHO DID IT?
♫
E-MAIL?
CLICK
Ko-chan, you're late! I'll be waiting in the usual spot for the next five minutes, so come on!
From Haru ♥

*SEE TRANSLATOR'S NOTES

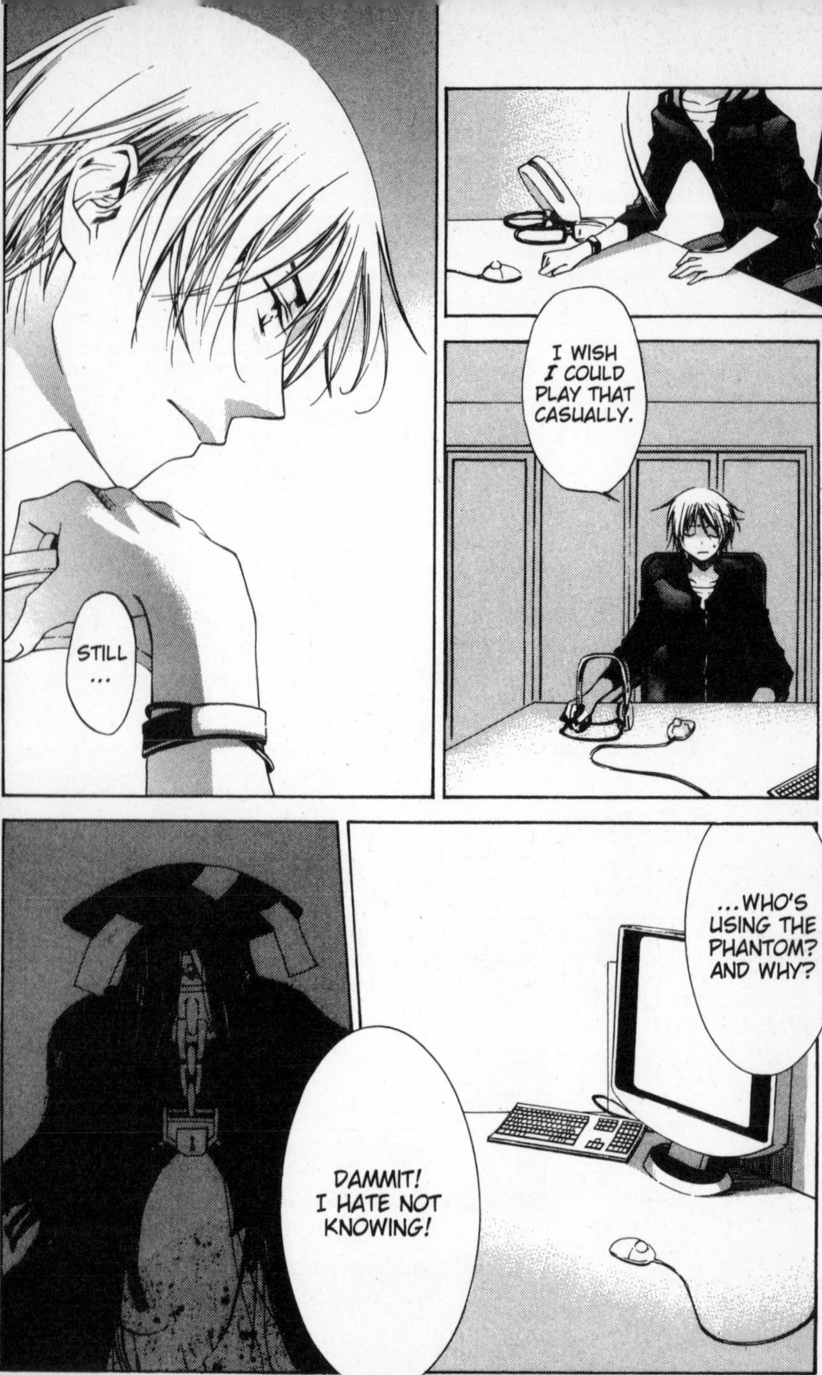
I WISH *I* COULD PLAY THAT CASUALLY.
STILL ...
...WHO'S USING THE PHANTOM? AND WHY?
DAMMIT! I HATE NOT KNOWING!

A Fruit of
Yggdrasil?

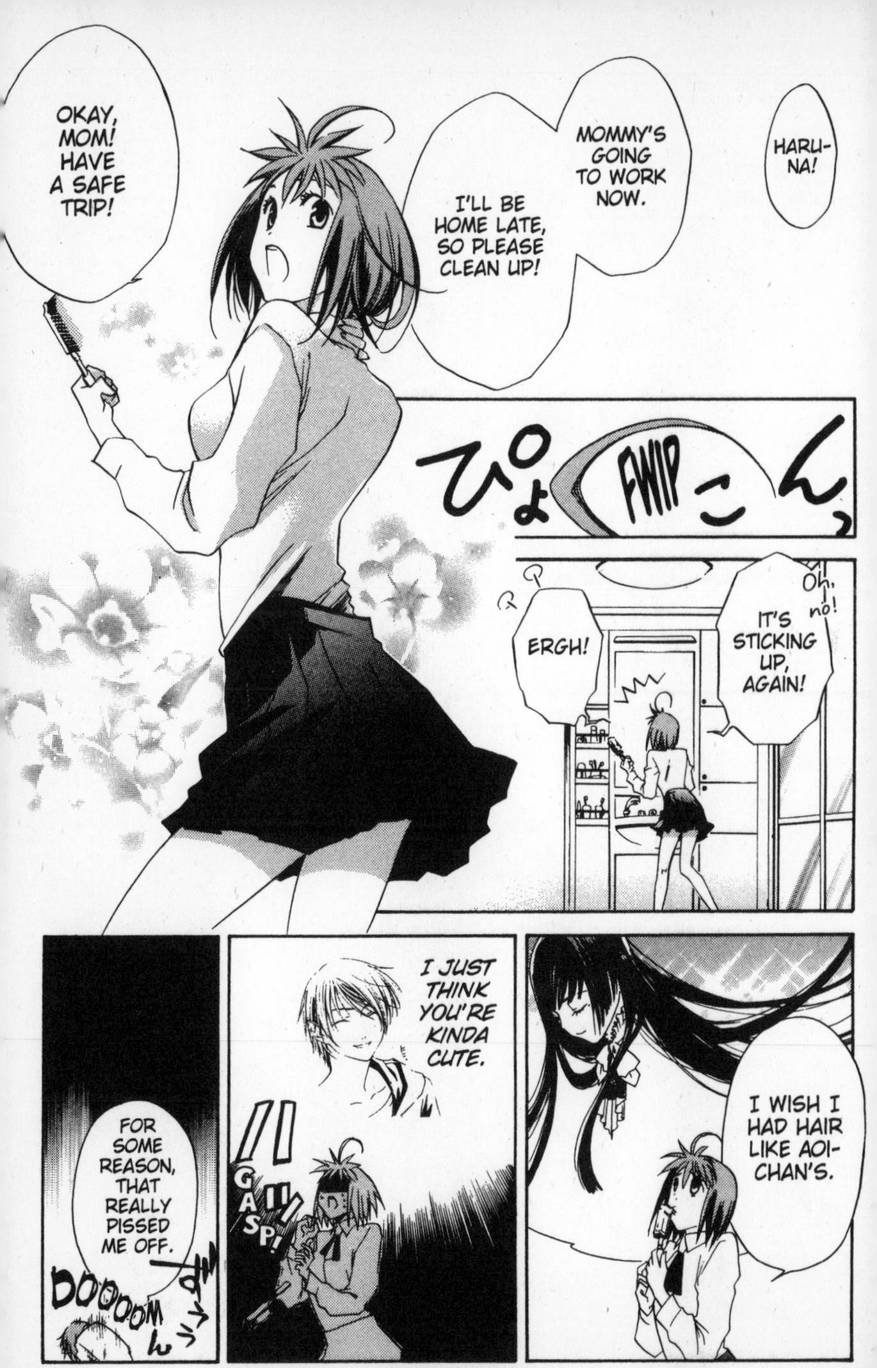
HARU-NA!
MOMMY'S GOING TO WORK NOW.
I'LL BE HOME LATE, SO PLEASE CLEAN UP!
OKAY, MOM! HAVE A SAFE TRIP!
ぴょこん
FWIP
Oh, no!
IT'S STICKING UP, AGAIN!
ERGH!
I WISH I HAD HAIR LIKE AOI-CHAN'S.
I JUST THINK YOU'RE KINDA CUTE.
GASP!
FOR SOME REASON, THAT REALLY PISSED ME OFF.
DOOOOM

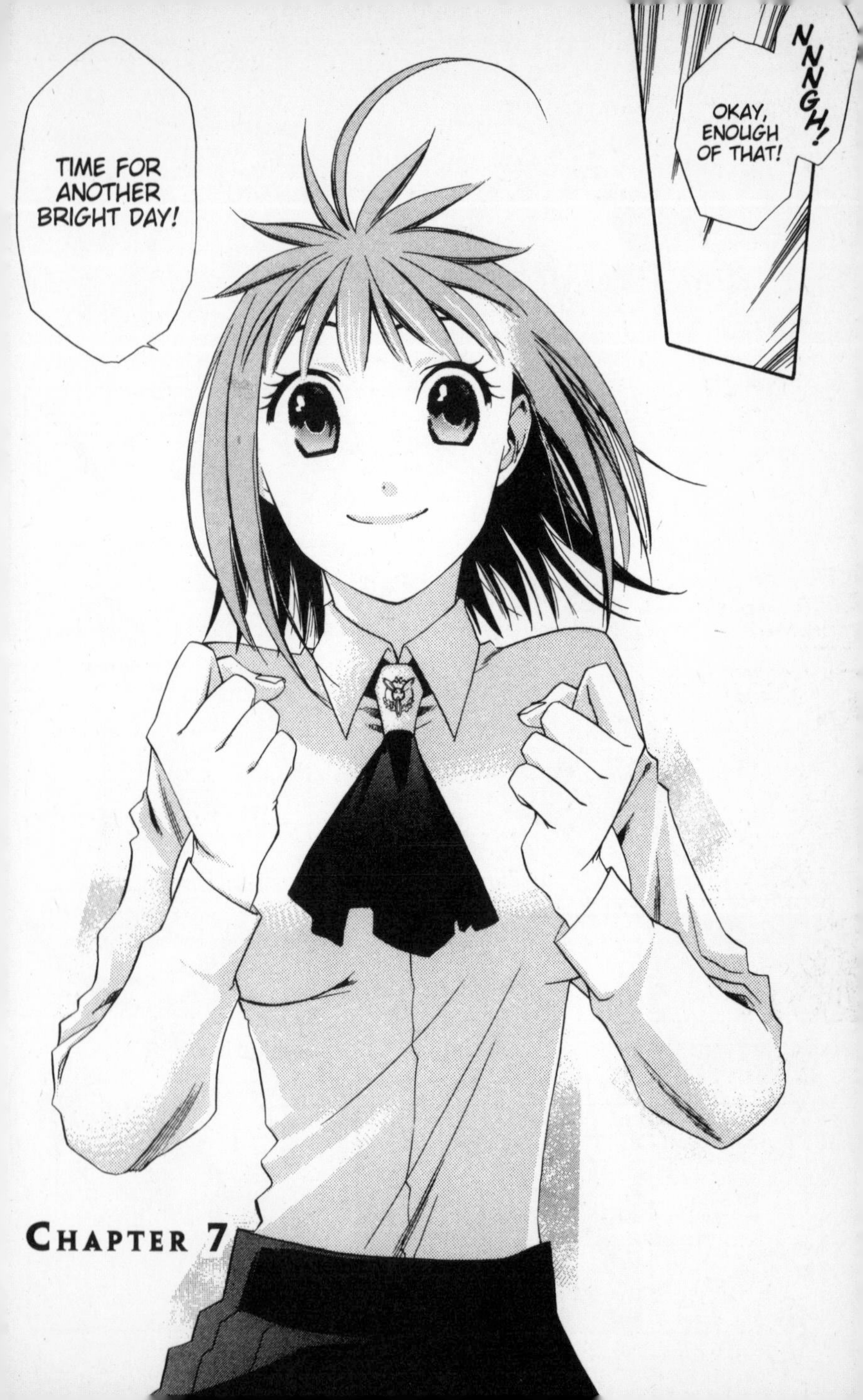
NNNGH!
OKAY, ENOUGH OF THAT!
TIME FOR ANOTHER BRIGHT DAY!

Chapter 7

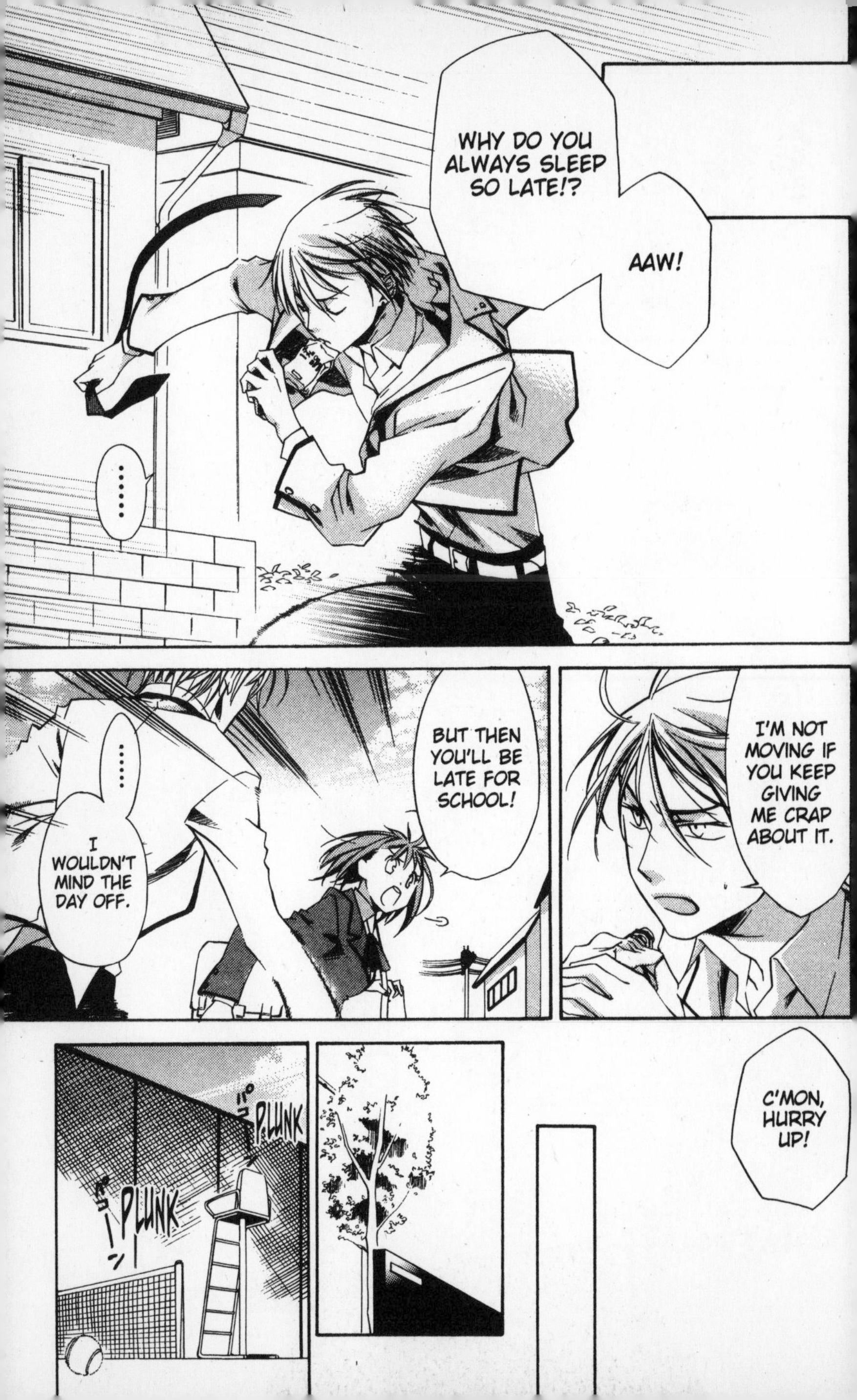
WHY DO YOU ALWAYS SLEEP SO LATE!?
AAW!
......
I'M NOT MOVING IF YOU KEEP GIVING ME CRAP ABOUT IT.
BUT THEN YOU'LL BE LATE FOR SCHOOL!
......
I WOULDN'T MIND THE DAY OFF.
C'MON, HURRY UP!
PLUNK
PLUNK

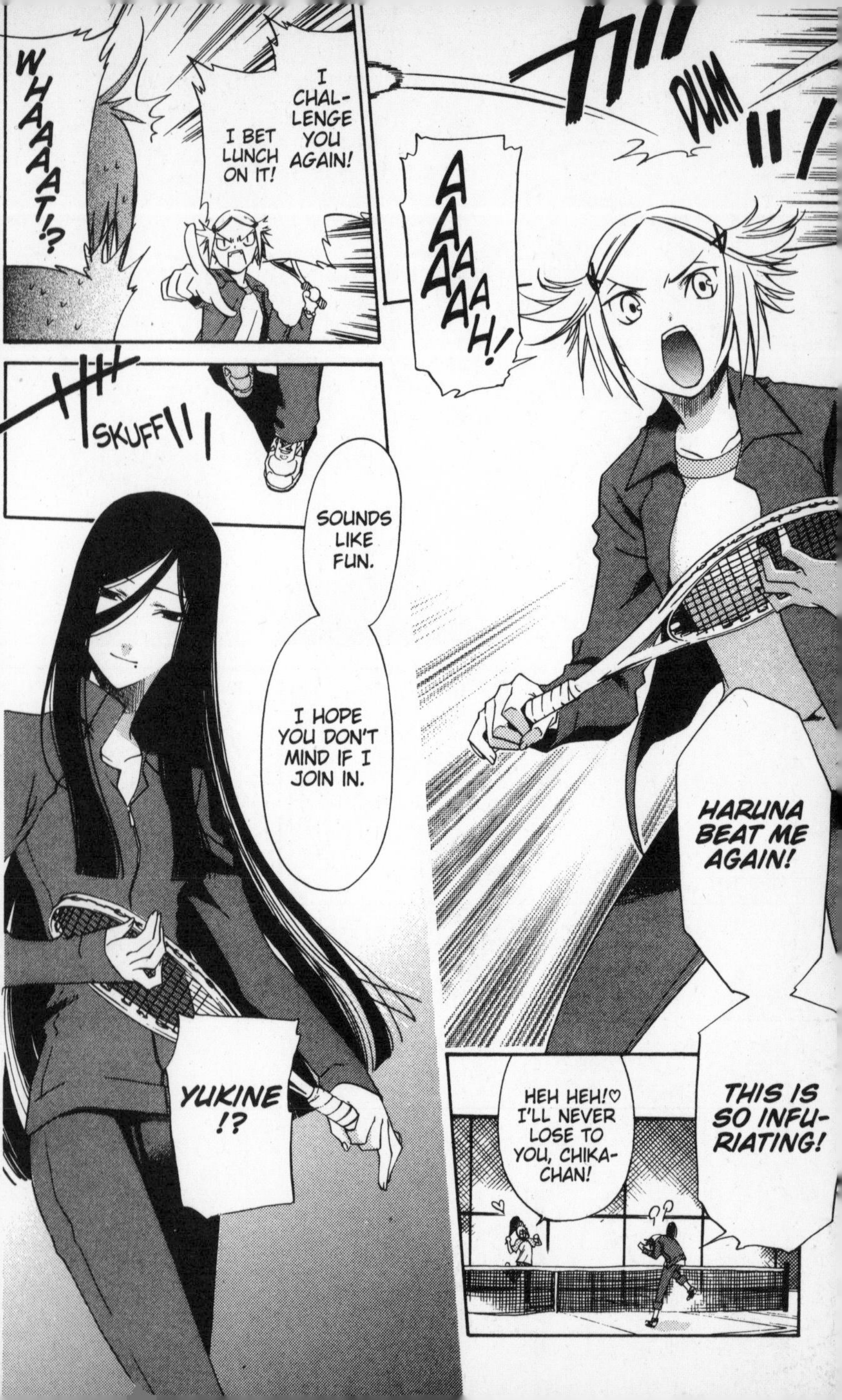
DUM
AAAAAAH!
HARUNA BEAT ME AGAIN!
THIS IS SO INFURIATING!
HEH HEH!♡ I'LL NEVER LOSE TO YOU, CHIKA-CHAN!
I CHALLENGE YOU AGAIN!
I BET LUNCH ON IT!
WHAAAAT!?
SKUFF
SOUNDS LIKE FUN.
I HOPE YOU DON'T MIND IF I JOIN IN.
YUKINE!?

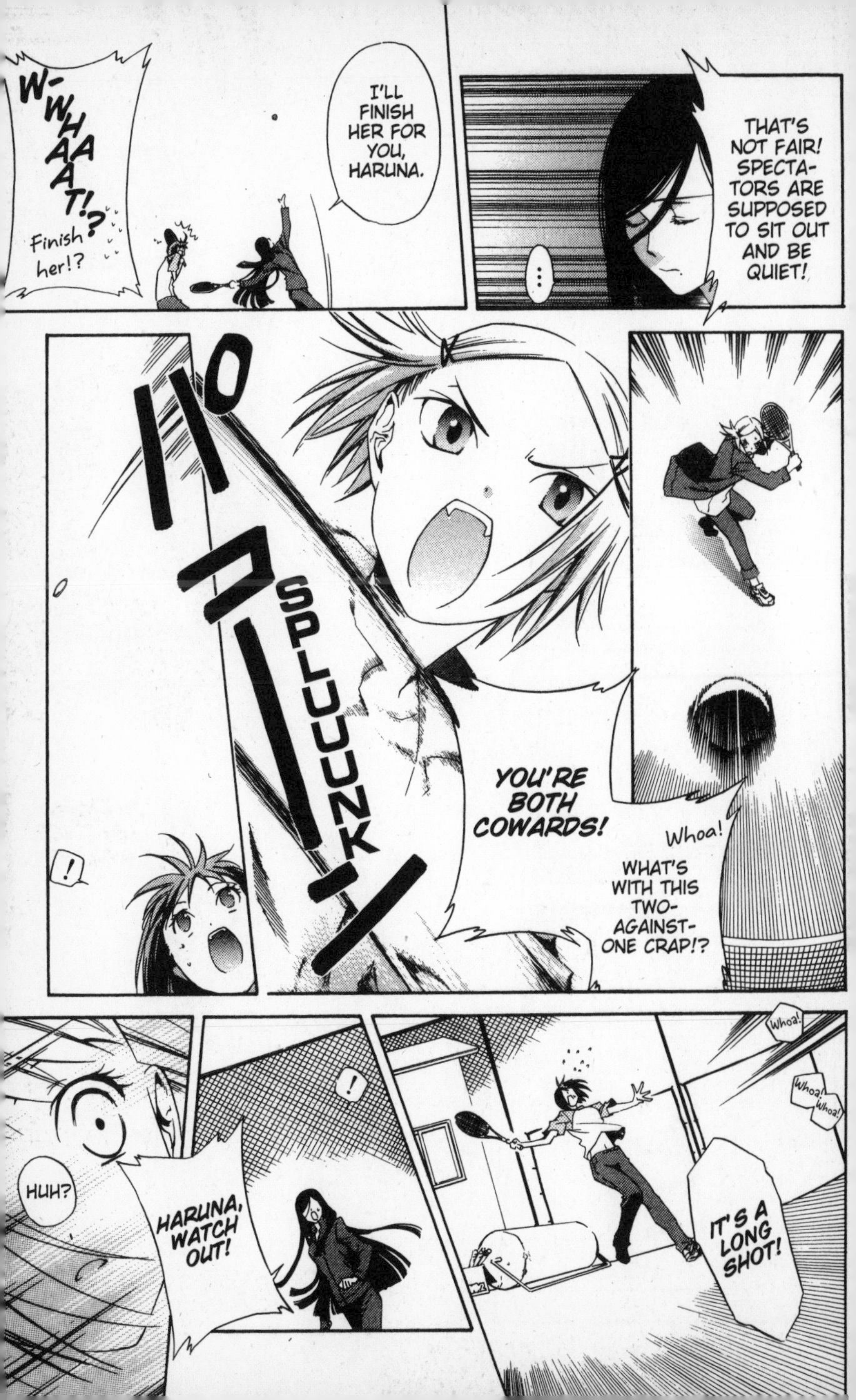
THAT'S NOT FAIR! SPECTATORS ARE SUPPOSED TO SIT OUT AND BE QUIET!
...
I'LL FINISH HER FOR YOU, HARUNA.
W-WHAAAT!?
Finish her!?
YOU'RE BOTH COWARDS!
Whoa!
WHAT'S WITH THIS TWO-AGAINST-ONE CRAP!?
SPLUUUNK
!
Whoa!
Whoa!
Whoa!
IT'S A LONG SHOT!
!
HARUNA, WATCH OUT!
HUH?

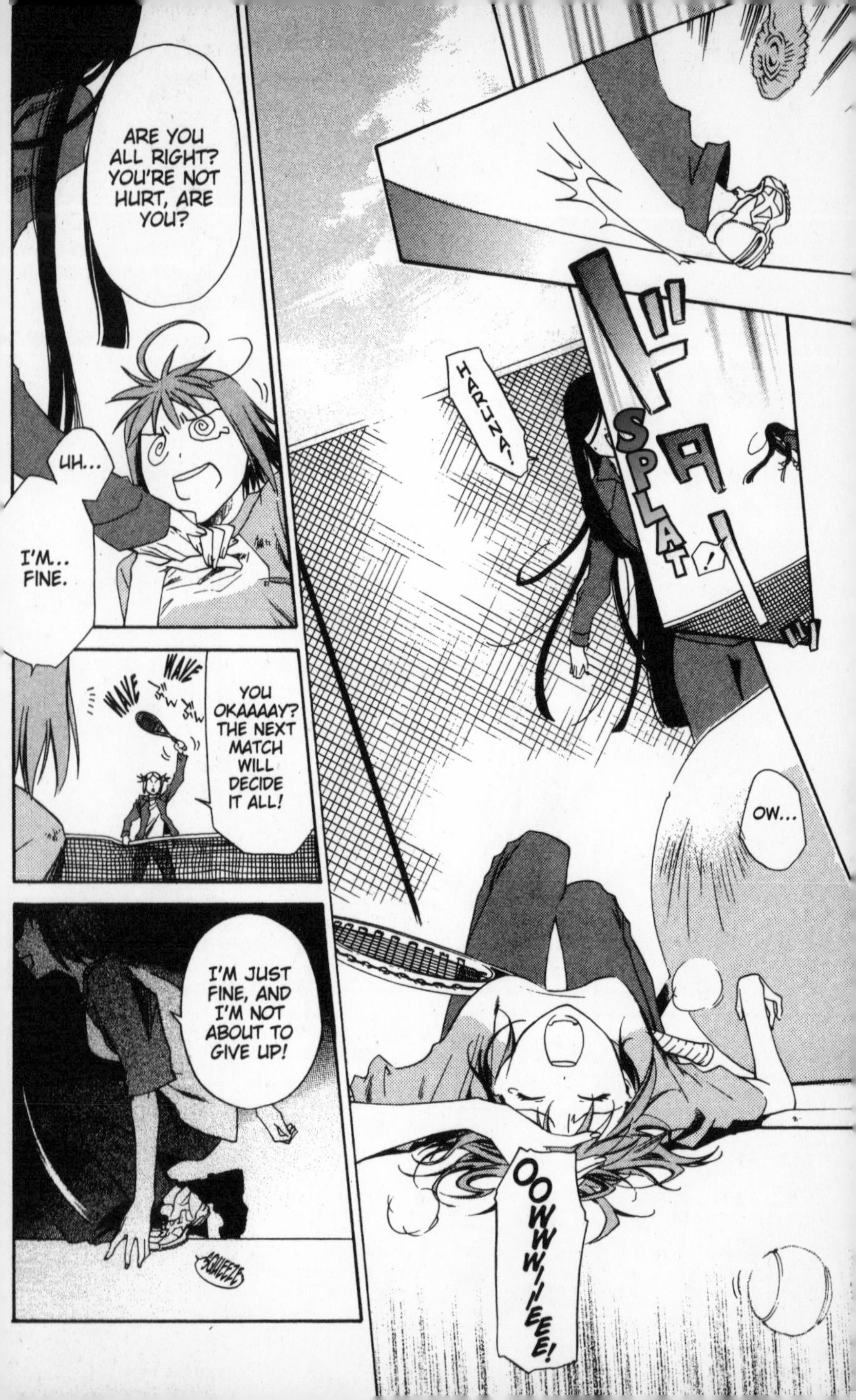
SPLAT!
HARUNA!
OW...
OOWWWIEEE!
ARE YOU ALL RIGHT? YOU'RE NOT HURT, ARE YOU?
UH...
I'M... FINE.
WAVE WAVE
YOU OKAAAAY? THE NEXT MATCH WILL DECIDE IT ALL!
I'M JUST FINE, AND I'M NOT ABOUT TO GIVE UP!
SQUEEZE

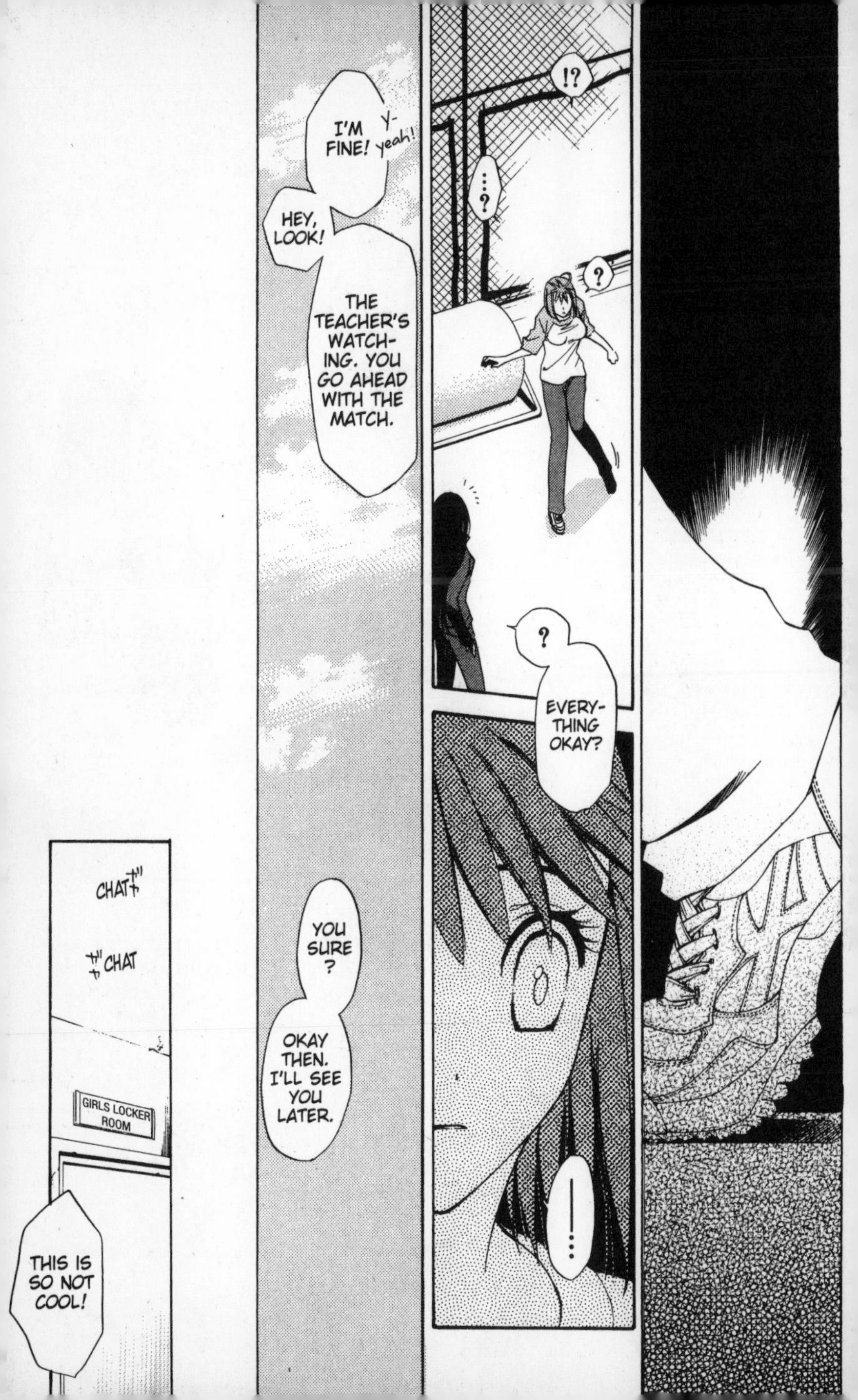

!?
...?
?
?
EVERY-THING OKAY?
!...
I'M FINE! Y-yeah!
HEY, LOOK!
THE TEACHER'S WATCHING. YOU GO AHEAD WITH THE MATCH.
YOU SURE?
OKAY THEN. I'LL SEE YOU LATER.
CHAT
CHAT
GIRLS LOCKER ROOM
THIS IS SO NOT COOL!

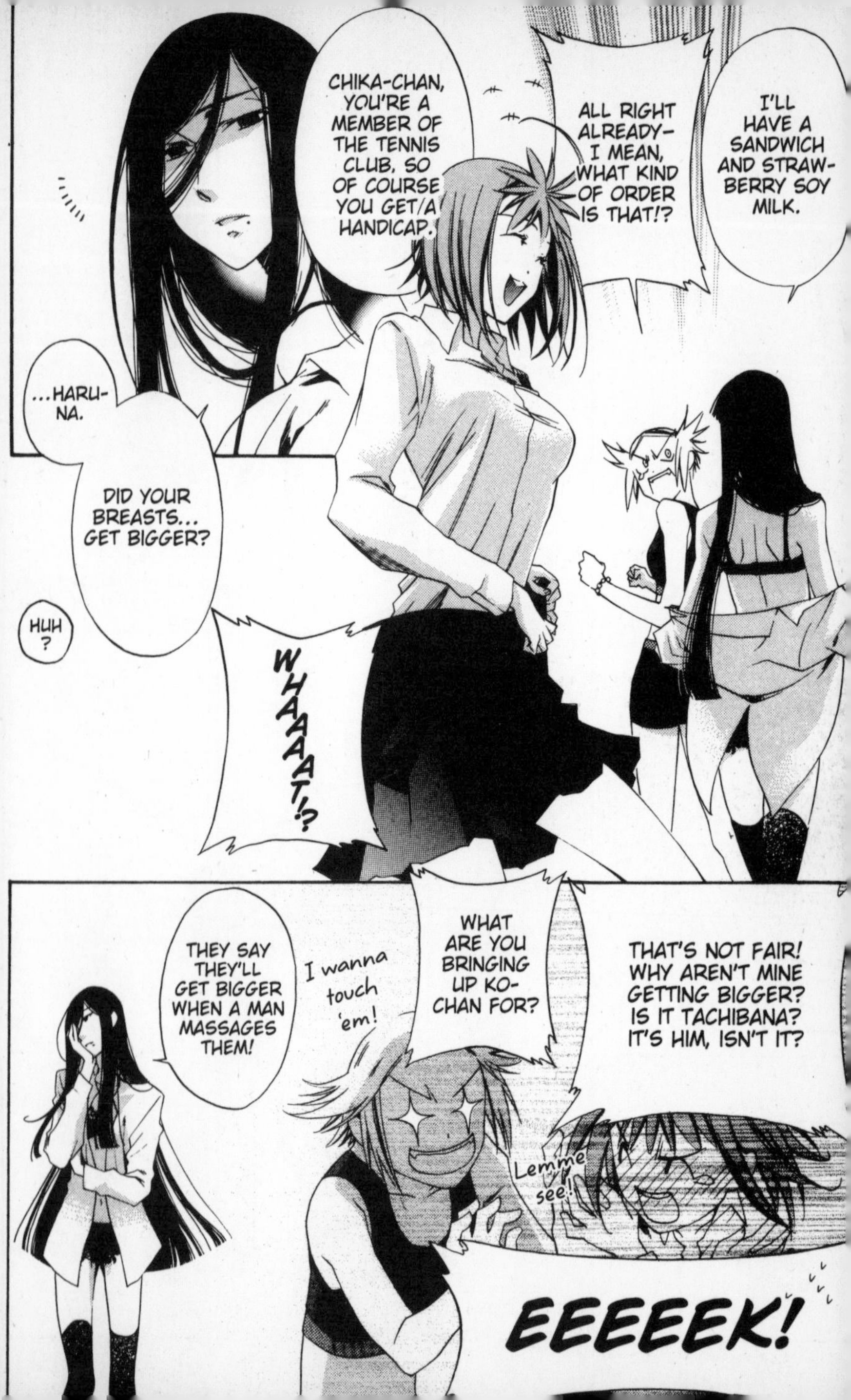
I'LL HAVE A SANDWICH AND STRAWBERRY SOY MILK.
ALL RIGHT ALREADY— I MEAN, WHAT KIND OF ORDER IS THAT!?
CHIKA-CHAN, YOU'RE A MEMBER OF THE TENNIS CLUB, SO OF COURSE YOU GET A HANDICAP.
...HARUNA.
DID YOUR BREASTS... GET BIGGER?
HUH?
WHAAAAT!?
THAT'S NOT FAIR! WHY AREN'T MINE GETTING BIGGER? IS IT TACHIBANA? IT'S HIM, ISN'T IT?
WHAT ARE YOU BRINGING UP KO-CHAN FOR?
Lemme see!
EEEEEK!
I wanna touch 'em!
THEY SAY THEY'LL GET BIGGER WHEN A MAN MASSAGES THEM!

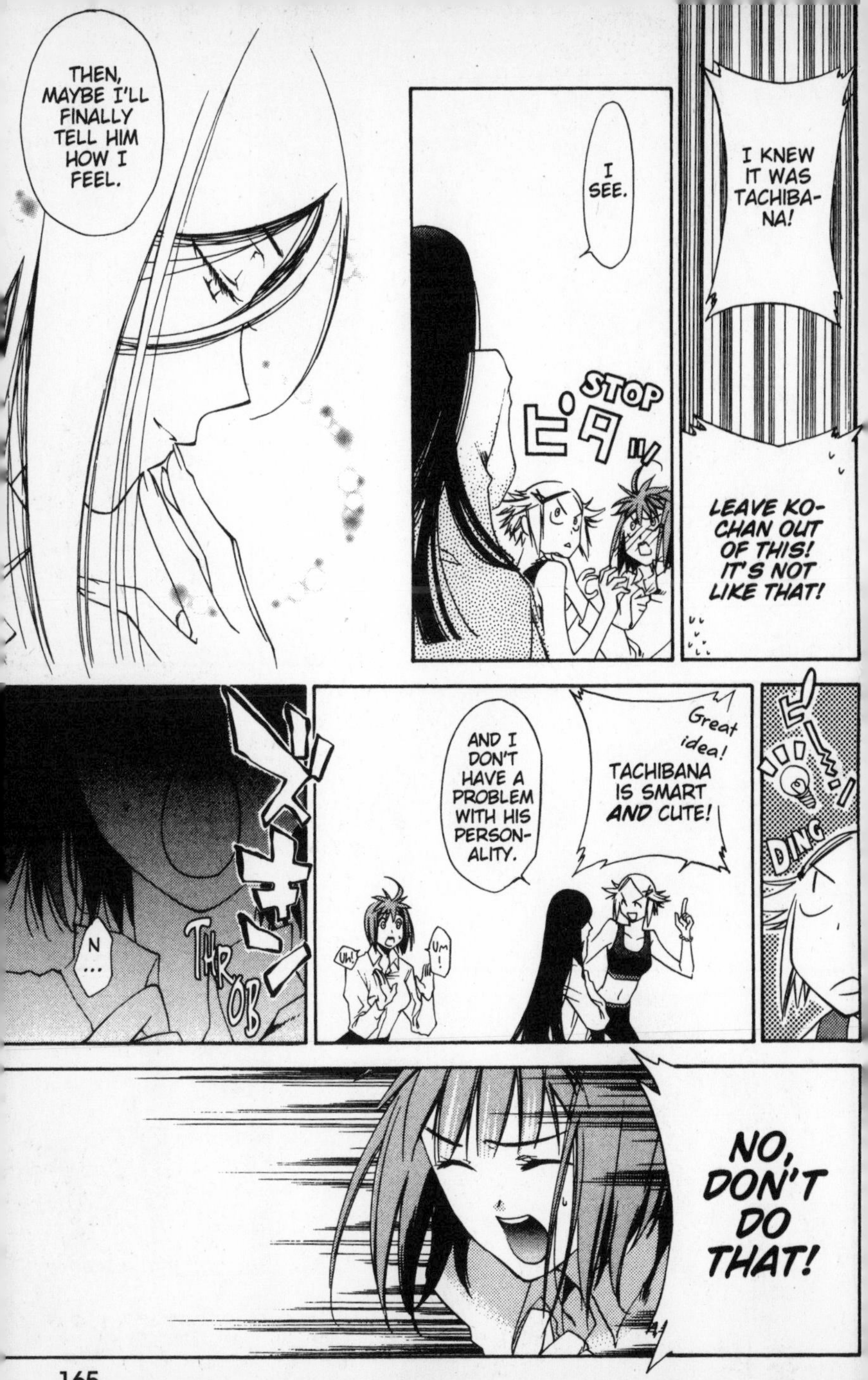
I KNEW IT WAS TACHIBA-NA!
LEAVE KO-CHAN OUT OF THIS! IT'S NOT LIKE THAT!
I SEE.
STOP
ピタッ
THEN, MAYBE I'LL FINALLY TELL HIM HOW I FEEL.
DING
Great idea!
TACHIBANA IS SMART AND CUTE!
AND I DON'T HAVE A PROBLEM WITH HIS PERSONALITY.
Um!
Uh!
THROB
N...
NO, DON'T DO THAT!

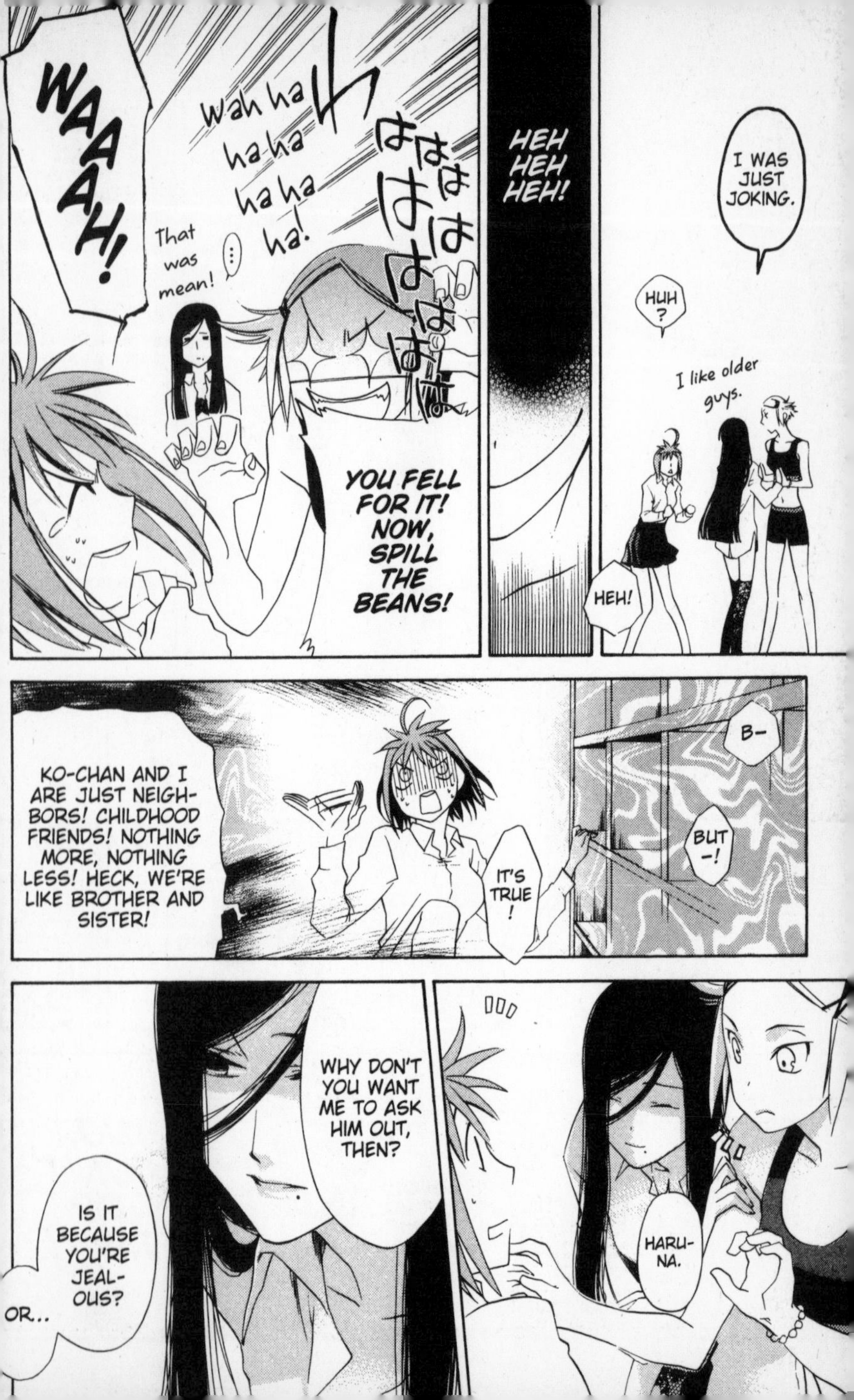
I WAS JUST JOKING.
HUH?
I like older guys.
HEH!
HEH HEH HEH!
わははははははは
wah ha ha ha ha ha ha!
YOU FELL FOR IT! NOW, SPILL THE BEANS!
That was mean!
...
WAAAAH!
B–
BUT –!
IT'S TRUE!
KO-CHAN AND I ARE JUST NEIGHBORS! CHILDHOOD FRIENDS! NOTHING MORE, NOTHING LESS! HECK, WE'RE LIKE BROTHER AND SISTER!
HARU-NA.
WHY DON'T YOU WANT ME TO ASK HIM OUT, THEN?
IS IT BECAUSE YOU'RE JEALOUS?
OR...

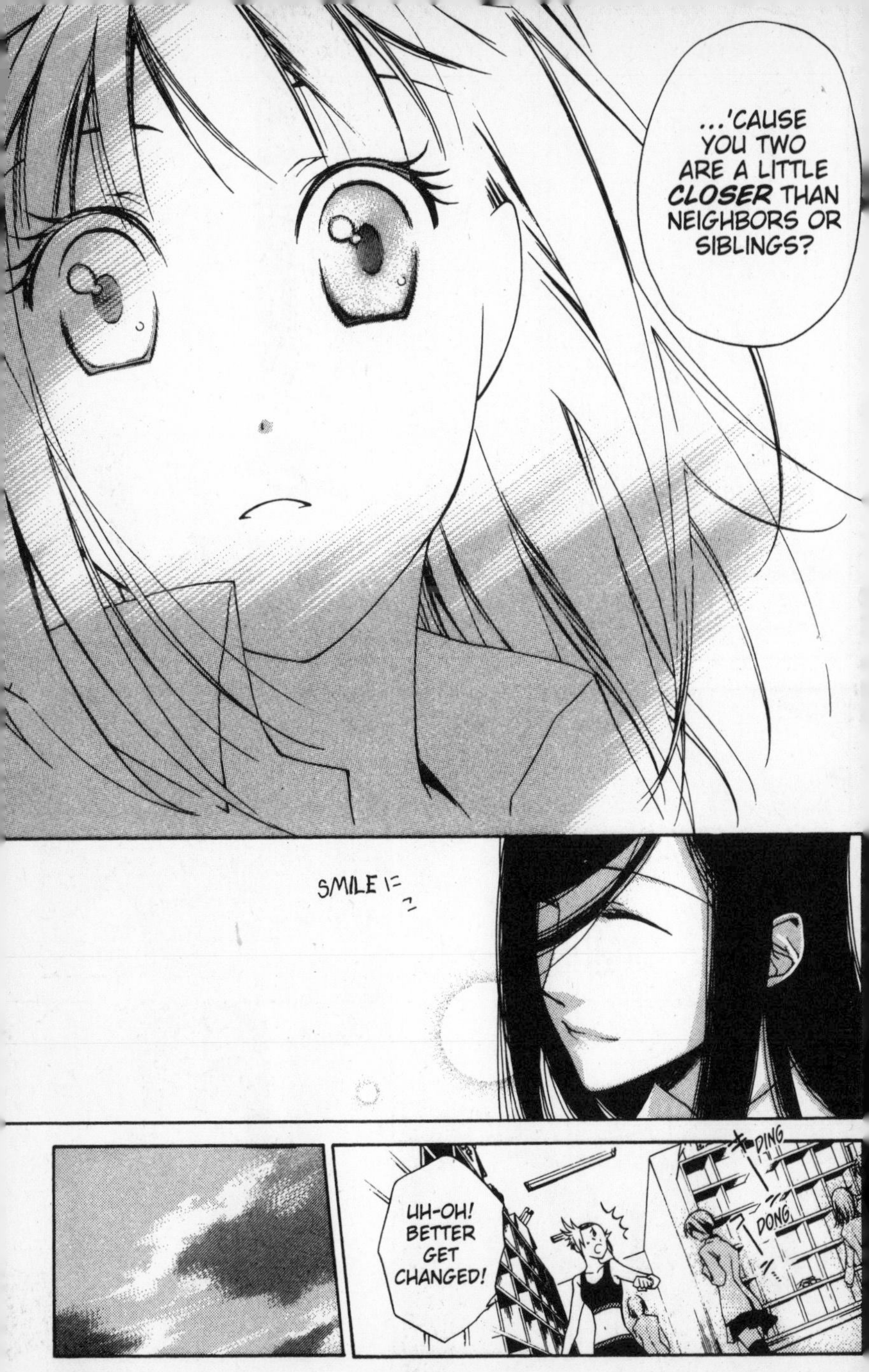
...'CAUSE YOU TWO ARE A LITTLE **CLOSER** THAN NEIGHBORS OR SIBLINGS?
SMILE
DING
DONG
UH-OH! BETTER GET CHANGED!

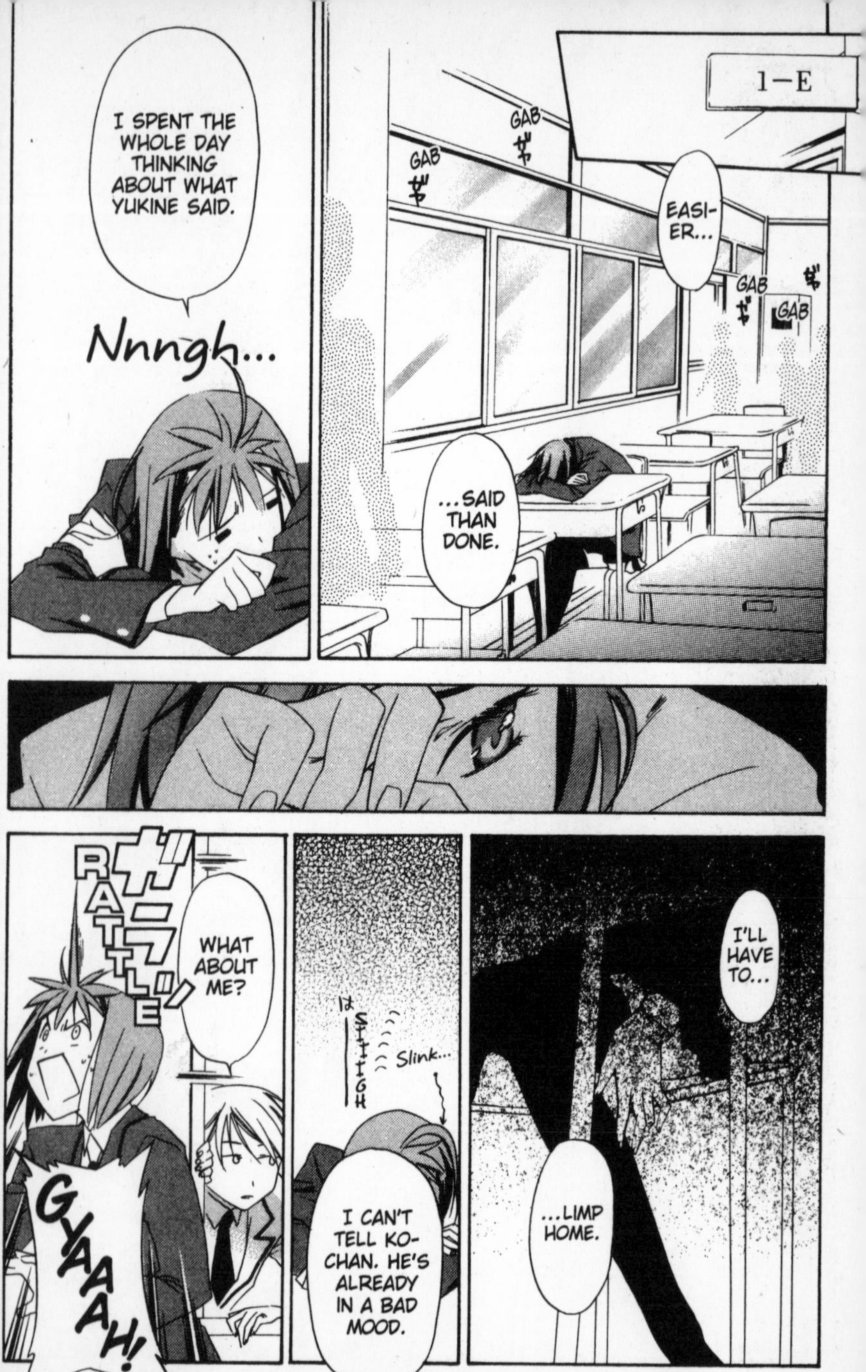
1—E
GAB
GAB
EASI-ER...
GAB
GAB
...SAID THAN DONE.
I SPENT THE WHOLE DAY THINKING ABOUT WHAT YUKINE SAID.
Nnngh...
I'LL HAVE TO...
...LIMP HOME.
SIIIGH
Slink...
I CAN'T TELL KO-CHAN. HE'S ALREADY IN A BAD MOOD.
RATTLE
WHAT ABOUT ME?
GYAAAH!

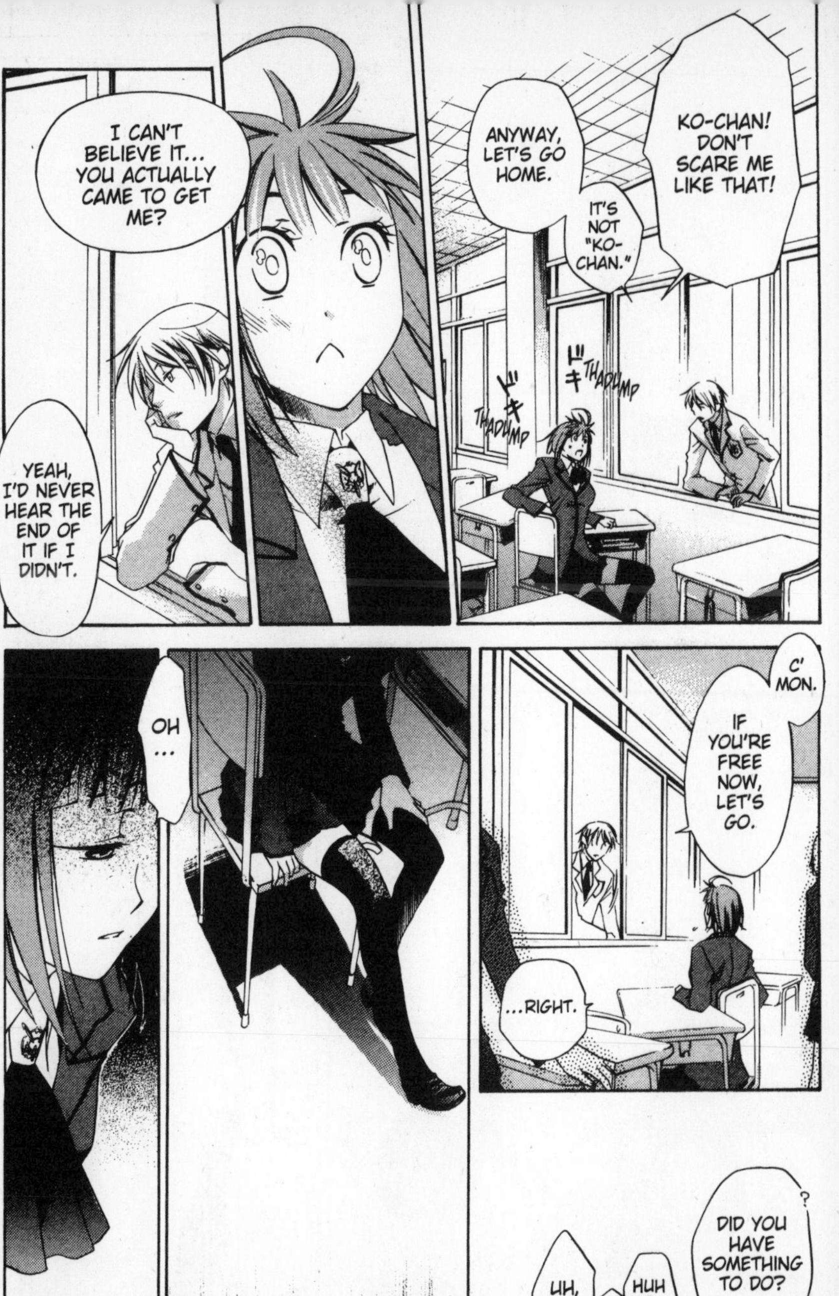
KO-CHAN! DON'T SCARE ME LIKE THAT!
IT'S NOT "KO-CHAN."
ANYWAY, LET'S GO HOME.
ドキ THADUMP
ドキ THADUMP
I CAN'T BELIEVE IT... YOU ACTUALLY CAME TO GET ME?
YEAH, I'D NEVER HEAR THE END OF IT IF I DIDN'T.
C'MON.
IF YOU'RE FREE NOW, LET'S GO.
...RIGHT.
DID YOU HAVE SOMETHING TO DO?
HUH?
OH.
UH, NO.
OH...

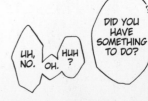

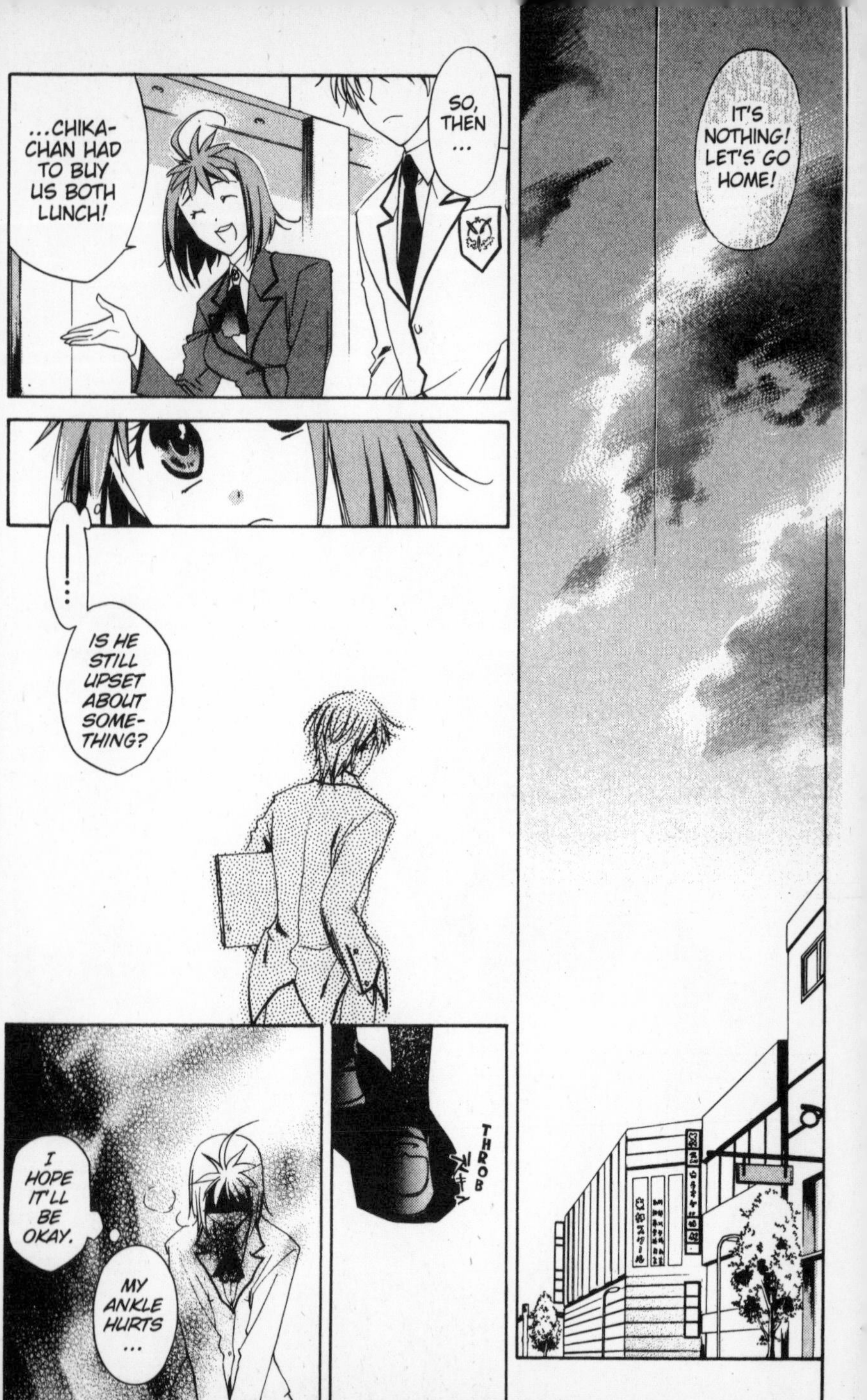
IT'S NOTHING! LET'S GO HOME!
SO, THEN ...
...CHIKA-CHAN HAD TO BUY US BOTH LUNCH!
......
IS HE STILL UPSET ABOUT SOMETHING?
THROB
I HOPE IT'LL BE OKAY.
MY ANKLE HURTS ...

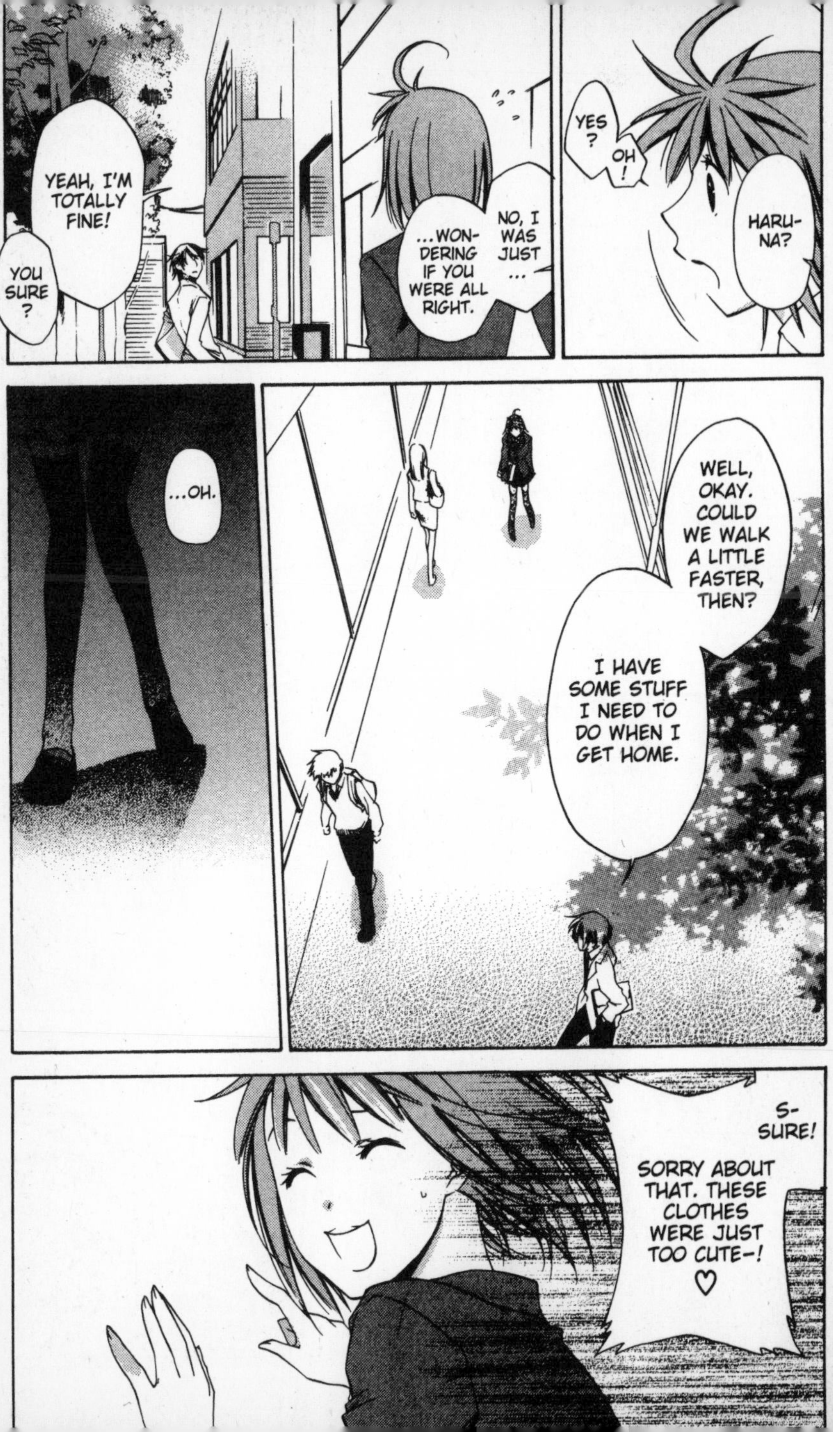
HARU-NA?
YES?
OH!
NO, I WAS JUST...
...WON-DERING IF YOU WERE ALL RIGHT.
YEAH, I'M TOTALLY FINE!
YOU SURE?
WELL, OKAY. COULD WE WALK A LITTLE FASTER, THEN?
I HAVE SOME STUFF I NEED TO DO WHEN I GET HOME.
...OH.
S-SURE!
SORRY ABOUT THAT. THESE CLOTHES WERE JUST TOO CUTE-! ♥

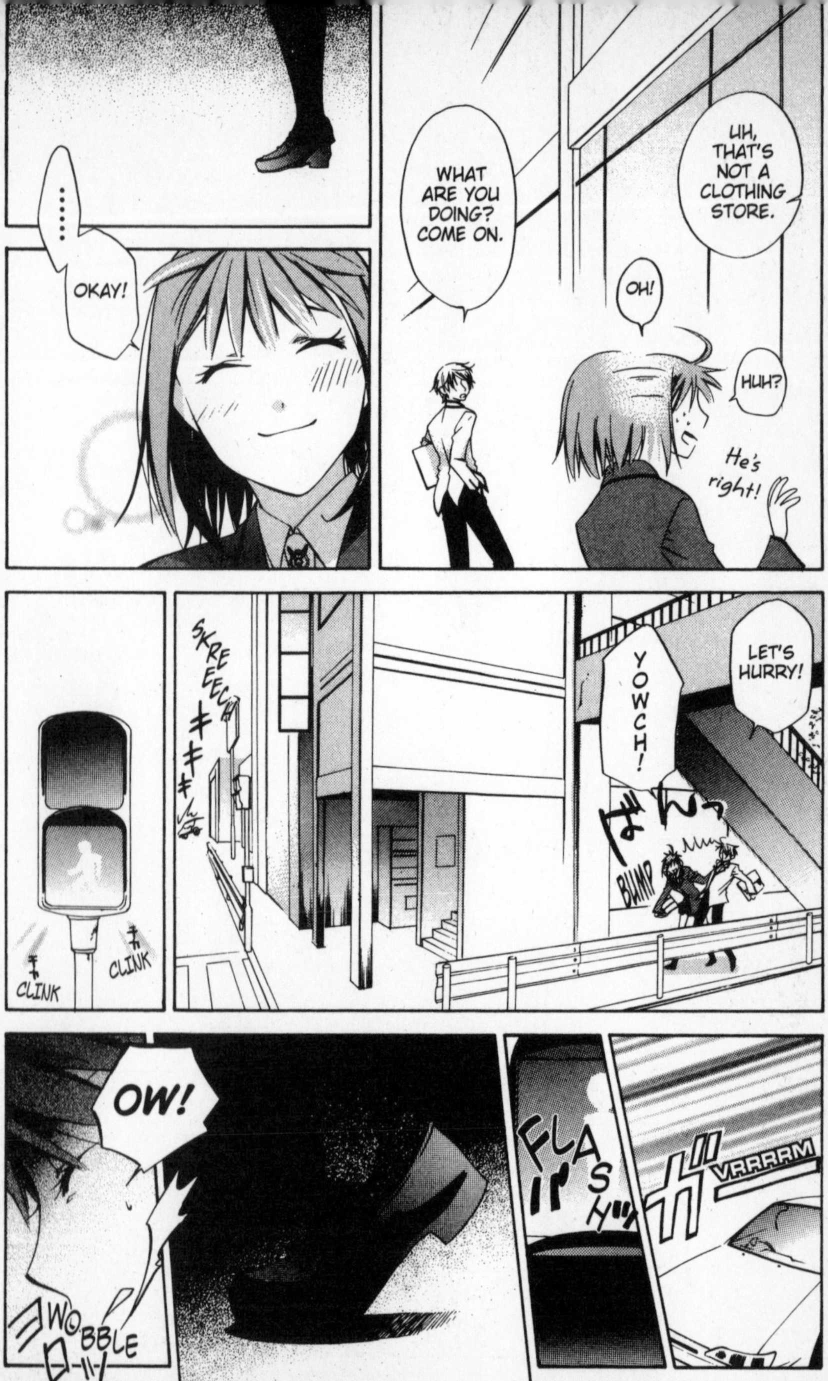
UH, THAT'S NOT A CLOTHING STORE.
WHAT ARE YOU DOING? COME ON.
OH!
HUH?
He's right!
......
OKAY!
LET'S HURRY!
YOWCH!
BUMP
SKREEECH
CLINK
CLINK
VRRRRM
FLASH
OW!
WOBBLE

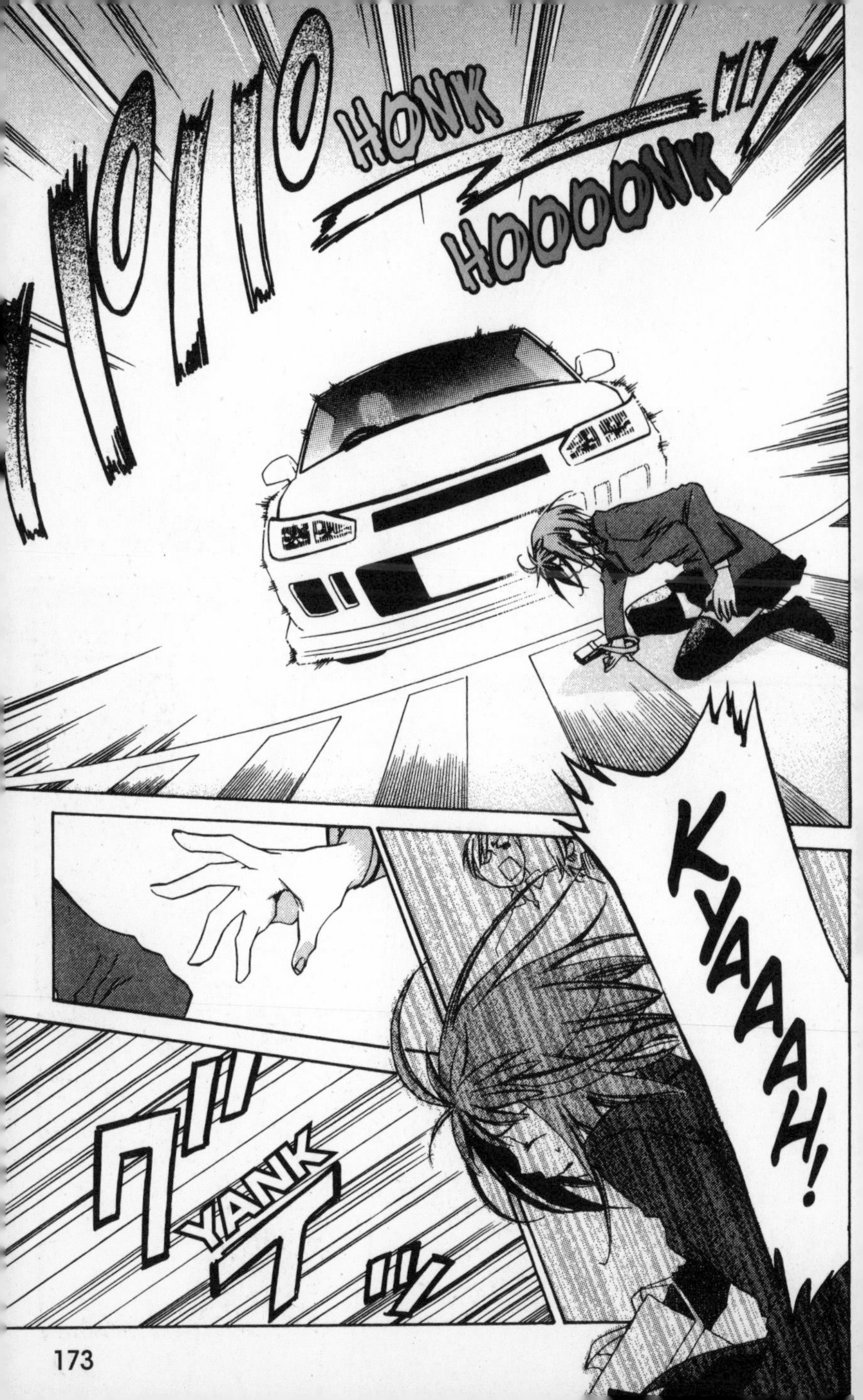
HONK
HOOOONK!!
KYAAAAH!
YANK

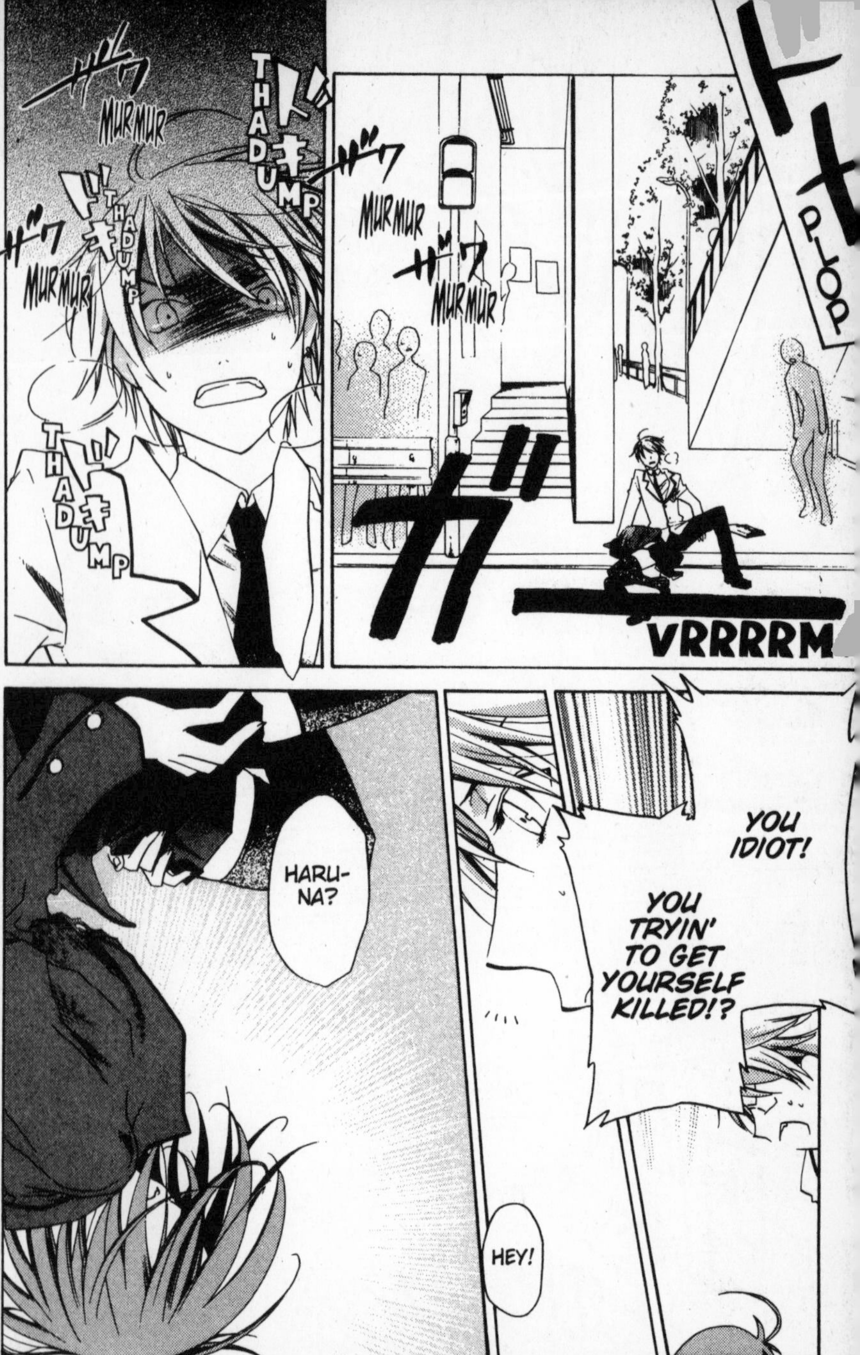
PLOP
MURMUR
MURMUR
VRRRRM
THADUMP
MURMUR
THADUMP
MURMUR
THADUMP
YOU IDIOT!
YOU TRYIN' TO GET YOURSELF KILLED!?
HEY!
HARU-NA?

A Fruit of Yggdrasil

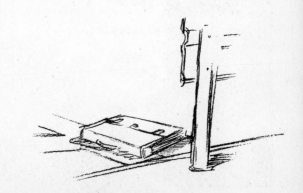

Chapter 8

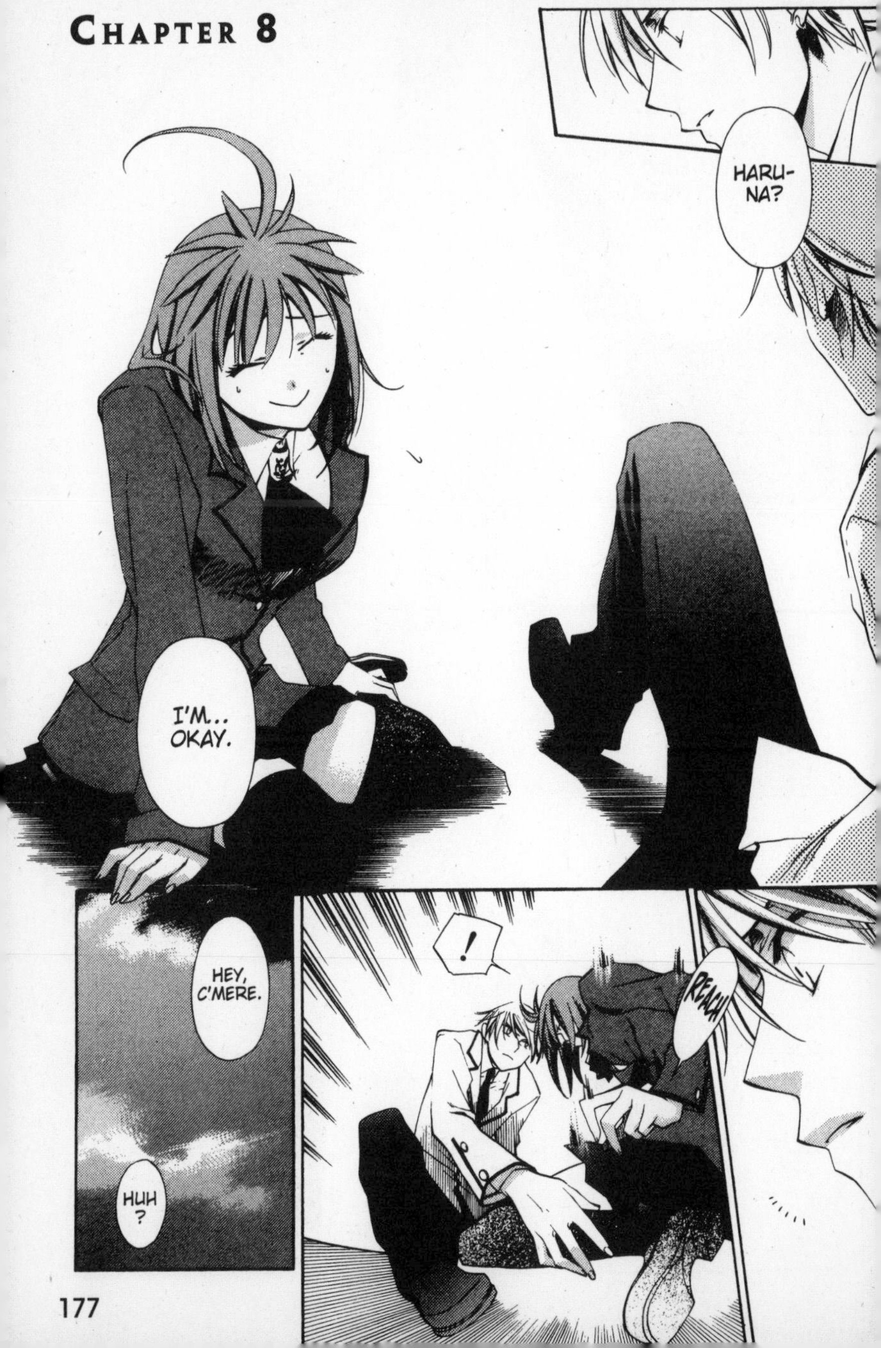

HARU-NA?
I'M... OKAY.
!
REACH
HEY, C'MERE.
HUH?

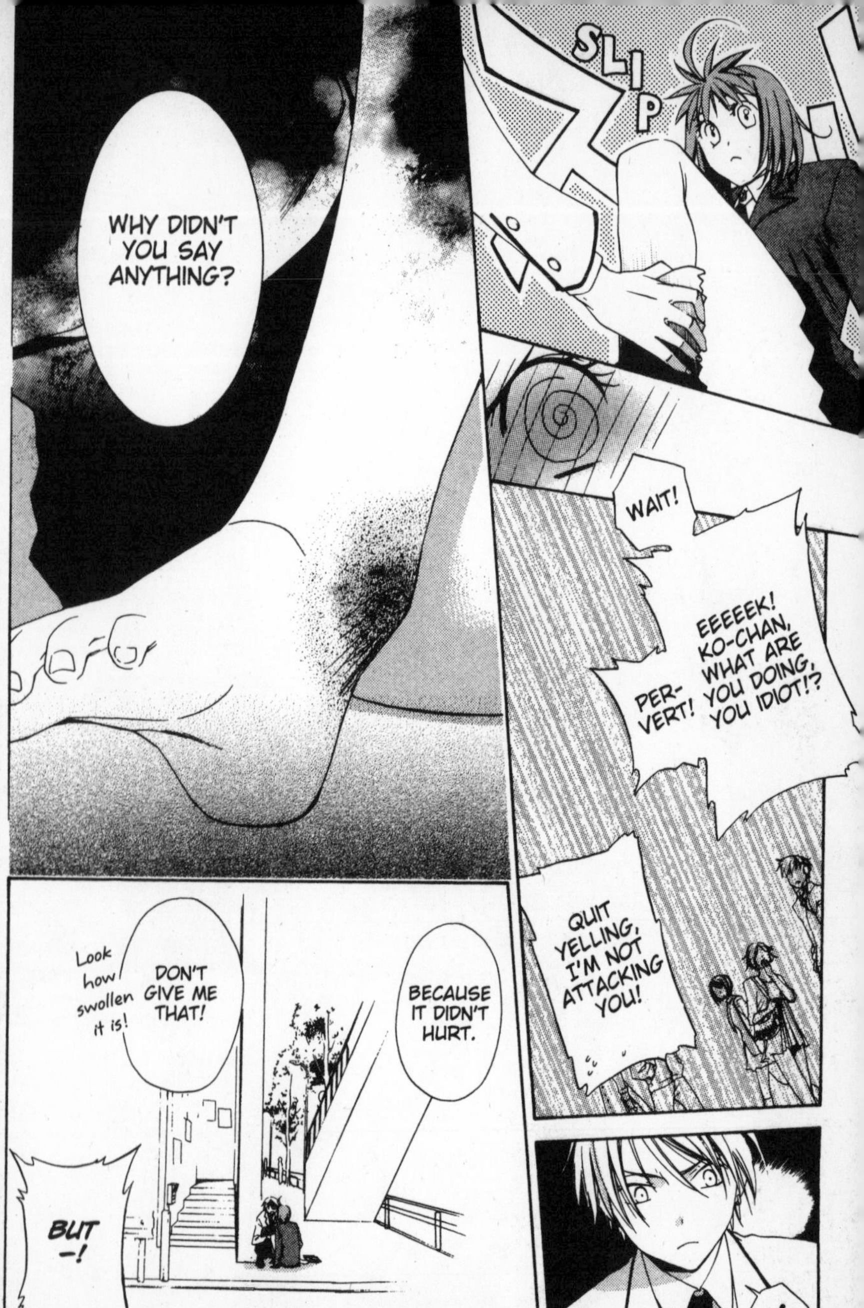
SLIP
WAIT!
EEEEEK! KO-CHAN, WHAT ARE YOU DOING, YOU IDIOT!?
PER-VERT!
QUIT YELLING, I'M NOT ATTACKING YOU!
!
WHY DIDN'T YOU SAY ANYTHING?
BECAUSE IT DIDN'T HURT.
DON'T GIVE ME THAT!
Look how swollen it is!
BUT-!

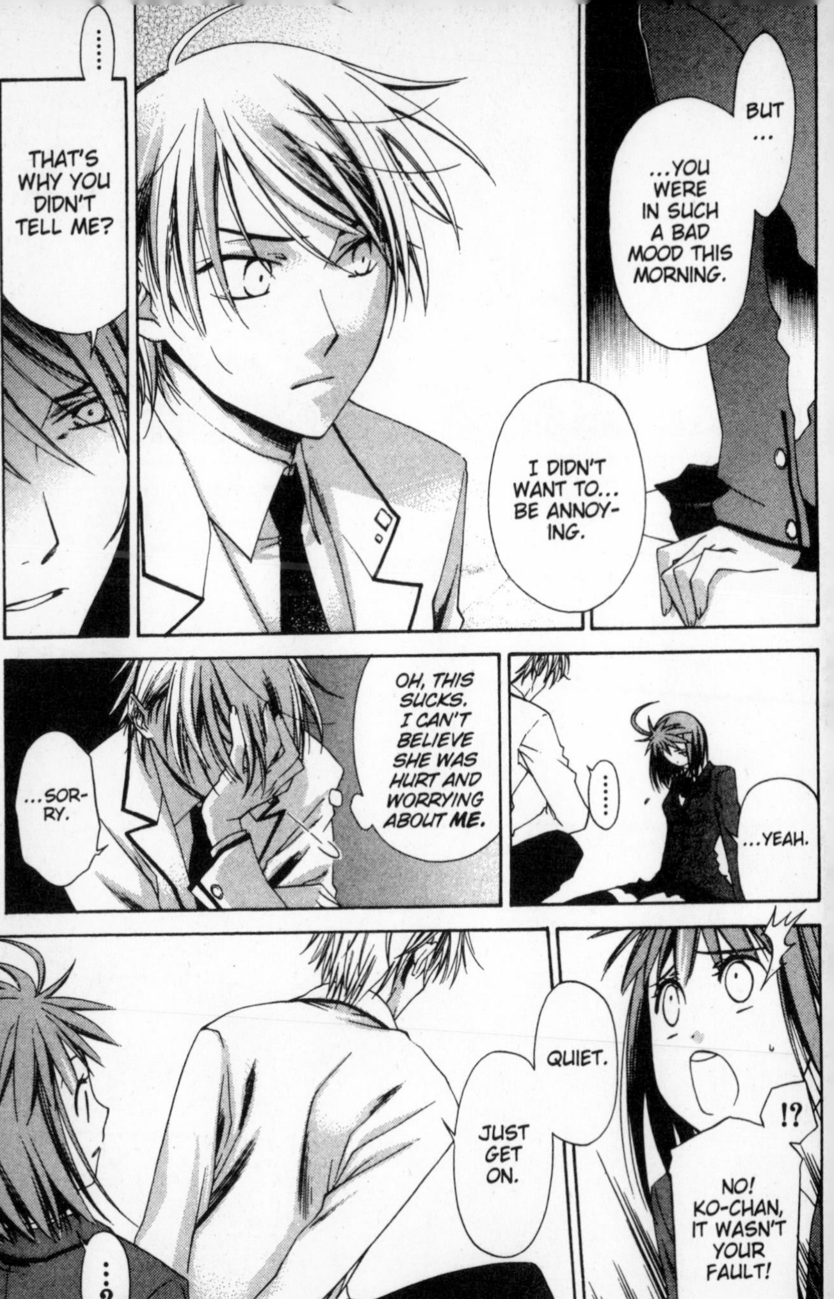
BUT ...
...YOU WERE IN SUCH A BAD MOOD THIS MORNING.
I DIDN'T WANT TO... BE ANNOY-ING.
......
THAT'S WHY YOU DIDN'T TELL ME?
......
...YEAH.
OH, THIS SUCKS. I CAN'T BELIEVE SHE WAS HURT AND WORRYING ABOUT ME.
...SOR-RY.
!?
NO! KO-CHAN, IT WASN'T YOUR FAULT!
QUIET.
JUST GET ON.
...?

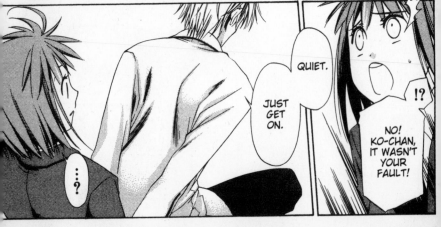

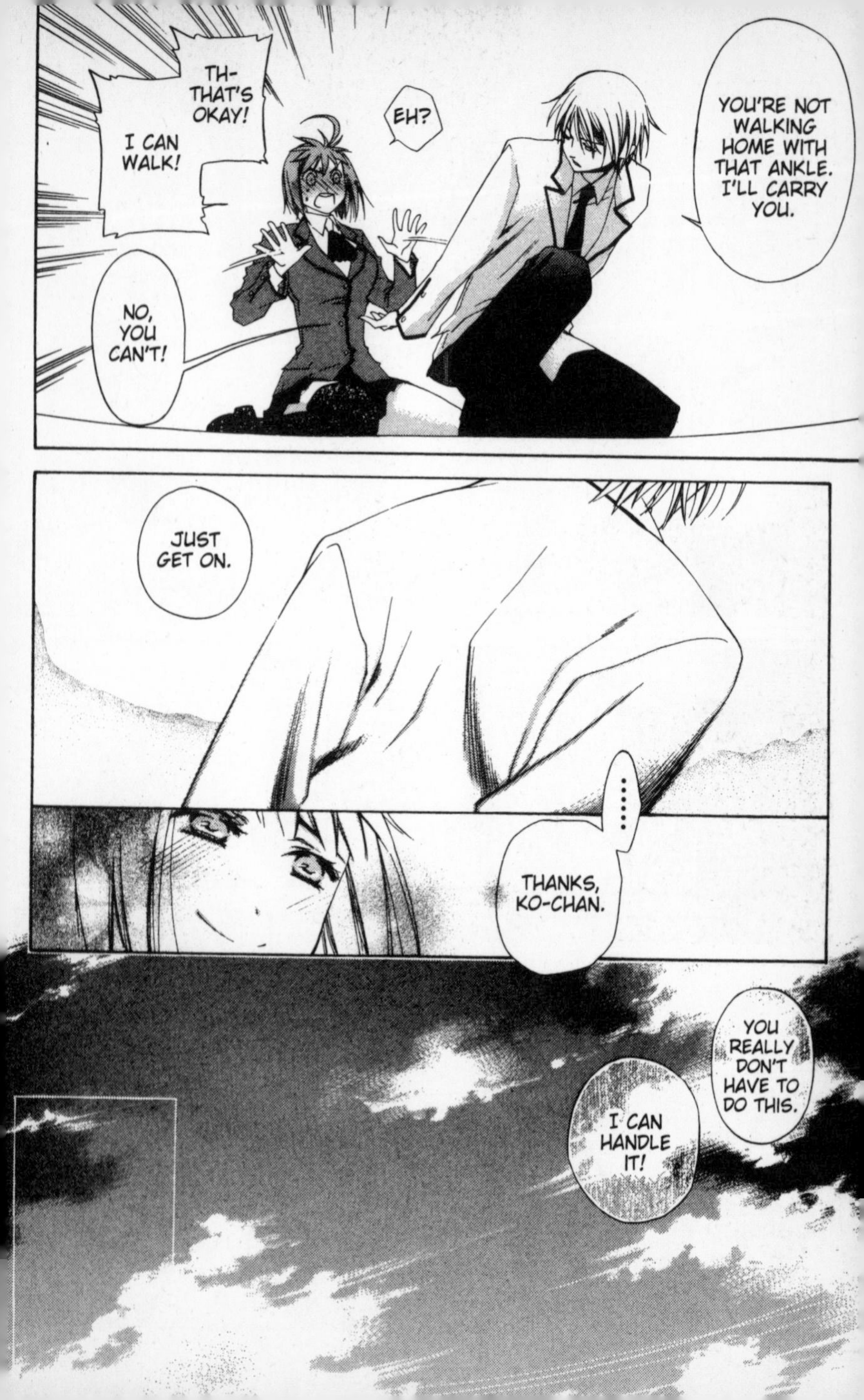
YOU'RE NOT WALKING HOME WITH THAT ANKLE. I'LL CARRY YOU.
EH?
TH-THAT'S OKAY!
I CAN WALK!
NO, YOU CAN'T!
JUST GET ON.
......
THANKS, KO-CHAN.
YOU REALLY DON'T HAVE TO DO THIS.
I CAN HANDLE IT!

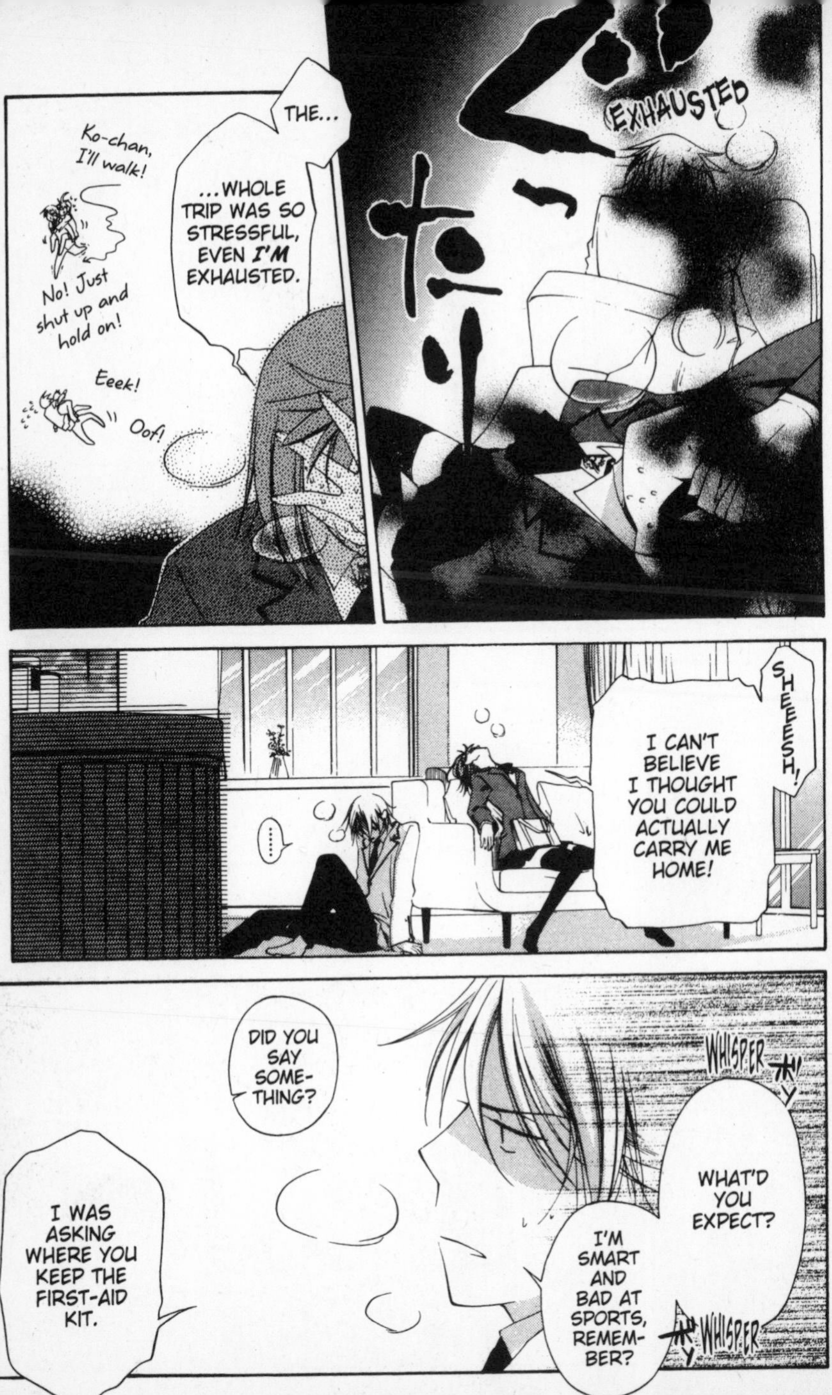
THE...
...WHOLE TRIP WAS SO STRESSFUL, EVEN ***I'M*** EXHAUSTED.
EXHAUSTED
Ko-chan, I'll walk!
No! Just shut up and hold on!
Eeek!
Oof!
SHEEESH!
I CAN'T BELIEVE I THOUGHT YOU COULD ACTUALLY CARRY ME HOME!
......
WHISPER
WHAT'D YOU EXPECT?
I'M SMART AND BAD AT SPORTS, REMEMBER?
WHISPER
DID YOU SAY SOMETHING?
I WAS ASKING WHERE YOU KEEP THE FIRST-AID KIT.

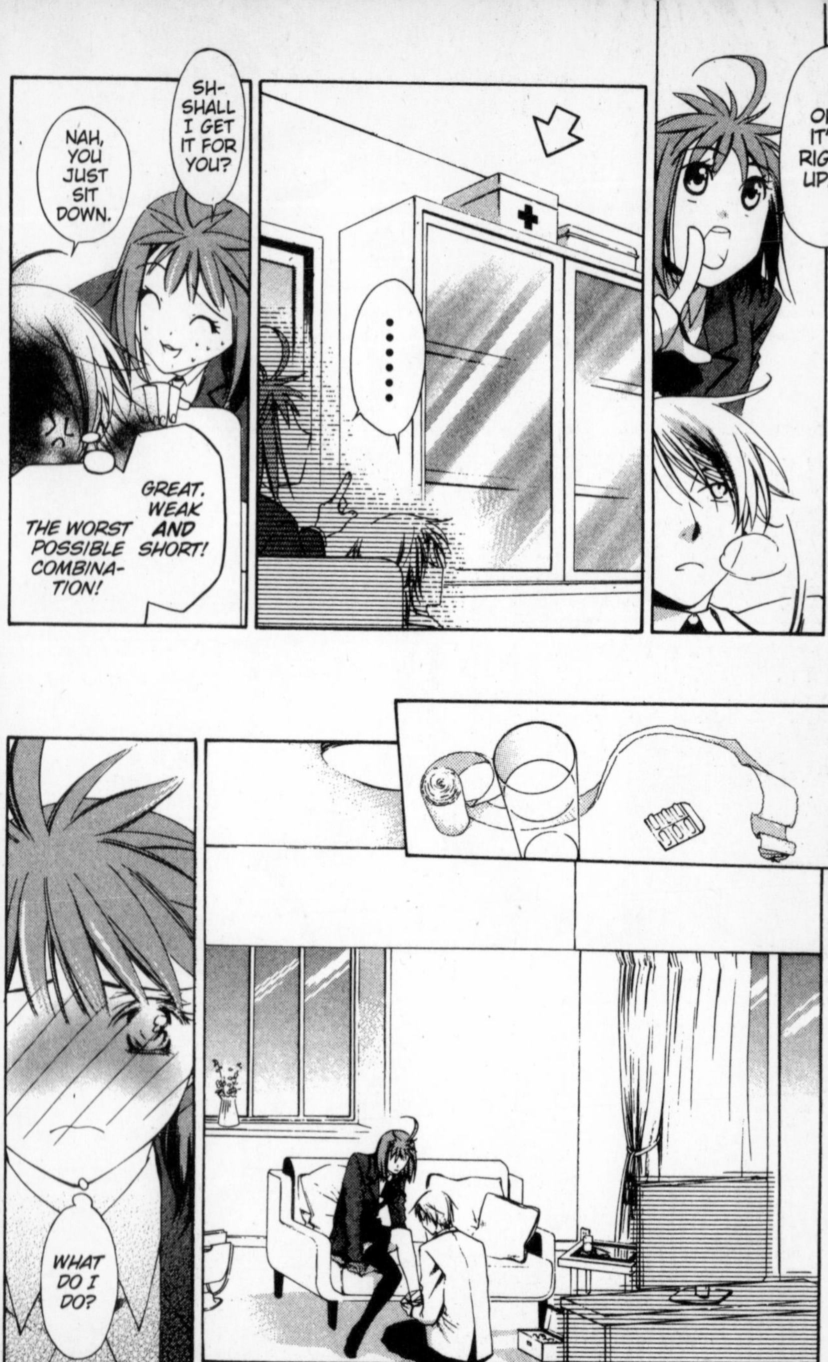
OH, IT'S RIGHT UP...
......
SH-SHALL I GET IT FOR YOU?
NAH, YOU JUST SIT DOWN.
GREAT. WEAK AND SHORT!
THE WORST POSSIBLE COMBINATION!
WHAT DO I DO?

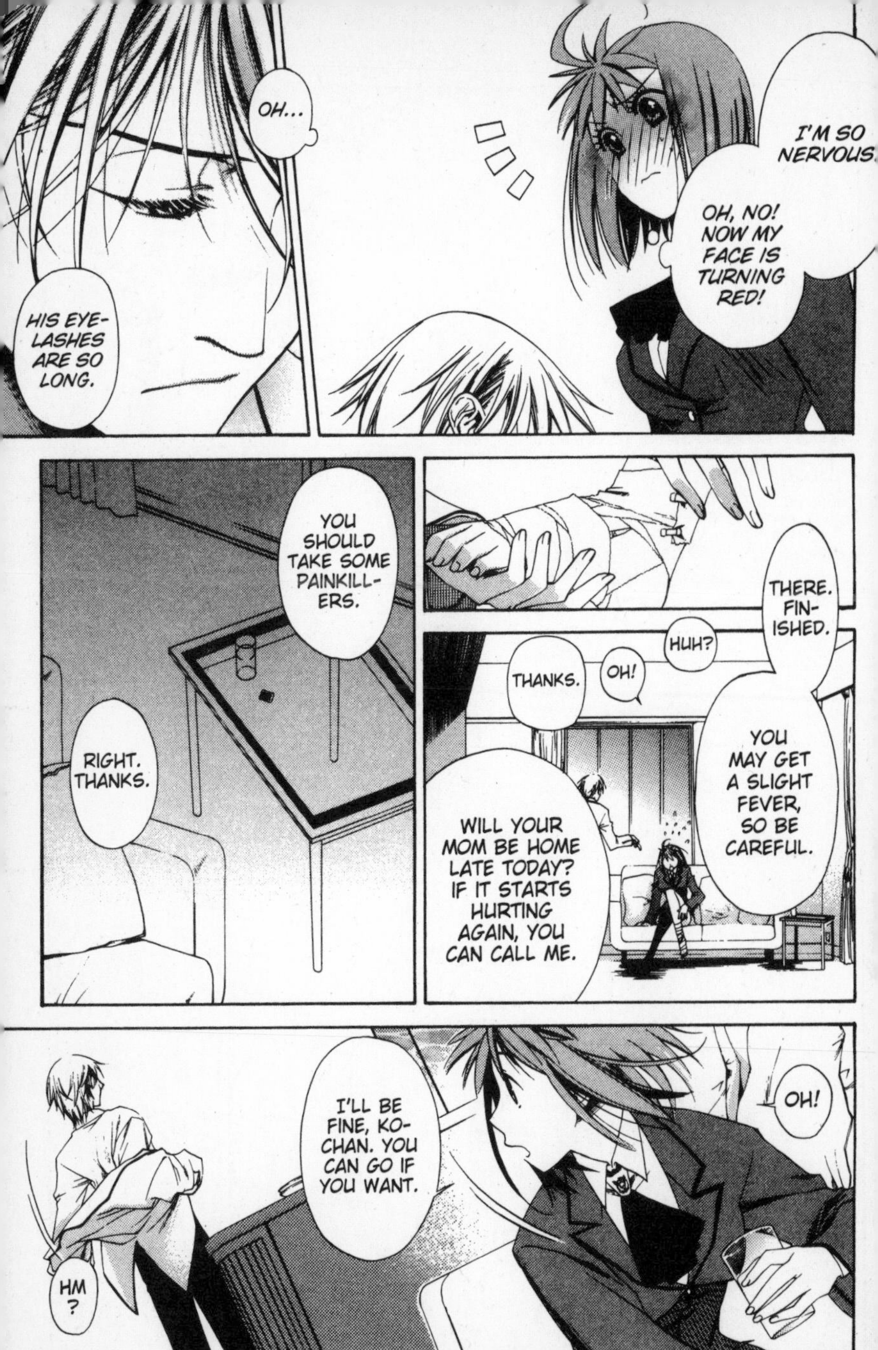
I'M SO NERVOUS.
OH, NO! NOW MY FACE IS TURNING RED!
OH...
HIS EYE-LASHES ARE SO LONG.
THERE. FIN-ISHED.
HUH?
OH!
THANKS.
YOU MAY GET A SLIGHT FEVER, SO BE CAREFUL.
WILL YOUR MOM BE HOME LATE TODAY? IF IT STARTS HURTING AGAIN, YOU CAN CALL ME.
YOU SHOULD TAKE SOME PAINKILL-ERS.
RIGHT. THANKS.
OH!
I'LL BE FINE, KO-CHAN. YOU CAN GO IF YOU WANT.
HM?

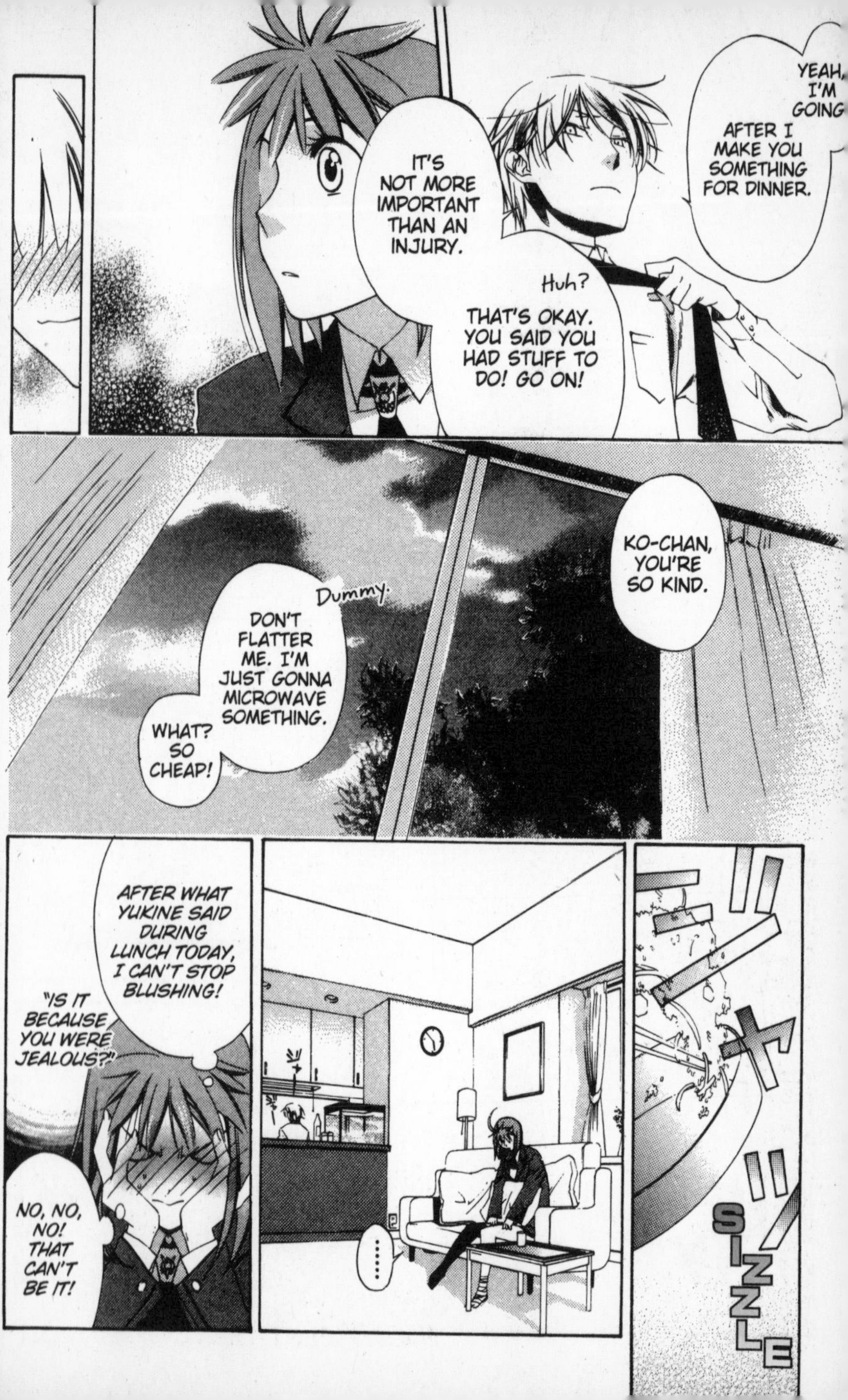
YEAH, I'M GOING AFTER I MAKE YOU SOMETHING FOR DINNER.
IT'S NOT MORE IMPORTANT THAN AN INJURY.
Huh?
THAT'S OKAY. YOU SAID YOU HAD STUFF TO DO! GO ON!
KO-CHAN, YOU'RE SO KIND.
Dummy.
DON'T FLATTER ME. I'M JUST GONNA MICROWAVE SOMETHING.
WHAT? SO CHEAP!
SIZZLE
......
AFTER WHAT YUKINE SAID DURING LUNCH TODAY, I CAN'T STOP BLUSHING!
"IS IT BECAUSE YOU WERE JEALOUS?"
NO, NO, NO! THAT CAN'T BE IT!

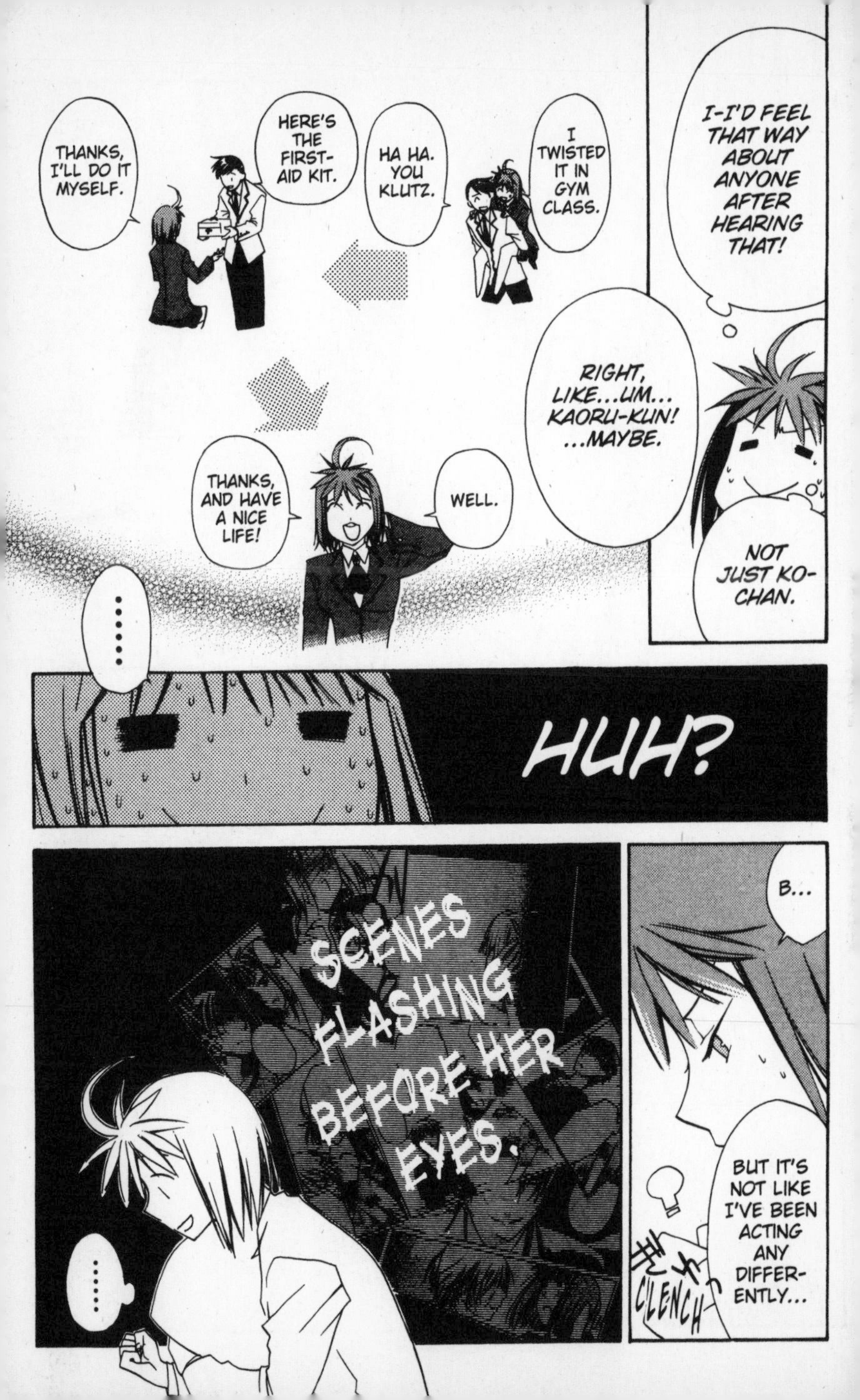
I-I'D FEEL THAT WAY ABOUT ANYONE AFTER HEARING THAT!
RIGHT, LIKE...UM... KAORU-KUN! ...MAYBE.
NOT JUST KO-CHAN.
I TWISTED IT IN GYM CLASS.
HA HA. YOU KLUTZ.
HERE'S THE FIRST-AID KIT.
THANKS, I'LL DO IT MYSELF.
WELL.
THANKS, AND HAVE A NICE LIFE!
......
HUH?
B...
BUT IT'S NOT LIKE I'VE BEEN ACTING ANY DIFFERENTLY...
CLENCH
SCENES FLASHING BEFORE HER EYES.
......

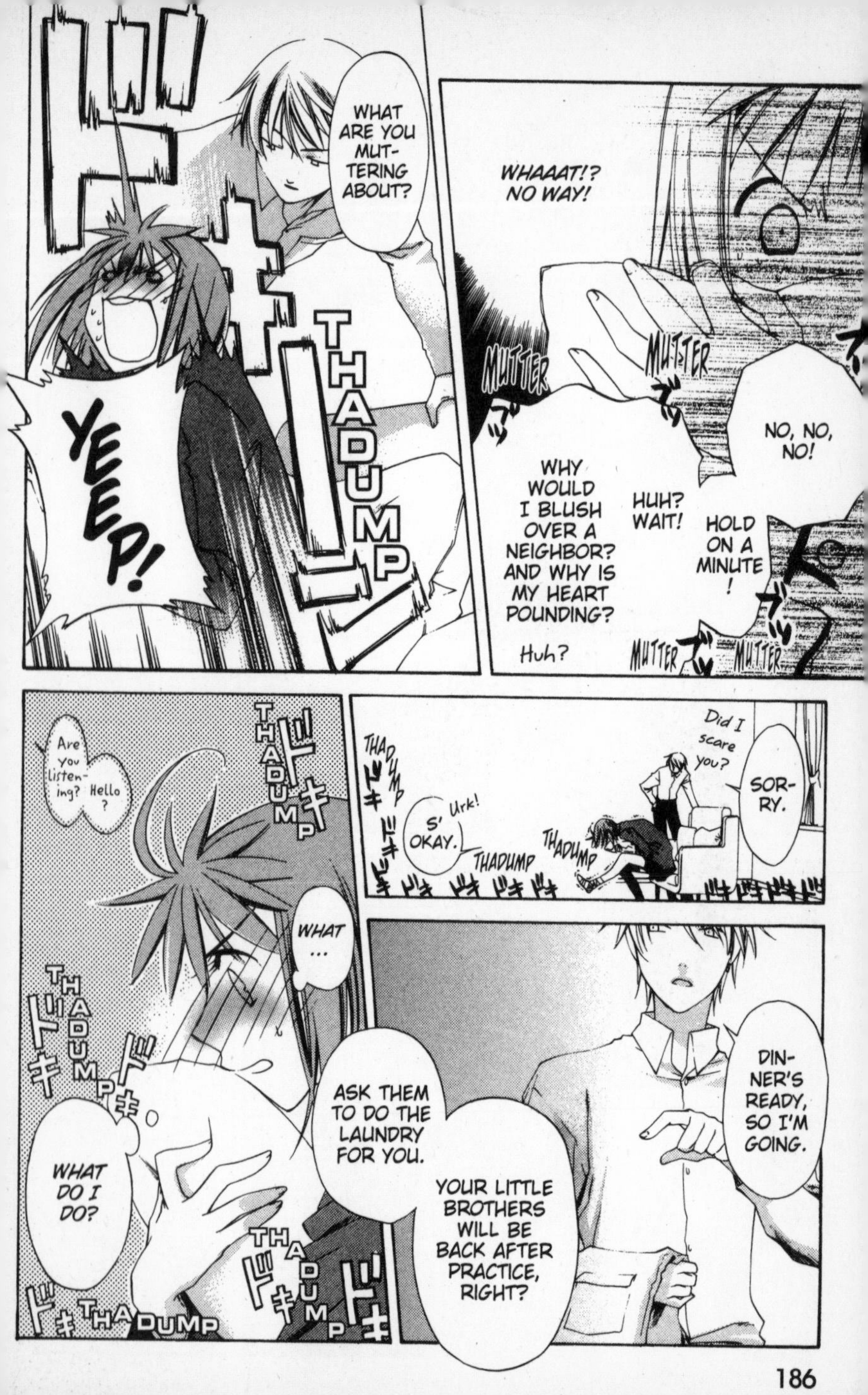
NO, NO, NO!
WHAAAT!? NO WAY!
MUTTER
MUTTER
HOLD ON A MINUTE!
HUH? WAIT!
WHY WOULD I BLUSH OVER A NEIGHBOR? AND WHY IS MY HEART POUNDING?
Huh?
MUTTER
MUTTER
WHAT ARE YOU MUT-TERING ABOUT?
THADUMP
YEEP!
Did I scare you?
SOR-RY.
THADUMP
Urk!
S' OKAY.
THADUMP
THADUMP
DIN-NER'S READY, SO I'M GOING.
YOUR LITTLE BROTHERS WILL BE BACK AFTER PRACTICE, RIGHT?
ASK THEM TO DO THE LAUNDRY FOR YOU.
THADUMP
Are you listen-ing? Hello?
WHAT ...
THADUMP
WHAT DO I DO?
THADUMP
THADUMP

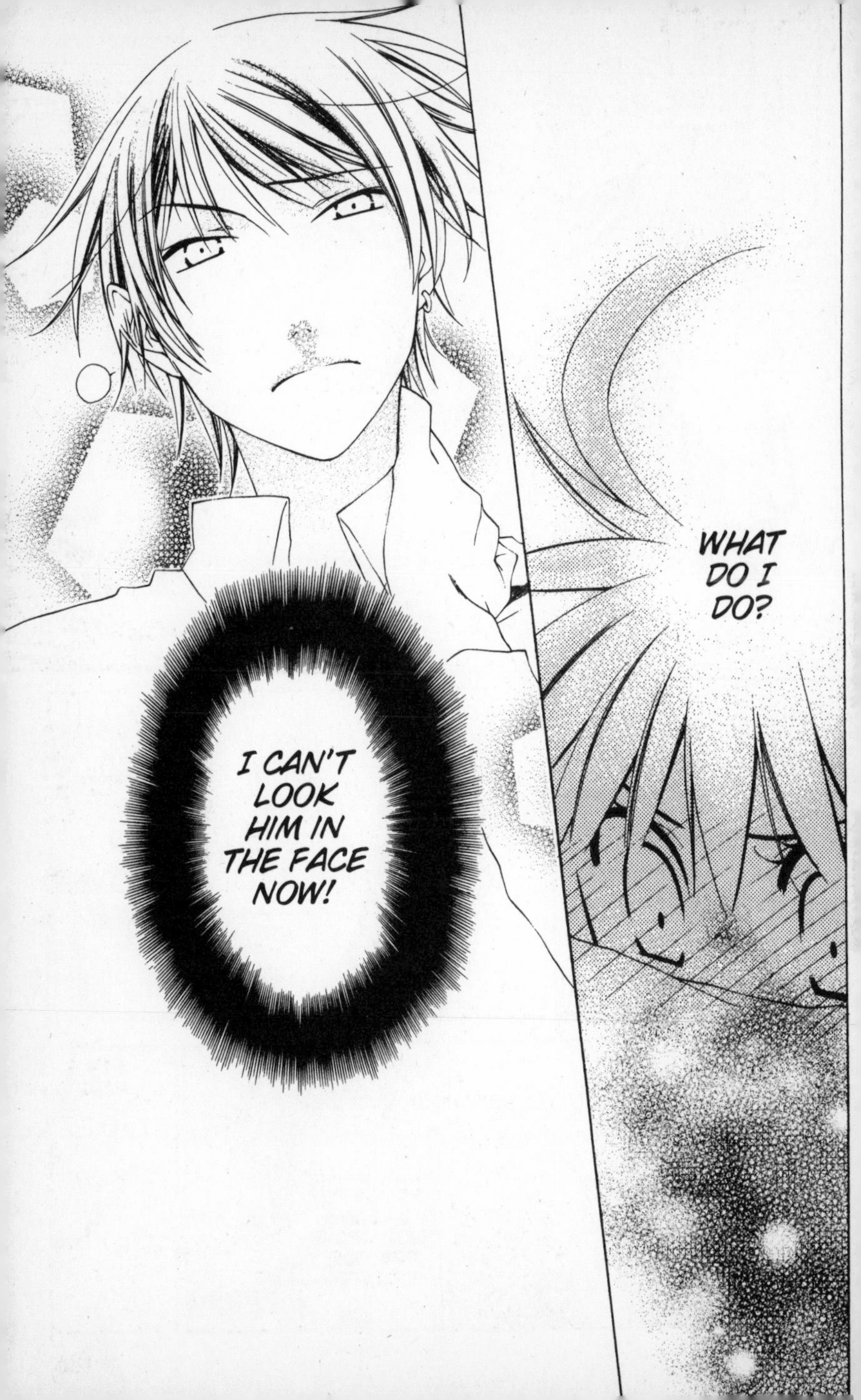
WHAT DO I DO?
I CAN'T LOOK HIM IN THE FACE NOW!

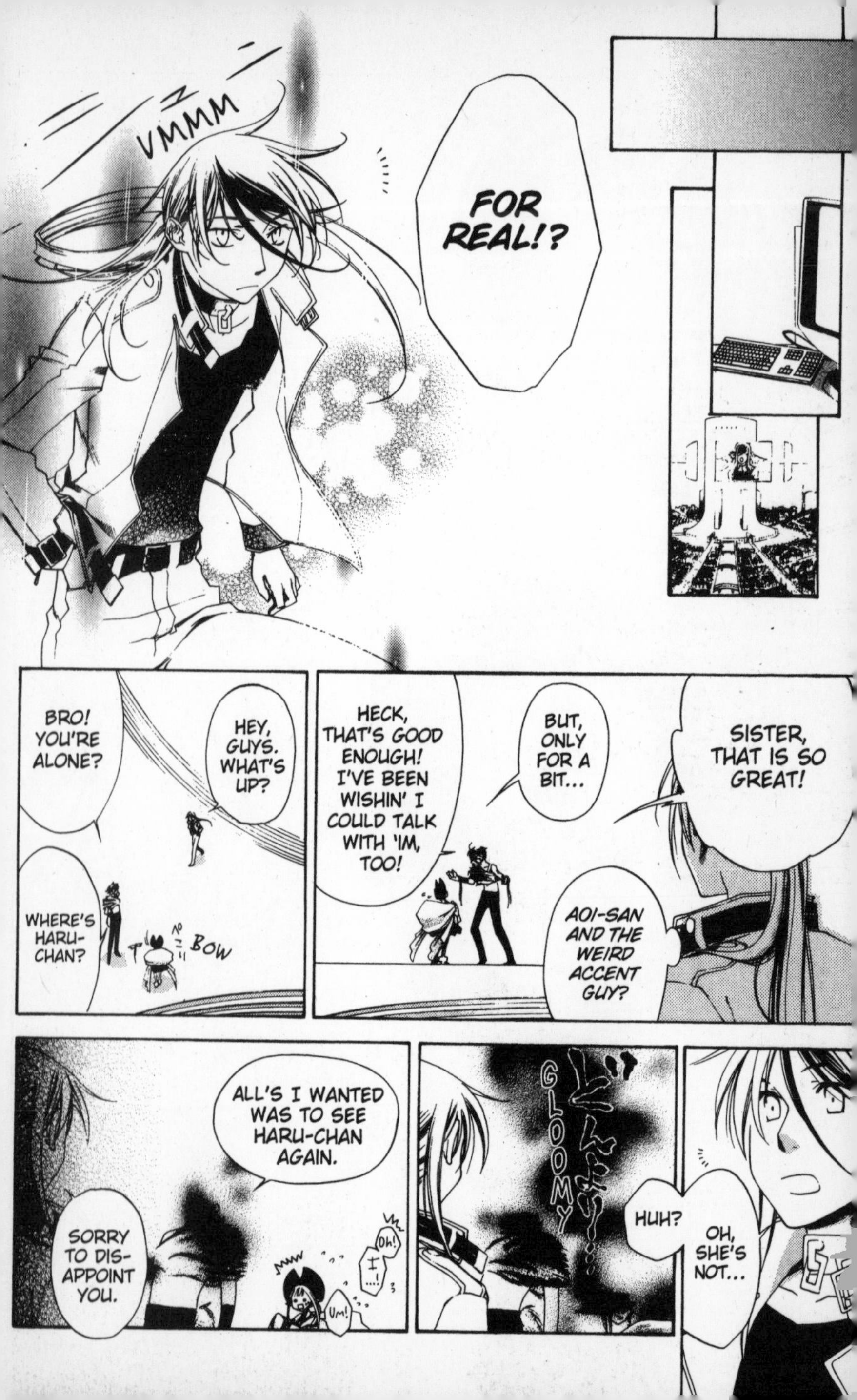
VMMM
FOR REAL!?
SISTER, THAT IS SO GREAT!
AOI-SAN AND THE WEIRD ACCENT GUY?
BUT, ONLY FOR A BIT...
HECK, THAT'S GOOD ENOUGH! I'VE BEEN WISHIN' I COULD TALK WITH 'IM, TOO!
HEY, GUYS. WHAT'S UP?
BRO! YOU'RE ALONE?
WHERE'S HARU-CHAN?
BOW
HUH?
OH, SHE'S NOT...
GLOOMY
ALL'S I WANTED WAS TO SEE HARU-CHAN AGAIN.
Oh!
Um!
SORRY TO DIS-APPOINT YOU.

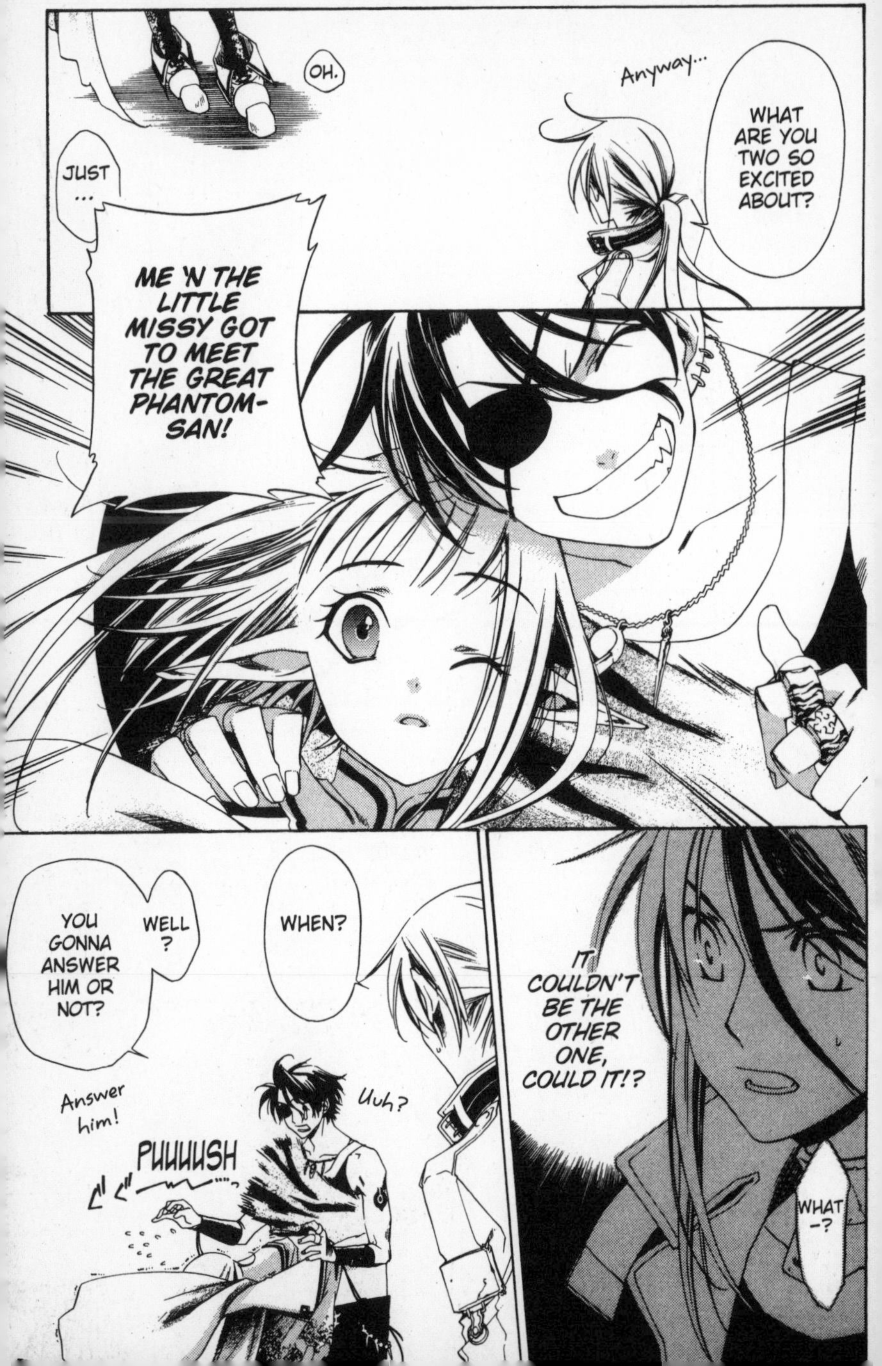

Anyway...
WHAT ARE YOU TWO SO EXCITED ABOUT?
OH.
JUST ...
ME 'N THE LITTLE MISSY GOT TO MEET THE GREAT PHANTOM-SAN!
IT COULDN'T BE THE OTHER ONE, COULD IT!?
WHAT -?
WHEN?
WELL ?
YOU GONNA ANSWER HIM OR NOT?
Uuh?
Answer him!
PUUUUSH

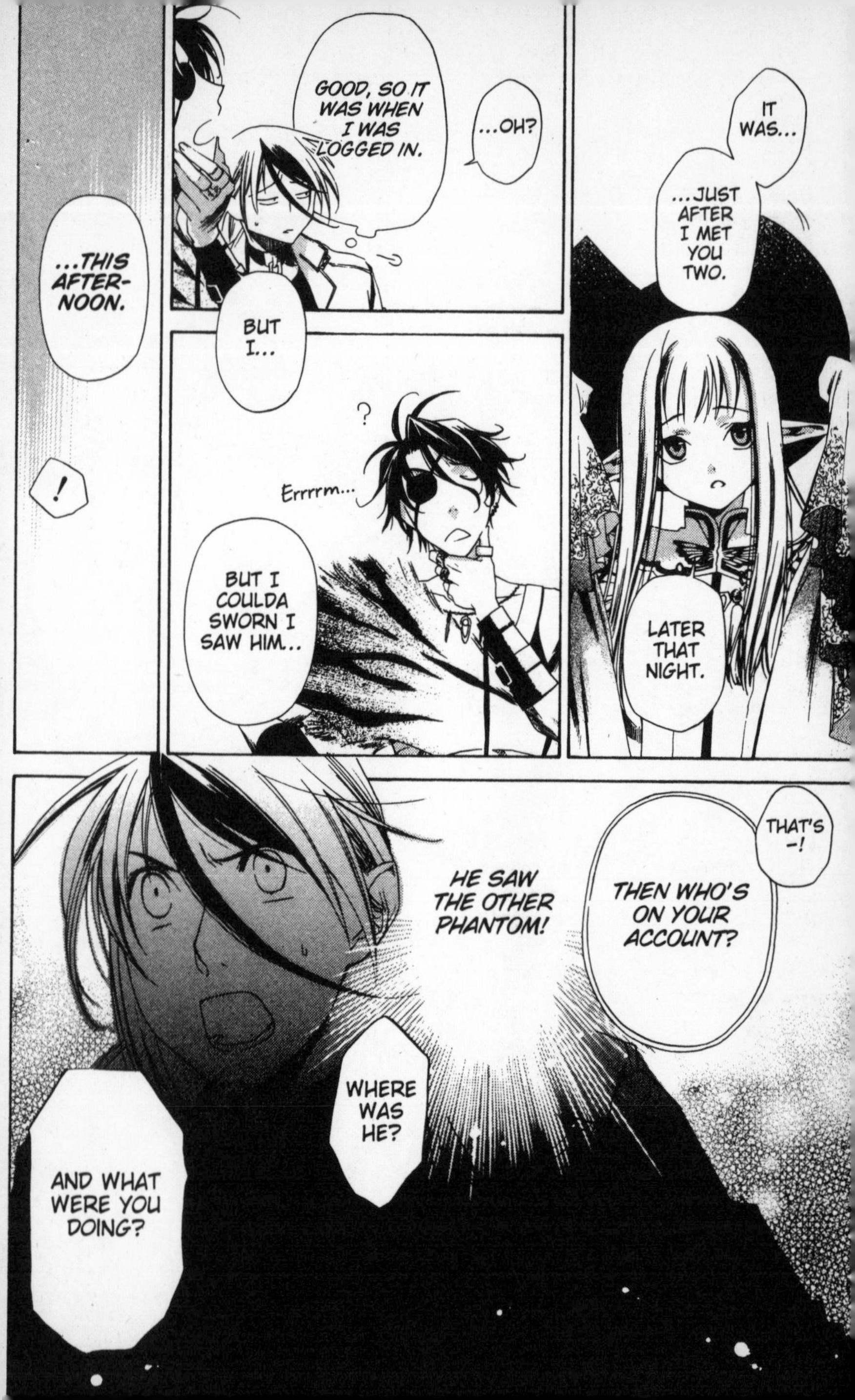
IT WAS...
...JUST AFTER I MET YOU TWO.
LATER THAT NIGHT.
...OH?
GOOD, SO IT WAS WHEN I WAS LOGGED IN.
BUT I...
?
Errrrm...
BUT I COULDA SWORN I SAW HIM...
...THIS AFTERNOON.
!
THAT'S-!
THEN WHO'S ON YOUR ACCOUNT?
HE SAW THE OTHER PHANTOM!
WHERE WAS HE?
AND WHAT WERE YOU DOING?

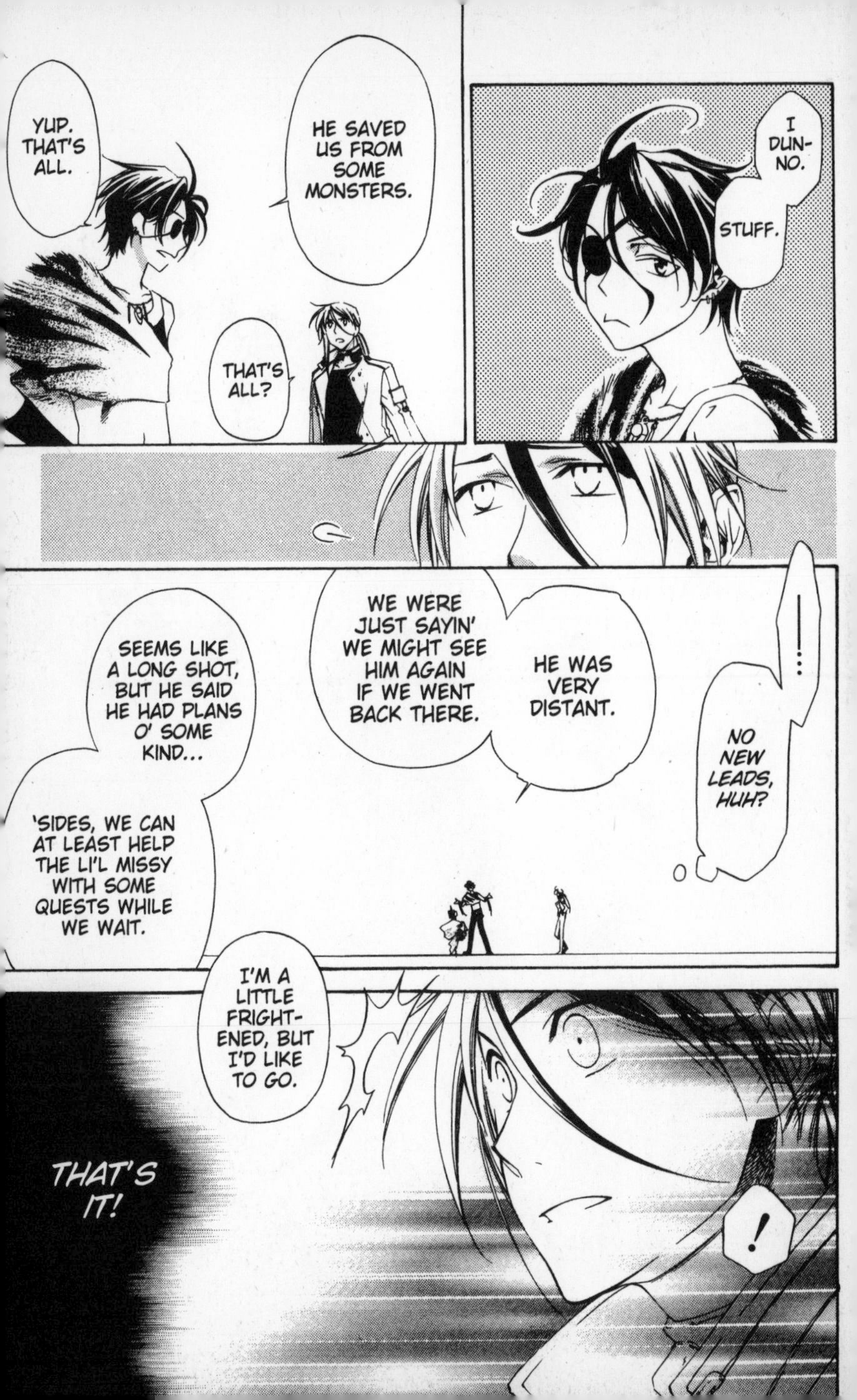
I DUN-NO.
STUFF.
HE SAVED US FROM SOME MONSTERS.
THAT'S ALL?
YUP. THAT'S ALL.
!...
NO NEW LEADS, HUH?
HE WAS VERY DISTANT.
WE WERE JUST SAYIN' WE MIGHT SEE HIM AGAIN IF WE WENT BACK THERE.
SEEMS LIKE A LONG SHOT, BUT HE SAID HE HAD PLANS O' SOME KIND...
'SIDES, WE CAN AT LEAST HELP THE LI'L MISSY WITH SOME QUESTS WHILE WE WAIT.
!
I'M A LITTLE FRIGHT-ENED, BUT I'D LIKE TO GO.
THAT'S IT!

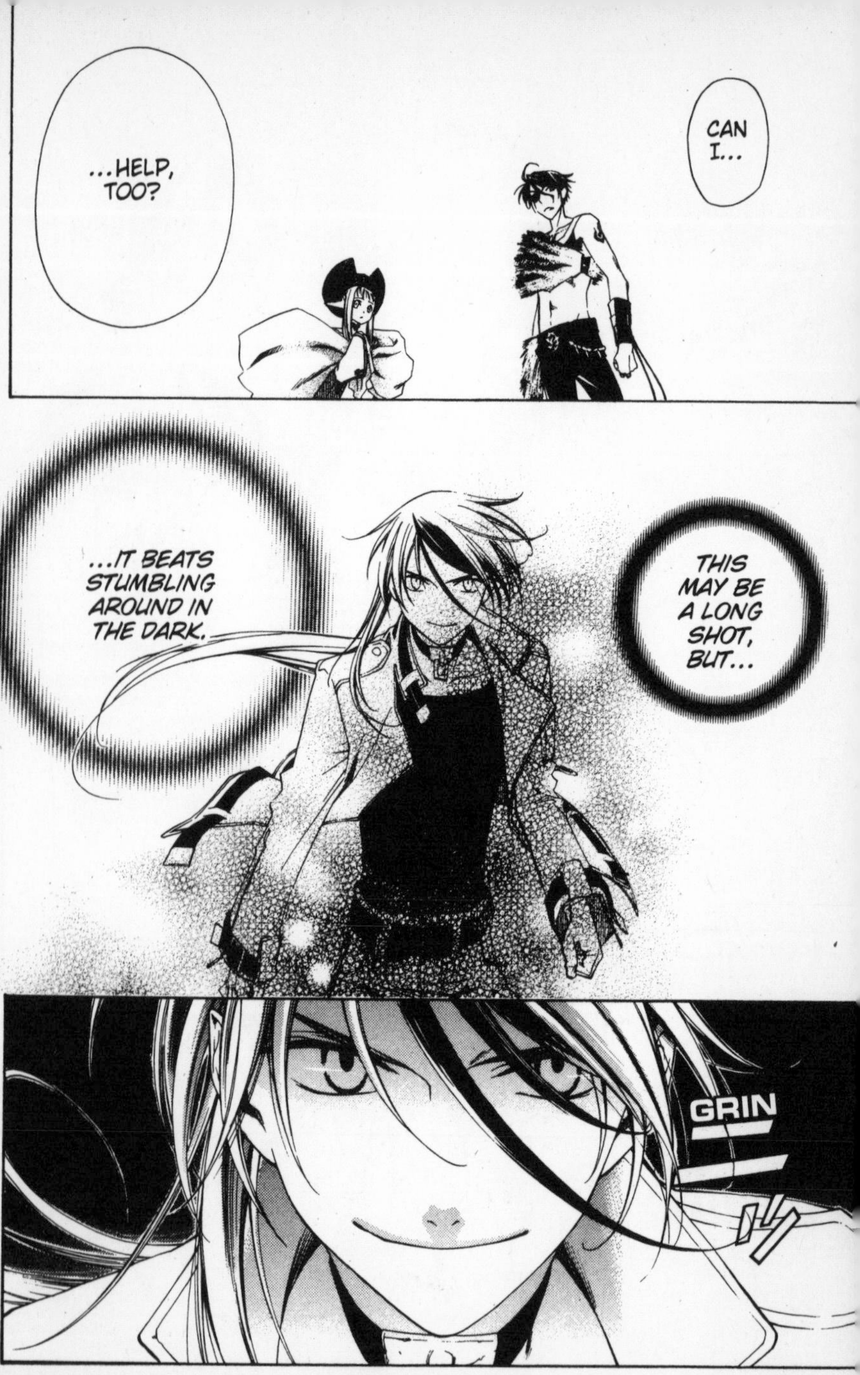
CAN I...
...HELP, TOO?
THIS MAY BE A LONG SHOT, BUT...
...IT BEATS STUMBLING AROUND IN THE DARK.
GRIN

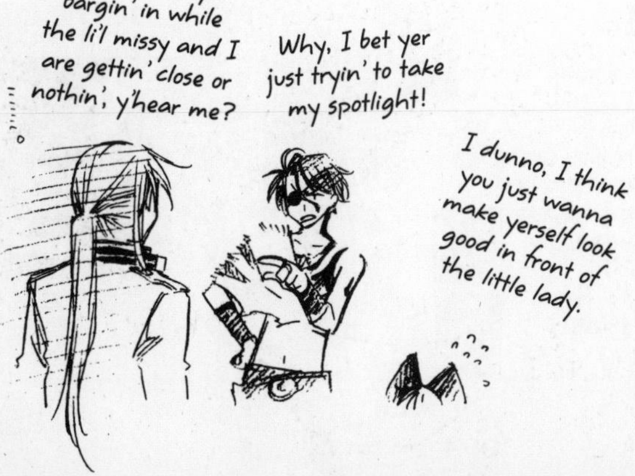
I don't want you bargin' in while the li'l missy and I are gettin' close or nothin', y'hear me?
Why, I bet yer just tryin' to take my spotlight!
I dunno, I think you just wanna make yerself look good in front of the little lady.

Yggdrasil Official Terminology

A

AOI - AOI KURENO'S AVATAR.

AVATAR - THE CHARACTER A PLAYER USES IN ONLINE COMMUNITIES TO REPRESENT HIM OR HERSELF. YGGDRASIL USES THESE COMMUNICATION TOOLS, AS WELL, SO THE CHARACTERS ARE CALLED THIS INSIDE THE GAME.

AOI KURENO - RELEASED THE SONGS FOR THE PERSONA KNOWN AS "TEAL" IN YGGDRASIL. NOW THAT SHE NO LONGER PLAYS TEAL, WILL SHE CONTINUE MAKING HER SONGS?

B

BETA TEST - THE MID-WAY PHASE OF TESTING DURING SOFTWARE DEVELOPMENT. JUST BEFORE A GAME'S OFFICIAL RELEASE, A TRIAL VERSION IS RELEASED TO TEST THE GAME'S ABILITIES AND FUNCTIONS, SUCH AS ITS USER-FRIENDLINESS AND TO CLEAN OUT ANY BUGS. KOKI TACHIBANA USED THE PHANTOM DURING THE BETA TESTING OF YGGDRASIL.

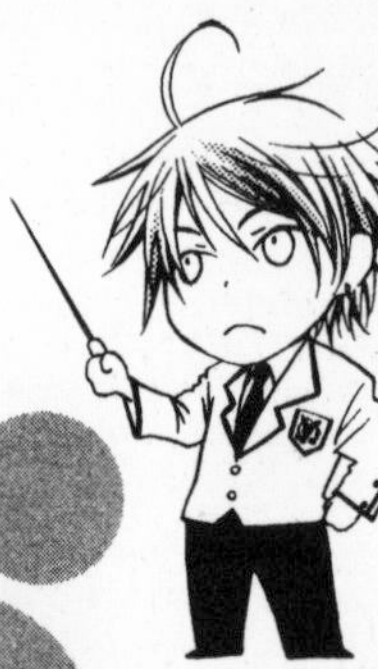

BUG - A FLAW IN A COMPUTER PROGRAM THAT CAUSES GLITCHES OR PROBLEMS.

C

CERBERUS - ONE OF THE STRONGEST MONSTERS IN THE GAME. THE PHANTOM USED A.I. TECHNOLOGY TO MAKE THEM INTO HIS PETS.

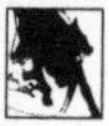

E

ENCOUNTER - WHEN A PLAYER COMES ACROSS A MONSTER IN THE GAME.

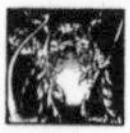

H

HARU - HARUNA FUJISAKI'S AVATAR.

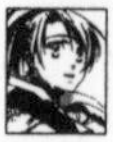

HARUNA FUJISAKI - KOKI TACHIBANA'S CHILDHOOD FRIEND. HER MOST REDEEMING QUALITIES ARE HER UNYIELDING ENERGY AND POSITIVE ATTITUDE. IT'S BECOME HER DAILY ROUTINE TO WAKE UP KOKI, WHO ALWAYS SLEEPS IN.

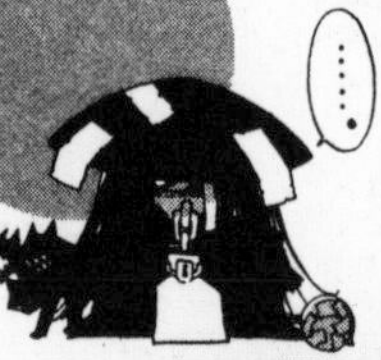

HOLO-MAIL - A PROGRAM IN YGGDRASIL THAT ALLOWS USERS TO SEND MESSAGES TO EACH OTHER, COMPLETE WITH A HOLOGRAPHIC REPRESENTATION OF THEIR AVATAR.

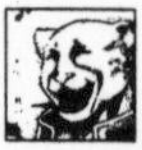

I

IRL MEETING - WHEN PLAYERS MEET OTHER PLAYERS FROM THE GAME IN REAL LIFE.

ITEM - IN YGGDRASIL, ITEMS CREATED BY PROGRAM LICENSED USERS CAN GO PUBLIC WITH APPROVAL.

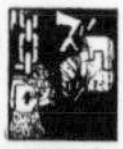

K

KO - KOKI TACHIBANA'S AVATAR. CREATED HIM AFTER HE STOPPED USING THE PHANTOM.

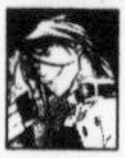

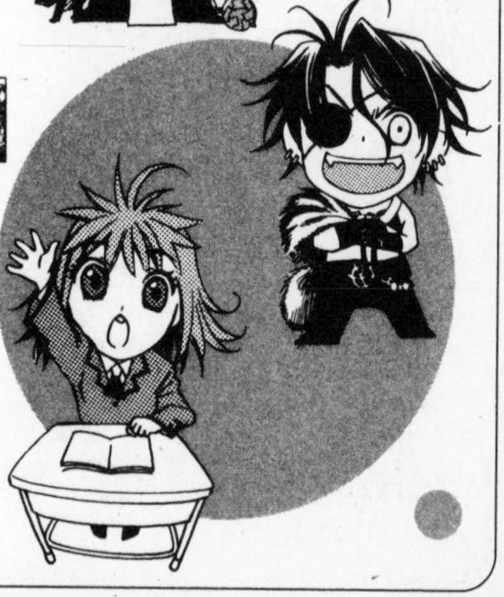

AND THE HIGHER UP YOU GO, THE HARDER IT IS TO ACT FREELY. THE RANKING SYSTEM WAS DESIGNED BY WOOD SOFT, INC.'S OWN TEAM OF ENGINEERS, AND THEY ARE THE ONES TO CAREFULLY SCRUTINIZE EACH ORIGINAL PROGRAM FOR ACCURACY AND CONTRIBUTION TO THE GAME. THE NUMBER OF SS-RANKING USERS IS VERY SMALL, AND SO ARE OFTEN THOUGHT TO BE RESERVED FOR PROFESSIONAL PROGRAMMERS ONLY.

SUPPORT PROGRAM - A GUIDE ABILITY FOR NEW PLAYERS IN YGGDRASIL. THEY OFTEN TAKE THE SHAPE OF A CUTE PET, AND HELP THE PLAYER THROUGH VARIOUS TASKS. AFTER THE 30-DAY TRIAL, THEY DISAPPEAR.

TACHIBANA SISTERS - KOKI TACHIBANA'S OLDER SISTERS. THEY'RE TWINS, BOTH OFFICEWORKERS, AND THEY BOTH LOVE TO TEASE THEIR POOR LITTLE BROTHER.

TEAL - THE SINGER/SONGWRITER OF YGGDRASIL, WHO CREATES AND PERFORMS ORIGINAL SONGS. HER TRUE IDENTITY IS YET UNKNOWN, BUT HER SONGS ARE OFTEN THE TOPIC OF CONVERSATION. THOUGH HER AVATAR'S IMAGE IS PUBLIC, HER TRUE AGE AND APPEARANCE ARE STILL HIDDEN FROM SIGHT. AFTER HER RECENT RELEASE, THERE ARE RUMORS THAT SHE MAY HAVE RETIRED FROM THE SPOTLIGHT.

WOOD SOFT, INC. - THE LEADING SOFTWARE COMPANY IN THE WORLD, STATIONED IN JAPAN. FAMOUS FOR THEIR LEAVES OPERATING SYSTEM THAT SPECIALIZES IN ENTERTAINMENT AND BUSINESS SOFTWARE.

YGGDRASIL - THE MMORPG BUNDLED TOGETHER WITH THE LEAVES OPERATING SYSTEM. IT CAN BASICALLY BE PLAYED FOR FREE. WOOD SOFT, INC. USES YGGDRASIL MORE AS A COMMUNICATION TOOL RATHER THAN A GAME. THAT'S WHY THE GAME'S SYSTEM COMES WITH A PUBLIC WEBSITE, ORIGINAL STORIES AND SONGS, AND ILLUSTRATIONS. MANY USERS MADE THEIR DEBUTS IN THE REAL WORLD AFTER ESTABLISHING A FANBASE IN YGGDRASIL.

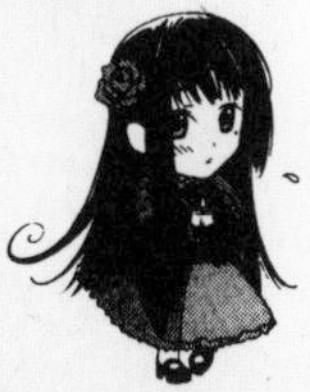

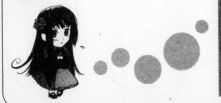

KOKI TACHIBANA - A FRESHMAN IN HIGH SCHOOL, HE'S VERY SMART BUT HORRIBLE AT SPORTS. LOSES HIS NERVE IN FRONT OF HIS TWO OLDER SISTERS. A REAL GENTLEMAN AT HEART.

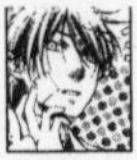

LEAVES - WOOD SOFT, INC.'S OPERATING SYSTEM. IT CARRIES A GRAPHICAL USER INTERFACE, AND IS BUNDLED WITH VARIOUS SOFTWARE.

LIBRARY - YGGDRASIL'S DATABASE. ALL OF YGGDRASIL'S HISTORY IS RECORDED WITHIN ITS WALLS.

MANGINA - A DEROGATORY TERM USED TO REFER TO MEN WHO PLAY FEMALE AVATARS ONLINE. MANY MEN CHOOSE TO PLAY FEMALE AVATARS BECAUSE THEY FIND THEY'RE REACTED TO BETTER, ARE MORE LIKELY TO BE GIVEN HELP OR ITEMS IF ASKED FOR, AND ARE GENERALLY TREATED WITH MORE COMPASSION. CONVERSELY, SOME WOMEN WILL CHOOSE TO PLAY MALE AVATARS TO DIVERT UNWANTED ATTENTION.

NPC - STANDS FOR NON-PLAYER CHARACTER, USUALLY REFERRING TO A COMPUTER-GENERATED AVATAR THAT HELPS MOVE THE GAME ALONG. THIS IS CONSIDERED TO BE THE "OPPOSITE" OF A PC (PLAYER CHARACTER).

ONE-SHOT - GENERALLY USED AS A VERB, THIS IS A TERM THAT MEANS 'TO BE KILLED WITH ONE HIT'; AS IN "I JUST GOT ONE-SHOT", OR "I TOTALLY ONE-SHOT YOU."

PC - PLAYER CHARACTER.

PHANTOM - ANOTHER OF KOKI TACHIBANA'S AVATARS. HE'S RELEASED DOZENS OF ORIGINAL PROGRAMS, AND IS SAID TO HAVE CREATED NEARLY 30% OF ALL OF YGGDRASIL'S MAGIC SPELLS. THIS SUCCESS AND PROGRAMMING PRECISION EARNED HIM THE SS-RANK IN THE PROGRAM LICENSE.

PROGRAM LICENSE - ASIDE FROM THE STANDARD PROGRAMMED MAGIC, MOST OF THE MAGIC IN YGGDRASIL IS CREATED THROUGH USER PROGRAMMING. THE USER MUST FIRST MAKE A REQUEST TO THE GM, RECEIVE HIS PROGRAM LICENSE AND HAVE HIS WRITTEN PROGRAMS PASS A SYSTEM CHECK, BEFORE HIS PROGRAMS CAN BE USED PUBLICLY. THERE ARE SEVEN RANKS INVOLVED.

RANK - THE PROGRAM LICENSE CAN BE BROKEN DOWN INTO SEVEN GROUPS: SS, S, A, B, D, C, AND E. EACH HAS A DETERMINED LEVEL OF INTERVENTION IN THE SYSTEM,

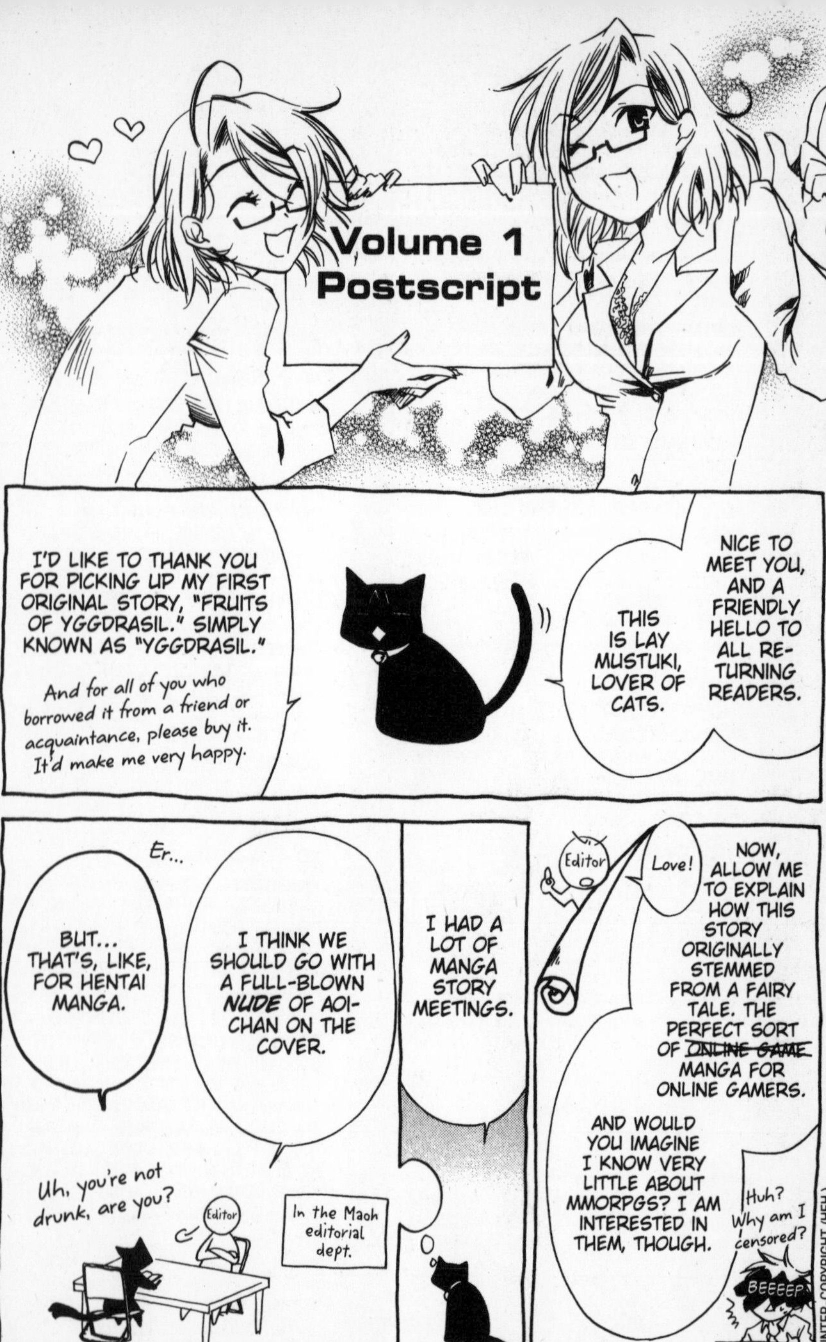
Volume 1 Postscript
NICE TO MEET YOU, AND A FRIENDLY HELLO TO ALL RE-TURNING READERS.
THIS IS LAY MUSTUKI, LOVER OF CATS.
I'D LIKE TO THANK YOU FOR PICKING UP MY FIRST ORIGINAL STORY, "FRUITS OF YGGDRASIL." SIMPLY KNOWN AS "YGGDRASIL."
And for all of you who borrowed it from a friend or acquaintance, please buy it. It'd make me very happy.
Editor
Love!
NOW, ALLOW ME TO EXPLAIN HOW THIS STORY ORIGINALLY STEMMED FROM A FAIRY TALE. THE PERFECT SORT OF ~~ONLINE GAME~~ MANGA FOR ONLINE GAMERS.
AND WOULD YOU IMAGINE I KNOW VERY LITTLE ABOUT MMORPGS? I AM INTERESTED IN THEM, THOUGH.
Huh? Why am I censored?
BEEEEP
Previous protagonist.
I HAD A LOT OF MANGA STORY MEETINGS.
I THINK WE SHOULD GO WITH A FULL-BLOWN NUDE OF AOI-CHAN ON THE COVER.
Er...
BUT... THAT'S, LIKE, FOR HENTAI MANGA.
Uh, you're not drunk, are you?
Editor
In the Maoh editorial dept.

*COUNTER-COPYRIGHT (HEH.)

I couldn't wrap my head around it! (Ha!)

I'm the type to get addicted to games to the point where I won't sleep or eat until I win, so I try to stay away from them.

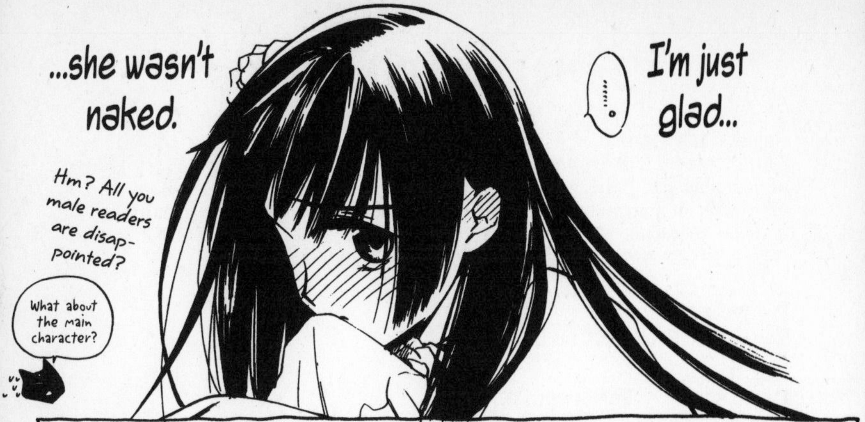
I'm just glad...
......
...she wasn't naked.
Hm? All you male readers are disap-pointed?
What about the main character?

Warning: And that's how my editor and I had such a fun time (?) completing the book. I'm sorry for never meeting my deadlines, though. And I'm sorry for being so slow. Thank you to Maoh's editorial department.

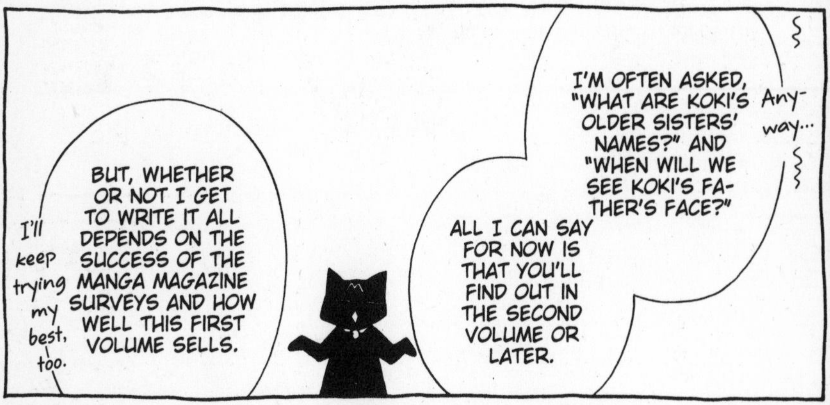
Any-way...
I'M OFTEN ASKED, "WHAT ARE KOKI'S OLDER SISTERS' NAMES?" AND "WHEN WILL WE SEE KOKI'S FA-THER'S FACE?"
ALL I CAN SAY FOR NOW IS THAT YOU'LL FIND OUT IN THE SECOND VOLUME OR LATER.
BUT, WHETHER OR NOT I GET TO WRITE IT ALL DEPENDS ON THE SUCCESS OF THE MANGA MAGAZINE SURVEYS AND HOW WELL THIS FIRST VOLUME SELLS.
I'll keep trying my best, too.

Now that I've taken all this time with useless rambling, I'll save this room for my special thanks.

- M. K.-san (#4, #5, #6)
- ototachibana-san (#4)
- REi-san (#4)
- Mizuho-san (#4)
- Mutsuki Tachibana-san
- (#4)
- E.SY (#7)
- Mom (#1–#8)

My mom always helped me erase my pencils (Ha.)

It's incred-ibly hard for a single person to release a monthly chapter, so I received a lot of help from other people. Thank you so very much!

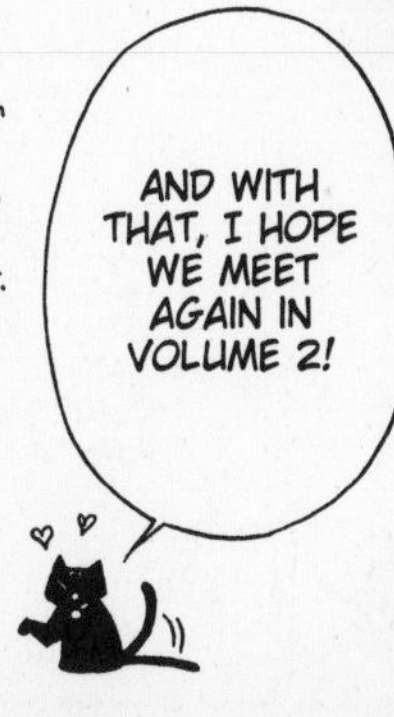
AND WITH THAT, I HOPE WE MEET AGAIN IN VOLUME 2!

I always set up my website to match with the manga's release. There's still not much left on it, but please come and check it out. I'd also love to hear any comments you have on my work.
http://replicazon.net
"Replica Zone"

Lay Mutsuki, XX '06

Lay Mutsuki '06

TRANSLATOR'S NOTES

Pg. 20 – MMORPG
This stands for Massive Multiplayer Online Role-playing Game, which is a kind of computer role-playing game that lets a huge number of people interact with each other in a virtual game world. The people who play take the identity of a fictional character. Unlike a computer or console game, the MMORPG world stays active even when the individual player is not playing.

Pg. 39 – IRL
The letters "IRL" stand for In Real Life.

Pg. 66 – "So Gyoku got gutted?"
This is a play on words, since the original word was "*gyokusai*" which means "to go down fighting".

Pg. 153 – *hentai*
A Japanese word that means both "abnormality" and "metamorphosis". It has a strong negative connotation in Japan, where its most common usage is "sexually perverted". It refers specifically to sexually explicit or pornographic anime, manga and computer games, in the West.